OLD LONDON
Cheapside and St Paul's

THE
'VILLAGE LONDON'
SERIES
from
THE ALDERMAN PRESS

OLD LONDON

Cheapside and St Paul's

by

WALTER THORNBURY

THE ALDERMAN PRESS

British Library Cataloguing in Publication Data.

Thornbury, Walter
    Old London: Cheapside and St. Pauls.
    1. London (England) ——————— History
    I. Title   2. Thornbury, Walter. Old and new London
    942.1   DA677

ISBN 0-946619-23-9

This edition published 1986
The Alderman Press, 1/7 Church Street,
Edmonton, London N9 9DR

Printed and bound in Great Britain
by The Camelot Press Ltd., Southampton.

CONTENTS.

CHAPTER XVII.
WHITEFRIARS.

The Present Whitefriars—The Carmelite Convent—Dr. Butts—The Sanctuary—Lord Sanquhar murders the Fencing-Master—His Trial—Bacon and Yelverton—His Execution—Sir Walter Scott's "Fortunes of Nigel"—Shadwell's *Squire of Alsatia*—A Riot in Whitefriars—Elizabethan Edicts against the Ruffians of Alsatia—Bridewell—A Roman Fortification—A Saxon Palace—Wolsey's Residence—Queen Katherine's Trial—Her Behaviour in Court—Persecution of the first Congregationalists—Granaries and Coal Stores destroyed by the Great Fire—The Flogging in Bridewell—Sermon on Madame Creswell—Hogarth and the "Harlot's Progress"—Pennant's Account of Bridewell—Bridewell in 1843—Its Latter Days—Pictures in the Court Room—Bridewell Dock—The Gas Works—Theatres in Whitefriars—Pepys' Visits to the Theatre—Dryden and the Dorset Gardens Theatre—Davenant—Kynaston—Dorset House—The Poet-Earl.   . 182

CHAPTER XVIII.
BLACKFRIARS.

Three Norman Fortresses on the Thames' Bank—The Black Parliament—The Trial of Katherine of Arragon—Shakespeare a Blackfriars Manager—The Blackfriars Puritans—The Jesuit Sermon at Hunsdon House—Fatal Accident—Extraordinary Escapes—Queen Elizabeth at Lord Herbert's Marriage—Old Blackfriars Bridge—Johnson and Mylne—Laying of the Stone—The Inscription—A Toll Riot—Failure of the Bridge—The New Bridge—Bridge Street—Sir Richard Phillips and his Works—Painters in Blackfriars—The King's Printing Office—Printing House Square—The *Times* and its History—Walter's Enterprise—War with the *Dispatch*—The gigantic Swindling Scheme exposed by the *Times*—Apothecaries' Hall—Quarrel with the College of Physicians   200

CHAPTER XIX.
LUDGATE HILL.

An Ugly Bridge and "Ye Belle Savage"—A Radical Publisher—The Principal Gate of London—From a Fortress to a Prison—"Remember the Poor Prisoners"—Relics of Early Times—St. Martin's, Ludgate—The London Coffee House—Celebrated Goldsmiths on Ludgate Hill—Mrs. Rundell's Cookery Book—Stationers' Hall—Old Burgavenny House and its History—Early Days of the Stationers' Company—The Almanacks—An Awkward Misprint—The Hall and its Decorations—The St. Cecilia Festivals—Dryden's "St. Cecilia's Day" and "Alexander's Feast"—Handel's Setting of them—A Modest Poet—Funeral Feasts and Political Banquets—The Company's Plate—Their Charities—The Pictures at Stationers' Hall—The Company's Arms—Famous Masters   220

CHAPTER XX.
ST. PAUL'S.

London's Chief Sanctuary of Religion—The Site of St. Paul's—The Earliest authenticated Church there—The Shrine of Erkenwald—St. Paul's Burnt and Rebuilt—It becomes the Scene of a Strange Incident—Important Political Meeting within its Walls—The Great Charter published there—St. Paul's and Papal Power in England—Turmoils around the Grand Cathedral—Relics and Chantry Chapels in St. Paul's—Royal Visits to St. Paul's—Richard, Duke of York, and Henry VI.—A Fruitless Reconciliation—Jane Shore's Penance—A Tragedy of the Lollards' Tower—A Royal Marriage—Henry VIII. and Cardinal Wolsey at St. Paul's—"Peter of Westminster"—A Bonfire of Bibles—The Cathedral Clergy Fined—A Miraculous Rood—St. Paul's under Edward VI. and Bishop Ridley—A Protestant Tumult at Paul's Cross—Strange Ceremonials—Queen Elizabeth's Munificence—The Burning of the Spire—Desecration of the Nave—Elizabeth and Dean Nowell—Thanksgiving for the Armada—The "Children of Paul's"—Government Lotteries—Executions in the Churchyard—Inigo Jones's Restorations and the Puritan Parliament—The Great Fire of 1666—Burning of Old St. Paul's, and Destruction of its Monuments—Evelyn's Description of the Fire—Sir Christopher Wren called in   234

CHAPTER XXI.
ST. PAUL'S (*continued*).

The Rebuilding of St. Paul's—Ill Treatment of its Architect—Cost of the Present Fabric—Royal Visitors—The First Grave in St. Paul's—Monuments in St. Paul's—Nelson's Funeral—Military Heroes in St. Paul's—The Duke of Wellington's Funeral—Other Great Men in St. Paul's—Proposal for the Completion and Decoration of the Building—Dimensions of St. Paul's—Plan of Construction—The Dome, Ball, and Cross—Mr. Horner and his Observatory—Two Narrow Escapes—Sir James Thornhill—Peregrine Falcons on St. Paul's—Nooks and Corners of the Cathedral—The Library, Model Room, and Clock—The Great Bell—A Lucky Error—Curious Story of a Monomaniac—The Poets and the Cathedral—The Festivals of the Charity Schools and of the Sons of the Clergy   240

CONTENTS.

CHAPTER XXII.
ST. PAUL'S CHURCHYARD.

St Paul's Churchyard and Literature—Queen Anne's Statue—Execution of a Jesuit in St. Paul's Churchyard—Miracle of the " Face in the Straw "—Wilkinson's Story—Newbery the Bookseller—Paul's Chain—" Cocker "—Chapter House of St. Paul's—St. Paul's Coffee House—Child's Coffee House and the Clergy—Garrick's Club at the " Queen's Arms," and the Company there—" Sir Benjamin " Figgins—Johnson the Bookseller—Hunter and his Guests—Fuseli—Bonnycastle—Kinnaird—Musical Associations of the Churchyard—Jeremiah Clark and his Works—Handel at Meares' Shop—Young the Violin Maker—The " Castle " Concerts—An Old Advertisement—Wren at the " Goose and Gridiron "—St. Paul's School—Famous Paulines—Pepys visiting his Old School—Milton at St. Paul's 262

CHAPTER XXIII.
PATERNOSTER ROW.

Its Successions of Traders—The House of Longman—Goldsmith at Fault—Tarleton, Actor, Host, and Wit—Ordinaries around St. Paul's : their Rules and Customs—The " Castle "—" Dolly's "—" The Chapter " and its Frequenters—Chatterton and Goldsmith—Dr. Buchan and his Prescriptions—Dr. Gower—Dr. Fordyce—The " Wittinagemot " at the " Chapter "—The " Printing Conger "—Mrs. Turner, the Poisoner—The Church of St. Michael " ad Bladum "—The Boy in Panier Alley 274

CHAPTER XXIV.
BAYNARD'S CASTLE AND DOCTORS' COMMONS.

Baron Fitzwalter and King John—The Duties of the Chief Bannerer of London—An Old-fashioned Punishment for Treason—Shakesperian Allusions to Baynard's " Castle "—Doctors' Commons and its Five Courts—The Court of Probate Act, 1857—The Court of Arches—The Will Office—Business of the Court—Prerogative Court—Faculty Office—Lord Stowell, the Admiralty Judge—Stories of him—His Marriage—Sir Herbert Jenner Fust—The Court " Rising "—Doctor Lushington—Marriage Licences—Old Weller and the " Touters "—Doctors' Commons at the Present Day 281

CHAPTER XXV.
HERALDS' COLLEGE.

Early Homes of the Heralds—The Constitution of the Heralds' College—Garter King at Arms—Clarencieux and Norroy—The Pursuivants—Duties and Privileges of Heralds—Good, Bad, and Jovial Heralds—A Notable Norroy King at Arms—The Tragic End of Two Famous Heralds—The College of Arms' Library 294

CHAPTER XXVI.
CHEAPSIDE—INTRODUCTORY AND HISTORICAL.

Ancient Reminiscences of Cheapside—Stormy Days therein—The Westchepe Market—Something about the Pillory—The Cheapside Conduits—The Goldsmiths' Monopoly—Cheapside Market—Gossip anent Cheapside by Mr. Pepys—A Saxon Rienzi—Anti-Free-Trade Riots in Cheapside—Arrest of the Rioters—A Royal Pardon—Jane Shore 304

CHAPTER XXVII.
CHEAPSIDE SHOWS AND PAGEANTS.

A Tournament in Cheapside—The Queen in Danger—The Street in Holiday Attire—The Earliest Civic Show on Record—The Water Processions—A Lord Mayor's Show in Queen Elizabeth's Reign—Gossip about Lord Mayors' Shows—Splendid Pageants—Royal Visitors at Lord Mayors' Shows—A Grand Banquet in Guildhall—George III. and the Lord Mayor's Show—The Lord Mayor's State Coach—The Men in Armour—Sir Claudius Hunter and Elliston—Stow and the Midsummer Watch 315

CHAPTER XXVIII.
CHEAPSIDE—CENTRAL.

Grim Chronicles of Cheapside—Cheapside Cross—Puritanical Intolerance—The Old London Conduits—Mediæval Water-carriers—The Church of St. Mary-le-Bow—" Murder will out "—The " Sound of Bow Bells "—Sir Christopher Wren's Bow Church—Remains of the Old Church—The Seldam—Interesting Houses in Cheapside and their Memories—Goldsmiths' Row—The " Nag's Head " and the Self-consecrated Bishops—Keats' House—Saddlers' Hall—A Prince Disguised—Blackmore, the Poet—Alderman Boydell, the Printseller—His Edition of Shakespeare—" Puck "—The Lottery—Death and Burial 332

CHAPTER XXIX.
CHEAPSIDE TRIBUTARIES—SOUTH.

The King's Exchange—Friday Street and the Poet Chaucer—The Wednesday Club in Friday Street—William Paterson, Founder of The Bank of England—How Easy it is to Redeem the National Debt—St. Matthew's and St. Margaret Moses—Bread Street and the Bakers' Shops—St. Austin's, Watling Street—The Fraternity of St. Austin's—St. Mildred's, Bread Street—The Mitre Tavern—A Priestly Duel—Milton's Birth-place—The " Mermaid "—Sir Walter Raleigh and the Mermaid Club—Thomas Coryatt, the Traveller—Bow Lane—Queen Street—Soper's Lane—A Mercer Knight—St. Bennet Sherehog—Epitaphs in the Church of St. Thomas Apostle—A Charitable Merchant 346

CHAPTER XXX.
CHEAPSIDE TRIBUTARIES—NORTH.

Goldsmiths' Hall—Its Early Days—Tailors and Goldsmiths at Loggerheads—The Goldsmiths' Company's Charters and Records—Their Great Annual Feast—They receive Queen Margaret of Anjou in State—A Curious Trial of Skill—Civic and State Duties—The Goldsmiths break up the Image of their Patron Saint—The Goldsmiths' Company's Assays—The Ancient Goldsmiths' Feasts—The Goldsmiths at Work—Goldsmiths' Hall at the Present Day—The Portraits—St. Leonard's Church—St. Vedast—Discovery of a Stone Coffin—Coach-makers' Hall 353

CONTENTS.

CHAPTER XXXI.
CHEAPSIDE TRIBUTARIES, NORTH :—WOOD STREET.

Wood Street—Pleasant Memories—St. Peter's in Chepe—St. Michael's and St. Mary Staining—St. Alban's, Wood Street—Some Quaint Epitaphs—Wood Street Compter and the Hapless Prisoners therein—Wood Street Painful, Wood Street Cheerful—Thomas Ripley—The Anabaptist Rising—A Remarkable Wine Cooper—St. John Zachary and St. Anne-in-the-Willows—Haberdashers' Hall—Something about the Mercers 364

CHAPTER XXXII.
CHEAPSIDE TRIBUTARIES, NORTH (*continued*).

Milk Street—Sir Thomas More—The City of London School—St. Mary Magdalen—Honey Lane—All Hallows' Church—Lawrence Lane and St. Lawrence Church—Ironmonger Lane and Mercers' Hall—The Mercers' Company—Early Life Assurance Companies—The Mercers' Company in Trouble—Mercers' Chapel—St. Thomas Acon—The Mercers' School—Restoration of the Carvings in Mercers' Hall—The Glories of the Mercers' Company—Ironmonger Lane 374

LIST OF ILLUSTRATIONS.

	PAGE
Yard of the Black Lion, Whitefriars	186
Bridewell, as Rebuilt after the Fire, from an Old Print	187
New Bridge Street in 1755	192
Interior of the Duke's Theatre	193
Baynard's Castle, from a View published in 1790	198
Falling-in of the Chapel at Blackfriars	199
Richard Burbage, from an Original Portrait	204
Laying the Foundation-stone of Blackfriars Bridge	205
Printing House Square and the "Times" Office	210
Blackfriars Old Bridge during its Construction, 1775	211
The College of Physicians, Warwick Lane	216
Outer Court of La Belle Sauvage in 1828	217
Inner Court of the Belle Sauvage	222
The North Side of Ludgate Hill	223
Old Lud Gate, from a Print published about 1750	226
Ruins of Barbican on Ludgate Hill	228
Interior of Stationers' Hall	229
Old St. Paul's, from a View by Hollar	234
Old St. Paul's—the Interior, looking East	235
The Church of St. Faith, the Crypt of Old St. Paul's	240
St. Paul's after the Fall of the Spire	241
The Chapter House of Old St. Paul's	246
St. Paul's from the South-west, 1800	247
The Rebuilding of St. Paul's	252
The Choir of St. Paul's, 1754	253
The Scaffolding and Observatory on St. Paul's in 1848	258
St. Paul's and the Neighbourhood in 1540	259
The Library of St. Paul's	264
The "Face in the Straw," 1613	265
St. Paul's Churchyard in 1820	270
Old St. Paul's School	271
Richard Tarleton, the Actor	276
Dolly's Coffee House	277
The Figure in Panier Alley	282

	PAGE
The Church of St. Michael ad Bladum	283
The Prerogative Office, Doctors' Commons, 1860	288
St. Paul's and Neighbourhood, from Aggas's Plan, 1563	289
Heralds' College (from an Old Print)	294
The Last Heraldic Court (from an Old Picture)	295
Sword, Dagger, and Ring of King James of Scotland	300
Linacre's House	301
Ancient View of Cheapside	307
Beginning of the Riot in Cheapside	312
Cheapside Cross, as it appeared in 1547	313
The Lord Mayor's Procession, after Hogarth	318
Bow Church and Cheapside in 1750	319
Figures of Gog and Magog set up in Guildhall	324
The Royal Banquet in Guildhall in 1761	325
The Lord Mayor's Coach	330
The Demolition of Cheapside Cross	331
Old Map of the Ward of Cheap—about 1750	336
The Seal of Bow Church	337
Bow Church, Cheapside, from a View taken about 1750	342
No. 73, Cheapside, from an Old View	343
The Door of Saddlers' Hall	348
Milton's House and Milton's Burial-place	349
Interior of Goldsmiths' Hall	354
Trial of the Pix	355
Exterior of Goldsmiths' Hall	360
Altar of Diana	361
Wood Street Compter, from a View published in 1793	366
The Tree at the Corner of Wood Street, 1870	367
Pulpit Hour-glass	370
Interior of St. Michael's, Wood Street	372
Interior of Haberdashers' Hall	373
The "Swan with Two Necks," Lad Lane	378
City of London School	379

LONDON AS IT WAS AND AS IT IS.

WRITING the history of a vast city like London is like writing a history of the ocean—the area is so vast, its inhabitants are so multifarious, the treasures that lie in its depths so countless. What aspect of the great chameleon city shall one select? for, as Boswell, with more than his usual sense, once remarked, "London is to the politician merely a seat of government, to the grazier a cattle market, to the merchant a huge exchange, to the dramatic enthusiast a congeries of theatres, to the man of pleasure an assemblage of taverns." If we follow one path alone, we must neglect other roads equally important; let us, then, consider the metropolis as a whole, for, as Johnson's friend well says, "the intellectual man is struck with London as comprehending the whole of human life in all its variety, the contemplation of which is inexhaustible." In histories, in biographies, in scientific records, and in chronicles of the past, however humble, let us gather materials for a record of the great and the wise, the base and the noble, the odd and the witty, who have inhabited London and left their names upon its walls. Wherever the glimmer of the cross of St. Paul's can be seen, we shall wander from street to alley, from alley to street, noting almost every event of interest that has taken place there since London became a city.

THE REBUILDING OF ST. PAUL'S. FROM AN ORIGINAL DRAWING IN THE POSSESSION OF J. G. CRACE, ESQ.

CHAPTER XVII.

WHITEFRIARS.

The Present Whitefriars—The Carmelite Convent—Dr. Butts—The Sanctuary—Lord Sanquhar Murders the Fencing-Master—His Trial—Bacon and Yelverton—His Execution— Sir Walter Scott's "Fortunes of Nigel"—Shadwell's *Squire of Alsatia*—A Riot in Whitefriars—Elizabethan Edicts against the Ruffians of Alsatia—Bridewell—A Roman Fortification—A Saxon Palace—Wolsey's Residence—Queen Katharine's Trial— Her Behaviour in Court— Persecution of the First Congregationalists—Granaries and Coal Stores destroyed by the Great Fire—The Flogging in Bridewell—Sermon on Madame Creswell—Hogarth and the "Harlot's Progress"—Pennant's Account of Bridewell—Bridewell in 1843— Its Latter Days—Pictures in the Court Room—Bridewell Dock—The Gas Works—Theatres in Whitefriars—Pepys' Visits to the Theatre— Dryden and the Dorset Gardens Theatre—Davenant—Kynaston—Dorset House—The Poet-Earl.

So rich is London in legend and tradition, that even some of the spots that now appear the blankest, baldest, and most uninteresting, are really vaults of entombed anecdote and treasure-houses of old story.

Whitefriars—that dull, narrow, uninviting lane sloping from Fleet Street to the river, with gas-works at its foot and mean shops on either side— was once the centre of a district full of noblemen's mansions ; but Time's harlequin wand by-and-by turned it into a debtors' sanctuary and thieves' paradise, and for half a century its bullies and swindlers waged a ceaseless war with their proud and rackety neighbours of the Temple. The dingy lane, now only awakened by the quick wheel of the swift newspaper cart or the ponderous tires of the sullen coal-wagon, was in olden times for ever ringing with clash of swords, the cries of quarrelsome gamblers, and the drunken songs of noisy Bobadils.

In the reign of Edward I., a certain Sir Robert Gray, moved by qualms of conscience or honest impulse, founded on the bank of the Thames, east of the well-guarded Temple, a Carmelite convent, with broad gardens, where the white friars might stroll, and with shady nooks where they might say their "office." Bouverie Street and Ram Alley were then part of their domain, and there they watched the river and prayed for their patrons' souls. In 1350 Courtenay, Earl of Devon, rebuilt the Whitefriars Church, and in 1420 a Bishop of Hereford added a steeple. In time, greedy hands were laid roughly on cope and chalice; and Henry VIII., seizing on the friars' domains, gave his physician—that Doctor Butts mentioned by Shakespeare—the chapter-house for a residence. Edward VI.—who, with all his promise, was as ready for such pillage as his tyrannical father—pulled down the church, and built noblemen's houses in its stead. The refectory of the convent, being preserved, afterwards became the Whitefriars Theatre. The mischievous right of sanctuary was preserved to the district, and confirmed by James I., in whose reign the slum became jocosely known as Alsatia— from Alsace, that unhappy frontier then, and later, contended for by French and Germans—just as Chandos Street and that shy neighbourhood at the north-west side of the Strand used to be called the Caribbee Islands, from its countless straits and intricate thieves' passages. The outskirts of the Carmelite monastery had no doubt become disreputable at an early time, for even in Edward III.'s reign the holy friars had complained of the gross temptations of Lombard Street (an alley near Bouverie Street). Sirens and Dulcineas of all descriptions were ever apt to gather round monasteries. Whitefriars, however, even as late as Cromwell's reign, preserved a certain respectability; for here, with his supposed wife, the Dowager Countess of Kent, Selden lived and studied.

In the reign of James I. a strange murder was committed in Whitefriars. The cause of the crime was highly singular. In 1607 young Lord Sanquhar, a Scotch nobleman, who with others of his countrymen had followed his king to England, had an eye put out by a fencing-master of Whitefriars. The young lord—a man of a very ancient, proud, and noble Scotch family, as renowned for courage as for wit—had striven to put some affront on the fencing-master at Lord Norris's house, in Oxfordshire, wishing to render him contemptible before his patrons and assistants—a common bravado of the rash Tybalts and hot-headed Mercutios of those fiery days of the duello, when even to crack a nut too loud was enough to make your tavern neighbour draw his sword. John Turner, the master, jealous of his professional honour, challenged the tyro with dagger and rapier, and, determined to chastise his ungenerous assailant, parried all his most skilful passadoes and staccatoes, and in his turn pressed Sanquhar with his foil so hotly and boldly that he unfortunately thrust out one of his eyes. The young baron, ashamed of his own rashness, and not convinced that Turner's thrust was only a slip and an accident, bore with patience several days of extreme danger. As for Turner, he displayed natural regret, and was exonerated by everybody. Some time after, Lord Sanquhar being in the court of Henry IV. of France, that chivalrous and gallant king, always courteous to strangers, seeing the patch of green taffeta, unfortunately, merely to make conversation, asked the young Scotchman how he lost his eye. Sanquhar, not willing to lose the credit of a wound, answered cannily, "It was done, your majesty, with a sword." The king replied, thoughtlessly, "Doth the man live?" and no more was said. This remark, however, awoke the viper of revenge in the young man's soul. He brooded over those words, and never ceased to dwell on the hope of some requital on his old opponent. Two years he remained in France, hoping that his wound might be cured, and at last, in despair of such a result, set sail for England, still brooding over revenge against the author of his cruel and, as it now appeared, irreparable misfortune. The King of Denmark, James's toss-pot father-in-law, was on a visit here at the time, and the court was very gay. The first news that Lord Sanquhar heard was, that the accursed Turner was down at Greenwich Palace, fencing there in public matches before the two kings. To these entertainments the young Scotchman went, and there, from some corner of a gallery, the man with a patch over his eye no doubt scowled and bit his lip at the fencing-master, as he strutted beneath, proud of his skill and flushed with triumph. The moment the prizes were given, Sanquhar hurried below, and sought Turner up and down, through court and corridor, resolved to stab him on the spot, though even drawing a sword in the precincts of the palace was an offence punishable with the loss of a hand. Turner, however, at that time escaped, for Sanquhar never came across him in the throng, though he beat it as a dog beats a covert. The next day, therefore, still on his trail, Lord Sanquhar went after him to London, seeking for him up and down the Strand, and in all the chief Fleet Street and Cheapside taverns. The Scot could not have come to a more dangerous place than London. Some, with malicious pity, would tell him that Turner had vaunted of his skilful thrust, and the way he had punished a man who tried to publicly shame him. Others would thoughtlessly lament the spoiling of a good swordsman and a brave soldier. The mere sight of the turnings to Whitefriars would rouse the evil spirit nestling in Sanquhar's heart. Eagerly he sought for Turner, till he found he was gone down to Norris's house, in Oxfordshire—the very place where the fatal wound had been inflicted. Being thus for the time foiled, Sanquhar returned to Scotland, and for the present delayed his revenge. On his next visit to London Sanquhar, cruel and steadfast as a bloodhound, again sought for Turner. Yet the difficulty was to surprise the man, for Sanquhar was well known in all the taverns and fencing-schools of Whitefriars, and yet did not remember Turner sufficiently well to be sure of him. He therefore hired two Scotchmen, who undertook his assassination; but, in spite of this, Turner somehow or other was hard to get at, and escaped his two pursuers and the relentless man whose money had bought them. Business then took Sanquhar again to France, but on his return the brooding revenge, now grown to a monomania, once more burst into a flame.

At last he hired Carlisle and Gray, two Scotchmen, who were to take a lodging in Whitefriars, to discover the best way for Sanquhar himself to strike a sure blow at the unconscious fencing-master. These men, after some reconnoitring, assured their employer that he could not himself get at Turner, but that they would undertake to do so, to which Sanquhar assented. But Gray's heart failed him after this, and he slipped away; and Turner went again out of town, to fence at some country mansion. Upon this Carlisle, a resolute villain, came to his employer and told him with grim set face that, as Gray had deceived him and there was "trust in no knave of them all," he would e'en have nobody but himself, and would assuredly kill Turner on his return, though it were with the loss of his own life. Irving, a Border lad, and page to Lord Sanquhar, ultimately joined Carlisle in the assassination.

On the 11th of May, 1612, about seven o'clock in the evening, the two murderers came to a tavern in Whitefriars, which Turner usually frequented as he returned from his fencing-school. Turner, sitting at the door with one of his friends, seeing the men, saluted them, and asked them to drink. Carlisle turned to cock the pistol he had prepared, then wheeled round, and drawing the pistol from under his coat, discharged it full at the unfortunate fencing-master, and shot him near the left breast. Turner had only time to cry, "Lord have mercy upon me—I am killed," and fell from the ale-bench, dead. Carlisle and Irving at once fled—Carlisle to the town, Irving towards the river; but the latter, mistaking a court where wood was sold for the turning into an alley, was instantly run down and taken. Carlisle was caught in Scotland, Gray as he was shipping at a sea-port for Sweden; and Sanquhar himself, hearing one hundred pounds were offered for his head, threw himself on the king's mercy by surrendering himself as an object of pity to the Archbishop of Canterbury. But no intercession could avail. It was necessary for James to show that he would not spare Scottish more than English malefactors.

Sanquhar was tried in Westminster Hall on the 27th of June, before Mr. Justice Yelverton. Sir Francis Bacon, the Solicitor-General, did what he could to save the revengeful Scot, but it was impossible to keep him from the gallows. Robert Creighton, Lord Sanquhar, therefore, confessed himself guilty, but pleaded extenuating circumstances. He had, he said, always believed that Turner boasted he had put out his eye of set purpose, though at the taking up the foils he (Sanquhar) had specially protested that he played as a scholar, and not as one able to contend with a master in the profession. The mode of playing among scholars was always to spare the face.

"After this loss of my eye," continued the quasi-repentant murderer, "and with the great hazard of the loss of life, I must confess that I ever kept a grudge of my soul against Turner, but had no purpose to take so high a revenge; yet in the course of my revenge I considered not my wrongs upon terms of Christianity—for then I should have sought for other satisfaction—but, being trained up in the courts of princes and in arms, I stood upon the terms of honour, and thence befell this act of dishonour, whereby I have offended—first, God; second, my prince; third, my native country; fourth, this country; fifth, the party murdered; sixth, his wife; seventh, posterity; eighth, Carlisle, now to be executed; and lastly, ninth, my own soul, and I am now to die for my offence. But, my lords," he added, "besides my own offence, which in its nature needs no aggravation, divers scandalous reports are given out which blemish my reputation, which is more dear to me than my life : first, that I made show of reconciliation with Turner, the which, I protest, is utterly untrue, for what I have formerly said I do again assure your good lordships, that ever after my hurt received I kept a grudge in my soul against him, and never made the least pretence of reconciliation with him. Yet this, my lords, I will say, that if he would have confessed and sworn he did it not of purpose, and withal would have foresworn arms, I would have pardoned him ; for, my lords, I considered that it must be done either of set purpose or ignorantly. If the first, I had no occasion to pardon him ; if the last, that is no excuse in a master, and therefore for revenge of such a wrong I thought him unworthy to bear arms."

Lord Sanquhar then proceeded to deny the aspersion that he was an ill-natured fellow, ever revengeful, and delighting in blood. He confessed, however, that he was never willing to put up with a wrong, nor to pardon where he had a power to retaliate. He had never been guilty of blood till now, though he had occasion to draw his sword, both in the field and on sudden violences, where he had both given and received hurts. He allowed that, upon commission from the king to suppress wrongs done him in his own country, he had put divers of the Johnsons to death, but for that he hoped he had need neither to ask God nor man for forgiveness. He denied, on his salvation, that by the help of his countrymen he had attempted to break prison and escape. The condemned prisoner finally begged the lords to let the following circumstances move them to pity and the king to mercy :—First, the indignity received from so mean a man ; second, that it was done willingly, for he had been informed that Turner had bragged of it after it was done ; third, the perpetual loss of his eye ; fourth, the want of law to give satisfaction in such a case ; fifth, the continued blemish he had received thereby.

The Solicitor-General (Bacon), in his speech, took the opportunity of fulsomely bepraising the king after his manner. He represented the sputtering, drunken, corrupt James as almost divine, in his energy and sagacity. He had stretched forth his long arms (for kings, he said, had long arms), and taken Gray as he shipped for Sweden, Carlisle ere he was yet warm in his house in Scotland. He had prosecuted the offenders "with the breath and blasts of his mouth ;" "so that," said this gross time-server, "I may conclude that his majesty hath showed himself God's true lieutenant, and that he is no respecter of persons, but English, Scots, noblemen, fencers (which is but an ignoble trade), are all to him alike in respect of justice. Nay, I may say further, that his majesty hath had in this matter a kind of prophetical spirit, for at what time Carlisle and Gray, and you, my lord, yourself, were fled no man knew whither, to the four winds, the king ever spoke in confident and undertaking manner, that wheresoever the offenders were in Europe, he would produce them to justice."

Mr. Justice Yelverton, though Bacon had altogether taken the wind out of his sails, summed up in the same vein, to prove that James was a Solomon and a prophet, and would show no favouritism to Scotchmen. He held out no hope of a reprieve. "The base and barbarous murder," he said, with ample legal verbiage, 'was exceeding strange ;—done upon the sudden ! done in an instant ! done with a pistol ! done with your own pistol ! under the colour of kindness. As Cain talked with his brother Abel, he rose up and slew him. Your executioners of the murder left the poor miserable man no time to defend himself, scarce any time to breathe out those last words, 'Lord, have mercy upon me !' The ground of the malice that you bore him grew not out of any offence that he ever willingly gave you, but out of the pride and haughtiness of your own self; for that in the false conceit of your own skill you would needs importune him to that action, the sequel whereof did most unhappily breed your blemish—the loss of your eye." The manner of his death would be, no doubt, as he (the prisoner) would think, unbefitting to a man of his honour and blood (a baron of 300 years' antiquity), but was fit enough for such an offender. Lord Sanquhar was then sentenced to be hung till he was dead. The populace, from whom he expected "scorn and disgrace," were full of pity for a man to be cut off, like Shakespeare's Claudio, in his prime, and showed great compassion.

On the 29th of June (St. Peter's Day) Lord Sanquhar was hung before Westminster Hall. On the ladder he confessed the enormity of his sins, but said that till his trial, blinded by the devil, he could not see he had done anything unfitting a man of his rank and quality, who had been trained up in the wars, and had lived the life of a soldier, standing more on points of honour than religion. He then professed that he died a Roman Catholic, and begged all Roman Catholics present to pray for him. He had long, he said, for worldly reasons, neglected the public profession of his faith, and he thought God was angry with him. His religion was a good religion—a saving religion—and if he had been constant to it he was verily persuaded he should never have fallen into that misery. He then prayed for the king, queen, their issue, the State of England and Scotland, and the lords of the Council and Church, after which the wearied executioner threw him from the ladder, suffering him to hang a long time to display the king's justice. The compassion and sympathy of

the series of the Waverley novels, and the best suited to dramatic adaptation. Sir Walter chooses a den of Alsatia as a sanctuary for young Nigel, after his duel with Dalgarno. At one stroke of Scott's pen, the foggy, crowded streets eastward of the Temple rise before us, and are thronged with shaggy, uncombed ruffians, with greasy shoulder-belts, discoloured scarves, enormous moustaches, and torn hats. With what a Teniers' pencil the great novelist sketches the dingy precincts, with its

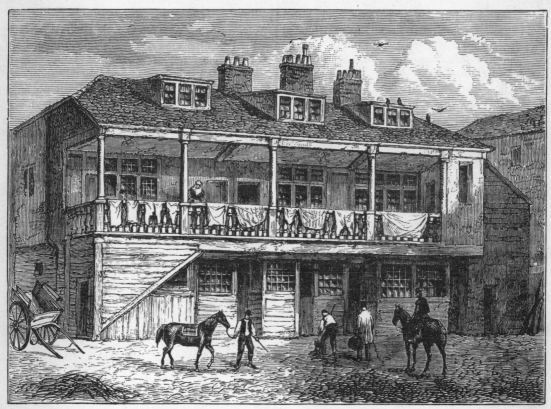

YARD OF THE BLACK LION, WHITEFRIARS (*see page* 195).
From a Drawing (1859) *in Mr. Crace's Collection.*

the people present had abated directly they found he was a Roman Catholic. The same morning, very early, Carlisle and Irving were hung on two gibbets in Fleet Street, over against the great gate of the Whitefriars. The page's gibbet was six feet higher than the serving-man's, it being the custom at that time in Scotland that, when a gentleman was hung at the same time with one of meaner quality, the gentleman had the honour of the higher gibbet, feeling much aggrieved if he had not.

The riotous little kingdom of Whitefriars, with all its frowzy and questionable population, has been admirably drawn by Scott in his fine novel of "The Fortunes of Nigel," one of the most graphic of all

blackguardly population :—" The wailing of children," says the author of "Nigel," "the scolding of their mothers, the miserable exhibition of ragged linen hung from the windows to dry, spoke the wants and distresses of the wretched inhabitants; while the sounds of complaint were mocked and overwhelmed by the riotous shouts, oaths, profane songs, and boisterous laughter that issued from the alehouses and taverns, which, as the signs indicated, were equal in number to all the other houses; and that the full character of the place might be evident, several faded, tinselled, and painted females looked boldly at the strangers from their open lattices, or more modestly seemed busied with the cracked

BRIDEWELL, AS REBUILT AFTER THE FIRE, FROM AN OLD PRINT (*see page 191*).

flower-pots, filled with mignonette and rosemary, which were disposed in front of the windows, to the great risk of the passengers." It is to a dilapidated tavern in the same foul neighbourhood that the gay Templar, it will be remembered, takes Nigel to be sworn in a brother of Whitefriars by drunken and knavish Duke Hildebrod, whom he finds surrounded by his councillors—a bullying Low Country soldier, a broken attorney, and a hedge parson; and it is here also, at the house of old Miser Trapbois, that the young Scot so narrowly escapes death at the hands of the poor old wretch's cowardly assassins.

The scoundrels and cheats of Whitefriars are admirably etched by Dryden's rival, Shadwell. That unjustly-treated writer (for he was by no means a fool) has called one of his comedies, in the Ben Jonson manner, *The Squire of Alsatia.* It paints the manners of the place at the latter end of Charles II.'s reign, when the dregs of an age that was indeed full of dregs were vatted in that disreputable sanctuary east of the Temple. The "copper captains," the degraded clergymen who married anybody, without inquiry, for five shillings, the broken lawyers, skulking bankrupts, sullen homicides, thievish money-lenders, and gaudy courtesans, Dryden's burly rival has painted with a brush full of colour, and with a brightness, clearness, and sharpness which are photographic in their force and truth. In his dedication, which is inscribed to that great patron of poets, the poetical Earl of Dorset, Shadwell dwells on the great success of the piece, the plot of which he had cleverly " adapted " from the *Adelphi* of Terence. In the prologue, which was spoken by Mountfort, the actor, whom the infamous Lord Mohun stabbed in Norfolk Street, the dramatist ridicules his tormentor Dryden, for his noise and bombast, and with some vigour writes—

> " With what prodigious scarcity of wit
> Did the new authors starve the hungry pit !
> Infected by the French, you must have rhyme,
> Which long to please the ladies' ears did chime.
> Soon after this came ranting fustian in,
> And none but plays upon the fret were seen,
> Such daring bombast stuff which fops would praise,
> Tore our best actors' lungs, cut short their days.
> Some in small time did this distemper kill ;
> And had the savage authors gone on still,
> Fustian had been a new disease i' the bill."

The moral of Shadwell's piece is the danger of severity in parents. An elder son, being bred up under restraint, turns a "rake-hell" in Whitefriars, whilst the younger, who has had his own way, becomes "an ingenious, well-accomplished gentleman, a man of honour in King's Bench Walk, and of excellent disposition and temper," in spite of a good deal more gallantry than our stricter age would pardon. The worst of it is that the worthy son is always being mistaken for the scamp, while the miserable Tony Lumpkin passes for a time as the pink of propriety. Eventually, he falls into the hands of some Alsatian tricksters. The first of these, Cheatley, is a rascal who, " by reason of debts, does not stir out of Whitefriars, but there inveigles young men of fortune, and helps them to goods and money upon great disadvantage, is bound for them, and shares with them till he undoes them." Shadwell tickets him, in his *dramatis personæ*, as " a lewd, impudent, debauched fellow." According to his own account, the cheat lies perdu, because his unnatural father is looking for him, to send him home into the country. Number two, Shamwell, is a young man of fortune, who, ruined by Cheatley, has turned decoy-duck, and lives on a share of the spoil. His ostensible reason for concealment is that an alderman's young wife had run away with him. The third rascal, Scrapeall, is a low, hypocritical money-lender, who is secretly in partnership with Cheatley. The fourth rascal is Captain Hackman, a bullying coward, whose wife keeps lodgings, sells cherry brandy, and is of more than doubtful virtue. He had formerly been a sergeant in Flanders, but ran from his colours, dubbed himself captain, and sought refuge in the Friars from a paltry debt. This blustering scamp stands much upon his honour, and is alternately drawing his enormous sword and being tweaked by the nose. A lion in the estimation of fools, he boasts over his cups that he has whipped five men through the lungs. He talks a detestable cant language, calling guineas " megs," and half-guineas " smelts." Money, with him is " the ready," " the rhino," " the darby ;" a good hat is " a rum nab ;" to be well off is to be " rhinocerical." This consummate scoundrel teaches young country Tony Lumpkins to break windows, scour the streets, to thrash the constables, to doctor the dice, and get into all depths of low mischief. Finally, when old Sir William Belfond, the severe old country gentleman, comes to confront his son, during his disgraceful revels at the "George" tavern, in Dogwell Court, Bouverie Street, the four scamps raise a shout of " An arrest ! an arrest ! A bailiff ! a bailiff !" The drawers join in the tumult ; the Friars, in a moment, is in an uproar ; and eventually the old gentleman is chased by all the scum of Alsatia, shouting at the top of their voices, " Stop ! stop ! A bailiff ! a bailiff !" He has a narrow escape of being pulled to pieces, and emerges in Fleet Street, hot, bespattered, and bruised. It was no joke then to threaten the privileges of Whitefriars.

Presently a horn is blown, there is a cry from Water Lane to Hanging-sword Alley, from Ashen-tree Court to Temple Gardens, of "Tip-staff! An arrest! an arrest!" and in a moment they are "up in the Friars," with a cry of "Fall on." The skulking debtors scuttle into their burrows, the bullies fling down cup and can, lug out their rusty blades, and rush into the *mêlée*. From every den and crib red-faced, bloated women hurry with fire-forks, spits, cudgels, pokers, and shovels. They're "up in the Friars," with a ven-geance. Pouring into the Temple before the Templars can gather, they are about to drag old Sir William under the pump, when the worthy son comes to the rescue, and the Templars, with drawn swords, drive back the rabble, and make the porters shut the gates leading into Alsatia. Cheatley, Shamwell, and Hackman, taken prisoners, are then well drubbed and pumped on by the Templars, and the gallant captain loses half his whiskers. "The terror of his face," he moans, "is gone." "Indeed," says Cheatley, "your magnanimous phiz is somewhat disfigured by it, captain." Cheatley threatened endless actions. Hackman swears his honour is very tender, and that this one affront will cost him at least five murders. As for Shamwell, he is inconsolable. "What reparation are actions?" he moans, as he shakes his wet hair and rubs his bruised back. "I am a gentleman, and can never show my face amongst my kindred more." When at last they have got free, they all console them-selves with cherry brandy from Hackman's shop, after which the "copper captain" observes, some-what in Falstaff's manner, "A fish has a cursed life on't. I shall have that aversion to water after this, that I shall scarce ever be cleanly enough to wash my face again."

Later in the play there is still another rising in Alsatia; but this time the musketeers come in force, in spite of all privileges, and the scuffle is greater than ever. Some debtors run up and down with-out coats, others with still more conspicuous de-ficiencies. Some cry, "Oars! oars! sculler; five pound for a boat; ten pound for a boat; twenty pound for a boat;" many leap from balconies, and make for the water, to escape to the Savoy or the Mint, also sanctuaries of that day. The play ends with a dignified protest, which doubtless proved thoroughly effective with the audience, against the privileges of places that harboured such knots of scoundrels. "Was ever," Shadwell says, "such im-pudence suffered in a Government? Ireland con-quered; Wales subdued; Scotland united. But there are some few spots of ground in London, just in the face of the Government, unconquered yet,

that hold in rebellion still. Methinks 'tis strange that places so near the king's palace should be no part of his dominions. 'Tis a shame in the society of law to countenance such practices. Should any place be shut against the king's writ or posse comitatus?"

Be sure the pugnacious young Templars present all rose at that, and great was the thundering of red-heeled shoes. King William probably agreed with Shadwell, for at the latter end of his reign the privilege of sanctuary was taken from Whitefriars, and the dogs were at last let in on the rats for whom they had been so long waiting. Two other places of refuge—the Mint and the Savoy—how-ever, escaped a good deal longer; and there the Hackmans and Cheatleys of the day still hid their ugly faces after daylight had been let into White-friars and the wild days of Alsatia had ceased for ever.

In earlier times there had been evidently special endeavours to preserve order in Whitefriars, for in the State Paper Office there exist the follow-ing rules for the inhabitants of the sanctuary in the reign of Elizabeth :—

"*Item.* Theise gates shalbe orderly shutt and opened at convenient times, and porters appointed for the same. Also, a scavenger to keep the pre-cincte clean.

"*Item.* Tipling houses shalbe bound for good order.

"*Item.* Searches to be made by the constables, with the assistance of the inhabitants, at the com-mandmente of the justices.

"*Item.* Rogues and vagabondes and other dis-turbers of the public peace shall be corrected and punished by the authoretie of the justices.

"*Item*. A bailife to be appointed for leavienge of such duties and profittes which apperteine unto her Matie; as also for returne of proces for execu-tion of justice.

"*Item.* Incontinent persons to be presented unto the Ordenary, to be tried, and punished.

"*Item.* The poore within the precincte shalbe provyded for by the inhabitantes of the same.

"*Item.* In tyme of plague, good order shalbe taken for the restrainte of the same.

"*Item.* Lanterne and light to be mainteined duringe winter time."

All traces of its former condition have long since disappeared from Whitefriars, and it is diffi-cult indeed to believe that the dull, uninteresting region that now lies between Fleet Street and the Thames was once the riotous Alsatia of Scott and Shadwell.

And now we come to Bridewell, first a palace, then

a prison. The palace of Bridewell (St. Bride's Well) was rebuilt upon the site of the old Tower of Montfichuet, a companion of the Conqueror, by Henry VIII., for the reception of Charles V. of France in 1522. There had been a Roman fortification in the same place, and a palace both of the Saxon and Norman kings. Henry I. partly rebuilt the palace; and in 1847 a vault with Norman billet moulding was discovered in excavating the site of a public-house in Bride Lane. It remained neglected till Cardinal Wolsey (*circa* 1512) came in pomp to live here. Here, in 1525, when Henry's affection for Anne Boleyn was growing, he made her father, Thomas Boleyn, Treasurer of the King's House, Viscount Rochford. A letter of Wolsey's, June 6, 1513, to the Lord Admiral, is dated from "my poor house at Bridewell;" and from 1515 to 1521 no less than £21,924 was paid in repairs. Another letter from Wolsey, at Bridewell, mentions that the house of the Lord Prior of St. John's Hospital, at Bridewell, had been granted by the king for a record office. The palace must have been detestable enough to the monks, for it was to his palace of Bridewell that Henry VIII. summoned the abbots and other heads of religious societies, and succeeded in squeezing out of them £100,000, the contumacious Cistercians alone yielding up £33,000.

It was at the palace at Bridewell (in 1528) that King Henry VIII. first disclosed the scruples that, after his acquaintance with Anne Boleyn, troubled his sensitive conscience as to his marriage with Katharine of Arragon. "A few days later," says Lingard, condensing the old chronicles, "the king undertook to silence the murmurs of the people, and summoned to his residence in the Bridewell the members of the Council, the lords of his Court, and the mayor, aldermen, and principal citizens. Before them he enumerated the several injuries which he had received from the emperor, and the motives which induced him to seek the alliance of France. Then, taking to himself credit for delicacy of conscience, he described the scruples which had long tormented his mind on account of his marriage with his deceased brother's widow. These he had at first endeavoured to suppress, but they had been revived and confirmed by the alarming declaration of the Bishop of Tarbes in the presence of his Council. To tranquillise his mind he had recourse to the only legitimate remedy: he had consulted the Pontiff, who had appointed two delegates to hear the case, and by their judgment he was determined to abide. He would therefore warn his subjects to be cautious how they ventured to arraign his conduct. The proudest among them

should learn that he was their sovereign, and should answer with their heads for the presumption of their tongues." Yet, notwithstanding he made all this parade of conscious superiority, Henry was prudent enough not by any means to refuse the aid of precaution. A rigorous search was made for arms, and all strangers, with the exception only of ten merchants from each nation, were ordered to leave the capital.

At the trial for divorce the poor queen behaved with much womanly dignity. "The judges," says Hall, the chronicler, and after him Stow, "commanded the crier to proclaim silence while their commission was read, both to the court and the people assembled. That done, the scribes commanded the crier to call the king by the name of 'King Henry of England, come into court,' &c. With that the king answered, and said, 'Here.' Then he called the queen, by the name of 'Katharine, Queen of England, come into court,' &c., who made no answer, but rose incontinent out of her chair, and because she could not come to the king directly, for the distance secured between them, she went about, and came to the king, kneeling down at his feet in the sight of all the court and people, to whom she said in effect these words, as followeth: 'Sir,' quoth she, 'I desire you to do me justice and right, and take some pity upon me, for I am a poor woman and a stranger, born out of your dominion, having here so indifferent counsel, and less assurance of friendship. Alas! sir, in what have I offended you? or what occasion of displeasure have I showed you, intending thus to put me from you after this sort? I take God to judge, I have been to you a true and humble wife, ever conformable to your will and pleasure; that never contrarised or gainsaid anything thereof; and being always contented with all things wherein you had any delight or dalliance, whether little or much, without grudge or countenance of discontent or displeasure. I loved for your sake all them you loved, whether I had cause or no cause, whether they were my friends or my enemies. I have been your wife these twenty years or more, and you have had by me divers children; and when ye had me at the first, I take God to be judge that I was a very maid; and whether it be true or not, I put it to your conscience. If there be any just cause that you can allege against me, either of dishonesty or matter lawful, to put me from you, I am content to depart, to my shame and rebuke; and if there be none, then I pray you to let me have justice at your hands. The king, your father, was, in his time, of such excellent wit, that he was accounted among all men for wisdom to be a second Solomon; and the

King of Spain, my father, Ferdinand, was reckoned one of the wisest princes that reigned in Spain many years before. It is not, therefore, to be doubted but that they had gathered as wise counsellors unto them of every realm as to their wisdom they thought meet; and as to me seemeth, there were in those days as wise and well-learned in both realms as now at this day, who thought the marriage between you and me good and lawful. Therefore it is a wonder to me to hear what new inventions are now invented against me, that never intended but honesty, and now to cause me to stand to the order and judgment of this court. Ye should, as seemeth me, do me much wrong, for ye may condemn me for lack of answer, having no counsel but such as ye have assigned me; ye must consider that they cannot but be indifferent on my part, where they be your own subjects, and such as ye have taken and chosen out of your council, whereunto they be privy, and dare not disclose your will and intent. Therefore, I humbly desire you, in the way of charity, to spare me until I may know what counsel and advice my friends in Spain will advertise me to take; and if you will not, then your pleasure be fulfilled.' With that she rose up, making a low curtsey to the king, and departed from thence, people supposing that she would have resorted again to her former place, but she took her way straight out of the court, leaning upon the arm of one of her servants, who was her receiver-general, called Master Griffith. The king, being advertised that she was ready to go out of the house where the court was kept, commanded the crier to call her again by these words, ' Katharine, Queen of England,' &c. With that, quoth Master Griffith, ' Madam, ye be called again.' ' Oh! oh!' quoth she, ' it maketh no matter; it is no indifferent (impartial) court for me, therefore I will not tarry: go on your ways.' And thus she departed without any further answer at that time, or any other, and never would appear after in any court."

Bridewell was endowed with the revenues of the Savoy. In 1555 the City companies were taxed for fitting it up; and the next year Machyn records that a thief was hung in one of the courts, and, later on, a riotous attempt was made to rescue prisoners.

In 1863 Mr. Lemon discovered in the State Paper Office some interesting documents relative to the imprisonment in Bridewell, in 1567 (Elizabeth), of many members of the first Congregational Church. Bishop Grindal, writing to Bullinger, in 1568 describes this schism, and estimates its adherents at about 200, but more women than men. Grindal says they held meetings and administered the

sacrament in private houses, fields, and even in ships, and ordained ministers, elders, and deacons, after their own manner. The Lord Mayor, in pity, urged them to recant, but they remained firm. Several of these sufferers for conscience' sake died in prison, including Richard Fitz, their minister, and Thomas Rowland, a deacon. In the year 1597, within two months, 5,468 prisoners, including many Spaniards, were sent to Bridewell.

The Bridewell soon proved costly and inconvenient to the citizens, by attracting idle, abandoned, and "masterless" people. In 1608 (James I.) the City erected at Bridewell twelve large granaries and two coal-stores; and in 1620 the old chapel was enlarged. In the Great Fire (six years after the Restoration) the buildings were nearly all destroyed, and the old castellated river-side mansion of Elizabeth's time was rebuilt in two quadrangles, the chief of which fronted the Fleet river (long a sewer under the centre of Bridge Street). We have already given on page 12 a view of Bridewell as it appeared previous to the. Great Fire; and the general bird's-eye view given on page 187 in the present number shows its appearance after it was rebuilt. Within the present century, Mr. Timbs says, the committee-rooms, chapel, and prisons were rebuilt, and the whole formed a large quadrangle, with an entrance from Bridge Street, the keystone of the arch being sculptured with the head of Edward VI. Bridewell stone bridge over the Fleet was painted by Hayman, Hogarth's friend, and engraved by Grignon, as the frontispiece to the third volume of " The Dunciad." In the burial-ground at Bridewell, now the coal-yard of the City Gas Company, was buried, in 1752, Dr. Johnson's friend and protégé, poor blameless Levett. The last interment took place here, Mr. Noble says, in 1844, and the trees and tombstones were then carted away. The gateway into Bridge Street is still standing, and such portions of the building as still remain are used for the house and offices of the treasury of the Bridewell Hospital property, which includes Bedlam.

The flogging at Bridewell is described by Ward, in his " London Spy." Both men and women, it appears, were whipped on their naked backs before the court of governors. The president sat with his hammer in his hand, and the culprit was taken from the post when the hammer fell. The calls to knock when women were flogged were loud and incessant. " Oh, good Sir Robert, knock! Pray, good Sir Robert, knock!" which became at length a common cry of reproach among the lower orders, to denote that a woman had been whipped in Bridewell. Madame Creswell, the celebrated procuress of King Charles II.'s reign, died a prisoner in Bridewell. She desired by *will* to have a sermon preached at her funeral, for which the preacher was to have £10, but upon this express condition, that he was to say nothing but what was well of her. A preacher was with some difficulty found who undertook the task. He, after a sermon preached on the general subject of mortality, concluded with saying, "By the will of the deceased, it is expected that I should mention her, and say

of £10 each. Many of these boys, says Hatton, "arrived from nothing to be governors." They wore a blue dress and white hats, and attended fires, with an engine belonging to the hospital. The lads at last became so turbulent, that in 1785 their special costume was abandoned. "Job's Pound" was the old cant name for Bridewell, and it is so called in "Hudibras."

The scene of the fourth plate of Hogarth's "Harlot's Progress," finished in 1733 (George II.),

NEW BRIDGE STREET AND THE OBELISK IN 1755.
From a Print published in 1800.

nothing but what was *well* of her. All that I shall say of her, therefore, is this : She was born *well*, she lived *well*, and she died *well;* for she was born with the name of Cres*well*, she lived in Clerken*well*, and she died in Bride*well*."

In 1708 (Queen Anne) Hatton describes Bridewell "as a house of correction for idle, vagrant, loose, and disorderly persons, and 'night walkers,' who are there set to hard labour, but receive clothes and diet." It was also a hospital for indigent persons. Twenty art-masters, decayed traders, were also lodged, and received about 140 apprentices. The boys, after learning tailoring, weaving, flax-dressing, &c., received the freedom of the City, and presents

.is laid in Bridewell. There, in a long, dilapidated, tiled shed, a row of female prisoners are beating hemp on wooden blocks, while a truculent-looking warder, with an apron on, is raising his rattan to strike a poor girl not without some remains of her youthful beauty, who seems hardly able to lift the heavy mallet, while the wretches around leeringly deride her fine apron, laced hood, and figured gown. There are two degraded men among the female hemp-beaters—one an old card-sharper in laced coat and foppish wig ; another who stands with his hands in a pillory, on which is inscribed the admonitory legend, "Better to work than stand thus." A cocked hat and a dilapidated hoop hang on the wall.

That excellent man, Howard, visiting Bridewell in 1783, gives it a bad name, in his book on "Prisons." He describes the rooms as offensive, the prisoners receiving only one penny loaf a day each. The steward received eightpence a day for each prisoner, and a hemp-dresser, paid a salary palace remaining, and a magnificent flight of ancient stairs leading to the court of justice. In the next room, where the whipping-stocks were, tradition says sentence of divorce was pronounced against Katherine of Arragon.

"The first time," says Pennant, "I visited the

INTERIOR OF THE DUKE'S THEATRE. *From Settle's "Empress of Morocco."* (*See page* 195.)

of £20, had the profit of the culprits' labour. For bedding the prisoners had fresh straw given them once a month. It was the only London prison where either straw or bedding was allowed. No out-door exercise was permitted. In the year 1782 there had been confined in Bridewell 659 prisoners.

In 1790, Pennant describes Bridewell as still having arches and octagonal towers of the old place, there was not a single male prisoner, but about twenty females. They were confined on a ground floor, and employed on the beating of hemp. When the door was opened by the keeper, they ran towards it like so many hounds in kennel, and presented a most moving sight. About twenty young creatures, the eldest not exceeding sixteen, many of them with angelic faces divested of every angelic expression, featured with impudence, impenitency, and profligacy, and clothed in the silken tatters of squalid finery. A magisterial—a national—opprobrium! What a disadvantageous contrast to the *Spinhaus*, in Amsterdam, where the confined sit under the eye of a matron, spinning or sewing, in plain and neat dresses provided by the public! No traces of their former lives appear in their countenances; a thorough reformation seems to have been effected, equally to the emolument and the honour of the republic. This is also the place of confinement for disobedient and idle apprentices. They are kept separate, in airy cells, and have an allotted task to be performed in a certain time. They, the men and women, are employed in beating hemp, picking oakum, and packing of goods, and are said to earn their maintenance."

A writer in "Knight's London" (1843) gives a very bad account of Bridewell. "Bridewell, another place of confinement in the City of London, is under the jurisdiction of the governors of Bridewell and Bethlehem Hospitals, but it is supported out of the funds of the hospital. The entrance is in Bridge Street, Blackfriars. The prisoners confined here are persons summarily convicted by the Lord Mayor and aldermen, and are, for the most part, petty pilferers, misdemeanants, vagrants, and refractory apprentices, sentenced to solitary confinement; which term need not terrify the said refractory offenders, for the persons condemned to solitude," says the writer, "can with ease keep up a conversation with each other from morning to night. The total number of persons confined here in 1842 was 1,324, of whom 233 were under seventeen, and 466 were known or reputed thieves. In 1818 no employment was furnished to the prisoners. The men sauntered about from hour to hour in those chambers where the worn blocks still stood and exhibited the marks of the toil of those who are represented in Hogarth's prints.

"'The treadmill has been now introduced, and more than five-sixths of the prisoners are sentenced to hard labour, the 'mill' being employed in grinding corn for Bridewell, Bethlehem, and the House of Occupation. The 'Seventh Report of the Inspectors of Prisons on the City Bridewell' is as follows:—'The establishment answers no one object of imprisonment except that of safe custody. It does not correct, deter, nor reform; but we are convinced that the association to which all but the City apprentices are subjected proves highly injurious, counteracts any efforts that can be made for the moral and religious improvement of the prisoners, corrupts the less criminal, and confirms the degradation of the more hardened offenders. The cells in the old part of the prison are greatly superior to those in the adjoining building, which is of comparatively recent erection, but the whole of the arrangements are exceedingly defective. It is quite lamentable to see such an injudicious and unprofitable expenditure as that which was incurred in the erection of this part of the prison.'"

Latterly Bridewell was used as a receptacle for vagrants, and as a temporary lodging for paupers on their way to their respective parishes. The prisoners sentenced to hard labour were put on a treadmill which ground corn. The other prisoners picked junk. The women cleaned the prison, picked junk, and mended the linen. In 1829 there was built adjoining Bedlam a House of Occupation for young prisoners. It was decided that from the revenue of the Bridewell hospital (£12,000) reformatory schools were to be built. The annual number of contumacious apprentices sent to Bridewell rarely exceeded twenty-five, and when Mr. Timbs visited the prison in 1863 he says he found only one lad out of the three thousand apprentices of the great City. In 1868 (says Mr. Noble) the governors refused to receive a convicted apprentice, for the very excellent reason that there was no cell to receive him.

The old court-room of Bridewell (84 by 29) was a handsome wainscoted room, adorned with a great picture, erroneously attributed to Holbein, and representing Edward VI. granting the Royal Charter of Endowment to the Mayor, which now hangs over the western gallery of the hall of Christ's Hospital. It was engraved by Vertue in 1750, and represents an event which happened ten years after the death of the supposed artist.

Beneath this was a cartoon of the "Good Samaritan," by Dadd, but this has since been removed to Bedlam.

There was a fine full-length of swarthy Charles II. by Lely, and full-lengths of George III. and Queen Charlotte, after Reynolds. There were murky portraits of past presidents, including an equestrian portrait of Sir William Withers (1708). Tables of benefactions also adorned the walls.

In this hall the governors of Bridewell dined annually, each steward contributing a sum of £15 towards the expenses, the dinner being dressed in a large kitchen below, which was used only for that purpose. The hall and kitchen were taken down so lately as 1862.

In the entrance corridor from Bridge Street (says Mr. Timbs) are the old chapel gates, of fine ironwork, originally presented by the equestrian Sir William Withers; and on the staircase is a bust of the venerable Chamberlain Clarke, who died in his ninety-third year.

The Bridewell prison was pulled down (except the hall, treasurer's house, and offices) in 1863, when its inmates were sent to Holloway.

Bridewell Dock, now covered by Tudor and William Streets, was long noted for its taverns, and was a favourite landing-place for the Thames watermen.

The "George" Tavern, in Whitefriars, before mentioned (see p. 188), figures in Mrs. Behn's "Lucky Chance" (1687); it was afterwards the printing-office of William Bowyer, whom Nichols commemorates in his "Literary Anecdotes;" it was next occupied by Thomas Davison, a well-known printer in his time, and latterly became the printing establishment of Messrs. Bradbury and Co. Another old and well-known tavern in this locality, but one that has remained to this day, in name, at least, is the "Black Lion," on the west side of Whitefriars Street. The old house, a quaint and picturesque edifice, of which we give a view on p. 186, was pulled down in 1877, and a large tavern, more in conformity with modern tastes, has been erected in its place.

The gas-works of Whitefriars, established in 1814, were removed about 1870 to Barking, in Essex. In 1807 Mr. Winsor, a German, first lit a part of London (Pall Mall) with gas, and in 1809 he applied for a charter. Yet, even as late as 1813, the inquest-men prosecuted two persons, named Sturt and Knight, for endangering the health of the inhabitants by the "making of gas-light;" but the latter, nevertheless, went on committing his harmless misdemeanour, and in the next year (1814) started a company and built gas-works on the bank of the river at Whitefriars. On a part of the site of these gas-works the governors of the City of London School are about to erect schools to accommodate six hundred day scholars.

The first theatre in Whitefriars seems to have been built in the hall of the old Whitefriars Monastery. Mr. J. P. Collier gives the duration of this theatre as from 1586 to 1613. A memorandum from the manuscript-book of Sir Henry Herbert, Master of the Revels to King Charles I., notes that "I committed Cromes, a broker in Long Lane, the 16th of February, 1634, to the Marshalsey, for lending a Church robe, with the name of Jesus upon it, to the players in Salisbury Court, to represent a flamen, a priest of the heathens. Upon his petition of submission and acknowledgment of his fault, I released him the 17th February, 1634."

The Whitefriars Theatre (erected originally in the precincts of the monastery, to be out of the jurisdiction of the Lord Mayor) seems to have become disreputable in 1609, and ruinous in 1619, when it is mentioned that "the rain hath made its way in, and if it be not repaired it must soon be plucked down, or it will fall." The Salisbury Court Theatre, which took its place, was erected about 1629, and the Earl of Dorset somewhat illegally let it for a term of sixty-one years and £950 down, Dorset House being afterwards sold for £4,000. The theatre was destroyed by the Puritan soldiers in 1649, and not rebuilt till the Restoration.

At the outbreak of pleasure and vice, after the Restoration, the actors, long starved and crestfallen, brushed up their plumes and burnished their tinsel. Killigrew, that clever buffoon of the Court, opened a new theatre in Drury Lane in 1663, with a play of Beaumont and Fletcher's; and Davenant (supposed to be Shakespeare's illegitimate son) opened the little theatre, long disused, in Salisbury Court, the rebuilding of which was commenced in 1660, on the site of the granary of Salisbury House. In time Davenant migrated to the old Tennis Court, in Portugal Street, on the south side of Lincoln's Inn Fields, and when the Great Fire came it erased the Granary Theatre. In 1671, on Davenant's death, the company (nominally managed by his widow) returned to the new theatre in Salisbury Court, designed by Wren, and decorated, it is said, by Grinling Gibbons. It opened with Dryden's *Sir Martin Marall*, which had already had a run, having been first played in 1668. On Killigrew's death, the King's and Duke's Servants united, and removed to Drury Lane in 1682; so that the Dorset Gardens Theatre flourished for only eleven years in all. It was subsequently let to wrestlers, fencers, and other brawny and wiry performers. The engraving on page 193, taken from Settle's "Empress of Morocco" (1678), represents the stage of the theatre in Lincoln's Inn Fields. Wren's new theatre in Dorset Gardens, an engraving of which is given on page 138, fronted the river, and had public stairs for the convenience of those who came by water. There was also an open place before the theatre for the coaches of the "quality." In 1698 it was used for the drawing of a penny lottery; but in 1703, when it threatened to re-open, Queen Anne finally closed it. It was standing, however, in 1720, when Strype drew up the continuation of Stow, but it was shortly after turned into a timber-yard. The New River Company next had their offices there, and in 1814 water was ousted by fire, and the City Gas Works were established in this quarter, with a dismal front to the bright and pleasant Embankment.

Pepys, the indefatigable, was a frequent visitor to the Whitefriars Theatre. A few of his quaint remarks will not be uninteresting :—

"1660.—By water to Salsbury Court Playhouse, where, not liking to sit, we went out again, and by coach to the theatre, &c.—To the playhouse, and there saw *The Changeling*, the first time it hath been acted these twenty years, and it takes exceedingly. Besides, I see the gallants do begin to be tyred with the vanity and pride of the theatre actors, who are indeed grown very proud and rich.

"1661.—To White-fryars, and saw *The Bondman* acted; an excellent play, and well done; but above all that I ever saw, Betterton do the Bondman the best.

"1661.—After dinner I went to the theatre, where I found so few people (which is strange, and the reason I do not know) that I went out again, and so to Salisbury Court, where the house as full as could be; and it seems it was a new play, *The Queen's Maske*, wherein there are some good humours; among others, a good jeer to the old story of the siege of Troy, making it to be a common country tale. But above all it was strange to see so little a boy as that was to act Cupid, which is one of the greatest parts in it.

"Creed and I to Salisbury Court, and there saw *Love's Quarrell* acted the first time, but I do not like the design or words. . . . . To Salsbury Court Playhouse, where was acted the first time a simple play, and ill acted, only it was my fortune to sit by a most pretty and most ingenuous lady, which pleased me much."

Dryden, in his prologues, makes frequent mention of the Dorset Gardens Theatre, more especially in the address on the opening of the new Drury Lane, March, 1674. The Whitefriars house, under Davenant, had been the first to introduce regular scenery, and it prided itself on stage pomp and show. The year before, in Shadwell's opera of *The Tempest, or the Enchanted Island*, the machinery was very costly; and one scene, in which the spirits flew away with the wicked duke's table and viands just as the company was sitting down, had excited the town to enthusiasm. *Psyche*, another opera by Shadwell, perhaps adapted from Molière's Court spectacle, had succeeded the *Tempest*. St. André and his French dancers were probably engaged in Shadwell's piece. The king, whose taste and good sense the poet praises, had recommended simplicity of dress and frugality of ornament. This Dryden took care to well remember. He says :—

"You who each day can theatres behold,
Like Nero's palace, shining all in gold,
Our mean, ungilded stage will scorn, we fear,
And for the homely room disdain the cheer."

Then he brings in the dictum of the king :—

"Yet if some pride with want may be allowed,
We in our plainness may be justly proud :
Our royal master willed it should be so ;
Whate'er he's pleased to own can need no show.
That sacred name gives ornament and grace,
And, like his stamp, makes basest metal pass.
'Twere folly now a stately pile to raise,
To build a playhouse, while you throw down plays.
While scenes, machines, and empty operas reign,
And for the pencil you the pen disdain :
While troops of famished Frenchmen hither drive,
And laugh at those upon whose alms they live,
Old English authors vanish, and give place
To these new conquerors of the Norman race."

And when, in 1671, the burnt-out Drury Lane company had removed to the Portugal Street Theatre, Dryden wrote, in the same strain,—

"So we expect the lovers, braves, and wits ;
The gaudy house with scenes will serve for cits."

In another epilogue Dryden alludes sarcastically to the death of Mr. Scroop, a young rake of fortune, who had just been run through by Sir Thomas Armstrong, a sworn friend of the Duke of Monmouth, in a quarrel at the Dorset Gardens Theatre, and died soon after. This fatal affray took place during the representation of Davenant's adaptation of *Macbeth*.

From Dryden's various prologues and epilogues we cull many sharply-outlined and bright-coloured pictures of the wild and riotous audiences of those evil days. We see again the "hot Burgundians" in the upper boxes wooing the masked beauties, crying "*bon*" to the French dancers and beating cadence to the music that had stirred even the stately Court of Versailles. Again we see the scornful critics, bunched with glistening ribbons, shaking back their cascades of blonde hair, lolling contemptuously on the foremost benches, and "looking big through their curls." There from "Fop's Corner" rises the tipsy laugh, the prattle, and the chatter, as the dukes and lords, the wits and courtiers, practise what Dryden calls "the diving bow," or "the toss and the new French wallow"—the diving bow being especially admired, because it—

"With a shug casts all the hair before,
Till he, with full decorum, brings it back,
And rises with a water-spaniel's shake."

Nor does the poet fail to recall the affrays in the upper boxes, when some quarrelsome rake was often pinned to the wainscot by the sword of his insulted rival. Below, at the door, the Flemish horses and the heavy gilded coach, lighted by flambeaux, are waiting for the noisy gallant, and will take back only his corpse.

Of Dryden's coldly licentious comedies and ranting bombastic tragedies a few only seem to have been produced at the Dorset Gardens Theatre. Among these we may mention *Limberham*, *Œdipus*, *Troilus and Cressida*, and *The Spanish Friar*. *Limberham* was acted at the Duke's Theatre, in Dorset Gardens; because, being a satire upon a Court vice, it was deemed peculiarly calculated for that playhouse. The concourse of the citizens thither is alluded to in the prologue to *Marriage à la Mode*. Ravenscroft, also, in his epilogue to the play of *Citizen Turned Gentleman*, which was acted at the same theatre, takes occasion to disown the patronage of the more dissolute courtiers, in all probability because they formed the minor part of his audience. The citizens were his great patrons.

In the *Postman*, December 8, 1679, there is the following notice, quoted by Smith:—"At the request of several persons of quality, on Saturday next, being the 9th instant, at the theatre in Dorset Gardens, the famous Kentish men, Wm. and Rich. Joy, design to show to the town before they leave it the same tryals of strength, both of them, that Wm. had the honour of showing before his majesty and their royal highnesses, with several other persons of quality, for which he received a considerable gratuity. The lifting a weight of two thousand two hundred and forty pounds. His holding an extraordinary large cart-horse; and breaking a rope which will bear three thousand five hundred weight. Beginning exactly at two, and ending at four. The boxes, 4s.; the pit, 2s. 6d.; first gallery, 2s.; upper gallery, 1s. Whereas several scandalous persons have given out that they can do as much as any of the brothers, we do offer to such persons £100 reward, if he can perform the said matters of strength as they do, provided the pretender will forfeit £20 if he doth not. The day it is performed will be affixed a signal-flag on the theatre. No money to be returned after once paid."

In 1681 Dr. Davenant seems, by rather unfair tactics, to have bought off and pensioned both Hart and Kynaston from the King's Company, and so to have greatly weakened his rivals. Of these two actors some short notice may not be uninteresting. Hart had been a Cavalier captain during the Civil Wars, and was a pupil of Robinson, the actor, who was shot down at the taking of Basing House. Hart was a tragedian who excelled in parts that required a certain heroic and chivalrous dignity. As a youth, before the Restoration, when boys played female parts, Hart was successful as the Duchess, in Shirley's *Cardinal*. In Charles's time he played Othello, by the king's command, and rivalled Betterton's Hamlet at the other house. He created the part of Alexander, was excellent as Brutus, and terribly and vigorously wicked as Ben Jonson's Cataline. Rymer, says Dr. Doran, styled Hart and Mohun the Æsopus and Roscius of their time. As Amintor and Melanthus, in *The Maid's Tragedy*, they were incomparable. Pepys is loud too in his praises of Hart. His salary, was, however, at the most, £3 a week, though he realised £1,000 yearly after he became a shareholder of the theatre. Hart died in 1683, within a year of his being bought off.

Kynaston, in his way, was also a celebrity. As a handsome boy he had been renowned for playing heroines, and he afterwards acquired celebrity by his dignified impersonation of kings and tyrants. Betterton, the greatest of all the Charles II. actors, also played occasionally at Dorset Gardens. Pope knew him; Dryden was his friend; Kneller painted him. He was probably the greatest Hamlet that ever appeared; and Cibber sums up all eulogy of him when he says, "I never heard a line in tragedy come from Betterton wherein my judgment, my ear, and my imagination were not fully satisfied, which since his time I cannot equally say of any one actor whatsoever." The enchantment of his voice was such, adds the same excellent dramatic critic, that the multitude no more cared for sense in the words he spoke, "than our musical connoiseurs think it essential in the celebrated airs of an Italian opera."

Even when Whitefriars was at its grandest, and plumes moved about its narrow river-side streets, Dorset House was its central and most stately mansion. It was originally a mansion with gardens, belonging to a Bishop of Winchester; but about the year 1217 (Henry III.) a lease was granted by William, Abbot of Westminster, to Richard, Bishop of Sarum, at the yearly rent of twenty shillings, the Abbot retaining the advowson of St. Bride's Church, and promising to impart to the said bishop any needful ecclesiastical advice. It afterwards fell into the hands of the Sackvilles, held at first by a long lease from the see, but was eventually alienated by Bishop Jewel. In 1611 a grant from James I. confirmed the manor of Salisbury Court to Richard, Earl of Dorset.

This Earl of Dorset, to whom Bishop Jewel alienated the Whitefriars House, was the father of the poet, Thomas Sackville, Lord High Treasurer to Queen Elizabeth. The bishop received in exchange for the famous old house a piece of land near Cricklade, in Wiltshire. The poet earl was that wise old statesman who began "The Mirror for Magistrates," an allegorical poem of gloomy power, in which the poet intended to make all the great statesmen of England since the Conquest pass one by one to tell their troublous stories. He, however, lived to write only one legend—that of Henry Stafford, Duke of Bucking-

> Went on three feet, and sometimes crept on four,
> With old lame bones, that rattled by his side;
> His scalp all pil'd, and he with eld forelore,
> His wither'd fist still knocking at death's door;
> Fumbling and drivelling, as he draws his breath;
> For brief, the shape and messenger of death."

At the Restoration, the Marquis of Newcastle,—the author of a magnificent book on horseman-

BAYNARD'S CASTLE, FROM A VIEW PUBLISHED IN 1790 (*see page* 200).

ham. One of his finest and most Holbeinesque passages relates to old age :—

> "And next in order sad, Old Age we found;
> His beard all hoar, his eyes hollow and blind;
> With drooping cheer still poring on the ground,
> As on the place where Nature him assigned
> To rest, when that the sisters had untwined
> His vital thread, and ended with their knife
> The fleeting course of fast declining life.
> Crooked-back'd he was, tooth-shaken, and blear-eyed,

ship—and his pedantic wife, whom Scott has sketched so well in "Peveril of the Peak," inhabited a part of Dorset House; but whether Great Dorset House or Little Dorset House, topographers do not record. "Great Dorset House," says Mr. Peter Cunningham, quoting Lady Anne Clifford's "Memoirs," "was the jointure house of Cicely Baker, Dowager Countess of Dorset, who died in it in 1615 (James I.)."

FALLING IN OF THE CHAPEL AT BLACKFRIARS (see page 202).

CHAPTER XVIII.

BLACKFRIARS.

Three Norman Fortresses on the Thames' Bank—The Black Parliament—The Trial of Katherine of Arragon—Shakespeare a Blackfriars Manager
—The Blackfriars Puritans—The Jesuit Sermon at Hunsdon House—Fatal Accident—Extraordinary Escapes—Queen Elizabeth at Lord
Herbert's Marriage—Old Blackfriars Bridge—Johnson and Mylne—Laying of the Stone—The Inscription—A Toll Riot—Failure of the
Bridge—The New Bridge—Bridge Street—Sir Richard Phillips and his Works—Painters in Blackfriars—The King's Printing Office—
Printing House Square—The *Times* and its History—Walter's Enterprise—War with the *Dispatch*—The Gigantic Swindling Scheme exposed
by the *Times*—Apothecaries' Hall—Quarrel with the College of Physicians.

ON the river-side, between St. Paul's and White-friars, there stood, in the Middle Ages, three Norman fortresses. Baynard Castle and the old tower of Mountfichuet were two of them. Baynard Castle, granted to the Earls of Clare and afterwards rebuilt by Humphrey, Duke of Gloucester, was the palace in which the Duke of Buckingham offered the crown to his wily confederate, Richard the Crookback. In Queen Elizabeth's time it was granted to the Earls of Pembroke, who lived there in splendour till the Great Fire melted their gold, calcined their jewels, and drove them into the fashionable flood that was already moving westward. Mountfichuet Castle was pulled down in 1276, when Hubert de Burgh, Earl of Kent, transplanted a colony of Black Dominican friars from Holborn, near Lincoln's Inn, to the river-side, south of Ludgate Hill. Yet so conservative is even Time in England, that a correspondent of *Notes and Queries* pointed out a piece of mediæval walling and the fragment of a buttress, still standing in 1874, near the *Times* Office, in Printing House Square, which seem to have formed part of the stronghold of the Mountfichuets. This interesting relic was visible on the north of Queen Victoria Street, going up from the bridge, just where there was formerly a picturesque but dangerous descent by a flight of break-neck stone steps. At the right-hand side of the same street stood an old rubble chalk wall, even older. It adjoined the new house of the Bible Society, and seemed to have formed part of the old City wall, which at first ended at Baynard Castle. The rampart advanced to Mountfichuet; and, lastly, to please and protect the Dominicans, was pushed forward outside Ludgate to the Fleet, which served as a moat, the Old Bailey being an advanced work.

King Edward I. and Queen Eleanor heaped many gifts on these sable friars. Charles V. of France was lodged at their monastery when he visited England; but his nobles resided in Henry's newly-built palace of Bridewell, a gallery being thrown over the Fleet and driven through the City wall, to serve as a communication between the two mansions. Henry held the "Black Parliament" in this monastery, and here Cardinal Campeggio presided at the trial which ended with the tyrant's divorce from the ill-used Katherine of Arragon. In the same house also sat the Parliament that condemned Wolsey, and sent him to beg "a little earth for charity" of the monks of Leicester. The rapacious king laid his rough hand on the treasures of the house in 1538; and Edward VI. sold the hall and prior's lodgings to Sir Francis Bryan, a courtier, afterwards granting to Sir Francis Cawarden, Master of the Revels, the whole house and precincts of the Preacher Friars, the yearly value being then estimated at nineteen pounds. The holy brothers were dispersed to beg or thieve, and the church was pulled down, but the mischievous right of sanctuary continued.

And now we come to the event which connects the old monastic ground with the name of the great genius of England. James Burbage (afterwards Shakespeare's friend and fellow-actor), and other servants of the Earl of Leicester, tormented out of the City by over-scrupulous Lord Mayors, took shelter in the Precinct, and there, in 1578, erected a playhouse, whence the place was called Playhouse Yard. Every attempt was in vain made to crush the intruders. About the year 1586, according to the best authorities, the young Shakespeare came to London, and joined the company at the Blackfriars Theatre. Only three years later we find the new arrival—and this is one of the unsolvable mysteries of Shakespeare's life—one of sixteen sharers in the prosperous though persecuted theatre. It is true that Mr. Halliwell has lately discovered that he was not exactly a proprietor, but only an actor, receiving a share of the profits of the house, exclusive of the galleries, the boxes and dress circle of those days. But this is, after all, only a lessening of the difficulty; and it is almost as remarkable that a young, unknown Warwickshire poet should receive such profits, as it is that he should have held a sixteenth of the whole property. Without the generous patronage of such friends as the Earl of Southampton or Lord Brooke, how could the young actor have thriven? He was only twenty-six, and may have written "Venus and

Adonis" or "Lucrece;" yet the first of these poems was not published till 1593. He may already, it is true, have adapted one or two tolerably successful historical plays, and, as Mr. Collier thinks, might have written *The Comedy of Errors, Love's Labour's Lost,* or *The Two Gentlemen of Verona.* One thing is certain, that in 1587 five companies of players, including the Blackfriars Company, performed at Stratford, and in his native town Mr. Collier thinks Shakespeare first proved himself useful to his new comrades.

In 1589 the Lord Mayor closed two theatres for ridiculing the Puritans. Burbage and his friends, alarmed at this, petitioned the Privy Council, and pleaded that they had never introduced into their plays matters of state or religion. The Blackfriars company, in 1593, began to build a summer theatre, the Globe, in Southwark; and Mr. Collier, remembering that this was the year in which "Venus and Adonis" was published, supposes that some great gift of the Earl of Southampton to Shakespeare immediately followed this poem, which was dedicated to him. By 1594 the poet had written *King Richard II.* and *King Richard III.,* and Burbage's son Richard had made himself famous as the first representative of the crook-backed king. In 1596 we find Shakespeare and his partners (only eight now) petitioning the Privy Council to allow them to repair and enlarge their theatre, which the Puritans of Blackfriars wanted to close. The Council allowed the repairs, but forbade the enlargement. At this time Shakespeare was living near the Bear Garden, Southwark, to be close to the Globe. He was now evidently a thriving, "warm" man, for in 1597 he purchased for £60 New Place, one of the best houses in Stratford. In 1613 we find Shakespeare purchasing a plot of ground not far from Blackfriars Theatre, and abutting on a street leading down to Puddle Wharf, "right against the king's majesty's wardrobe;" but he had retired to Stratford, and given up London and the stage before this. The deed of this sale was sold in 1841 for £162 5s.

In 1608 the Lord Mayor and aldermen of London made a final attempt to crush the Blackfriars players, but failing to prove to the Lord Chancellor that the City had ever exercised any authority within the precinct and liberty of Blackfriars, their cause fell to the ground. The Corporation then opened a negotiation for purchase with Burbage, Shakespeare, and the other (now nine) shareholders. The players asked about £7,000, Shakespeare's four shares being valued at £1,433 6s. 8d., including the wardrobe and properties, estimated at £500. The poet's income at this time Mr. Collier esti-

mates at £400 a year. The Blackfriars Theatre was pulled down in Cromwell's time (1655), and houses built in its room.

Randolph, the dramatist, a pupil of Ben Jonson, ridicules, in that strange "morality" play, *The Muses' Looking-Glass,* the Puritan feather-sellers of Blackfriars, whom Ben Jonson also taunts; Randolph's pretty Puritan, Mrs. Flowerdew, says of the ungodly of Blackfriars:—

> "Indeed, it sometimes pricks my conscience,
>   I come to sell 'em pins and looking-glasses."

To which her friend, Mr. Bird, replies, with the sly sanctity of Tartuffe:—

> "I have this custom, also, for my feathers;
>   'Tis fit that we, which are sincere professors,
>   Should gain by infidels."

Ben Jonson, that smiter of all such hypocrites, wrote *Volpone* at his house in Blackfriars, where he laid the scene of *The Alchymist.* The Friars were fashionable, however, in spite of the players, for Vandyke lived in the precinct for nine years (he died in 1641); and the wicked Earl and Countess of Somerset resided in the same locality when they poisoned their former favourite, Sir Thomas Overbury. As late as 1735, Mr. Peter Cunningham says, there was an attempt to assert precinct privileges, but years before sheriffs had arrested in the Friars.

In 1623 Blackfriars was the scene of a most fatal and extraordinary accident. It occurred in the chief house of the Friary, then a district declining fast in respectability. Hunsdon House derived its name from Queen Elizabeth's favourite cousin, the Lord Chamberlain, Henry Carey, Baron Hunsdon, and was at the time occupied by Count de Tillier, the French ambassador. About three o'clock on Sunday, October 26th, a large Roman Catholic congregation of about three hundred persons, worshipping to a certain degree in stealth, not without fear from the Puritan feathermakers of the theatrical neighbourhood, had assembled in a long garret on the third and uppermost storey. Master Drury, a Jesuit preacher of celebrity, had drawn together this crowd of timid people. The garret, looking over the gateway, was approached by a passage having a door opening into the street, and also by a corridor from the ambassador's withdrawing-room. The garret was about seventeen feet wide and forty feet long, with a vestry for a priest partitioned off at one end. In the middle of the garret, and near the wall, stood a raised table and chair for the preacher. The gentry sat on chairs and stools facing the pulpit, the rest stood behind, crowding as far as the head of the stairs. At the appointed hour Master Drury, the priest, came from the inner room in white robe and scarlet stole, an attendant carrying a book and an hour-glass, by which to measure his sermon. He knelt down at the chair for about an Ave Maria, but uttered no audible prayer. He then took the Jesuits' Testament, and read for the text the Gospel for the day, which was, according to the Gregorian Calendar, the twenty-first Sunday after Pentecost—"Therefore is the kingdom of heaven like unto a man being a king that would make an account of his servants. And when he began to make account there was one presented unto him that owed him ten thousand talents." Having read the text, the Jesuit preacher sat down, and putting on his head a red quilt cap, with a white linen one beneath it, commenced his sermon. He had spoken for about half an hour when the calamity happened. The great weight of the crowd in the old room suddenly snapped the main summer beam of the floor, which instantly crashed in and fell into the room below. The main beams there also snapped and broke through to the ambassador's drawing-room over the gate-house, a distance of twenty-two feet. Only a part, however, of the gallery floor, immediately over Father Rudgate's chamber, a small room used for secret mass, gave way. The rest of the floor, being less crowded, stood firm, and the people on it, having no other means of escape, drew their knives and cut a way through a plaster wall into a neighbouring room.

A contemporary pamphleteer, who visited the ruins and wrote fresh from the first outburst of sympathy, says : "What ear without tingling can bear the doleful and confused cries of such a troop of men, women, and children, all falling suddenly in the same pit, and apprehending with one horror the same ruin ? What eye can behold without inundation of tears such a spectacle of men overwhelmed with breaches of mighty timber, buried in rubbish and smothered with dust ? What heart without evaporating in sighs can ponder the burden of deepest sorrows and lamentations of parents, children, husbands, wives, kinsmen, friends, for their dearest pledges and chiefest comforts ? This world all bereft and swept away with one blast of the same dismal tempest."

The news of the accident fast echoing through London, Serjeant Finch, the Recorder, and the Lord Mayor and aldermen at once provided for the safety of the ambassador's family, who were naturally shaking in their shoes, and shutting up the gates to keep off the curious and thievish crowd, set guards at all the Blackfriars passages. Workmen were employed to remove the *débris* and rescue the sufferers who were still alive. The pamphleteer,

again rousing himself to the occasion, and turning on his tears, says :—"At the opening hereof what a chaos ! what fearful objects ! what lamentable representations ! Here some buried, some dismembered, some only parts of men ; here some wounded and weltering in their own and others' blood ; others putting forth their fainting hands and crying out for help. Here some gasping and panting for breath ; others stifled for want of air. So the most of them being thus covered with dust, their death was a kind of burial." All that night and part of the next day the workmen spent in removing the bodies, and the inquest was then held. It was found that the main beams were only ten inches square, and had two mortise-holes, where the girders were inserted, facing each other, so that only three inches of solid timber were left. The main beam of the lower room, about thirteen inches square, without mortise-holes, broke obliquely near the end. No wall gave way, and the roof and ceiling of the garret remained entire. Father Drury perished, as did also Father Rudgate, who was in his own apartment, underneath. Lady Webb, of Southwark, Lady Blackstone's daughter, from Scroope's Court, Mr. Fowell, a Warwickshire gentleman, and many tradesmen, servants, and artisans—ninety-five in all—perished. Some of the escapes seemed almost miraculous. Mistress Lucie Penruddock fell between Lady Webb and a servant, who were both killed, yet was saved by her chair falling over her head. Lady Webb's daughter was found alive near her dead mother, and a girl named Elizabeth Sanders was also saved by the dead who fell and covered her. A Protestant scholar, though one of the very undermost, escaped by the timbers arching over him and some of them slanting against the wall. He tore a way out through the laths of the ceiling by main strength, then crept between two joists to a hole where he saw light, and was drawn through a door by one of the ambassador's family. He at once returned to rescue others. There was a girl of ten who cried to him, "Oh, my mother !—oh, my sister !— they are down under the timber." He told her to be patient, and by God's grace they would be quickly got forth. The child replied, "This will be a great scandal to our religion." One of the men that fell said to a fellow-sufferer, "Oh, what advantage our adversaries will take at this !" The other replied, "If it be God's will this should befall us, what can we say to it ?" One gentleman was saved by keeping near the stairs, while his friend, who had pushed near the pulpit, perished.

Many of those who were saved died in a few hours after their extrication. The bodies of Lady

Webb, Mistress Udall, and Lady Blackstone's daughter, were carried to Ely House, Holborn, and there buried under the chapel. In the fore court-yard, by the French ambassador's house, a huge grave, eighteen feet long and twelve feet broad, was dug, and forty-four corpses piled within it. In another pit, twelve feet long and eight feet broad, in the ambassador's garden, were buried fifteen more. Others were interred in St. Andrew's, St. Bride's, and Blackfriars churches. The list of the killed and wounded is curious, from its topo-graphical allusions. Amongst other entries, we find "John Halifax, a water-bearer" (in the old times of street conduits the water-bearer was an important person); "a son of Mr. Flood, the scrivener, in Holborn; a man of Sir Ives Pemberton; Thomas Brisket, his wife, son, and maid, in Montague Close; Richard Fitzgarret, of Gray's Inn, gentle-man; Davie, an Irishman, in Angell Alley, Gray's Inn, gentleman; Sarah Watson, daughter of Master Watson, chirurgeon; Master Grimes, near the 'Horse Shoe' tavern, in Drury Lane; John Bevan, at the 'Seven Stars', in Drury Lane; Francis Man, Thieving Lane, Westminster," &c. As might have been expected, the fanatics of both parties had much to say about this terrible accident. The Catholics declared that the Protestants, knowing this to be a chief place of meeting for men of their faith, had secretly drawn out the pins, or sawn the supporting timbers partly asunder. The Pro-testants, on the other hand, lustily declared that the planks would not bear such a weight of Romish sin, and that God was displeased with their pulpits and altars, their doctrine and sacrifice. One zealot remembered that, at the return of Prince Charles from the madcap expedition to Spain, a Catholic had lamented, or was said to have lamented, the street bonfires, as there would be never a fagot left to burn the heretics. "If it had been a Pro-testant chapel," the Puritans cried, "the Jesuits would have called the calamity an omen of the speedy downfall of heresy." A Catholic writer replied "with a word of comfort," and pronounced the accident to be a presage of good fortune to Catholics and of the overthrow of error and heresy. This zealous, but not well-informed, writer compared Father Drury's death with that of Zuinglius, who fell in battle, and with that of Calvin, "who, being in despair, and calling upon the devil, gave up his wicked soul, swearing, cursing, and blas-pheming." So intolerance, we see, is neither specially Protestant nor Catholic, but of every party. "The Fatal Vespers," as that terrible day at Blackfriars was afterwards called, were long **remembered with a shudder by Catholic England.**

In a curious old pamphlet entitled "Something Written by Occasion of that Fatall and Memorable Accident in the Blacke-friers, on Sonday, being the 26th October, 1623, *stilo antiquo*, and the 5th November, *stilo novo*, or *Romano*," the author re-lates a singular escape of one of the listeners. "When all things were ready," he says, "and the prayer finished, the Jesuite tooke for his text the gospell of the day, being (as I take it) the 22nd Sunday after Trinity, and extracted out of the 18th of Matthew, beginning at the 21st verse, to the end. The story concerns forgiveness of sinnes, and de-scribeth the wicked cruelty of the unjust steward, whom his maister remitted, though he owed him 10,000 talents, but he would not forgive his fellow a 100 pence, whereupon he was called to a new reckoning, and cast into prison, and then the par-ticular words are, which he insisted upon, the 34th verse: 'So his master was wroth, and delivered him to the jaylor, till he should pay all that was due to him.' For the generall, he urged many good doctrines and cases; for the particular, he modelled out that fantasie of purgatory, which he followed with a full crie of pennance, satisfaction, paying of money, and such like.

"While this exercise was in hand, a gentleman brought up his friend to see the place, and bee partaker of the sermon, who all the time he was going up stairs cried out, 'Whither doe I goe? I protest my heart trembles;' and when he came into the roome, the priest being very loud, he whis-pered his friend in the eare that he was afraid, for, as he supposed, the room did shake under him; at which his friend, between smiling and anger, left him, and went close to the wall behind the preacher's chaire. The gentleman durst not stirre from the staires, and came not full two yards in the roome, when on a sudden there was a kinde of murmuring amongst the people, and some were heard to say, 'The roome shakes;' which words being taken up one of another, the whole company rose up with a strong suddainnesse, and some of the women screeched. I cannot compare it better than to many passengers in a boat in a tempest, who are commanded to sit still and let the waterman alone with managing the oares, but some unruly people rising overthrowes them all. So was this company served; for the people thus affrighted started up with extraordinary quicknesse, and at an instant the maine summer beame broke in sunder, being mortised in the wall some five foot from the same; and so the whole roofe or floore fell at once, with all the people that stood thronging on it, and with the violent impetuosity drove downe the nether roome quite to the ground, so that they fell twenty-four foot high, and were most of them buried and bruised betweene the rubbish and the timber; and though some were questionlesse smothered, yet for the most part they were hurt and bled, and being taken forth the next day, and laid all along in the gallery, presented to the lookers-on a wofull spectacle of fourscore and seventeen dead persons, besides eight or nine which perished since, unable to recover themselves.

of a grand festivity at the house of Lord Herbert, which the Queen honoured by her attendance. The account is worth inserting, if only for the sake of a characteristic bit of temper which the Queen exhibited on the occasion.

"Lord Herbert, son of William, fourth Earl of Worcester," says Pennant, "had a house in Black-friars, which Queen Elizabeth, in 1600, honoured with her presence, on occasion of his nuptials

RICHARD BURBAGE. *From the Original Portrait in Dulwich College.* (*See page* 201.)

"They that kept themselves close to the walls, or remained by the windows, or held by the rafters, or settled themselves by the stayres, or were driven away by fear and suspition, sauved themselves without further hurt; but such as seemed more devoute, and thronged neere the preacher, perished in a moment with himselfe and other priests and Jesuites; and this was the summe of that unhappy disaster."

In earlier days Blackfriars had been a locality much inhabited by fashionable people, especially about the time of Queen Elizabeth. Pennant quotes from the *Sydney Papers* a curious account

with the daughter and heiress of John, Lord Russell, son of Francis, Earl of Bedford. The queen was met at the water-side by the bride, and carried to her house in a *lectica* by six knights. Her majesty dined there, and supped in the same neighbourhood with Lord Cobham, where there was 'a memorable maske of eight ladies, and a strange dawnce new invented. Their attire is this: each hath a skirt of cloth of silver, a mantell of coruscian taffete, cast under the arme, and their haire loose about their shoulders, curiously knotted and interlaced. Mrs. Fitton leade. These eight ladys maskers choose eight ladies more to dawnce the measures. Mrs. Fitton went to the queen and woed her dawnce. Her majesty (the love of Essex rankling in her heart) asked what she was? "*Affection*," she said. "*Affection !*" said the queen; "*affection* is false; yet her majestie rose up and dawnced.' At this

Sunday, November 19, 1769. It was built from the design of Robert Mylne, a clever young Scotch engineer, whose family had been master masons to the kings of Scotland for five hundred years. Mylne had just returned from a professional tour in Italy, where he had followed in

LAYING THE FOUNDATION-STONE OF BLACKFRIARS BRIDGE, 1760. *From a Contemporary Print.*
(*See page* 206.)

time the queen was sixty. Surely, as Mr. Walpole observed, it was at that period as natural for her as to be in love! I must not forget that in her passage from the bride's to Lord Cobham's she went through the house of Dr. Puddin, and was presented by the doctor with a fan."

Old Blackfriars Bridge, pulled down a few years since, was begun in 1760, and first opened on

the footsteps of Vitruvius, and gained the first prize at the Academy of St. Luke. He arrived in London friendless and unknown, and at once entered into competition with twenty other architects for the new bridge. Among these rivals was Smeaton, the great engineer (a *protegé* of Lord Bute), and Dr. Johnson's friend, Gwynn, well known for his admirable work on London improvements. The committee were, however, just enough to be unanimous in favouring the young unknown Scotchman, and he carried off the prize. Directly it was known that Mylne's arches were to be elliptical, every one unacquainted with the subject began to write in favour of the semi-circular arch. Among the champions Dr. Johnson was, if not the most ignorant, the most rash. He wrote three letters to the printer of the *Gazetteer*, praising Gwynn's plans and denouncing the Scotch conqueror. Gwynn had "coached" the learned Doctor in a very unsatisfactory way. In his early days the giant of Bolt Court had been accustomed to get up subjects rapidly, but the science of architecture was not so easily digested. The Doctor contended " that the first excellence of a bridge built for commerce over a large river is strength." So far so good ; but he then went on to try and show that the pointed arch is necessarily weak, and here he himself broke down. He allowed that there was an elliptical bridge at Florence, but he said carts were not allowed to go over it, which proved its fragility. He also condemned a proposed cast-iron parapet, in imitation of one at Rome, as too poor and trifling for a great design. He allowed that a certain arch of Perault's was elliptical, but then he contended that it had to be held together by iron clamps. He allowed that Mr. Mylne had gained the prize at Rome, but the competitors, the arrogant despot of London clubs asserted, were only boys ; and, moreover, architecture had sunk so low at Rome, that even the Pantheon had been deformed by petty decorations. In his third letter the Doctor grew more scientific, and even more confused. He was very angry with Mr. Mylne's friends for asserting that though a semi-ellipse might be weaker than a semicircle, it had quite strength enough to support a bridge. "I again venture to declare," he wrote—"I again venture to declare, in defiance of all this contemptuous superiority" (how arrogant men hate other people's arrogance !), " that a straight line will bear no weight. Not even the science of Vasari will make that form strong which the laws of nature have condemned to weakness. By the position that a straight line will bear nothing is meant that it receives no strength from straightness ; for that many bodies laid in straight lines will support weight by the cohesion of their parts, every one has found who has seen dishes on a shelf, or a thief upon the gallows. It is not denied that stones may be so crushed together by enormous pressure on each side, that a heavy mass may be safely laid upon them ; but the strength must be derived merely from the lateral resistance, and the line so

loaded will be itself part of the load. The semi-elliptical arch has one recommendation yet unexamined. We are told that it is difficult of execution."

In the face of this noisy newspaper thunder, Mylne went on, and produced one of the most beautiful bridges in England for £152,640 3s. 10d., actually £163 less than the original estimate—an admirable example for all architects, present and to come. The bridge, which had nine arches, and was 995 yards from wharf to wharf, was erected in ten years and three quarters. Mylne received £500 a year and ten per cent. on the expenditure. His claims, however, were disputed, and not allowed by the grateful City till 1776. The bridge-tolls were bought by Government in 1785, and the passage then became free. It was afterwards lowered, and the open parapet, condemned by Johnson, removed. It was supposed that Mylne's mode of centreing was a secret, but in contempt of all quackery he deposited exact models of his system in the British Museum. He was afterwards made surveyor of St. Paul's Cathedral, and in 1811 was interred near the tomb of Wren. He was a despot amongst his workmen, and ruled them with a rod of iron. However, the foundations of this bridge were never safely built, and latterly the piers began visibly to subside. The semi-circular arches would have been far stronger.

The foundation-stone of Blackfriars Bridge was laid by Sir Thomas Chitty, Lord Mayor, on the 31st of October, 1760. Horace Walpole, always Whiggish, describing the event, says :—"The Lord Mayor laid the first stone of the new bridge yesterday. There is an inscription on it in honour of Mr. Pitt, which has a very Roman air, though very unclassically expressed. They talk of the contagion of his public spirit ; I believe they had not got rid of their panic about mad dogs." Several gold, silver, and copper coins of the reign of George II. (just dead) were placed under the stone, with a silver medal presented to Mr. Mylne by the Academy of St. Luke's, and upon two plates of tin —Bonnel Thornton said they should have been lead—was engraved a very shaky Latin inscription, thus rendered into English :—

On the last day of October, in the year 1760,
And in the beginning of the most auspicious reign of
GEORGE the Third,
Sir THOMAS CHITTY, Knight, Lord Mayor,
laid the first stone of this Bridge,
undertaken by the Common Council of London
(amidst the rage of an extensive war)
for the public accommodation
and ornament of the City ;
ROBERT MYLNE being the architect.

And that there might remain to posterity
a monument of this city's affection to the man
who, by the strength of his genius,
the steadiness of his mind,
and a certain kind of happy contagion of his
Probity and Spirit
(under the Divine favour
and fortunate auspices of GEORGE the Second)
recovered, augmented, and secured
the British Empire
in Asia, Africa, and America,
and restored the ancient reputation
and influence of his country
amongst the nations of Europe ;
the citizens of London have unanimously voted this
Bridge to be inscribed with the name of
WILLIAM PITT.

On this pretentious and unlucky inscription, that reckless wit, Bonnel Thornton, instantly wrote a squib, under the obvious pseudonym of the " Rev. Busby Birch." In these critical and political remarks (which he entitled " City Latin ") the gay scoffer professed in his preface to prove " almost every word and every letter to be erroneous and contrary to the practice of both ancients and moderns in this kind of writing," and appended a plan or pattern for a new inscription. The clever little lampoon soon ran to three editions. The ordinary of Newgate, my lord's chaplain, or the masters of Merchant Taylors', Paul's, or Charter-house schools, who produced the wonderful pontine inscription, must have winced under the blows of this jester's bladderful of peas. Thornton laughed most at the awkward phrase implying that Mr. Pitt had caught the happy contagion of his own probity and spirit. He said that " Gulielmi Pitt" should have been "Gulielmi Fossæ." Lastly, he proposed, for a more curt and suitable inscription, the simple words—

" GUIL. FOSSÆ,
Patri Patriæ D.D.D. (i.e., Datur, Dicatur, Dedicatur)."

Party feeling, as usual at those times, was rife. Mylne was a friend of Paterson, the City solicitor, an apt scribbler and a friend of Lord Bute, who no doubt favoured his young countryman. For, being a Scotchman, Johnson no doubt took pleasure in opposing him, and for the same reason Churchill, in his bitter poem on the Cock Lane ghost, after ridiculing Johnson's credulity, goes out of his way to sneer at Mylne :—

" What of that bridge which, void of sense,
But well supplied with impudence,
Englishmen, knowing not the Guild,
Thought they might have the claim to build ;
Till Paterson, as white as milk,
As smooth as oil, as soft as silk,
In solemn manner had decreed
That, on the other side the Tweed,

Art, born and bred and fully grown,
Was with one Mylne, a man unknown ?
But grace, preferment, and renown
Deserving, just arrived in town ;
One Mylne, an artist, perfect quite,
Both in his own and country's right,
As fit to make a bridge as he,
With glorious Patavinity,
To build inscriptions, worthy found
To lie for ever underground."

In 1766 the bridge was opened for foot passengers, the completed portion being connected with the shore by a wooden structure ; two years later it was made passable for horses, and in 1769 it was fully opened. An unpopular toll of one halfpenny on week-days for every person, and of one penny on Sundays, was exacted. The result of this was that while the Gordon Riots were raging, in 1780, the too zealous Protestants, forgetting for a time the poor tormented Papists, attacked and burned down the toll-gates, stole the money, and destroyed all the account-books. Several rascals lost their lives, and one rioter, being struck with a bullet, ran howling for thirty or forty yards, and then dropped down dead. Nevertheless, the obnoxious toll continued until 1785, when it was redeemed by Government.

The bridge, according to the order of Common Council, was first named Pitt Bridge, and the adjacent streets (in honour of the great earl) Chatham Place, William Street, and Earl Street. But the first name of the bridge soon dropped off, and the monastic locality asserted its prior right. This is the more remarkable (as Mr. Timbs judiciously observes), because with another Thames bridge the reverse change took place. Waterloo Bridge was first called Strand Bridge, but it was soon dedicated by the people to the memory of the most famous of British victories.

The £152,640 that the bridge cost does not include the £5,830 spent in altering and filling up the Fleet Ditch, or the £2,167 the cost of the temporary wooden bridge. The piers, of bad Portland stone, were decorated by some columns of unequal sizes, and the line of parapet was low and curved. The approaches to the bridge were also designed by Mylne, who built himself a house at the corner of Little Bridge Street. The walls of the rooms were adorned with classical medallions, and on the exterior was the date (1780), with Mylne's crest, and the initials " R. M." Dr. Johnson became a friend of Mylne, and dined with him at this residence at least on one occasion. The house afterwards became the " York Hotel," and eventually was taken down in 1863.

The repairs of the Bridge between 1833 and

1840, by Walker and Burgess, engineers, at an expense of £74,000, produced a loss to the contractors; and the removal of the cornice and balustrade spoiled the bridge whither old Richard Wilson, the landscape-painter, used to come and admire the grand view of St. Paul's. The bridge seemed to be as unlucky as if it had incurred Dr. Johnson's curse. In 1843 the Chamberlain reported to the Common Council that the sum of £100,960 had been already expended in repairing Mylne's faulty work, besides the £800 spent in procuring a local Act (4 William IV.). According to a subsequent report, £10,200 had been spent in six years in repairing one arch alone. From 1851 to 1859 the expenditure had been at the rate of £600 a year. Boswell, indeed, with all his zealous partiality for the Scotch architect, had allowed that the best Portland stone belonged to Government quarries, and from this Parliamentary interest had debarred Mylne.

The tardy Common Council was at last forced, in common decency, to build a new bridge. The architect began by building a temporary structure of great strength. It consisted of two storeys— the lower for carriages, the upper for pedestrians— and stretching 990 feet from wharf to wharf. The lower piles were driven ten feet into the bed of the river, and braced with horizontal and diagonal bracings. The demolition began with vigour in 1864. In four months only, the navigators' brawny arms had removed twenty thousand tons of earth, stone, and rubble above the turning of the arches, and the pulling down those enemies of Dr. Johnson commenced by the removal of the key-stone of the second arch on the Surrey side. The masonry of the arches proved to be rather thinner than it appeared to be, and was stuffed with river ballast, mixed with bones and small old-fashioned pipes. The bridge had taken nearly ten years to build; it was entirely demolished in less than a year, and rebuilt in two. In some cases the work of removal and re-construction went on harmoniously and simultaneously side by side. Ingenious steam cranes travelled upon rails laid on the upper scaffold beams, and lifted the blocks of stone with playful ease and speed. In December, 1864, the men worked in the evenings, by the aid of naphtha lamps.

According to a report printed in the *Times*, Blackfriars Bridge had suffered from the removal of London Bridge, which served as a mill-dam, to restrain the speed and scour of the river.

Twelve designs had been sent in at the competition, and, singularly enough, among the competitors was a Mr. Mylne, grandson of Johnson's foe. The design of Mr. Page was first selected, as the handsomest and cheapest. It consisted of only three arches. Ultimately Mr. Joseph Cubitt won the prize. Cubitt's bridge has five arches, the centre one eighty-nine feet span; the style, Venetian Gothic; the cost, £265,000. The piers are grey, the columns red, granite; the bases and capitals are of carved Portland stone; the bases, balustrades, and roads of somewhat over-ornamented iron.

The *Quarterly Review*, of April, 1872, contains the following bitter criticisms of the new double bridge :—" With Blackfriars Bridge," says the writer, " we find the public thoroughly well pleased, though the design is really a wonder of depravity. Polished granite columns of amazing thickness, with carved capitals of stupendous weight, all made to give shop-room for an apple-woman, or a convenient platform for a suicide. The parapet is a fiddle-faddle of pretty cast-iron arcading, out of scale with the columns, incongruous with the capitals, and quite unsuited for a work that should be simply grand in its usefulness ; and at each corner of the bridge is a huge block of masonry, *àpropos* of nothing, a well-known evidence of desperate imbecility."

Bridge Street is too new for many traditions. Its chief hero is that active-minded and somewhat shallow speculator, Sir Richard Phillips, the book-seller and projector. An interesting memoir by Mr. Timbs, his friend, furnishes us with many curious facts about him, and shows how the publisher of Bridge Street impinged on many of the most illustrious of his contemporaries, and how in a way he pushed forward the good work which afterwards owed so much to Mr. Charles Knight. Phillips, born in London in 1767, was educated in Soho Square, and afterwards at Chiswick, where he remembered often seeing Hogarth's widow and Dr. Griffith, of the *Monthly Review* (Goldsmith's tyrant), attending church. He was brought up to be a brewer, but in 1788 settled as a schoolmaster, first at Chester and afterwards at Leicester. At Leicester he opened a bookseller's shop, started a newspaper (the *Leicester Herald*), and established a philosophical society. Obnoxious as a Radical, he was at last entrapped for selling Tom Paine's " Rights of Man," and was sent to gaol for eighteen months, where he was visited by Lord Moira, the Duke of Norfolk, and other advanced men of the day. His house being burned down, he removed to London, and projected a Sunday newspaper, but eventually Mr. Bell stole the idea and started the *Messenger*. In 1795 this restless and energetic man commenced the *Monthly Magazine*. Before this he had already been a hosier, a tutor, and a speculator in canals. The politico-literary magazine was advertised by circulars sent to eminent men of the opposition in commercial parcels, to save the enormous postage of those unregenerate days. Dr. Aiken, the literary editor, afterwards started a rival magazine, called the *Athenæum*. The *Gentleman's Magazine* never rose to a circulation above 10,000, which soon sank to 3,000. Phillips's magazine sold about 3,750. With all these multifarious pursuits, Phillips was an antiquary—purchasing Wolsey's skull for a shilling, a portion of his stone coffin, that had been turned into a horse-trough at the "White Horse" inn, Leicester; and Rufus's stirrup, from a descendant of the charcoal-burner who drove the body of the slain king to Winchester.

As a pushing publisher Phillips soon distinguished himself, for the Liberals came to him, and he had quite enough sense to discover if a book was good. He produced many capital volumes of "Ana," on the French system, and memoirs of Foote, Monk Lewes, Wilkes, and Lady Mary Wortley Montagu. He published Holcroft's "Travels," Godwin's best novels, and Miss Owenson's (Lady Morgan's) first work, "The Novice of St. Dominick." In 1807, when he removed to New Bridge Street, he served the office of sheriff; was knighted on presenting an address, and effected many reforms in the prisons and lock-up houses. In his useful "Letter to the Livery of London" he computes the number of writs then annually issued at 24,000; the sheriffs' expenses at £2,000. He also did his best to repress the cruelties of the mob to poor wretches in the pillory. He was a steady friend of Alderman Waithman, and was with him in the carriage at the funeral of Queen Caroline, in 1821, when a bullet from a soldier's carbine passed through the carriage window near Hyde Park. In 1809 Phillips had some reverses, and breaking up his publishing-office in Bridge Street, devoted himself to the profitable reform of school-books, publishing them under the names of Goldsmith, Mavor, and Blair.

This active-minded man was the first to assert that Dr. Wilmot wrote "Junius," and to start the celebrated scandal about George III. and the young Quakeress, Hannah Lightfoot, daughter of a linendraper, at the corner of Market Street, St. James's. She afterwards, it is said, married a grocer, named Axford, on Ludgate Hill, was then carried off by the prince, and bore him three sons, who in time became generals. The story is perhaps traceable to Dr. Wilmot, whose daughter married the Duke of Cumberland. Phillips found time to attack the Newtonian theory of gravitation, to advocate a memorial to Shakespeare, to compile a book containing a million of facts, to write on

Divine philosophy, and to suggest (as he asserted) to Mr. Brougham, in 1825, the first idea of the Society for Useful Knowledge. Almost ruined by the failures during the panic in 1826, he retired to Brighton, and there pushed forward his books and his interrogative system of education. Sir Richard's greatest mistakes, he used to say, had been the rejection of Byron's early poems, of "Waverley," of Bloomfield's "Farmer's Boy," and O'Meara's "Napoleon in Exile." He always stoutly maintained his claim to the suggestion of the "Percy Anecdotes." Phillips died in 1840. Superficial as he was, and commercial as were his literary aims, we nevertheless cannot refuse him the praise awarded in his epitaph :—" He advocated civil liberty, general benevolence, ascendancy of justice, and the improvement of the human race."

The old monastic ground of the Black Friars seems to have been beloved by painters, for, as we have seen, Vandyke lived luxuriously here, and was frequently visited by Charles I. and his Court. Cornelius Jansen, the great portrait-painter of James's Court, arranged his black draperies and ground his fine carnations in the same locality; and at the same time Isaac Oliver, the exquisite Court miniature-painter, dwelt in the same place. It was to him Lady Ayres, to the rage of her jealous husband, came for a portrait of Lord Herbert of Cherbury, an imprudence that very nearly led to the assassination of the poet-lord, who believed himself so specially favoured of Heaven.

The king's printing-office for proclamations, &c., used to be in Printing-house Square, but was removed in 1770; and we must not forget that where a Norman fortress once rose to oppress the weak, to guard the spoils of robbers, and to protect the oppressor, the *Times* printing-office now stands, to diffuse its ceaseless floods of knowledge, to spread its resistless ægis over the poor and the oppressed, and ever using its vast power to extend liberty and crush injustice, whatever shape the Proteus assumes, whether it sits upon a throne or lurks in a swindler's office.

This great paper was started in the year 1785, by Mr. John Walter, under the name of the *Daily Universal Register*. It was first called the *Times*, January 1, 1788, when the following prospectus appeared :—

"The *Universal Register* has been a name as injurious to the logographic newspaper as Tristram was to Mr. Shandy's son; but old Shandy forgot he might have rectified by confirmation the mistake of the parson at baptism, and with the touch of a bishop changed Tristram into Trismegistus. The *Universal Register*, from the day of its first appearance to the day of its confirmation, had, like Tristram, suffered from innumerable casualties, both laughable and serious, arising from its name, which in its introduction was immediately curtailed of its fair proportions by all who called for it, the word 'Universal' being universally omitted, and

him with the *Court and City Register*, the *Old Annual Register*, or the *New Annual Register*, or, if the house be within the purlieus of Covent Garden or the hundreds of Drury, slips into the politician's hand *Harris's Register of Ladies*.

"For these and other reasons the printer of the

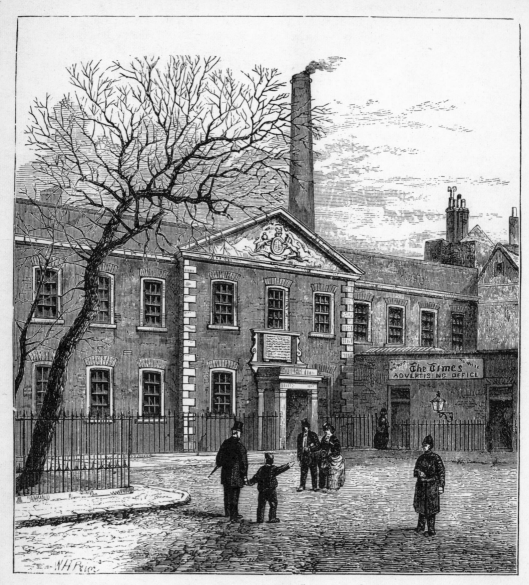

PRINTING HOUSE SQUARE AND THE "TIMES" OFFICE, 1870 (*see page* 209).

the word 'Register' only retained. 'Boy, bring me the *Register*.' The waiter answers, 'Sir, we have no library; but you may see it in the "New Exchange" coffee-house.' 'Then I will see it there,' answers the disappointed politician; and he goes to the 'New Exchange' coffee-house, and calls for the *Register*, upon which the waiter tells him he cannot have it, as he is not a subscriber, or presents

Universal Register has added to its original name that of the *Times*, which, being a monosyllable, bids defiance to the corruptions and mutilations of the language.

"The *Times!* what a monstrous name! Granted —for the Times is a many-headed monster, that speaks with a hundred tongues, and displays a thousand characters; and in the course of its

BLACKFRIARS OLD BRIDGE DURING ITS CONSTRUCTION, SHOWING THE TEMPORARY FOOT BRIDGE. *From a Print of 1775.* (*See page 207.*)

transitions in life, assumes innumerable shapes and humours.

" The critical reader will observe, we personify our new name; but as we give it no distinction of sex, and though it will be active in its vocation, yet we apply to it the neuter gender.

"The *Times*, being formed of and possessing qualities of opposite and heterogeneous natures, cannot be classed either in the animal or vegetable genus, but, like the polypus, is doubtful; and in the discussion, description, and illustration, will employ the pens of the most celebrated *literati*.

" The heads of the *Times*, as has already been said, are many; these will, however, not always appear at the same time, but casually, as public or private affairs may call them forth.

" The principal or leading heads are—the literary, political, commercial, philosophical, critical, theatrical, fashionable, humorous, witty, &c., each of which is supplied with a competent share of intellect for the pursuit of their several functions, an endowment which is not in all cases to be found, even in the heads of the State, the heads of the Church, the heads of the law, the heads of the navy, the heads of the army, and, though last not least, the great heads of the universities.

" The political head of the *Times*—like that of Janus, the Roman deity—is double-faced. With one countenance it will smile continually on the friends of Old England, and with the other will frown incessantly on her enemies.

" The alteration we have made in our paper is not without precedents. The *World* has parted with half its *caput mortuum* and a moiety of its brains; the *Herald* has cut off one half of its head and has lost its original humour; the *Post*, it is true, retains its whole head and its old features; and as to the other public prints, they appear as having neither heads nor tails.

"On the Parliamentary head, every communication that ability and industry can produce may be expected. To this great national object the *Times* will be most sedulously attentive, most accurately correct, and strictly impartial in its reports."

Both the *Times* and its predecessor were printed " logographically," Mr. Walter having obtained a patent for his peculiar system. The plan consisted in abridging the compositors' labour by casting all the more frequently recurring words in metal. It was, in fact, a system of partial stereotyping. The English language, said the sanguine inventor, contained above 90,000 words. This number Walter had reduced to about 5,000. The projector was assailed by the wits, who declared that his orders to the type-founders ran,—" Send me a

hundredweight, in separate pounds, of *heat, cold, wet, dry, murder, fire, dreadful robbery, atrocious outrage, fearful calamity*, and *alarming explosion*." But nothing could daunt or stop Walter. One eccentricity of the *Daily Register* was that on red-letter days the title was printed in red ink, and the character of the day stated under the date-line. For instance, on Friday, August 11, 1786, there is a red heading, and underneath the words—

" Princess of Brunswick born.
Holiday at the Bank, Excise offices, and the Exchequer."

The first number of the *Times* is not so large as the *Morning Herald* or *Morning Chronicle* of the same date, but larger than the *London Chronicle*, and of the same size and shape as the *Public Advertiser.*

The first Walter lived in rough times, and suffered from the political storms that then prevailed. He was several times imprisoned for articles against great people, and it has been asserted that he stood in the pillory in 1790 for a libel against the Duke of York. This is not, however, true; but it is a fact that he was sentenced to such a punishment, and remained sixteen months in Newgate, till released at the intercession of the Prince of Wales. The first Walter died in 1812. The second Mr. Walter, who came to the helm in 1803, was the real founder of the future greatness of the *Times;* and he, too, had his rubs. In 1804 he offended the Government by denouncing the foolish Catamaran expedition. For this the Government meanly deprived his family of the printing for the Customs, and also withdrew their advertisements. During the war of 1805 the Government stopped all the foreign papers sent to the *Times*. Walter, stopped by no obstacle, at once contrived other means to secure early news, and had the triumph of announcing the capitulation of Flushing forty-eight hours before the intelligence had arrived through any other channel.

There were no reviews of books in the *Times* till long after it was started, but it paid great attention to the drama from its commencement. There were no leading articles for several years, yet in the very first year the *Times* displays threefold as many advertisements as its contemporaries. For many years Mr. Walter, with his usual sagacity and energy, endeavoured to mature some plan for printing the *Times* by steam. As early as 1804 a compositor named Martyn had invented a machine for the purpose of superseding the hand-press, which took hours struggling over the three or four thousand copies of the *Times*. The pressmen threatened destruction to the new machine, and it had to be smuggled piecemeal into the premises, while Martyn sheltered himself under various disguises to escape the vengeance of the workmen. On the eve of success, however, Walter's father lost courage, stopped the supplies, and the project was for the time abandoned. In 1814 Walter, however, returned to the charge. Kœnig and Barnes put their machinery in premises adjoining the *Times* office, to avoid the violence of the pressmen. At one time the two inventors are said to have abandoned their machinery in despair, but a clerical friend of Walter examined the difficulty and removed it. The night came at last when the great experiment was to be made. The unconscious pressmen were kept waiting in the next office for news from the Continent. At six o'clock in the morning Mr. Walter entered the press-room, with a wet paper in his hand, and astonished the men by telling them that the *Times* had just been printed by steam. If they attempted violence, he said, there was a force ready to suppress it; but if they were peaceable their wages should be continued until employment was found for them. He could now print 1,100 sheets an hour. By-and-by Kœnig's machine proved too complicated, and Messrs. Applegarth and Cowper invented a cylindrical one, that printed 8,000 an hour. Then came Hoe's process, which is now said to print at the rate of from 18,000 to 22,000 copies an hour (Grant). The various improvements in steam-printing have altogether cost the *Times*, according to general report, not less than £80,000.

About 1813 Dr. Stoddart, the brother-in-law of Hazlitt (afterwards Sir John Stoddart, a judge in Malta), edited the *Times* with ability, till his almost insane hatred of Bonaparte, "the Corsican fiend," as he called him, led to his secession in 1815 or 1816. Stoddart was the "Doctor Slop" whom Tom Moore derided in his gay little Whig lampoons. The next editor was Thomas Barnes, a better scholar and a far abler man. He had been a contemporary of Lamb at Christ's Hospital, and a rival of Blomfield, afterwards Bishop of London. While a student in the Temple he wrote for the *Times* a series of political letters in the manner of "Junius," and was at once placed as a reporter in the gallery of the House. Under his editorship Walter secured some of his ablest contributors, including that Captain Stirling, "The Thunderer," whom Carlyle has sketched so happily. Stirling was an Irishman, who had fought with the Royal troops at Vinegar Hill, then joined the line, and afterwards turned gentleman farmer in the Isle of Bute. He began writing for the *Times* about 1815, and, it is said, eventually received £2,000 a year as a writer of dashing and effective leaders.

Lord Brougham also, it is said, wrote occasional articles. Tom Moore was even offered £100 a month if he would contribute, and Southey declined an offer of £2,000 a year for editing the *Times*. Macaulay in his day wrote many brilliant squibs in the *Times;* amongst them one containing the line,

"Ye diners out, from whom we guard our spoons."

Barnes died in 1841, and was succeeded in the editorial chair by Mr. John Delane, who retained that post till 1877, when, owing to failing health, he retired into private life. Under Mr. Delane's hands the *Times* held undisputed sway in the newspaper world; and instead of containing the fierce declamations for which it was once famous, became "mild, argumentative, and discriminating." Mr. Delane died in November, 1879.

One of the longest wars the *Times* ever carried on was that against Alderman Harmer. It was Harmer's turn, in due order of rotation, to become Lord Mayor. A strong feeling had arisen against Harmer because, as the avowed proprietor of the *Weekly Dispatch*, he inserted certain letters of the late Mr. Williams ("Publicola"), which were said to have had the effect of preventing Mr. Walter's return for Southwark (see page 59). The *Times* upon this wrote twelve powerful leaders against Harmer, which at once decided the question. This was a great assertion of power, and raised the *Times* in the estimation of all England. For these twelve articles, originally intended for letters, the writer (says Mr. Grant) received £200. But in 1841 the extraordinary social influence of this giant paper was even still more shown. Mr. O'Reilly, their Paris correspondent, obtained a clue to a vast scheme of fraud concocting in Paris by a gang of fourteen accomplished swindlers, who had already netted £10,700 of the million for which they had planned. At the risk of assassination, O'Reilly exposed the scheme in the *Times*, dating the *exposé* from Brussels, in order to throw the swindlers on the wrong scent.

At a public meeting of merchants, bankers, and others held in the Egyptian Hall, Mansion House, October 1, 1841, the Lord Mayor (Thomas Johnson) in the chair, it was unanimously resolved to thank the proprietors of the *Times* for the services they had rendered in having exposed the most remarkable and extensively fraudulent conspiracy (the famous "Bogle" swindle) ever brought to light in the mercantile world, and to record in some substantial manner the sense of obligation conferred by the proprietors of the *Times* on the commercial world. The proprietors of the *Times* declining to receive the £2,625 subscribed by the London merchants to recompense them for doing their duty, it was resolved, in 1842, to set apart the funds for the endowment of two scholarships, one at Christ's Hospital, and one at the City of London School. In both schools a commemorative tablet was put up, as well as one at the Royal Exchange and over the entrance of the *Times* printing-office.

At various periods the *Times* has had to endure violent attacks in the House of Commons, and many strenuous efforts to restrain its vast powers. In 1819 John Payne Collier, one of their Parliamentary reporters, and better known as one of the greatest of Shakesperian critics, was committed into the custody of the Serjeant-at-Arms for a report in which he had attacked Canning. The *Times*, however, had some powerful friends in the House; and in 1821 we find Mr. Hume complaining that the Government advertisements were systematically withheld from the *Times*. In 1831 Sir R. H. Inglis complained that the *Times* had been guilty of a breach of privilege, in asserting that there were borough nominees and lackeys in the House. Sir Charles Wetherell, that titled, incomparable old Tory, joined in the attack, which Burdett chivalrously cantered forward to repel. Sir Henry Hardinge wanted the paper prosecuted; Lord John Russell, Orator Hunt, and O'Connell, however, moved the previous question, and the great debate on the Reform Bill then proceeded. The same year the House of Lords flew at the great paper. The Earl of Limerick had been called "an absentee, and a thing with human pretensions." The Marquis of Londonderry joined in the attack. The next day Mr. Lawson, printer of the *Times*, was examined and worried by the House; and Lord Wynford moved that Mr. Lawson, as printer of a scandalous libel, should be fined £100, and committed to Newgate till the fine be paid. The next day Mr. Lawson handed in an apology, but Lord Brougham generously rose and denied the power of the House to imprison and fine without a trial by jury. The Tory lords spoke angrily; the Earl of Limerick called the press a tyrant that ruled all things, and crushed everything under its feet; and the Marquis of Londonderry complained of the coarse and virulent libels against Queen Adelaide, for her supposed opposition to Reform.

In 1833 O'Connell attributed dishonest motives to the London reporter who had suppressed his speeches, and the reporters in the *Times* expressed their resolution not to report any more of his speeches unless he retracted. O'Connell then moved in the House that the printer of the *Times* be summoned to the bar for printing their resolution, but his motion was rejected. In 1838 Mr. Lawson

was fined £200 for accusing Sir John Conroy, treasurer of the household of the Duchess of Kent, of peculation. In 1840 an angry member brought a breach of privilege motion against the *Times*, and advised every one who was attacked in that paper to horsewhip the editor.

In January, 1829, the *Times* came out with a double sheet, consisting of eight pages, or forty-eight columns. In 1830 it paid £70,000 advertisement duty. In 1800 its sale had been below that of the *Morning Chronicle, Post, Herald*, and *Advertiser*.

The *Times*, according to Mr. Grant, in one day of 1870, received no less than £1,500 for advertisements. On June 22, 1862, it produced a paper containing no less than twenty-four pages, or 144 columns. In 1854 the *Times* had a circulation of 51,000 copies; in 1860, 60,000. For special numbers its sale is enormous. The biography of Prince Albert sold 90,000 copies; the marriage of the Prince of Wales, 110,000 copies. The income of the *Times* from advertisements alone has been calculated at £260,000. A writer in a Philadelphia paper of 1867 estimates the paper consumed weekly by the *Times* at seventy tons; the ink at two tons. There are employed in the office ten stereotypers, sixteen firemen and engineers, ninety machine-men, six men who prepare the paper for printing, and seven to transfer the papers to the news-agents. The new Walter press prints 22,000 to 24,000 impressions an hour, or 12,000 perfect sheets printed on both sides. It prints from a roll of paper three-quarters of a mile long, and cuts the sheets and piles them without help. It is a self-feeder, and requires only a man and two boys to guide its operations. A copy of the *Times* has been known to contain 4,000 advertisements; and for every daily copy it is computed that the compositors mass together not less than 2,500,000 separate types.

The number of persons engaged in daily working for the *Times* is put at nearly 350.

In the annals of this paper we must not forget the energy that, in 1834, established a system of home expresses, which enabled them to give the earliest intelligence before any other paper; and at an expence of £200 brought a report of Lord Durham's speech at Glasgow to London at the then unprecedented rate of fifteen miles an hour; nor should we forget their noble disinterestedness during the railway mania of 1845, when, although they were receiving more than £3,000 a week for railway advertisements, they warned the country unceasingly of the misery and ruin that must inevitably follow. The *Times* proprietors are known to pay the highest sums for articles, and to be uniformly generous in pensioning men who have spent their lives in its service.

The late Mr. Walter, even when M.P. for Berkshire and Nottingham, never forgot Printing-house Square when the debate, however late, had closed. One afternoon, says Mr. Grant, he came to the office and found the compositors gone to dinner. Just at that moment a parcel, marked "immediate and important," arrived. It was news of vast importance. He at once slipped off his coat, and set up the news with his own hands; a pressman was at his post, and by the time the men returned a second edition was actually printed and published. But his foresight and energy was most conspicuously shown in 1845, when the jealousy of the French Government had thrown obstacles in the way of the *Times'* couriers, who brought their Indian despatches from Marseilles. What were seas and deserts to Walter? He at once took counsel with Lieutenant Waghorn, who had opened up the overland route to India, and proposed to try a new route by Trieste. The result was that Waghorn reached London two days before the regular mail—the usual mail aided by the French Government. The *Morning Herald* was at first forty-eight hours before the *Times*, but after that the *Times* got a fortnight ahead; and although the Trieste route was abandoned, the *Times*, eventually, was left alone as a troublesome and invincible adversary.

Apothecaries' Hall, the grave stone and brick building, in Water Lane, Blackfriars, was erected in 1670 (Charles II.), as the dispensary and hall of the Company of Apothecaries, incorporated by a charter of James I., at the suit of Gideon Delaune, the king's own apothecary. Drugs in the Middle Ages were sold by grocers and pepperers, or by the doctors themselves, who, early in James's reign, formed one company with the apothecaries; but the ill-assorted union lasted only eleven years, for the apothecaries were then fast becoming doctors themselves.

Garth, in his "Dispensary," describes, in the Hogarthian manner, the topographical position of Apothecaries' Hall:—

"Nigh where Fleet Ditch descends in sable streams,
To wash the sooty Naiads in the Thames,
There stands a structure on a rising hill,
Where tyros take their freedom out to kill."

Gradually the apothecaries, refusing to be merely "the doctors' tools," began to encroach more and more on the doctors' province, and to prescribe for and even cure the poor. In 1687 (James II.) open war broke out. First Dryden, then Pope, fought on the side of the doctors against the humbler men, whom they were taught to consider as mere greedy mechanics and empirics. Dryden first let fly his mighty shaft :—

"The apothecary tribe is wholly blind;
From files a random recipe they take,
And many deaths from one prescription make.
Garth, generous as his muse, prescribes and gives;
The shopman sells, and by destruction lives."

Pope followed with a smaller but keener arrow :—

"So modern 'pothecaries, taught the art
By doctors' bills to play the doctor's part,
Bold in the practice of mistaken rules,
Prescribe, apply, and call their masters fools."

The origin of the memorable affray between the College of Physicians and the Company of Apothecaries is admirably told by Mr. Jeaffreson, in his "Book of Doctors." The younger physicians, impatient at beholding the increasing prosperity and influence of the apothecaries, and the older ones indignant at seeing a class of men they had despised creeping into their quarters, and craftily laying hold of a portion of their monopoly, concocted a scheme to reinstate themselves in public favour. Without a doubt, many of the physicians who countenanced this scheme gave it their support from purely charitable motives; but it cannot be questioned that, as a body, the dispensarians were only actuated in their humanitarian exertions by a desire to lower the apothecaries and raise themselves in the eyes of the world. In 1687 the physicians, at a college meeting, voted "that all members of the college, whether fellows, candidates, or licentiates, should give their advice gratis to all their sick neighbouring poor, when desired, within the city of London, or seven miles round." The poor folk carried their prescriptions to the apothecaries, to learn that the trade charge for dispensing them was beyond their means. The physicians asserted that the demands of the drug-vendors were extortionate, and were not reduced to meet the finances of the applicants, to the end that the undertakings of benevolence might prove abortive. This was, of course, absurd. The apothecaries knew their own interests better than to oppose a system which at least rendered drug-consuming fashionable with the lower orders. Perhaps they regarded the poor as their peculiar property as a field of practice, and felt insulted at having the same humble people for whom they had pompously prescribed, and put up boluses at twopence apiece, now entering their shops with papers dictating what the twopenny bolus was to be composed of. But the charge preferred against them was groundless. Indeed, a numerous body of the apothecaries expressly offered to sell medicines "to the poor within their respective parishes at such rates as the committee of physicians should think reasonable."

But this would not suit the game of the physicians. " A proposal was started by a committee of the college that the college should furnish the medicines of the poor, and perfect alone that

paring and delivering medicines at their intrinsic value."

Such was the version of the affair given by the college apologists. The plan was acted upon, and a dispensary was eventually established (some nine years after the vote of 1687) at the College

THE COLLEGE OF PHYSICIANS, WARWICK LANE, 1868 (*see page* 216).

charity which the apothecaries refused to concur in; and, after divers methods ineffectually tried, and much time wasted in endeavouring to bring the apothecaries to terms of reason in relation to the poor, an instrument was subscribed by divers charitably-disposed members of the college, now in numbers about fifty, wherein they obliged themselves to pay ten pounds apiece towards the pre-

of Physicians, Warwick Lane, where medicines were vended to the poor at cost price. This measure of the college was impolitic and unjustifiable. It was unjust to that important division of the trade who were ready to vend the medicines at rates to be paid by the college authorities, for it took altogether out of their hands the small amount of profit which they, as *dealers*, could have realised on those terms. It was also an eminently unwise course. The College sank to the level of the Apothecaries' Hall, becoming an emporium for the sale of medicines. It was all very well to say that no profit was made on such sale, the censorious world would not believe it. The apothecaries and their friends denied that such was the fact, and vowed that the benevolent dispensarians were bent only on underselling and ruining them.

fees. They therefore joined in the cry against the dispensary. The profession was split up into two parties—Dispensarians and Anti-Dispensarians. The apothecaries combined, and agreed not to recommend the Dispensarians. The Anti-Dispensarians repaid this ill service by refusing to

OUTER COURT OF LA BELLE SAUVAGE IN 1828. (*See page* 221.)
(*From an Original Drawing in Mr. Gardner's Collection.*)

their friends denied that such was the fact, and vowed that the benevolent dispensarians were bent only on underselling and ruining them.

Again, the movement introduced dissensions within the walls of the college. Many of the first physicians, with the conservatism of success, did not care to offend the apothecaries, who were continually calling them in and paying them

meet Dispensarians in consultation. Sir Thomas Millington, the President of the College, Hans Sloane, John Woodward, Sir Edmund King, and Sir Samuel Garth, were amongst the latter. Of these the last named was the man who rendered the most efficient service to his party. For a time Garth's great poem, "The Dispensary," covered the apothecaries and Anti-Dispensarians with ridicule. It rapidly passed through numerous editions. To say that of all the books, pamphlets, and broadsheets thrown out by the combatants on both sides, it is by far the one of the greatest merit, would be scant justice, when it might almost be said that it is the only one of them that can now be read by a gentleman without a sense of annoyance and disgust. There is no point of view from which the medical profession appears in a more humiliating and contemptible light than that which the literature of this memorable squabble presents to the student. Charges of ignorance, dishonesty, and extortion were preferred on both sides. And the Dispensarian physicians did not hesitate to taunt their brethren of the opposite camp with playing corruptly into the hands of the apothecaries —prescribing enormous and unnecessary quantities of medicine, so that the drug-vendors might make heavy bills, and, as a consequence, recommend in all directions such complacent superiors to be called in. Garth's, unfair and violent though it is, nowhere offends against decency. As a work of art it cannot be ranked high, and is now deservedly forgotten, although it has many good lines and some felicitous satire. Garth lived to see the apothecaries gradually emancipate themselves from the ignominious regulations to which they consented when their vocation was first separated from the grocery trade. Four years after his death they obtained legal acknowledgment of their right to dispense and sell medicines without the prescription of a physician; and six years later the law again decided in their favour with regard to the physicians' right of examining and condemning their drugs. In 1721, Mr. Rose, an apothecary, on being prosecuted by the college for prescribing as well as compounding medicines, carried the matter into the House of Lords, and obtained a favourable decision; and from 1727, in which year Mr. Goodwin, an apothecary, obtained in a court of law a considerable sum for an illegal seizure of his wares (by Drs. Arbuthnot, Bale, and Levit), the physicians may be said to have discontinued to exercise their privileges of inspection.

In his elaborate poem Garth cruelly caricatures the apothecaries of his day :—

" Long has he been of that amphibious fry,
    Bold to prescribe, and busy to apply ;
His shop the gazing vulgar's eyes employs,
    With foreign trinkets and domestic toys.
Here mummies lay, most reverently stale,
    And there the tortoise hung her coat of mail ;
Not far from some huge shark's devouring head
    The flying-fish their finny pinions spread.
Aloft in rows large poppy-heads were strung,
    And near, a scaly alligator hung.

In this place drugs in musty heaps decay'd,
    In that dried bladders and false teeth were laid.

" An inner room receives the num'rous shoals
    Of such as pay to be reputed fools ;
Globes stand by globes, volumes on volumes lie,
    And planetary schemes amuse the eye.
The sage in velvet chair here lolls at ease,
    To promise future health for present fees ;
Then, as from tripod, solemn shams reveals,
    And what the stars know nothing of foretells.
Our manufactures now they merely sell,
    And their true value treacherously tell ;
Nay, they discover, too, their spite is such,
    That health, than crowns more valued, cost not much ;
Whilst we must steer our conduct by these rules,
    To cheat as tradesmen, or to starve as fools."

Before finally leaving Blackfriars, let us gather up a few reminiscences of the King's and Queen's printers who here first worked their inky presses.

Queen Anne, by patent in 1713, constituted Benjamin Tooke, of Fleet Street, and John Barber (afterwards Alderman Barber), Queen's printers for thirty years. This Barber, a high Tory and suspected Jacobite, was Swift's printer and warm friend. A remarkable story is told of Barber's dexterity in his profession. Being threatened with a prosecution by the House of Lords, for an offensive paragraph in a pamphlet which he had printed, and being warned of his danger by Lord Bolingbroke, he called in all the copies from the publishers, cancelled the leaf which contained the obnoxious passage, and returned them to the booksellers with a new paragraph supplied by Lord Bolingbroke; so that when the pamphlet was produced before the House, and the passage referred to, it was found unexceptionable. He added greatly to his wealth by the South Sea Scheme, which he had prudence enough to secure in time, and purchased an estate at East Sheen with part of his gain. In principles he was a Jacobite; and in his travels to Italy, whither he went for the recovery of his health, he was introduced to the Pretender, which exposed him to some danger on his return to England ; for, immediately on his arrival, he was taken into custody by a King's messenger, but was released without punishment. After his success in the South Sea Scheme, he was elected Alderman of Castle Baynard Ward, 1722 ; sheriff, 1730 ; and, in 1732–3, Lord Mayor of London.

John Baskett subsequently purchased both shares of the patent, but his printing-offices in Blackfriars (now Printing House Square) were soon afterwards destroyed by fire. In 1739 George II. granted a fresh patent to Baskett for sixty years, with the privilege of supplying Parliament with stationery. Half this lease Baskett sold to Charles Eyre, who eventually appointed William Strahan his printer.

Strahan soon after brought in Mr. Eyre, and in 1770 erected extensive premises in Printer Street, New Street Square, between Gough Square and Fetter Lane, near the present offices of Mr. Spottiswoode, one of whose family married Mr. Strahan's daughter. Strahan died a year after his old friend, Dr. Johnson, at his house in New Street, leaving £1,000 to the Stationers' Company, which his son Andrew augmented with £2,000 more. This son died in 1831, aged eighty-three.

William Strahan, the son of a Scotch Custom-house officer, had come up to London a poor printers' boy, and worked his way to wealth and social distinction. He was associated with Cadell in the purchase of copyrights, on the death of Cadell's partner and former master, Andrew Millar, who died *circa* 1768. The names of Strahan and Cadell appeared on the title-pages of the great works of Gibbon, Robertson, Adam Smith, and Blackstone. In 1776 Hume wrote to Strahan, "There will be no books of reputation now to be printed in London, but through your hands and Mr. Cadell's." Gibbon's history was a vast success. The first edition of 1,000 went off in a few days. This produced £490, of which Gibbon received £326 13s. 4d. The great history was finished in 1788, by the publication of the fourth quarto volume. It appeared on the author's fifty-first birthday, and the double festival was celebrated by a dinner at Mr. Cadell's, when complimentary verses from that second-rate poet, Hayley, made the great man with the button-hole mouth blush or feign to blush. That was a proud day for Gibbon, and a proud day for Messrs. Cadell and Strahan.

The first Strahan, Johnson's friend, was M.P. for Malmesbury and Wootton Bassett (1775-84), and his taking to a carriage was the subject of a recorded conversation between Boswell and Johnson, who gloried in his friend's success. It was Strahan who, with Johnston and Dodsley, purchased, in 1759, for £100, the first edition of Johnson's "Rasselas, Prince of Abyssinia," that sententious story, which Johnson wrote in a week, to defray the expenses of his mother's funeral.

Boswell has recorded several conversations between Dr. Johnson and Strahan. Strahan, at the doctor's return from the Hebrides, asked him, with a firm tone of voice, what he thought of his country. "That it is a very vile country, to be sure, sir," Dr. Johnson returned for answer. "Well, sir," replied the other, somewhat mortified, "God made it." "Certainly he did," answered Dr. Johnson again; "but we must always remember that he made it for Scotchmen, and — comparisons are odious, Mr. Strahan—God made hell!"

Boswell has also a pretty anecdote relating to one of the doctor's visits to Strahan's printing-office, which shows the "Great Bear" in a very amiable light, and the scene altogether is not unworthy of the artist's pencil.

"Mr. Strahan," says Boswell, "had taken a poor boy from the country as an apprentice, upon Johnson's recommendation. Johnson having inquired after him, said, 'Mr. Strahan, let me have five guineas on account, and I'll give this boy one. Nay, if a man recommends a boy, and does nothing for him, it is a sad work. Call him down.' I followed him into the court-yard, behind Mr. Strahan's house, and there I had a proof of what I heard him profess—that he talked alike to all. 'Some people will tell you that they let themselves down to the capacity of their hearers. I never do that. I speak uniformly in as intelligible a manner as I can.' 'Well, my boy, how do you go on?' 'Pretty well, sir; but they are afraid I'm not strong enough for some parts of the business.' Johnson: 'Why, I shall be sorry for it; for when you consider with how little mental power and corporal labour a printer can get a guinea a week, it is a very desirable occupation for you. Do you hear? Take all the pains you can; and if this does not do, we must think of some other way of life for you. There's a guinea.' Here was one of the many instances of his active benevolence. At the same time the slow and sonorous solemnity with which, while he bent himself down, he addressed a little thick, short-legged boy, contrasted with the boy's awkwardness and awe, could not but excite some ludicrous emotions."

In Ireland Yard, on the west side of St. Andrew's Hill, and in the parish of St. Anne, Blackfriars, stood the house which Shakespeare bought, in the year 1612, and which he bequeathed by will to his daughter, Susanna Hall. In the deed of conveyance to the poet, the house is described as "abutting upon a street leading down to Puddle Wharf, and now or late in the tenure or occupation of one William Ireland" (hence, we suppose, Ireland Yard), "part of which said tenement is erected over a great gate leading to a capital messuage, which some time was in the tenure of William Blackwell, Esq., deceased, and since that in the tenure or occupation of the Right Honourable Henry, now Earl of Northumberland." The original deed of conveyance is shown in the City of London Library, at Guildhall, under a handsome glass case.

The street leading down to Puddle Wharf is called St. Andrew's Hill, from the Church of St. Andrew's-in-the-Wardrobe. The proper name (says Cunningham) is Puddle Dock Hill.

CHAPTER XIX.

LUDGATE HILL.

An Ugly Bridge and "Ye Belle Savage"—A Radical Publisher—The Principal Gate of London—From a Fortress to a Prison—"Remember the Poor Prisoners"— Relics of Early Times—St. Martin's, Ludgate—The London Coffee House—Celebrated Goldsmiths on Ludgate Hill— Mrs. Rundell's Cookery Book—Stationers' Hall—Old Burgavenny House and its History—Early Days of the Stationers' Company—The Almanacks—An Awkward Misprint—The Hall and its Decorations—The St. Cecilia Festivals—Dryden's "St. Cecilia's Day" and "Alexander's Feast"—Handel's Setting of them—A Modest Poet—Funeral Feasts and Political Banquets—The Company's Plate—Their Charities—The Pictures at Stationers' Hall—The Company's Arms—Famous Masters.

OF all the eyesores of modern London, surely the most hideous is the Ludgate Hill Viaduct— that enormous flat iron which lies across the chest of Ludgate Hill, like a bar of metal on the breast of a wretch in a torture-chamber. Let us hope that a time will come when all designs for City improvements will be compelled to endure the scrutiny and win the approval of a committee of taste. The useful and the beautiful must not for ever be divorced. The railway bridge lies flat across the street, only eighteen feet above the roadway, and is a miracle of clumsy and stubborn ugliness, entirely spoiling the approach to one of the finest buildings in London. The five girders of wrought iron cross the street, here only forty-two feet wide, and the span is sixty feet, in order to allow of future enlargement of the street. Absurd lattice-work, decorative brackets, bronze armorial medallions, and gas lanterns and standards, form a combination that only the unsettled and imitative art of the ruthless nineteenth century could have put together. Think of what the Egyptians in the times of the Pharaohs did with granite ! and observe what we Englishmen of the present day do with iron. Observe this vulgar daubing of brown paint and barbaric gilding, and think of what the Moors did with colour in the courts of the Alhambra! A viaduct was necessary, we allow, but such a viaduct even the architect of the National Gallery would have shuddered at. The difficulties, we however allow, were great. The London, Chatham, and Dover Company, eager for dividends, was bent on wedding the Metropolitan Railway near Smithfield; but how could the hands of the affianced couple be joined ? If there was no viaduct, there must be a tunnel. Now, the bank of the river being a very short distance from Smithfield, a very steep and dangerous gradient would have been required to effect the junction. Moreover, had the line been carried under Ludgate Hill, there must have been a slight detour to ease the ascent, the cost of which detour would have been enormous. The tunnel proposed would have involved the destruction of a few trifles —such, for instance, as Apothecaries' Hall, the churchyard adjoining, the *Times* printing office—

besides doing injury to the foundations of St. Martin's Church, the Old Bailey Sessions House, and Newgate. Moreover, no station would have been possible between the Thames and Smithfield. The puzzled inhabitants, therefore, ended in despair by giving evidence in favour of the viaduct. The stolid hammermen went to work, and the iron nightmare was set up in all its Babylonian hideousness.

The enormous sum of upwards of £10,000 was awarded as the Metropolitan Board's quota for removing the hoarding, for widening the pavement a few feet under the railway bridge over Ludgate Hill, and for rounding off the corner.

An incredible quantity of ink has been shed about the origin of the sign of the "Belle Sauvage" inn, and even now the controversy is scarcely settled. Mr. Riley records that in 1380 (Richard II.) a certain William Lawton was sentenced to an uncomfortable hour in the pillory for trying to obtain, by means of a forged letter, twenty shillings from William Savage, Fleet Street, in the parish of St. Bridget. This at least shows that Savage was the name of a citizen of the locality. In 1453 (Henry VI.) a clause roll quoted by Mr. Lysons notices the bequest of John French to his mother, Joan French, widow, of "Savage's Inn," otherwise called the "Bell in the Hoop," in the parish of St. Bride's. Stow (Elizabeth) mentions a Mrs. Savage as having given the inn to the Cutlers' Company, which, however, the books of that company disprove. This, anyhow, is certain, that in 1568 (Elizabeth) a John Craythorne gave the reversion of the "Belle Sauvage" to the Cutlers' Company, on condition that two exhibitions to the university and certain sums to poor prisoners be paid by them out of the estate. A portrait of Craythorne's wife still hangs in Cutler's Hall. In 1584 the inn was described as "Ye Belle Savage." In 1648 and 1672 the landlords' tokens exhibited (says Mr. Noble) an Indian woman holding a bow and arrow. The sign in Queen Anne's time was a savage man standing by a bell. The question, therefore, is, whether the name of the inn was originally derived from Isabel (Bel) Savage, the landlady, or the sign of the bell and savage ; or whether it was, as the *Spectator* cleverly suggests, from La Belle Sauvage, "the beautiful savage," which is a derivation very generally received. There is an old French romance formerly popular in this country, the heroine of which was known as La Belle Sauvage ; and it is possible that Mrs. Isabel Savage, the ancient landlady, might have become in time confused with the heroine of the old romance.

In the ante-Shakespearean days our early actors performed in inn-yards, the court-yard representing the pit, the upper and lower galleries the boxes and gallery of the modern theatre. The "Belle Sauvage," says Mr. Collier, was a favourite place for these performances. There was also a school of defence, or fencing school, here in Queen Elizabeth's time ; so many a hot Tybalt and fiery Mercutio have here crossed rapiers, and many a silk button has been reft from gay doublets by the quick passadoes of the young swordsmen who ruffled it in the Strand. This quondam inn was also the place where Banks, the showman (so often mentioned by Nash and others in Elizabethan pamphlets and lampoons), exhibited his wonderful trained horse "Marocco," the animal which once ascended the tower of St. Paul's, and who on another occasion, at his master's bidding, delighted the mob by selecting Tarleton, the low comedian, as the greatest fool present. Banks eventually took his horse, which was shod with silver, to Rome, and the priests, frightened at the circus tricks, burnt both "Marocco" and his master for witchcraft. At No. 11 in this yard—now such a little world of industry, although it no longer rings with the stage-coach horn—lived in his obscurer days that great carver in wood, Grinling Gibbons, whose genius Evelyn first brought under the notice of Charles II. Horace Walpole says that, as a sort of advertisement, Gibbons carved an exquisite pot of flowers in wood, which stood on his window-sill, and shook surprisingly with the motion of the coaches that passed beneath. No man (says Walpole) before Gibbons had "ever given to wood the loose and airy lightness of flowers, or linked together the various productions of the elements with a free disorder natural to each species." His *chef d'œuvre* of skill was an imitation point-lace cravat, which he carved at Chatsworth for the Duke of Devonshire. Petworth is also garlanded with Gibbons' fruit, flowers, and dead game.

Belle Sauvage Yard no longer re-echoes with the guard's rejoicing horn, and the old coaching interest is now only represented by a railway parcel office huddled up in the left-hand corner. The old galleries are gone over which pretty chambermaids leant and waved their dusters in farewell greeting to the handsome guards or smart coachmen. Industries of a very different character have now turned the old yard into a busy hive. It is not for us to dilate upon the firm whose operations are carried on here, but it may interest the reader to know that the very sheet he is now perusing was printed on the site of the old coaching inn, and published very near the old tap-room of La Belle Sauvage ; for where coach-wheels once rolled and clattered, only printing-press wheels now revolve.

The old inn-yard is now very much altered in plan from what it was in former days. Originally it consisted of two courts. Into the outer one of these the present archway from Ludgate Hill led. It at one period certainly had contained private houses, in one of which Grinling Gibbons had lived. The inn stood round an inner court, entered by a second archway which stood about half-way up the present yard. Over the archway facing the outer court was the sign of "The Bell," and all round the interior ran those covered galleries, so prominent a feature in old London inns.

Near the "Belle Sauvage" resided that proud cobbler mentioned by Steele, who has recorded his eccentricities. This man had bought a wooden figure of a beau of the period, who stood before him in a bending position, and humbly presented him with his awl, wax, bristles, or whatever else his tyrannical master chose to place in his hand.

To No. 45 (south side), Ludgate Hill, that strange, independent man, Lamb's friend, William Hone, the Radical publisher, came from Ship Court, Old Bailey, where he had published those blasphemous "Parodies," for which he was three times tried and acquitted, to the vexation of Lord Ellenborough. Here, having sown his seditious wild oats and broken free from the lawyers, Hone continued his occasional clever political satires, sometimes suggested by bitter Hazlitt and illustrated by George Cruikshank's inexhaustible fancy. Here Hone devised those delightful miscellanies, the "Every-Day Book" and "Year Book," into which Lamb and many young poets threw all their humour and power. The books were commercially not very successful, but they have delighted generations, and will delight generations to come. Mr. Timbs, who saw much of Hone, describes him as sitting in a second-floor back room, surrounded by rare books and black-letter volumes. His conversion from materialism to Christianity was apparently sudden, though the process of change had no doubt long been maturing. The story of his conversion is thus related by Mr. Timbs :—" Hone was once called to a house, in a certain street in a part of the world of London entirely unknown

THE INNER COURT OF THE "BELLE SAUVAGE." (From an Original Drawing in Mr. Crace's Collection.)

to him. As he walked he reflected on the entirely unknown region. He arrived at the house, and was shown into a room to wait. All at once, on looking round, to his astonishment and almost horror, every object he saw seemed familiar to him. He said to himself, 'What is this? I was never here before, and yet I have seen all this before; and as a

the knot in the particular place was a mere coincidence. But, considering that Hone was a self-educated man, and, like many sceptics, was incredulous only with regard to Christianity, and even believed he once saw an apparition in Ludgate Hill, who can be surprised?

At No. 7, opposite Hone's, "The Percy Anec-

THE NORTH SIDE OF LUDGATE HILL.—THE CAMBRIDGE COACH STARTING.
(*From a Coloured Print after a Drawing in Mr. Crace's Collection.*)

proof I have I now remember a very peculiar knot behind the shutters.' He opened the shutters, and found the very knot. 'Now then,' he thought, 'here is something I cannot explain on any principle—there must be some power beyond matter.'" The argument that so happily convinced Hone does not seem to us in itself as very convincing. Hone's recognition of the room was but some confused memory of an analogous place. Knots are not uncommon in deal shutters, and the discovery of

dotes," that well-chosen and fortunate selection of every sort of story, were first published.

Lud Gate, which Stow in his "Survey" designates the sixth and principal gate of London, taken down in 1760 at the solicitation of the chief inhabitants of Farringdon Without and Farringdon Within, stood between the old London Coffee House and the church of St. Martin. According to old Geoffry of Monmouth's fabulous history of England, this entrance to London was first built by King Lud, a British monarch, sixty-six years before Christ. Our later antiquaries, ruthless as to legends, however romantic, consider its original name to have been the Flood or Fleet Gate, which is far more feasible. Lud Gate was either repaired or rebuilt in the year 1215, when the armed barons, under Robert Fitzwalter, repulsed at Northampton, were welcomed to London, and there awaited King John's concession of the Magna Charta. While in the metropolis these greedy and fanatical barons spent their time in spoiling the houses of the rich Jews, and used the stones in strengthening the walls and gates of the City. That this tradition is true was proved in 1586, when, as Stow says, all the gate was rebuilt. Embedded among other stones was found one on which was engraved, in Hebrew characters, the words "This is the ward of Rabbi Moses, the son of the honourable Rabbi Isaac." This stone was probably the sign of one of the Jewish houses pulled down by Fitzwalter, Magnaville, and the Earl of Gloucester, perhaps for the express purpose of obtaining ready materials for strengthening the bulwarks of London. In 1260 (Henry III.) Lud Gate was repaired, and beautified with images of King Lud and other monarchs. In the reign of Edward VI. the citizens, zealous against everything that approached idolatry, smote off the heads of Lud and his family; but Queen Mary, partial to all images, afterwards replaced the heads on the old bodies.

In 1554 King Lud and his sons looked down on a street seething with angry men, and saw blood shed upon the hill leading to St. Paul's. Sir Thomas Wyat, a Kentish gentleman, urged by the Earl of Devon, and led on by the almost universal dread of Queen Mary's marriage with the bigoted Philip of Spain, assembled 1,500 armed men at Rochester Castle, and, aided by 500 Londoners, who deserted to him, raised the standard of insurrection. Five vessels of the fleet joined him, and with seven pieces of artillery, captured from the Duke of Norfolk, he marched upon London. Soon followed by 15,000 men, eager to save the Princess Elizabeth, Wyat marched through Dartford to Greenwich and Deptford. With a force now dwindled to 7,000 men, Wyat attacked London Bridge. Driven from there by the Tower guns, he marched to Kingston, crossed the river, resolving to beat back the Queen's troops at Brentford, and attempt to enter the City by Lud Gate, which some of the Protestant citizens had offered to throw open to him. The Queen, with true Tudor courage, refused to leave St. James's, and in a council of war it was agreed to throw a strong force into Lud Gate, and, per-

mitting Wyat's advance up Fleet Street, to enclose him like a wild boar in the toils. At nine on a February morning, 1554, Wyat reached Hyde Park Corner, was cannonaded at Hay Hill, and further on towards Charing Cross he and some three or four hundred men were cut off from his other followers. Rushing on with a standard through Piccadilly, Wyat reached Lud Gate. There (says Stow) he knocked, calling out, "I am Wyat; the Queen has granted all my petitions."

But the only reply from the strongly-guarded gate was the rough, stern voice of Lord William Howard—"Avaunt, traitor; thou shalt have no entrance here."

No friends appearing, and the Royal troops closing upon him, Wyat said, "I have kept my promise," and retiring, silent and desponding, sat down to rest on a stall opposite the gate of the "Belle Sauvage." Roused by the shouts and sounds of fighting, he fought his way back, with forty of his staunchest followers, to Temple Bar, which was held by a squadron of horse. There the Norroy King-of-Arms exhorted him to spare blood and yield himself a prisoner. Wyat then surrendered himself to Sir Maurice Berkeley, who just then happened to ride by, ignorant of the affray, and, seated behind Sir Maurice, he was taken to St. James's. On April 11th Wyat perished on the scaffold at Tower Hill. This rash rebellion also led to the immediate execution of the innocent and unhappy Lady Jane Grey and her husband, Guilford Dudley, endangered the life of the Princess Elizabeth, and hastened the Queen's marriage with Philip, which took place at Winchester, July 25th of the same year.

In the reign of Elizabeth (1586), the old gate, being "sore decayed," was pulled down, and was newly built, with images of Lud and others on the east side, and a "picture of the lion-hearted queen" on the west, the cost of the whole being over £1,500.

Lud Gate became a free debtors' prison the first year of Richard II., and was enlarged in 1463 (Edward IV.) by that "well-disposed, blessed, and devout woman," the widow of Stephen Forster, fishmonger, Mayor of London in 1454. Of this benefactress of Lud Gate, Maitland (1739) has the following legend. Forster himself, according to this story, in his younger days had once been a pining prisoner in Lud Gate. Being one day at the begging grate, a rich widow asked how much would release him. He said, "Twenty pounds." She paid it, and took him into her service, where, by his indefatigable application to business, he so gained her affections that she married him, and he earned so great riches by commerce that she concurred with him to make his former prison more commodious, and to endow a new chapel, where, on a wall, there was this inscription on a brass plate :—

" Devout souls that pass this way,
For Stephen Forster, late Lord Mayor, heartily pray,
And Dame Agnes, his spouse, to God consecrate,
That of pity this house made for Londoners in Lud Gate ;
So that for lodging and water prisoners here nought pay,
As their keepers shall all answer at dreadful doomsday."

This legend of Lud Gate is also the foundation of Rowley's comedy of *A Woman Never Vext ; or, The Widow of Cornhill*, which has in our times been revived, with alterations, by Mr. Planché. In the first scene of the fifth act occurs the following passage:—

" *Mrs. S. Forster.* But why remove the prisoners from Ludgate ?
" *Stephen Forster.* To take the prison down and build it new,
With leads to walk on, chambers large and fair ;
For when myself lay there the noxious air
Choked up my spirits.   None but captives, wife,
Can know what captives feel."

Stow, however, seems to deny this story, and suggests that it arose from some mistake. The stone with the inscription was preserved by Stow when the gate was rebuilt, together with Forster's arms, " three broad arrow-heads," and was fixed over the entry to the prison. The enlargement of the prison on the south-east side formed a quadrant thirty-eight feet long and twenty-nine feet wide. There were prisoners' rooms above it, with a leaden roof, where the debtors could walk, and both lodging and water were free of charge.

Strype says the prisoners in Ludgate were chiefly merchants and tradesmen, who had been driven to want by losses at sea. When King Philip came to London after his marriage with Mary in 1554 thirty prisoners in Lud Gate, who were in gaol for £10,000, compounded for at £2,000, presented the king a well-penned Latin speech, written by " the curious pen " of Roger Ascham, praying the king to redress their miseries, and by his royal generosity to free them, inasmuch as the place was not *sceleratorum carcer, sed miserorum custodia* (not a dungeon for the wicked, but a place of detention for the wretched).

Marmaduke Johnson, a poor debtor in Lud Gate the year before the Restoration, wrote a curious account of the prison, which Strype printed. The officials in " King Lud's House " seem to have been—1, a reader of Divine service ; 2, the upper steward, called the master of the box ; 3, the under steward ; 4, seven assistants—that is, one for every day of the week ; 5, a running

assistant ; 6, two churchwardens ; 7, a scavenger ; 8, a chamberlain ; 9, a runner ; 10, the cryers at the grate, six in number, who by turns kept up the ceaseless cry to the passers-by of " Remember the poor prisoners ! " The officers' charge (says Johnson) for taking a debtor to Ludgate was sometimes three, four, or five shillings, though their just due is but twopence ; for entering name and address, fourteen pence to the turnkey ; a lodging is one penny, twopence, or threepence ; for sheets to the chamberlain, eighteenpence ; to chamber-fellows a garnish of four shillings (for non-payment of this his clothes were taken away, or " mobbed," as it was called, till he did pay) ; and the next day a due of sixteen pence to one of the stewards, which was called table money. At his discharge the several fees were as follows :—Two shillings the master's fee ; fourteen pence for the turning of the key ; twelve pence for every action that lay against him. For leave to go out with a keeper upon security (as formerly in the Queen's Bench) the prisoners paid for the first time four shillings and tenpence, and two shillings every day afterwards. The exorbitant prison fees of three shillings a day swallowed up all the prison bequests, and the miserable debtors had to rely on better means from the Lord Mayor's table, the light bread seized by the clerk of the markets, and presents of under-sized and illegal fish from the water-bailiffs.

A curious handbill of the year 1664, preserved by Mr. Collier, and containing the petition of 180 poor Ludgate prisoners, seems to have been a circular taken round by the alms-seekers of the prison, who perambulated the streets with baskets at their backs and a sealed money-box in their hands. "We most humbly beseech you," says the handbill, " even for God's cause, to relieve us with your charitable benevolence, and to put into this bearer's box—the same being sealed with the house seal, as it is figured upon this petition."

A quarto tract, entitled " Prison Thoughts," by Thomas Browning, citizen and cook of London, a prisoner in Lud Gate, "where poor citizens are confined and starve amidst copies of their freedom," was published in that prison, by the author, in 1682. It is written both in prose and verse, and probably gave origin to Dr. Dodd's more elaborate work on the same subject. The following is a specimen of the poetry :—

" ON PATIENCE.

" Patience is the poor man's walk,
Patience is the dumb man's talk,
Patience is the lame man's thighs,
Patience is the blind man's eyes,
Patience is the poor man's ditty,
Patience is the exil'd man's city,

Patience is the sick man's bed of down,
Patience is the wise man's crown,
Patience is the live man's story,
Patience is the dead man's glory.

" When your troubles do controul,
In Patience then possess your soul."

In the *Spectator* (Queen Anne) a writer says: " Passing under Lud Gate the other day, I heard a voice bawling for charity which I thought I had heard somewhere before. Coming near to the grate, the prisoner called me by my name, and desired I would throw something into the box."

The prison at Lud Gate was gutted by the Great Fire of 1666, and in 1760, the year of George III.'s accession, the gate, impeding traffic, was taken down, and the materials sold for £148. The prisoners were removed to the London Workhouse, in Bishopsgate Street, a part whereof was fitted up for that purpose, and Lud Gate prisoners continued to be received there until the year 1794, when they were removed to the prison of Lud Gate, adjoining the compter in Giltspur Street.

When old Lud Gate was pulled down, Lud and his worthy sons were given by the City to Sir Francis Gosling, who intended to set them up at the east end of St. Dunstan's. Nevertheless the royal effigies, of very rude workmanship, were sent to end their days in the parish bone-house ; a better fate, however, awaited them, for the late Marquis of Hertford eventually purchased them, and they are now, with St. Dunstan's clock, in Hertford Villa, Regent's Park. The statue of Elizabeth was placed in a niche in the outer wall of old St. Dunstan's Church, and it still adorns the new church, as we have before mentioned in our chapter on Fleet Street.

In 1792 an interesting discovery was made in St. Martin's Court, Ludgate Hill. Workmen came upon the remains of a small barbican, or watchtower, part of the old City wall of 1276; and in a

OLD LUD GATE, FROM A PRINT PUBLISHED ABOUT 1750
(*see page* 223).

line with the Old Bailey they found another outwork. A fragment of it in a court is now built up. A fire which took place on the premises of Messrs. Kay, Ludgate Hill, May 1, 1792, disclosed these interesting ruins, probably left by the builders after the fire of 1666 as a foundation for new buildings. The tower projected four feet from the wall into the City ditch, and measured twenty-two feet from top to bottom. The stones were of different sizes, the largest and the corner rudely squared. They had been bound together with cement of hot lime, so that wedges had to be used to split the blocks asunder. Small square holes in the sides of the tower seemed to have been used either to receive floor timbers, or as peep-holes for the sentries. The adjacent part of the City wall was about eight feet thick, and of rude workmanship, consisting of irregular-sized stones, chalk, and flint. The only bricks seen in this part of the wall were on the south side, bounding Stone-cutters' Alley. On the east half of Chatham Place, by Blackfriars Bridge, stood the tower built by order of Edward I., at the end of a continuation of the City wall, running from Lud Gate behind the houses in Fleet Ditch to the Thames. A rare plan of London, by Hollar (says Mr. J. T. Smith), marks this tower. Roman monuments have been so frequently dug up near St. Martin's Church, that there is no doubt that a Roman extra-mural cemetery once existed here ; in the same locality, in 1800, a sepulchral monument was dug up, dedicated to Claudina Mertina, by her husband, a Roman soldier. A fragment of a statue of Hercules and a female head were also found, and were preserved at the " London " Coffee House.

Ludgate Hill and Street is probably the greatest thoroughfare in London. Through Ludgate Hill and Street there have passed in twelve hours 8,752 vehicles, 13,025 horses, and 105,352 persons.

St. Martin's, Ludgate, though one of Wren's

churches, is not a romantic building; yet it has its legends. Robert of Gloucester, a rhyming chronicler, describes it as built by Cadwallo, a British prince, in the seventh century :—

> " A chirch of Sent Martyn livying he let rere,
> In whyche yet man should Goddy's seruys do,
> And singe for his soule, and al Christine also."

The church seems to have been rebuilt in 1437 (Henry VI.). From the parish books, which commence in 1410, we find the old church to have had several chapels, and to have been well furnished with plate, paintings, and vestments, and to have had two projecting porches on the south side, next Ludgate Hill. The right of presentation to St. Martin's belonged to the Abbot of Westminster, but Queen Mary granted it to the Bishop of London. The following curious epitaph in St. Martin's, found also elsewhere, has been beautifully paraphrased by the Quaker poet, Bernard Barton :—

Earth goes to		As mold to mold,	
Earth treads on	Earth,	Glittering in gold,	
Earth as to		Return nere should,	
Earth shall to		Goe ere he would.	

Earth upon		Consider may,	
Earth goes to	Earth,	Naked away,	
Earth though on		Be stout and gay,	
Earth shall from		Passe poore away.	

Strype says of St. Martin's—" It is very comely, and ascended up by stone steps, well finished within; and hath a most curious spire steeple, of excellent workmanship, pleasant to behold." The new church stands farther back than the old. The little black spire that adorns the tower rises from a small bulb of a cupola, round which runs a light gallery. Between the street and the body of the church Wren, always ingenious, contrived an ambulatory the whole depth of the tower, to deaden the sound of passing traffic. The church is a cube, the length 57 feet, the breadth 66 feet; the spire, 168 feet high, is dwarfed by St. Paul's. The church cost in erection £5,378 18s. 8d.

The composite pillars, organ balcony, and oaken altar-piece are tasteless and pagan. The font was the gift of Thomas Morley, in 1673, and is encircled by a favourite old Greek palindrome, that is, a puzzle sentence that reads equally well backwards or forwards—

> " Tripson anomeema me monan opsin."
> (Cleanse thy sins, not merely thy outward self.)

This inscription, according to Mr. G. Godwin (" Churches of London "), is also found on the font in the basilica of St. Sophia, Constantinople. In the vestry-room, approached by a flight of stairs at the north-east angle of the church, there is a carved seat (date 1690) and several chests, covered with curious indented ornaments.

On this church, and other satellites of St. Paul's, a poet has written—

> " So, like a bishop upon dainties fed,
> St. Paul's lifts up his sacerdotal head;
> While his lean curates, slim and lank to view,
> Around him point their steeples to the blue."

Coleridge used to compare a Mr. H——, who was always putting himself forward to interpret Fox's sentiments, to the steeple of St. Martin's, which is constantly getting in the way when you wish to see the dome of St. Paul's.

One great man, at least, has been connected with this church, where the Knights Templars were put to trial, and that was good old Purchas, the editor and enlarger of " Hakluyt's Voyages." He was rector of this parish. Hakluyt was a prebendary of Westminster, who, with a passion for geographical research, though he himself never ventured farther than Paris, had devoted his life, encouraged by Drake and Raleigh, in collecting from old libraries and the lips of venturous merchants and sea-captains travels in various countries. The manuscript remains were bought by Purchas, who, with a veneration worthy of that heroic and chivalrous age, wove them into his " Pilgrims " (five vols., folio), which are a treasury of travel, exploit, and curious adventures. It has been said that Purchas ruined himself by this publication, and that he died in prison. This is not, however, true. He seems to have impoverished himself chiefly by taking upon himself the care and cost of his brother and brother-in-law's children. He appears to have been a single-minded man, with a thorough devotion to geographic study. Charles I. promised him a deanery, but Purchas did not live to enjoy it.

There is an architectural tradition that Wren purposely designed the spire of St. Martin's, Ludgate, small and slender, to give a greater dignity to the dome of St. Paul's.

The London Coffee House, 24 to 26, Ludgate Hill, a place of celebrity in its day, was first opened in May, 1731. The proprietor, James Ashley, in his advertisement announcing the opening, professes cheap prices, especially for punch. The usual price of a quart of arrack was then eight shillings, and six shillings for a quart of rum made into punch. This new punch house, Dorchester beer, and Welsh ale warehouse, on the contrary, professed to charge six shillings for a quart of arrack made into punch; while a quart of rum or brandy made into punch was to be four shillings, and half a quartern fourpence halfpenny, and gentlemen were to have punch as quickly made as a gill of wine could be drawn. After Roney and Ellis, the house, according to Mr. Timbs, was taken by Messrs. Leech and Dallimore. Mr. Leech was the father of one of the most admirable caricaturists of modern times. Then came Mr. Lovegrove, from the "Horn," Doctors' Commons. In 1856 Mr. Robert Clarke took possession, and was the last tenant, the house being closed in 1867, and pur-

Prison. At the bar of the London Coffee House was sold Rowley's British Cephalic Snuff. A singular incident occurred here many years since. Mr. Brayley, the topographer, was present at a party, when Mr. Broadhurst, the famous tenor, by singing a high note caused a wine-glass on the table to break, the bowl being separated from the stem.

At No. 32 (north side) for many years Messrs.

RUINS OF THE BARBICAN ON LUDGATE HILL (*see page* 226).

chased by the Corporation for £38,000. Several lodges of Freemasons and sundry clubs were wont to assemble here periodically—among them "The Sons of Industry," to which many of the influential tradesmen of the wards of Farringdon have been long attached. Here, too, in the large hall, the juries from the Central Criminal Court were lodged during the night when important cases lasted more than one day. During the Exeter Hall May meetings the London Coffee House was frequently resorted to as a favourite place of meeting. It was also noted for its publishers' sales of stocks and copyrights. It was within the rules of the Fleet

Rundell and Bridge, the celebrated goldsmiths and diamond merchants, carried on their business. Here Flaxman's *chef d'œuvre*, the Shield of Achilles, in silver gilt, was executed; also the crown worn by that august monarch, George IV. at his coronation, for the loan of the jewels of which £7,000 was charged, and among the elaborate luxuries a gigantic silver wine-cooler (now at Windsor), that took two years in chasing. Two men could be seated inside that great cup, and on grand occasions it has been filled with wine and served round to the guests. Two golden salmon, leaning against each other, was the sign of this old shop, now removed. Mrs. Rundell met a great want of her day by writing her well-known book, "The Art of Cookery," published in 1806, and which has gone through countless editions. Up to 1833 she had received no remuneration for it, but she ultimately obtained 2,000 guineas. People had no idea of cooking in those days; and she laments in her preface the scarcity of good melted butter, good toast and water, and good coffee. Her directions were sensible and clear; and she studied

was first incorporated. The old house had been, in the reign of Edward III., the palace of John, Duke of Bretagne and Earl of Richmond. It was afterwards occupied by the Earls of Pembroke. In Elizabeth's reign it belonged to Lord Abergavenny, whose daughter married Sir Thomas Vane. In 1611 (James I.) the Stationers' Company purchased it and took complete possession. The house was swept away in the Great Fire of 1666, when the Stationers — the greatest sufferers on that

INTERIOR OF STATIONERS' HALL (*see page 230*).

economical cooking, which great cooks like Ude and Francatelli despised. It is not every one who can afford to prepare for a good dish by stewing down half-a-dozen hams.

The hall of the Stationers' Company hides itself with the modesty of an author in Stationers' Hall Court, Ludgate Hill, close abutting on Paternoster Row, a congenial neighbourhood. This hall of the master, and keepers or wardens, and commonalty of the mystery or art of a Stationer of the City of London stands on the site of Burgavenny House, which the Stationers modified and re-erected in the third and fourth years of Philip and Mary—the dangerous period when the company

occasion — lost property to the amount of £200,000.

The fraternity of the Stationers ot London (says Mr. John Gough Nichols, F.S.A., who has written a most valuable and interesting historical notice of the Worshipful Company) is first mentioned in the fourth year of Henry IV., when their bye-laws were approved by the City authorities, and they are then described as "writers (transcribers), lymners of books and dyverse things for the Church and other uses." In early times all special books were protected by special letters patent, so that the early registers of Stationers' Hall chiefly comprise books of entertainment, sermons, pamphlets, and ballads.

Mary originally incorporated the society in order to put a stop to heretical writings, and gave the Company power to search in any shop, house, chamber, or building of printer, binder, or seller, for books published contrary to statutes, acts, and proclamations. King James, in the first year of his reign, by letters-patent, granted the Stationers' Company the exclusive privilege of printing Almanacs, Primers, Psalters, the A B C, the "Little Catechism," and Nowell's Catechism.

The Stationers' Company, for two important centuries in English history (says Mr. Cunningham), had pretty well the monopoly of learning. Printers were obliged to serve their time to a member of the Company; and almost every publication, from a Bible to a ballad, was required to be "entered at Stationers' Hall." The service is now unnecessary, but Parliament still requires, under the present Copyright Act, that the proprietor of every published work should register his claim in the books of the Stationers' Company, and pay a fee of five shillings to the Registering Officer before he can commence any proceedings to protect his property. The Company do not derive any pecuniary benefit from the Registry; and have to forward the copies of new books lodged at Stationers' Hall to various public libraries. The number of the freemen of the Company is between 1,000 and 1,100, and of the livery, or leading persons, about 450. The capital of the Company amounts to upwards of £40,000, divided into shares, varying in amount from £40 to £400 each. A considerable sum out of the profit from this capital is annually distributed amongst the poor freemen and their widows. The great treasure of the Stationers' Company is its series of registers of works entered for publication. This valuable collection of entries commences in 1557, and, though often consulted and quoted, was never properly understood till Mr. J. Payne Collier published two carefully-edited volumes of extracts from its earlier pages. Since then the registers from 1557 to 1640 have been printed *in extenso* by Mr. Edward Arber.

The celebrated Bible of the year 1632, with the important word "not" omitted in the seventh commandment—"Thou shalt *not* commit adultery"—was printed by the Stationers' Company. Archbishop Laud made a Star-Chamber matter of the omission, and a heavy fine was laid upon the Company for their neglect. And in another later edition in Psalm xiv. the text ran, "The fool hath said in his heart, There is a God." For the substitution of "a" for the important word "no" the printer was fined £3,000. Several other errors

have occurred, but the wonder is that they have not been more frequent.

The only publications which the Company continues to issue are a Latin gradus and almanacs, of which it had at one time the entire monopoly. A few years since Almanac-day at Stationers' Hall (every 22nd of November, at three o'clock) was a sight worth seeing, from the bustle of the porters anxious to get off with early supplies. The Stationers' Company's almanacs have much improved in late years. Formerly the Company was not ashamed to publish in their almanacs nonsensical, old astrological tables, describing the moon's influence on various parts of the human body; but this farrago, with the monkish hieroglyphics which accompanied it, has now disappeared; and in place of these obsolete productions the Company continue the publication of the "British Almanac and Companion," which were started by the late Mr. Charles Knight, who worked so strenuously and so successfully for the spread of popular education. Two "Charles Knight" scholarships have been founded in the Company's School in commemoration of this great benefactor.

The first Stationers' Hall was in Milk Street. In 1553 they removed to St. Peter's College, near St. Paul's Deanery, where the chantry priests of St. Paul's had previously resided. The present hall closely resembles the hall at Bridewell, having a row of oval windows above the lower range, which were fitted up by Mr. Mylne in 1800, when the chamber was cased with Portland stone and the lower windows lengthened.

The great window at the upper end of the hall was erected in 1801, at the expense of Mr. Alderman Cadell. It includes some older glass blazoned with the arms and crest of the Company, the two emblematic figures of Religion and Learning being designed by Smirke. Like most ancient halls, it had a raised dais, or haut place, which was occupied by the Court table at the two great dinners in August and November; but this was removed in 1866. On the wall, above the wainscoting that has glowed red with the reflection of many a bumper of generous wine, are hung in decorous state the pavises or shields of arms of members of the court, which in civic processions were usually borne by a body of pensioners, the number of whom, when the Lord Mayor is a member of the Company, corresponded with the years of that august dignitary's age. In the old water-show these escutcheons decorated the sides of the Company's barge when they accompanied the Lord Mayor to Westminster, and called at the landing of Lambeth Palace to pay their respects to the representative of their former ecclesiastical censors. On this occasion the Archbishop usually sent out the thirsty Stationers a hamper of wine, while the rowers of the barge had bread and cheese and ale to their hearts' content. It is still the custom (says Mr. Nichols) to forward the Archbishop annually a set of the Company's almanacs, and some also to the Lord Chancellor and the Master of the Rolls. Formerly the twelve judges and various other persons received the same compliment. Alas for the mutation of other things than almanacs, however; for in 1850 the Company's barge, being sold, was taken to Oxford, where it may still be seen on the Isis, the property of one of the College boat clubs. At the upper end of the hall is a court cupboard or buffet for the display of the Company's plate, and at the lower end, on either side of the doorway, is a similar recess. The entrance-screen of the hall, guarded by allegorical figures, and crowned by the royal arms (with the inescutcheon of Nassau—William III.), is richly adorned with carvings.

Stationers' Hall was in 1677 used for Divine service by the parish of St. Martin's, Ludgate, and towards the end of the seventeenth century an annual musical festival was instituted on the 22nd of November, in commemoration of Saint Cecilia, and as an excuse for some good music. A splendid entertainment was provided in the hall, preceded by a grand concert of vocal and instrumental music, which was attended by people of the first rank. The special attraction was always an ode to Saint Cecilia, set by Purcell, Blow, or some other eminent composer of the day. Dryden's and Pope's odes are almost too well known to need mention; but Addison, Yalden, Shadwell, and even D'Urfey, tried their hands on praises of the same musical saint.

After several odes by the mediocre satirist, Oldham, and that poor verse-maker, Nahum Tate, who scribbled upon King David's tomb, came Dryden. The music to the first ode, says Scott, was first written by Percival Clarke, who killed himself in a fit of lovers' melancholy in 1707. It was then reset by Draghi, the Italian composer, and in 1711 was again set by Clayton for one of Sir Richard Steele's public concerts. The first ode (1687) contains those fine lines :—

> " From harmony, from heavenly harmony,
>   This universal frame began;
>   From harmony to harmony,
> Through all the compass of the notes it ran,
>   The diapason closing full in man."

Of the composition of this ode, for which Dryden received £40, and which was afterwards eclipsed by the glories of its successor, the following interesting anecdote is told :—

" Mr. St. John, afterwards Lord Bolingbroke, happening to pay a morning visit to Dryden, whom he always respected, found him in an unusual agitation of spirits, even to a trembling. On inquiring the cause, 'I have been up all night,' replied the old bard. 'My musical friends made me promise to write them an ode for their feast of St. Cecilia. I have been so struck with the subject which occurred to me, that I could not leave it till I had completed it. Here it is, finished at one sitting.' And immediately he showed him the ode."

Dryden's second ode, " Alexander's Feast; or, the Power of Music," was written for the St. Cecilian Feast at Stationers' Hall in 1697. This ode ends with those fine and often-quoted lines on the fair saint :—

> " Let old Timotheus yield the prize,
>   Or both divide the crown ;
>   He raised a mortal to the skies,
>   She drew an angel down."

Handel, in 1736, set this ode, and reproduced it at Covent Garden, with deserved success. Not often do such a poet and such a musician meet at the same anvil. The great German also set the former ode, which is known as " The Ode on St. Cecilia's Day." Dryden himself told Tonson that he thought with the town that this ode was the best of all his poetry; and he said to a young flatterer at Will's, with honest pride—" You are right, young gentleman; a nobler never was produced, nor ever will."

Many magnificent funerals have been marshalled in the Stationers' Hall; it has also been used for several great political banquets. In September, 1831, the Reform members of the House of Commons gave a dinner to the Chancellor of the Exchequer, Lord Althorp, and to Lord John Russell—Mr. Abercromby (afterwards Speaker) presiding. In May, 1842, the Duke of Wellington presided here over a dinner for the Infant Orphan Asylum, and in June, 1847, a dinner for the King's College Hospital was given under Sir Robert Peel's presidency. In the great kitchen below the hall, Mr. Nichols, long an honorary member of the Company, says there have been sometimes seen at the same time as many as eighteen haunches of venison, besides a dozen necks and other joints; for these companies are as hospitable as they are rich.

The funeral feast of Thomas Sutton, of the Charterhouse, was given May 28th, 1612, in Stationers' Hall, the procession having started from Doctor Law's, in Paternoster Row. For the repast were provided "32 neats' tongues, 40 stone of beef, 24 marrow-bones, 1 lamb, 46 capons, 32 geese, 4 pheasants, 12 pheasants' pullets, 12 godwits, 24 rabbits, 6 hearnshaws, 43 turkey-chickens, 48 roast chickens, 18 house pigeons, 72 field pigeons, 36 quails, 48 ducklings, 160 eggs, 3 salmon, 4 congers, 10 turbots, 2 dories, 24 lobsters, 4 mullets, a firkin and keg of sturgeon, 3 barrels of pickled oysters, 6 gammon of bacon, 4 Westphalia gammons, 16 fried tongues, 16 chicken pies, 16 pasties, 16 made dishes of rice, 16 neats'-tongue pies, 16 custards, 16 dishes of bait, 16 mince pies, 16 orange pies, 16 gooseberry tarts, 8 redcare pies, 6 dishes of whitebait, and 6 grand salads."

To the west of the hall is the handsome court-room, where the meetings of the Company are held. The wainscoting, &c., were renewed in the year 1757, and an octagonal card-room was added by Mr. Mylne in 1828. On the opposite side of the hall is the stock-room, adorned by beautiful carvings of the school of Grinling Gibbons. Here the commercial committees of the Company usually meet.

The nine painted storeys which stood in the old hall, above the wainscot in the council parlour, probably crackled to dust in the Great Fire, which also rolled up and took away the portraits of John Cawood, printer to Philip and Mary, and his master, John Raynes. This same John Cawood seems to have been specially munificent in his donations to the Company, for he gave two new stained-glass windows to the hall; also a hearse-cover, of cloth and gold, powdered with blue velvet and bordered with black velvet, embroidered and stained with blue, yellow, red, and green, besides considerable plate.

The Company's curious collection of plate is carefully described by Mr. Nichols. In 1581 it seems every master on quitting the chair was required to give a piece of plate, weighing fourteen ounces at least; and every upper or under warden a piece of plate of at least three ounces. In this accumulative manner the Worshipful Company soon became possessed of a glittering store of "salts," gilt bowls, college pots, snuffers, cups, and flagons. Their greatest trophy seems to have been a large silver-gilt bowl, given in 1626 by a Mr. Hulet (Owlett), weighing sixty ounces, and shaped like an owl, in allusion to the donor's name. In the early Civil War, when the Company had to pledge their plate to meet the heavy loans exacted by Charles the Martyr from a good many of his unfortunate subjects, the cherished Owlett was specially excepted. Among other memorials in the posses-

sion of the Company was a silver college cup bought in memory of Mr. John Sweeting, who, dying in 1659 (the year before the Restoration), founded by will the pleasant annual venison dinner of the Company in August.

It is supposed that all the great cupboards of plate were lost in the fire of 1666, for there is no piece now existing (says Mr. Nichols) of an earlier date than 1676. It has been the custom also from time to time to melt down obsolete plate into newer forms and more useful vessels. Thus salvers and salt-cellars were in 1720–21 turned into monteaths, or bowls, filled with water, to keep the wine-glasses cool; and in 1844 a handsome rose-water dish was made out of a silver bowl, and an old tea-urn and coffee-urn. This custom is rather too much like Saturn devouring his own children, and has led to the destruction of many curious old relics. The massive old plate now remaining is chiefly of the reign of Charles II. High among these presents tower the quaint silver candlesticks bequeathed by Mr. Richard Royston, twice Master of the Stationers' Company, who died in 1686, and had been bookseller to three kings—James I., Charles I., and Charles II. The ponderous snuffers and snuffer-box are gone. There were also three other pairs of candlesticks, given by Mr. Nathanael Cole, who had been clerk of the Company, at his death in 1760. A small two-handled cup was bequeathed in 1771 by that worthy old printer, William Bowyer, as a memorial of the Company's munificence to his father after his loss by fire in 1712–13.

The Stationers are very charitable. Their funds spring chiefly from £1,150 bequeathed to them by Mr. John Norton, the printer to the learned Queen Elizabeth in Latin, Greek, and Hebrew, alderman of London in the reign of James I., and thrice Master of this Company. The money laid out by Norton's wish in the purchase of estates in fee-simple in Wood Street has grown and grown. One hundred and fifty pounds out of this bequest the old printer left to the minister and church-wardens of St. Faith, in order to have distributed weekly to twelve poor persons—six appointed by the parish, and six by the Stationers' Company—twopence each and a penny loaf, the vantage loaf (the thirteenth allowed by the baker) to be the clerk's; ten shillings to be paid for an annual sermon on Ash Wednesday at St. Faith's; the residue to be laid out in cakes, wine, and ale for the Company of Stationers, either before or after the sermon. The liverymen still (according to Mr. Nichols) enjoy this annual dole of well-spiced and substantial buns. The sum of £1,000 was left for the generous purpose of advancing small loans to struggling young men in business. In 1861, however, the Company, under the direction of the Court of Chancery, devoted the sum to the founding of a commercial school in Bolt Court for the sons of liverymen and freemen of the Company, and £8,500 were spent in purchasing Mr. Bensley's premises and Dr. Johnson's old house. The doctor's usual sitting-room is now occupied by the head master. The school itself is built on the site formerly occupied by Johnson's garden. The boys pay a quarterage not exceeding £2. The school has four exhibitions.

The pictures at Stationers' Hall are worthy of mention. In the stock-room are portraits, after Kneller, of Prior and Steele, which formerly belonged to Harley, Earl of Oxford, Swift's great patron. The best picture in the room is a portrait by an unknown painter of Tycho Wing, the astronomer, holding a celestial globe. Tycho was the son of Vincent Wing, the first author of the almanacks still published under his name, and who died in 1668. There are also portraits of that worthy old printer, Samuel Richardson and his wife; Archbishop Tillotson, by Kneller; Bishop Hoadley, prelate of the Order of the Garter; Robert Nelson, the author of the "Fasts and Festivals," who died in 1714-15, by Kneller; and one of William Bowyer, the Whitefriars printer, with a posthumous bust beneath it of his son, the printer of the votes of the House of Commons. There was formerly a brass plate beneath this bust expressing the son's gratitude to the Company for their munificence to his father after the fire which destroyed his printing-office.

In the court-room hangs a portrait of John Boydell, who was Lord Mayor of London in the year 1791. This picture, by Graham, was formerly surrounded by allegorical figures of Justice, Prudence, Industry, and Commerce; but they have been cut out to reduce the canvas to Kit-cat size. There is a portrait, by Owen, of Lord Mayor Domville, Master of the Stationers' Company, in the actual robe he wore when he rode before the Prince Regent and the Allies in 1814 to the Guildhall banquet and the Peace thanksgiving. In the card-room is an early picture, by West, of King Alfred dividing his loaf with the pilgrim— a representation, by the way, of a purely imaginary occurrence—in fact, the old legend is that it was really St. Cuthbert who executed this generous partition. There are also portraits of the two Strahans, Masters in 1774 and 1816; one of Alderman Cadell, Master in 1798, by Sir William Beechey; and one of John Nicholls, Master of the

Company in 1804, after a portrait by Jackson. In the hall, over the gallery, is a picture, by Graham, of Mary Queen of Scots escaping from the Castle of Lochleven. It was engraved by Dawe, afterwards a Royal Academician, when he was only fourteen years of age.

The arms of the Company appear from a Herald visitation of 1634 to have been azure on a chevron, an eagle volant, with a diadem between two red roses, with leaves vert, between three books clasped gold; in chief, issuing out of a cloud, the sun-beams gold, a holy spirit, the wings displayed silver, with a diadem gold. In later times the books have been blazoned as Bibles. In a "tricking" in the volume before mentioned, in the College of Arms, St. John the Evangelist stands behind the shield in the attitude of benediction, and bearing in his left hand a cross with a serpent rising from it (much more suitable for the scriveners or law writers, by the bye). On one side of the shield stands the Evangelist's emblematic eagle, holding an inkhorn in his beak. The Company never received any grant of arms or supporters, but about the year 1790 two angels seem to have been used as supporters. About 1788 the motto "Verbum Domini manet in eternum" (The word of the Lord endureth for ever) began to be adopted, and in the same year the crest of an eagle was used. On the silver badge of the Company's porter the supporters are naked winged boys, and the eagle on the chevron is turned into a dove holding an olive-branch. Some of the buildings of the present hall are still let to Paternoster Row booksellers as warehouses.

The list of masters of this Company includes Sir John Key, Bart. ("Don Key"), Lord Mayor in 1831–1832. In 1712 Thomas Parkhurst, who had been Master of the Worshipful Company in 1683, left £37 to purchase Bibles and Psalters, to be annually given to the poor; hence the old custom of giving Bibles to apprentices bound at Stationers' Hall.

This is the first of the many City companies of which we shall have by turns to make mention in the course of this work. Though no longer useful as a guild to protect a trade which now needs no fostering, we have seen that it still retains some of its mediæval virtues. It is hospitable and charitable as ever, if not so given to grand funeral services and ecclesiastical ceremonials. Its privileges have grown out of date and obsolete, but they harm no one but authors, and to the wrongs of authors both Governments and Parliaments have been from time immemorial systematically indifferent.

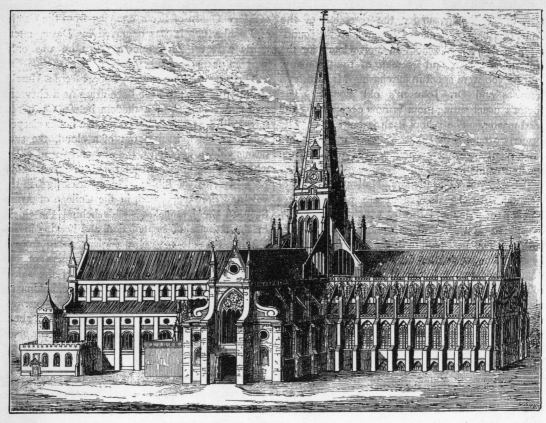

OLD ST. PAUL'S. (*From a View by Hollar.*)

CHAPTER XX.

ST. PAUL'S.

London's chief Sanctuary of Religion—The Site of St. Paul's—The Earliest authenticated Church there—The Shrine of Erkenwald—St. Paul's Burnt and Rebuilt—It becomes the Scene of a Strange Incident—Important Political Meeting within its Walls—The Great Charter published there—St. Paul's and Papal Power in England—Turmoils around the Grand Cathedral—Relics and Chantry Chapels in St. Paul's—Royal Visits to St. Paul's—Richard, Duke of York, and Henry VI.—A Fruitless Reconciliation—Jane Shore's Penance—A Tragedy of the Lollards' Tower—A Royal Marriage—Henry VIII. and Cardinal Wolsey at St. Paul's—"Peter of Westminster"—A Bonfire of Bibles—The Cathedral Clergy Fined—A Miraculous Rood—St. Paul's under Edward VI. and Bishop Ridley—A Protestant Tumult at Paul's Cross—Strange Ceremonials—Queen Elizabeth's Munificence—The Burning of the Spire—Desecration of the Nave—Elizabeth and Dean Nowell—Thanksgiving for the Armada—The "Children of Paul's"—Government Lotteries—Executions in the Churchyard—Inigo Jones's Restorations and the Puritan Parliament—The Great Fire of 1666—Burning of Old St. Paul's, and Destruction of its Monuments—Evelyn's Description of the Fire—Sir Christopher Wren called in.

STOOPING under the flat iron bar that lies like a bone in the mouth of Ludgate Hill, we pass up the gentle ascent between shops hung with gold chains, brimming with wealth, or crowded with all the luxuries that civilisation has turned into necessities; and once past the impertinent black spire of St. Martin's, we come full-butt upon the great grey dome. The finest building in London, with the worst approach; the shrine of heroes; the model of grace; the *chef-d'œuvre* of a great genius, rises

before us, and between its sable Corinthian pillars we have now to thread our way in search of the old legends of St. Paul's.

The old associations rise around us as we pass across the paved area that surrounds Queen Anne's mean and sooty statue. From the times of the Saxons to the present day, London's chief sanctuary of religion has stood here above the river, a landmark to the ships of all nations that have floated on the welcoming waters of the Thames. That great dome, circled with its coronet of gold, is the first object the pilgrim traveller sees, whether he approach by river or by land; the sparkle of that golden cross is seen from many a distant hill and plain. St. Paul's is the central object—the very palladium—of modern London.

of London from two Welsh words, "Llan-den"—church of Diana. Dugdale, to confirm these traditions, drags a legend out of an obscure monkish chronicle, to the effect that during the Diocletian persecution, in which St. Alban, a centurion, was martyred, the Romans demolished a church stand-

OLD ST. PAUL'S.—THE INTERIOR, LOOKING EAST.

Camden, the Elizabethan historian, revived an old tradition that a Roman temple to Diana once stood where St. Paul's was afterwards built; and he asserts that in the reign of Edward III. an incredible quantity of ox-skulls, stag-horns, and boars' tusks, together with some sacrificial vessels, were exhumed on this site. Selden, a better Orientalist than Celtic scholar (Charles I.), derived the name

ing on the site of St. Paul's, and raised a temple to Diana on its ruins, while in Thorny Island, Westminster, St. Peter, in the like manner, gave way to Apollo. These myths are, however, more than doubtful.

Sir Christopher Wren's excavations for the foundation of modern St. Paul's entirely refuted these confused stories, to which the learned and the credulous had paid too much deference. He dug down to the river-level, and found neither ox-bone nor stag-horn. What he did find, however, was curious. It was this :—1. Below the mediæval graves Saxon stone coffins and Saxon tombs, lined with slabs of chalk. 2. Lower still, British graves, and in the earth around the ivory and box-wood skewers that had fastened the Saxons' woollen shrouds. 3. At the same level with the Saxon graves, and also deeper, Roman funeral urns. These were discovered as deep as eighteen feet. Roman lamps, tear vessels, and fragments of sacrificial vessels of Samian ware were met with chiefly towards the Cheapside corner of the church-yard.

There had evidently been a Roman cemetery out-side this Prætorian camp, and beyond the ancient walls of London, the wise nation, by the laws of the Twelve Tables, forbidding the interment of the dead within the walls of a city. There may have been a British or a Saxon temple here; for the Church tried hard to conquer and consecrate places where idolatry had once triumphed. But the Temple of Diana was doubtful from the beginning, and doubt-ful it will ever remain. The antiquaries were, however, angry with Wren for the logical refutation of their belief. Dr. Woodward (the "Martinus Scriblerus" of Pope and his set) was especially vehement at the slaying of his hobby, and produced a small brass votive image of Diana, that had been found between the Deanery and Blackfriars. Wren, who could be contemptuous, disdained a reply, and so the matter remained till 1830, when the discovery of a rude stone altar, with an image of Diana, under the foundation of the new Goldsmith's Hall, Foster Lane, Cheapside, revived the old dispute, yet did not help a whit to prove the existence of the supposed temple to the goddess of moonshine.

The earliest authenticated church of St. Paul's was built and endowed by Ethelbert, King of East Kent, with the sanction of Sebert, King of the East Angles; and the first bishop who preached within its walls was Mellitus, the companion of St. Augustine, the first Christian missionary who visited the heathen Saxons. The visit of St. Paul to England in the time of Boadicea's war, and that of Joseph of Arimathea, are mere monkish legends. The Londoners again became pagan, and for thirty-eight years there was no bishop at St. Paul's, till a brother of St. Chad of Lichfield came and set his foot on the images of Thor and Wodin. With the fourth successor of Mellitus, Saint Erkenwald, wealth and splendour returned to St. Paul's. This zealous man worked miracles both before and after his death. He used to be driven about in a cart, and one legend says that he often preached to the woodmen in the wild forests that lay to the north of London. On a certain day one of the cart-wheels came off in a slough. The worthy confessor was in a dilemma. The congre-gation under the oaks might have waited for ever, but the one wheel left was equal to the occasion, for it suddenly grew invested with special powers of balancing, and went on as steadily as a velocipede with the smiling saint. This was pretty well, but still nothing to what happened after the good man's death.

St. Erkenwald departed at last in the odour of sanctity at his sister's convent at Barking. Eager to get hold of so valuable a body, the Chertsey monks instantly made a dash for it, pursued by the equally eager clergy of St. Paul's, who were fully alive to the value of their dead bishop, whose shrine would become a money-box for pilgrim's offerings. The London priests, by a forced march, got first to Barking and bore off the body; but the monks of Chertsey and the nuns of Barking followed, wringing their hands and loudly protesting against the theft. The river Lea, sympathising with their prayers, rose in a flood. There was no boat, no bridge, and a fight for the body seemed imminent. A pious man present, however, exhorted the monks to peace, and begged them to leave the matter to heavenly decision. The clergy of St. Paul's then broke forth into a litany. The Lea at once subsided, the cavalcade crossed at Stratford, the sun cast down its benediction, and the clergy passed on to St. Paul's with their holy spoil. From that time the shrine of Erkenwald became a source of wealth and power to the cathedral.

The Saxon kings, according to Dean Milman, were munificent to St. Paul's. The clergy claimed Tillingham, in Essex, as a grant from King Ethel-bert, and that place still contributes to the mainte-nance of the cathedral. The charters of Athel-stane are questionable, but the places mentioned in them certainly belonged to St. Paul's till the Eccle-siastical Commissioners broke in upon that wealth; and the charter of Canute, still preserved, and no doubt authentic, ratifies the donations of his Saxon predecessors.

William the Conqueror's Norman Bishop of London was a good, peace-loving man, who inter-ceded with the stern monarch, and recovered the forfeited privileges of the refractory London citizens. For centuries—indeed, even up to the end of Queen Mary's reign—the mayor, aldermen, and crafts used to make an annual procession to St. Paul's, to visit the tomb of good Bishop William in the nave. In 1622 the Lord Mayor, Edward

Barkham, caused these quaint lines to be carved on the bishop's tomb :—

> " Walkers, whosoe'er ye bee,
> If it prove you chance to see,
> Upon a solemn scarlet day,
> The City senate pass this way,
> Their grateful memory for to show,
> Which they the reverent ashes owe
> Of Bishop Norman here inhumed,
> By whom this city has assumed
> Large privileges ; those obtained
> By him when Conqueror William reigned.
> This being by Barkham's thankful mind renewed,
> Call it the monument of gratitude."

The ruthless Conqueror granted valuable privileges to St. Paul's. He freed the church from the payment of Danegeld, and all services to the Crown. His words (if they are authentic) are—" Some lands I give to God and the church of St. Paul's, in London, and special franchises, because I wish that this church may be free in all things, as I wish my soul to be on the day of judgment." In this same reign the Primate Lanfranc held a great council at St. Paul's—a council which Milman calls "the first full Ecclesiastical Parliament of England." Twelve years after (1087), the year in which the Conqueror died, fire, that persistent enemy of St. Paul's, almost entirely consumed the cathedral.

Bishop Maurice set to work to erect a more splendid building, with a vast crypt, in which the valuable remains of St. Erkenwald were enshrined. William of Malmesbury ranked it among the great buildings of his time. One of the last acts of the Conqueror was to give the stone of a Palatine tower (on the subsequent site of Blackfriars) for the building. The next bishop, De Balmeis, is said to have devoted the whole of his revenues for twenty years to this pious work. Fierce Rufus— no friend of monks—did little ; but the milder monarch, Henry I., granted exemption of toll to all vessels, laden with stone for St. Paul's, that entered the Fleet.

To enlarge the area of the church, King Henry gave part of the Palatine Tower estate, which was turned into a churchyard and encircled with a wall, which ran along Carter Lane to Creed Lane, and was freed of buildings. The bishop, on his part, contributed to the service of the altar the rents of Paul's Wharf, and for a school gave the house of Durandus, at the corner of Bell Court. On the bishop's death, the Crown seized his wealth, and the bishop's boots were carried to the Exchequer full of gold and silver. St. Bernard, however, praises him, and says : " It was not wonderful that Master Gilbert should be a bishop ; but that the

Bishop of London should live like a poor man, that was magnificent."

In the reign of Stephen a dreadful fire broke out and raged from London Bridge to St. Clement Danes. In this fire St. Paul's was partially destroyed. The Bishop, in his appeals for contributions to the church, pleaded that this was the only London church specially dedicated to St. Paul. The citizens of London were staunch advocates of King Stephen against the Empress Maud, and at their folkmote, held at the Cheapside end of St. Paul's, claimed the privilege of naming a monarch.

In the reign of Henry II. St. Paul's was the scene of a strange incident connected with the quarrel between the King and that ambitious Churchman, the Primate Becket. Gilbert Foliot, the learned and austere Bishop of London, had sided with the King and provoked the bitter hatred of Becket. During the celebration of mass a daring emissary of Becket had the boldness to thrust a roll, bearing the dreaded sentence of excommunication against Foliot, into the hands of the officiating priest, and at the same time to cry aloud—" Know all men that Gilbert, Bishop of London, is excommunicated by Thomas, Archbishop of Canterbury !" Foliot for a time defied the interdict, but at last bowed to his enemy's authority, and refrained from entering the Church of St. Paul's.

The reign of Richard I. was an eventful one to St. Paul's. In 1191, when Cœur de Lion was in Palestine, Prince John and all the bishops met in the nave of St. Paul's to arraign William de Longchamp, one of the King's regents, of many acts of tyranny. In the reign of their absentee monarch the Londoners grew mutinous, and their leader, William Fitzosbert, or Longbeard, denounced their oppressors from Paul's Cross. These disturbances ended in the siege of Bow Church, where Fitzosbert had fortified himself, and by the burning alive of him and other ringleaders. It was at this period that Dean Radulph de Diceto, a monkish chronicler of learning, built the Deanery, "inhabited," says Milman, " after him, by many men of letters ;" before the Reformation, by the admirable Colet ; after the Reformation by Alexander Nowell, Donne, Sancroft (who rebuilt the mansion after the Great Fire), Stillingfleet, Tillotson, W. Sherlock, Butler, Secker, Newton, Van Mildert, Copleston, Milman, and Mansel.

St. Paul's was also the scene of one of those great meetings of prelates, abbots, deans, priors, and barons that finally led to King John's concession of Magna Charta. On this solemn occasion—so important for the progress of England—the Primate Langton displayed the old charter of Henry I. to the chief barons, and made them sacredly pledge themselves to stand up for Magna Charta and the liberties of England.

One of the first acts of King Henry III. was to hold a council in St. Paul's, and there publish the Great Charter. Twelve years after, when a Papal Legate enthroned himself in St. Paul's, he was there openly resisted by Cantelupe, Bishop of Worcester.

In this reign Papal power attained its greatest height in England. On the death of Bishop Roger, an opponent of these inroads, the King gave orders that out of the episcopal revenue 1,500 poor should be feasted on the day of the conversion of St. Paul, and 1,500 lights offered in the church. The country was filled with Italian prelates. An Italian Archbishop of Canterbury, coming to St. Paul's, with a cuirass under his robes, to demand first-fruits from the Bishop, found the doors closed in his face; and two canons of the Papal party, endeavouring to install themselves at St. Paul's, were in 1259 killed by the angry populace.

In the reign of this weak king several folkmotes of the London citizens were held at Paul's Cross, in the churchyard. On one occasion the king himself, and his brother, the King of Almayne, were present. All citizens, even to the age of twelve, were sworn to allegiance, for a great outbreak for liberty was then imminent. The inventory of the goods of Bishop Richard de Gravesend, Bishop of London for twenty-five years of this reign, is still preserved in the archives of St. Paul's. It is a roll twenty-eight feet long. The value of the whole property was nearly £3,000, and this sum (says Milman) must be multiplied by about fifteen to bring it to its present value.

When the citizens of London justly ranged themselves on the side of Simon de Montfort, who stood up for their liberties, the great bell of St. Paul's was the tocsin that summoned the burghers to arms, especially on that memorable occasion when Queen Eleanor tried to escape by water from the Tower to Windsor, where her husband was, and the people who detested her tried to sink her barge as it passed London Bridge.

In the equally troublous reign of Edward II. St. Paul's was again splashed with blood. The citizens, detesting the king's foreign favourites, rose against the Bishop of Exeter, Edward's regent in London. A letter from the queen, appealing to them, was affixed to the cross in Cheapside. The bishop demanded the City keys of the Lord Mayor, and the people sprang to arms, with cries

of "Death to the queen's enemies!" They cut off the head of a servant of the De Spensers, burst open the gates of the Bishop of Exeter's palace (Essex Street, Strand), and plundered, sacked, and destroyed everything. The bishop, at the time riding in the Islington fields, hearing the danger, dashed home, and made straight for sanctuary in St. Paul's. At the north door, however, the mob thickening, tore him from his horse, and, hurrying him into Cheapside, proclaimed him a traitor, and beheaded him there, with two of his servants. They then dragged his body back to his palace, and flung the corpse into the river.

In the inglorious close of the glorious reign of Edward III., Courtenay, Bishop of London, an inflexible prelate, did his best to induce some of the London rabble to plunder the Florentines, at that time the great bankers and money-lenders of the metropolis, by reading at Paul's Cross the interdict Gregory XI. had launched against them; but on this occasion the Lord Mayor, leading the principal Florentine merchants into the presence of the aged king, obtained the royal protection for them.

Wycliffe and his adherents (amongst whom figured Chaucer's patron, John of Gaunt—" old John of Gaunt, time-honoured Lancaster "—) soon brewed more trouble in St. Paul's for the proud bishop. The great reformer being summoned to an ecclesiastical council at St. Paul's, was accompanied by his friends, John of Gaunt and the Earl Marshal, Lord Percy. When in the lady chapel Percy demanded a soft seat for Wycliffe. The bishop said it was law and reason that a cited man should stand before the ordinary. Angry words ensued, and the Duke of Lancaster taunted Courtenay with his pride. The bishop answered, " I trust not in man, but in God alone, who will give me boldness to speak the truth." A rumour was spread that John of Gaunt had threatened to drag the bishop out of the church by the hair, and that he had vowed to abolish the title of Lord Mayor. A tumult began. All through the City the billmen and bowmen gathered. The Savoy, John of Gaunt's palace, would have been burned but for the intercession of the bishop. A priest mistaken for Percy was murdered. The duke fled to Kennington, and joined the Princess of Wales.

Richard II., that dissolute, rash, and unfortunate monarch, once only (alive) came to St. Paul's in great pomp, his robes hung with bells, and afterwards feasted at the house of his favourite, Sir Nicholas Brember. who was eventually put to death.

The Lollards were now making way, and Arch-bishop Courtenay had a great barefooted proces-sion to St. Paul's to hear a famous Carmelite preacher inveigh against the Wycliffe doctrines. A Lollard, indeed, had the courage to nail to the doors of St. Paul's twelve articles of the new creed denouncing the mischievous celibacy of the clergy, transubstantiation, prayers for the dead, pilgrim-ages, and other mistaken and idolatrous usages. When Henry Bolingbroke (not yet crowned Henry IV.) came to St. Paul's to offer prayer for the dethronement of his ill-fated cousin, Richard, he paused at the north side of the altar to shed tears over the grave of his father, John of Gaunt, interred early that very year in the Cathedral. Not long after the shrunken body of the dead king, on its way to the Abbey, was exposed in St. Paul's, to prove to the populace that Richard was not still alive. Hardynge, in his chronicles (quoted by Milman), says that the usurping king and his nobles spread—some seven, some nine—cloths of gold on the bier of the murdered king.

Bishop Braybroke, in the reign of Edward IV., was strenuous in denouncing ecclesiastical abuses. Edward III. himself had denounced the resort of mechanics to the refectory, the personal vices of the priests, and the pilfering of sacred vessels. He restored the communion-table, and insisted on daily alms-giving. But Braybroke also condemned worse abuses. He issued a prohibition at Paul's Cross against barbers shaving on Sundays; he forbade the buying and selling in the Cathedral, the flinging stones and shooting arrows at the pigeons and jackdaws nestling in the walls of the church, and the playing at ball, both within and without the church, a practice which led to the breaking of many beautiful and costly painted windows.

But here we stop awhile in our history of St. Paul's, on the eve of the sanguinary wars of the Roses, to describe mediæval St. Paul's, its structure, and internal government. Foremost among the relics were two arms of St. Mellitus (miraculously enough, of quite different sizes). Behind the high altar—what Dean Milman justly calls "the pride, glory, and fountain of wealth" to St. Paul's—was the body of St. Erkenwald, covered with a shrine which three London goldsmiths had spent a whole year in chiselling; and this shrine was covered with a grate of tinned iron. The very dust of the chapel floor, mingled with water, was said to work instantaneous cures. On the anniversary of St. Erkenwald the whole clergy of the diocese attended in procession in their copes. When King John of France was made captive at Poictiers, and paid his orisons at St. Paul's, he presented four golden basins to the high altar, and twenty-two nobles at the shrine of St. Erkenwald. Milman calcu-lates that in 1344 the oblation-box alone at St. Paul's produced an annual sum to the dean and chapter of £9,000. Among other relics that were milch cows to the monks were a knife of our Lord, some hair of Mary Magdalen, blood of St. Paul, milk of the Virgin, the hand of St. John, pieces of the impetuous skull of Thomas à Becket, and the head and jaw of King Ethelbert. These were all preserved in jewelled cases. One hun-dred and eleven anniversary masses were cele-brated. The chantry chapels in the Cathedral were very numerous, and they were served by an army of idle and often dissolute mass priests. There was one chantry in Pardon Churchyard, on the north side of St. Paul's, east of the bishop's chapel, where St. Thomas Becket's ancestors were buried. The grandest was one near the nave, built by Bishop Kemp, to pray for himself and his royal master, Edward IV. Another was founded by Henry IV. for the souls of his father, John of Gaunt, and his mother, Blanche of Castile. A third was built by Lord Mayor Pulteney, who was buried in St. Lawrence Pulteney, so called from him. The revenues of these chantries were vast.

But to return to our historical sequence. During the ruthless Wars of the Roses St. Paul's became the scene of many curious ceremonials, on which Shakespeare himself has touched, in his early his-torical plays. It was on a platform at the cathedral door that Roger Bolingbroke, the spurious necro-mancer who was supposed to have aided the am-bitious designs of the Duke and Duchess of Glou-cester, was exhibited. The Duchess's penance for the same offence, according to Milman's opinion, commenced or closed near the cathedral, in that shameful journey when she was led through the streets wrapped in a sheet, and carrying a lighted taper in her hand. The duke, her husband, was eventually buried at St. Paul's, where his tomb became the haunt of needy men about town, whence the well-known proverb of "dining with Duke Humphrey."

Henry VI.'s first peaceful visit to St. Paul's is quaintly sketched by that dull old poet, Lydgate, who describes "the bishops *in pontificalibus*, the Dean of Paules and canons, every one who con-veyed the king"

> "Up into the church, with full devout singing;
> And when he had made his offering,
> The mayor, the citizens, bowed and left him."

While all the dark troubles still were pending, we find the Duke of York taking a solemn oath on the host of fealty to King Henry. Six years later, after the battle of St. Albans, the Yorkists and Lancastrians met again at the altar of St. Paul's in feigned unity. The poor weak monarch was crowned, and had sceptre in hand, and his proud brilliant queen followed him in smiling converse with the Duke of York. Again the city poet broke into rejoicing at the final peace :—

"At Paul's in London, with great renown,
    On Lady Day in Lent, this peace was wrought ;

knelt before the primate, and swore allegiance to the king ; and the duke's two sons, March and Rutland, took the same oath. Within a few months the battle of Wakefield was fought ; Richard was slain, and the duke's head, adorned with a mocking paper crown, was sent, by the she-wolf of a queen, to adorn the walls of York.

The next year, however, fortune forsook Henry for ever, and St. Paul's welcomed Edward IV. and the redoubtable "king-maker," who had won the

THE CHURCH OF ST. FAITH, THE CRYPT OF OLD ST. PAUL'S, FROM A VIEW BY HOLLAR.

The King, the Queen, with lords many an one,
    To worship the Virgin as they ought,
Went in procession, and spared right nought
    In sight of all the commonalty ;
In token this love was in heart and thought,
    Rejoice England in concord and unity."

Alas for such reconciliations ! Four years later more blood had been shed, more battle-fields strewn with dead. The king was a captive, had disinherited his own son, and granted the succession to the Duke of York, whose right a Parliament had acknowledged. His proud queen was in the North rallying the scattered Lancastrians. York and Warwick, Henry's deadly enemies,

crown for him at the battle of Mortimer's Cross ; and no Lancastrian dared show his face on that triumphant day. Ten years later Warwick, veering to the downfallen king, was slain at Barnet, and the body of the old warrior, and that of his brother, were exposed, barefaced, for three days in St. Paul's, to the delight of all true Yorkists. Those were terrible times, and the generosity of the old chivalry seemed now despised and forgotten. The next month there was even a sadder sight, for the body of King Henry himself was displayed in the Cathedral. Broken-hearted, said the Yorkists ; but the Lancastrian belief (favoured by Shakespeare) was that Richard Duke of Gloucester, the wicked Crookback, stabbed him with his own hand in the Tower, and it was said that blood poured from the body when it lay in the Cathedral. Again St. Paul's was profaned at the death of Edward IV., when Richard came to pay his ostentatious orisons in the Cathedral, while he was already planning the removal of the princes to the Tower. Always anxious to please the London citizens, it was to St. Paul's Cross that Richard sent Dr. Shaw to accuse Clarence of illegitimacy. At St. Paul's, too, according to Shakespeare, who in his historic plays often follows traditions now forgotten, or chronicles that have perished, the charges against Hastings

mangled, and ill-shaped body thrown, like carrion, across a pack-horse and driven off to Leicester, and Henry VII., the astute, the wily, the thrifty, reigned in his stead. After Henry's victory over Simnel he came two successive days to St. Paul's to offer his thanksgiving, and Simnel, afterwards a scullion in the royal kitchen, rode humbly at his conqueror's side.

The last ceremonial of the reign of Henry VII. that took place at St. Paul's was the ill-fated marriage of Prince Arthur—a mere boy, who died six months after—with Katharine of Arragon The whole church was hung with tapestry, and there

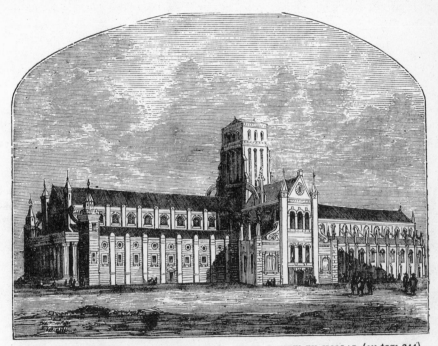

ST. PAUL'S AFTER THE FALL OF THE SPIRE, FROM A VIEW BY HOLLAR (*see page* 244).

were publicly read. Jane Shore, the mistress, and supposed accomplice of Hastings in bewitching Richard, did penance in St. Paul's. She was the wife of a London goldsmith, and had been mistress of Edward IV. Her beauty, as she walked downcast with shame, is said to have moved every heart to pity. On his accession, King Richard, nervously fingering his dagger, as was his wont to do according to the chronicles, rode to St. Paul's, and was received by procession, amid great congratulation and acclamation from the fickle people. Kemp, who was the Yorkist bishop during all these dreadful times, rebuilt St. Paul's Cross, which then became one of the chief ornaments of London.

Richard's crown was presently beaten into a hawthorn bush on Bosworth Field, and his defaced,

was a huge scaffold, with seats round it, reaching from the west door to the choir. On this platform the ceremony was performed. All day, at several places in the city, and at the west door of the Cathedral, the conduits ran for the delighted people with red and white wine. The wedded children were lodged in the bishop's palace, and three days later returned by water to Westminster. When Henry VII. died, his body lay in state in St. Paul's, and from thence it was taken to Windsor, to remain there till the beautiful chapel he had endowed at Westminster was ready for his reception. The Dean and Chapter of St. Paul's were among the trustees for the endowment he left, and the Cathedral still possesses the royal testament.

A Venetian ambassador who was present has

left a graphic description of one of the earliest ceremonies (1514) which Henry VIII. witnessed at St. Paul's. The Pope, Leo X., had sent the young and chivalrous king a sword and cap of maintenance, as a special mark of honour. The cap was of purple satin, covered with embroidery and pearls, and decked with ermine. The king rode from the bishop's palace to the cathedral on a beautiful black palfrey, the nobility walking before him in pairs. At the high altar the king donned the cap, and was girt with the sword. The procession then made the entire circuit of the church. The king wore a gown of purple satin and gold in chequer, and a jewelled collar; his cap of purple velvet had two jewelled rosettes, and his doublet was of gold brocade. The nobles wore massive chains of gold, and their chequered silk gowns were lined with sables, lynx-fur, and swansdown.

In the same reign Richard Fitz-James, the fanatical Bishop of London, persecuted the Lollards, and burned two of the most obstinate at Smithfield. It is indeed, doubtful, even now, if Fitz-James, in his hatred of the reformers, stopped short of murder. In 1514 Richard Hunn, a citizen who had disputed the jurisdiction of the obnoxious Ecclesiastical Court, was thrown into the Lollards' Tower, the bishop's prison, at the south-west corner of the Cathedral. A Wycliffe Bible had been found in his house; he was adjudged a heretic, and one night this obstinate man was found hung in his cell. The clergy called it suicide, but the coroner brought in a verdict of wilful murder against the Bishop's Chancellor, the sumner, and the bell-ringer of the Cathedral. The king, however, pardoned them all on their paying £1,500 to Hunn's family. The bishop, still furious, burned Hunn's body sixteen days after, as that of a heretic, in Smithfield. This fanatical bishop was the ceaseless persecutor of Dean Colet, that excellent and enlightened man, who founded St. Paul's School, and was the untiring friend of Erasmus, whom he accompanied on his memorable visit to Becket's shrine at Canterbury.

In 1518 Wolsey, proud and portly, appears upon the scene, coming to St. Paul's to sing mass and celebrate eternal peace between France, England, and Spain, and the betrothal of the beautiful Princess Mary to the Dauphin of France. The large chapel and the choir were hung with gold brocade, blazoned with the king's arms. Near the altar was the king's pew, formed of cloth of gold, and in front of it a small altar covered with silver-gilt images, with a gold cross in the centre. Two low masses were said at this before the king,

while high mass was being sung before the rest. On the opposite side of the altar, on a raised and canopied chair, sat Wolsey; further off stood the legate Campeggio. The twelve bishops and six abbots present all wore their jewelled mitres, while the king himself shone out in a tunic of purple velvet, "powdered" with pearls and rubies, sapphires and diamonds. His collar was studded with carbuncles as large as walnuts. A year later Charles V. was proclaimed emperor by the heralds at St. Paul's. Wolsey gave the benediction, no doubt with full hope of the Pope's tiara.

In 1521, but a little later, Wolsey, "Cardinal of St. Cecilia and Archbishop of York," was welcomed by Dean Pace to St. Paul's. He had come to sit near Paul's Cross, to hear Fisher, Bishop of Rochester, by the Pope's command, denounce "Martinus Eleutherius" and his accursed works, many of which were burned in the churchyard during the sermon, no doubt to the infinite alarm of all heretical booksellers in the neighbouring street. Wolsey had always an eye to the emperor's helping him to the papacy; and when Charles V. came to England to visit Henry, in 1522, Wolsey said mass, assisted by more than twenty obsequious prelates. It was Wolsey who first, as papal legate, removed the Convocation entirely from St. Paul's to Westminster, to be near his house at Whitehall. His ribald enemy, Skelton, then hiding from the cardinal's wrath in the Sanctuary at Westminster, wrote the following rough distich on the arbitrary removal:—

"Gentle Paul, lay down thy sword,
 For Pêter of Westminster hath shaven thy beard."

On the startling news of the battle of Pavia, when Francis I. was taken prisoner by his great rival of Spain, a huge bonfire illumined the west front of St. Paul's, and hogsheads of claret were broached at the Cathedral door, to celebrate the welcome tidings. On the Sunday after, the bluff king, the queen, and both houses of Parliament, attended a solemn "Te Deum" at the cathedral; while on St. Matthew's Day there was a great procession of all the religious orders in London, and Wolsey, with his obsequious bishops, performed service at the high altar. Two years later Wolsey came here again, to lament or rejoice over the sack of Rome by the Constable Bourbon, and the captivity of the Pope.

Singularly enough, the fire lighted by Wolsey in St. Paul's Churchyard had failed totally to burn up Luther and all his works; and on Shrove Tuesday, 1527, Wolsey made another attempt to reduce the new-formed Bible to ashes. In the great procession that came on this day to St. Paul's there were six Lutherans in penitential dresses, carrying terribly symbolical fagots and huge lighted tapers. On a platform in the nave sat the portly and proud cardinal, supported by thirty-six zealous bishops, abbots, and priests. At the foot of the great rood over the northern door the heretical tracts and Testaments were thrown into a fire. The prisoners, on their knees, begged pardon of God and the Catholic Church, and were then led three times round the fire, which they fed with the fagots they had carried.

Four years later, after Wolsey's fall, the London clergy were summoned to St. Paul's Chapter-house, on the south side. The king, offended at the Church having yielded to Wolsey's claims as a papal legate, by which the penalty of præmunire had been incurred, had demanded from Convocation the alarming fine of £100,000. Immediately six hundred clergy of all ranks thronged riotously to the chapter-house, to resist this outrageous tax. The bishop was all for concession ; "their goods and lands were forfeit, their bodies liable to imprisonment." The humble clergy cried out, "We have never meddled in the cardinal's business. Let the bishops and abbots, who have offended, pay." Blows were struck, and eventually fifteen priests and four laymen were condemned to terms of imprisonment in the Fleet and Tower, for their resistance to despotic power.

In 1535 nineteen German Anabaptists were examined in St. Paul's, and fourteen of them sent to the stake. Then came plain signs that the Reformation had commenced. The Pope's authority had been denied at Paul's Cross in 1534. A miraculous rood from Kent was brought to St. Paul's, and the machinery that moved the eyes and lips was shown to the populace, after which it was thrown down and broken amid contemptuous laughter. Nor would this chapter be complete if we did not mention a great civic procession at the close of the reign of Henry VIII. On Whit Sunday, 1546, the children of St. Paul's School, with parsons and vicars of every London church, in their copes, went from St. Paul's to St. Peter's, Cornhill, Bishop Bonner bearing the sacrament under a canopy ; and at the Cross, before the mayor, aldermen, and all the crafts, heralds proclaimed perpetual peace between England, France, and the Emperor. Two months after, the ex-bishop of Rochester preached a sermon at Paul's Cross recanting his heresy, four of his late fellow-prisoners in Newgate having obstinately perished at the stake.

In the reign of Edward VI. St. Paul's witnessed far different scenes. The year of the accession of the child-king a funeral service was celebrated in memory of Francis I., Latin dirges were chanted, and eight mitred bishops sang a requiem to the monarch lately deceased. At his Coronation, while the guilds were marshalled along Cheapside, and tapestries hung from every window, an acrobat descended by a cable from St. Paul's steeple to the anchor of a ship near the Deanery door. In November of the next year, at night, the crucifixes and images in St. Paul's were pulled down and removed, to the horror of the faithful, and all obits and chantreys were confiscated, and the vestments and altar cloths were sold. The early reformers were backed by greedy partisans. The Protector Somerset, who was desirous of building rapidly a sumptuous palace in the Strand, pulled down the chapel and charnel-house in the Pardon churchyard, and carted off the stones of St. Paul's cloister. When the good Ridley was installed Bishop of London, he would not enter the choir until the lights on the altar were extinguished. Very soon a table was substituted for the altar, and there was an attempt made to remove the organ. The altar, and chapel, and tombs, all but John of Gaunt's, were then ruthlessly destroyed.

During the Lady Jane Grey rebellion, Ridley denounced Mary and Elizabeth as bastards. The accession of gloomy Queen Mary soon turned the tables. As the Queen passed to her Coronation, a daring Dutchman stood on the cross of St. Paul's waving a long streamer, and shifting from foot to foot as he shook two torches which he held over his head.

But the citizens were Protestants at heart. At the first sermon preached at St. Paul's Cross in this reign, Dr. Bourne, an Essex clergyman, prayed for the dead, praised Bonner, and denounced Ridley. The mob, inflamed to madness, shouted, "He preaches damnation ! Pull him down ! pull him down !" A dagger, thrown at the preacher, stuck quivering in a side-post of the pulpit. With difficulty two good men dragged the rash zealot safely into St. Paul's School. For this riot several persons were sent to the Tower, and a priest and a barber had their ears nailed to the pillory at St. Paul's Cross. The crosses were raised again in St. Paul's, and the old ceremonies and services revived. On St. Katharine's Day, in honour of the queen's mother's patron saint there was a procession with lights and the image of St. Katharine, round St. Paul's steeple, and the bells rang. Not long after this, when a Dr. Pendleton preached the "old doctrines" at St. Paul's Cross, a gun was fired at him. When Bonner was released from the Marshalsea and restored to his see, the people shouted, " Welcome home ;" and a woman ran forward and kissed him. We are told that he knelt in prayer on the Cathedral steps.

In 1554, at the reception in St. Paul's of Cardinal Pole, King Philip attended with English, Spanish, and German guards, and a great retinue of nobles. Bishop Gardiner preached on the widening heresy till the audience groaned and wept. Of the cruel persecutions of the Protestants in this reign, St. Paul's was now and then a witness, and likewise of the preparations for the execution of Protestants, which Bonner's party called " trials." Thus we find Master Cardmaker, vicar of St. Bride's, and Warne, an upholsterer in Walbrook, both arraigned at St. Paul's before the bishop for heresy, and carried back from there to Newgate, to be shortly after burned alive in Smithfield.

In the midst of these horrors, a strange ceremony took place at St. Paul's, far more worthy, indeed, of the supposed temple of Diana than of a Christian cathedral, did it not remind us that Popery was always strangely intermingled with fragments of old paganism. In June, 1557 (St. Paul's Day, says Machyn, an undertaker and chronicler of Mary's reign), a fat buck was presented to the dean and chapter, according to an annual grant made by Sir Walter le Baud, an Essex knight, in the reign of Edward I. A priest from each London parish attended in his cope, and the Bishop of London wore his mitre, while behind the burly, bullying, persecutor Bonner came a fat buck, his head with his horns borne upon a pole, while forty huntsmen's horns blew a rejoicing chorus.

The last event of this blood-stained reign was the celebration at St. Paul's of the victory over the French at the battle of St. Quintin by Philip and the Spaniards. A sermon was preached before the city authorities at Paul's Cross, bells were rung, and bonfires blazed in every street.

At Elizabeth's accession its new mistress soon purged St. Paul's of all its images : copes and shaven crowns disappeared. The first ceremony of the new reign was the performance of the obsequies of Henry II. of France. An empty hearse was hung with cloth of gold, the choir draped in black, the clergy appearing in plain black gowns and caps. And now, what the Catholics called a great judgment fell on the old Cathedral. During a great storm in 1561, St. Martin's Church, Ludgate, was struck by lightning ; immediately after, the wooden steeple of St. Paul's started into a flame. The fire burned downwards furiously for four hours, the bells were melted, the lead poured in torrents ; the roof fell in, and the whole Cathedral became for a time a ruin.

Soon after, at the Cross, Dean Nowell rebuked the Papists for crying out "a judgment." In papal times the church had also suffered. In Richard I.'s reign an earthquake shook down the spire, and in Stephen's time fire had also brought destruction. The Crown and City were roused by this misfortune. Thrifty Elizabeth gave 1,000 marks in gold, and 1,000 marks' worth of timber ; the City gave a great benevolence, and the clergy subscribed £1,410. In one month a false roof was erected, and by the end of the year the aisles were leaded in. On the 1st of November, the same year, the mayor, aldermen, and crafts, with eighty torchbearers, went to attend service at St. Paul's. The steeple, however, was never rebuilt, in spite of Queen Elizabeth's angry remonstrances.

In the first year of Philip and Mary, the Common Council of London passed an act which shows the degradation into which St. Paul's had sunk even before the fire. It forbade the carrying of beer-casks, or baskets of bread, fish, flesh, or fruit, or leading mules or horses through the Cathedral, under pain of fines and imprisonment. Elizabeth also issued a proclamation to a similar effect, forbidding a fray, drawing of swords in the church, or shooting with hand-gun or dagg within the church or churchyard, under pain of two months' imprisonment. Neither were agreements to be made for the payment of money within the church. Soon after the fire, a man that had provoked a fray in the church was set in the pillory in the churchyard, and had his ears nailed to a post, and then cut off. These proclamations, however, led to no reform. Cheats, gulls, assassins, and thieves thronged the middle aisle of St. Paul's ; advertisements of all kinds covered the walls, the worst class of servants came there to be hired ; worthless rascals and disreputable flaunting women met there by appointment. Parasites, hunting for a dinner, hung about a monument of the Beauchamps, foolishly believed to be the tomb of the good Duke Humphrey. Shakespeare makes Falstaff hire red-nosed Bardolph in St. Paul's, and Ben Jonson lays the third act of his *Every Man in his Humour* in the middle aisle. Bishop Earle, in his " Microcosmography," describes the noise of the crowd of idlers in Paul's " as that of bees, a strange hum mixed of walking tongues and feet, a kind of still roar or loud whisper." He describes the crowd of young curates, "copper" captains, thieves, and dinnerless adventurers and gossip-mongers. Bishop Corbet, that jolly prelate, speaks of

" The walk,
Where all our British sinners swear and talk,
Old hardy ruffians, bankrupts, soothsayers,
And youths whose cousenage is old as theirs."

On the eve of the election of Sandys as Bishop of London, May, 1570, all London was roused by a papal bull against Elizabeth being found nailed on the gates of the bishop's palace. It declared her crown forfeited and her people absolved from their oaths of allegiance. The fanatic maniac, Felton, was soon discovered, and hung on a gallows at the bishop's gates.

One or two anecdotes of interest specially connect Elizabeth with St. Paul's. On one occasion Dean Nowell placed in the queen's closet or pew a splendid prayer-book, full of German scriptural engravings, richly illuminated. The zealous queen was furious; the book seemed to her of Catholic tendencies.

"Who placed this book on my cushion? You know I have an aversion to idolatry. The cuts resemble angels and saints—nay, even grosser absurdities."

The frightened dean pleaded innocence of all evil intentions. The queen prayed God to grant him more wisdom for the future, and asked him where they came from. When told Germany, she replied, "It is well it was a stranger. Had it been one of my subjects, we should have questioned the matter."

Once again Dean Nowell vexed the queen—this time by being too strongly Puritan. On Ash Wednesday, 1572, the dean preaching before her, he denounced certain popish superstitions in a book recently dedicated to her majesty. He specially denounced the use of the sign of the cross. Suddenly a harsh voice was heard in the royal closet. It was Elizabeth's. She chidingly bade Mr. Dean return from his ungodly digression and revert to his text. The next day the frightened dean wrote a most abject apology to the high-spirited queen.

The victory over the Armada was, of course, not forgotten at St. Paul's. When the thanksgiving sermon was preached at Paul's Cross, eleven Spanish ensigns waved over the cathedral battlements, and one painted streamer with an image of the Virgin fluttered over the preacher. That was in September; the queen herself came in November, drawn by four white horses, and with her privy council and all the nobility. Elizabeth heard a sermon, and dined at the bishop's palace.

The "aery of children" whom Shakespeare, in *Hamlet*, mentions with the jealousy of a rival manager, were, as Dean Milman has proved, the chorister-boys of St. Paul's. They acted, it is supposed, in their singing-school. The play began at four p.m., after prayers, and the price of admission was 4d. They are known at a later period to have acted some of Lily's Euphuistic plays, and one of Middleton's.

In this reign lotteries for Government purposes were held at the west door of St. Paul's, where a wooden shed was erected for drawing the prizes, which were first plate and then suits of armour. In the first lottery (1569) there were 40,000 lots at 10s. a lot, and the profits were applied to repairing the harbours of England.

In the reign of James I. blood was again shed before St. Paul's. Years before a bishop had been murdered at the north door; now, before the west entrance, in January, 1605-6, four of the desperate Gunpowder Plot conspirators, Sir Everard Digby, Winter, Grant, and Bates, were there hung, drawn, and quartered. Their attempt to restore the old religion by one blow ended in the hangman's strangling rope and the executioner's cruel knife. In the May following a man of less-proven guilt, Garnet, the Jesuit, suffered the same fate in St. Paul's Churchyard; and zealots of his faith affirmed that on straws saved from the scaffold miraculous portraits of their martyr were discovered.

The ruinous state of the great cathedral, still without a tower, now aroused the king. He tried to saddle the bishop and chapter with its restoration, but Lord Southampton, Shakespeare's friend, interposed to save them. Then the matter went to sleep for twelve years. In 1620 the king again awoke, and came in state with all his lords on horseback, to hear a sermon at the Cross and to view the church. A royal commission followed, Inigo Jones, the king's *protégé*, whom James had brought from Denmark, being one of the commissioners. The sum required was estimated at £22,536. But the king's zeal ended here; his favourite, Buckingham, borrowed, for his Strand palace, the stone collected for St. Paul's, and from parts of it was raised that fine water-gate still existing in the Thames Embankment gardens.

When Charles I. made that narrow-minded churchman, Laud, Bishop of London, one of Laud's first endeavours was to restore St. Paul's. Charles I. was a man of taste, and patronised painting and architecture. Inigo Jones was already building the Banqueting House at Whitehall. The king was so pleased with Inigo's design for the new portico of St. Paul's, that he proposed to pay for that himself. Laud gave £1,200. The fines of the obnoxious and illegal High Commission Court were set apart for the same object. The small sheds and houses round the west front were ruthlessly cleared away. All shops in Cheapside and Lombard Street, except goldsmiths, were to be shut up, that the eastern approach to St. Paul's might appear more splendid. The church of St. Gregory, at the south-west wing of the cathedral, was removed and rebuilt. Inigo Jones cut away all the decayed stone and crumbling Gothic work of the Cathedral, and on the west portico expended all the knowledge he had acquired in his visit to Rome. The result was a pagan composite, beautiful but incongruous. The front, 161 feet long and 162 feet high, was supported by fourteen Corinthian columns. On the parapet above the pillars Inigo proposed that there should stand ten statues of

1639, a paper was found in the yard of the deanery, before Laud's house, inscribed—"Laud, look to thyself. Be assured that thy life is sought, as thou art the fountain of all wickedness;" and in October, 1640, the High Commission sitting at St. Paul's, nearly 2,000 Puritans made a tumult, tore down the benches in the consistory, and shouted, "We will have no bishops and no High Commission."

The Parliament made short work with St. Paul's, of Laud's projects, and Inigo Jones's classicalisms. They at once seized the £17,000 or so left of the

THE CHAPTER HOUSE OF OLD ST. PAUL'S, FROM A VIEW BY HOLLAR (*see page* 243).

princely benefactors of St. Paul's. At each angle of the west front there was a tower. The portico was intended for a Paul's Walk, to drain off the profanation from within.

Nor were the London citizens backward. One most large-hearted man, Sir Paul Pindar, a Turkey merchant who had been ambassador at Constantinople, and whose house is still to be seen in Bishopsgate Street, contributed £10,000 towards the screen and south transept. The statues of James and Charles were set up over the portico, and the steeple was begun, when the storm arose that soon whistled off the king's unlucky head. The coming troubles cast shadows around St. Paul's. In March,

subscription. To Colonel Jephson's regiment, in arrears for pay, £1,746, they gave the scaffolding round St. Paul's tower, and in pulling it to pieces down came part of St. Paul's south transept. The copes in St. Paul's were burnt, to extract the gold, and the money sent to the unfortunate Protestant poor in Ireland. The silver vessels were sold to buy artillery for Cromwell. There was a story current that Cromwell intended to sell St. Paul's to the Jews for a synagogue. The east end of the church was walled in for a Puritan lecturer; the graves were desecrated; the choir became a cavalry barrack; the portico was let out to sempsters and hucksters, who lodged in rooms above; James and Charles

EXTERIOR OF ST. PAUL'S FROM THE SOUTH-WEST, 1800.

were toppled from the portico; while the pulpit and cross were entirely destroyed. The dragoons in St. Paul's became so troublesome to the inhabitants by their noisy brawling games and their rough interruption of passengers, that in 1651 we find them forbidden to play at ninepins from six a.m. to nine p.m.

When the Restoration came, sunshine again fell upon the ruins. Wren, that great genius, was called in. His report was not very favourable. The pillars were giving way; the whole work had been from the beginning ill designed and ill built; the tower was leaning. He proposed to have a rotunda, with cupola and lantern, to give the church light, "and incomparable more grace" than the lean shaft of a steeple could possibly afford. He closed his report by a eulogy on the portico of Inigo Jones, as "an absolute piece in itself." Some of the stone collected for St. Paul's went, it is said, to build Lord Clarendon's house, near Albemarle Street. On August 27, 1661, good Mr. Evelyn, one of the commissioners, describes meeting Wren, the Bishop and Dean of St. Paul's, &c., and resolving finally on a new foundation. But on Sunday, September 2, the Great Fire drew a red cancelling line over Wren's half-drawn plans. The old cathedral passed away, like Elijah, in flames. The fire broke out about ten o'clock on Saturday night at a bakehouse in Pudding Lane, near East Smithfield. On Sunday afternoon Pepys found all the goods carried that morning to Cannon Street now removing to Lombard Street. At St. Paul's Wharf he takes water, follows the king's party, and lands at Bankside. "In corners and upon steeples, and between churches and houses, as far as we could see up the city, a most horrid, bloody, malicious flame, not like the flame of an ordinary fire." On the 7th he saw St. Paul's Church with all the roof off, and the body of the choir fallen into St. Faith's.

On Monday, the 3rd, Mr. Evelyn describes the whole north of the City on fire, the sky ablaze for ten miles round, and the scaffolds round St. Paul's in flames. On the 4th he saw the stones of St. Paul's flying like grenades, the melting lead running in streams down the streets, the very pavements too hot for the feet, and the approaches too blocked for any help to be applied. A Westminster boy named Taswell, quoted by Dean Milman from "Camden's Miscellany," vol. ii., p. 12, has also sketched the scene. On Monday, the 3rd, from Westminster he saw, about eight o'clock, the fire burst forth, and before nine he could read by the blaze a 16mo "Terence" which he had with him. The boy at once set out for St. Paul's, resting by the way upon Fleet Bridge, being almost faint with the intense heat of the air. The bells were melting, and vast avalanches of stones were pouring from the walls. Near the east end he found the body of an old woman, who had cowered there, burned to a coal. Taswell also relates that the ashes of the books kept in St. Faith's were blown as far as Eton and Windsor.

On the 7th (Friday) Evelyn again visited St. Paul's. The portico he found rent in pieces, the vast stones split asunder, and nothing remaining entire but the inscription on the architrave, not one letter of which was injured. Six acres of lead on the roof were all melted. The roof of St. Faith's had fallen in, and all the stores and books from Paternoster Row were consumed, burning for a week together. Singularly enough, the lead over the altar at the east end was untouched, and among the monuments the body of one bishop, Braybroke (Richard II.) remained entire. The old tombs nearly all perished; amongst them those of two Saxon kings, John of Gaunt, his wife Constance of Castile, poor St. Erkenwald, and scores of bishops, good and bad; Sir Nicholas Bacon, Elizabeth's Lord Keeper, and father of the great philosopher; the last of the true knights, the gallant Sir Philip Sidney; and Walsingham, that astute counsellor of Elizabeth. Then there was Sir Christopher Hatton, the dancing chancellor, whose proud monument crowded back Walsingham's and Sidney's. According to the old scoffing distich,

"Philip and Francis they have no tomb,
   For great Christopher takes all the room."

Men of letters in old St. Paul's, says Dean Milman, there were few. The chief were Lily, the grammarian, second master of St. Paul's; and Linacre, the physician, the friend of Colet and Erasmus. Of artists there was at least one great man— Vandyck, who was buried near John of Gaunt. Among citizens, the chief was Sir William Hewet, whose daughter married Osborne, the apprentice who saved her from drowning, and who was the ancestor of the Dukes of Leeds.

After the fire Bishop Sancroft preached in a patched-up part of the west end of the ruins. All hopes of restoration were soon abandoned, as Wren had, with his instinctive genius, predicted. Sancroft at once wrote to the great architect, "What you last whispered in my ear is now come to pass. A pillar has fallen, and the rest threatens to follow." The letter concludes thus: "You are so absolutely necessary to us, that we can do nothing, resolve on nothing, without you." There was plenty of zeal in London still; but, nevertheless, after all, nothing was done in the way of rebuilding till the year 1673.

CHAPTER XXI.

ST. PAUL'S (continued).

The Rebuilding of St. Paul's—Ill Treatment of its Architect—Cost of the Present Fabric—Royal Visitors—The First Grave in St. Paul's—Monuments in St. Paul's—Nelson's Funeral—Military Heroes in St. Paul's—The Duke of Wellington's Funeral—Other Great Men in St. Paul's—Proposals for the Completion and Decoration of the Building—Dimensions of St. Paul's—Plan of Construction—The Dome, Ball, and Cross—Mr. Horner and his Observatory—Two Narrow Escapes—Sir James Thornhill—Peregrine Falcons on St. Paul's—Nooks and Corners of the Cathedral—The Library, Trophy Room, and Clock—The Great Bell—The New Peal of Bells—Curious Story of a Monomaniac—The Poets and the Cathedral—Discovery of Ancient Foundations—St. Paul's Churchyard Gardens.

TOWARDS the rebuilding of St. Paul's Cathedral, Charles II., generous as usual in promises, offered an annual contribution of £1,000; but this, however, never seems to have been paid. It, no doubt, went to pay Nell Gwynne's losses at the gambling-table, or to feed the Duchess of Portsmouth's lap-dogs. Some £1,700 in fines, however, were set apart for the new building. The Primate Sheldon gave £2,000. Many of the bishops contributed largely, and there were parochial collections all over England. But the bulk of the money was obtained from the City duty on coals, which, as Dean Milman remarks, in time had their revenge by destroying the stone-work of the Cathedral. It was only by a fortunate accident that Wren became the builder; for Charles II., whose tastes and vices were all French, had in vain invited over Perrault, the designer of one of the fronts of the Louvre.

The great architect, Wren, was the son of a Dean of Windsor, and nephew of a Bishop of Norwich whom Cromwell had imprisoned for his Romish tendencies. From a boy Wren had shown a genius for scientific discovery. He distinguished himself in almost every branch of knowledge, and to his fruitful brain we are indebted for some fifty-two suggestive discoveries. He now hoped to rebuild London on a magnificent scale; but it was not to be. Even in the plans for the new cathedral Wren was from the beginning thwarted and impeded. Ignorance, envy, jealousy, and selfishness met him at every line he drew. He made two designs—the first a Greek, the second a Latin cross. The Greek cross the clergy considered as unsuitable for a cathedral. The model for it, which is still preserved in the Cathedral, was for some time on view at the South Kensington Museum, having been lent for that purpose by the Dean and Chapter. The interior of the first design is by many considered superior to the present interior. The present recesses along the aisles of the nave, tradition says, were insisted on by James II., who thought they would be useful as side chapels when masses were once more introduced.

The first stone was laid by Wren on the 21st June, 1675, but there was no public ceremonial. Soon after the great geometrician had drawn the circle for the beautiful dome, he sent a workman for a stone to mark the exact centre. The man returned with a fragment of a tombstone, on which was the one ominous word, as every one observed, "Resurgam!" The ruins of old St. Paul's were stubborn. When they tried to blow up the tower, a passer-by was killed, and Wren, with his usual ingenuity, resorted successfully to the old Roman battering-ram, which soon cleared a way. "I build for eternity," said Wren, with the true confidence of genius, as he searched for a firm foundation. Below the Norman, Saxon, and Roman graves he dug and probed till he could find the most reliable stratum. Below the loam was sand; under the sand a layer of fresh-water shells; under these were sand, gravel, and London clay. At the north-east corner of the dome Wren was vexed by coming upon a pit dug by the Roman potters in search of clay. He, however, began from the solid earth a strong pier of masonry, and above turned a short arch to the former foundation. He also slanted the new building more to the north-east than its predecessor, in order to widen the street south of St. Paul's.

Well begun is half done. The Cathedral grew fast, and in two-and-twenty years from the laying of the first stone the choir was opened for Divine service. The master mason who helped to lay the first stone assisted in fixing the last in the lantern. A great day was chosen for the opening of St. Paul's. December 2nd, 1697, was the thanksgiving day for the Peace of Ryswick—the treaty which humbled France, and seated William firmly and permanently on the English throne. The king, much against his will, was persuaded to stay at home by his courtiers, who dreaded armed Jacobites among the 300,000 people who would throng the streets. Worthy Bishop Compton, who, dressed as a trooper, had guarded the Princess Anne in her flight from her father, preached that inspiring day on the text, "I was glad when they said unto me, Let us go into the house of the Lord." From then till now the daily voice of prayer and praise has never ceased in St. Paul's.

Queen Anne, during her eventful reign, went seven times to St. Paul's in solemn procession, to commemorate victories over France or Spain. The first of these (1702) was a jubilee for Marlborough's triumph in the Low Countries and Rooke's destruction of the Spanish fleet at Vigo. The Queen sat on a raised and canopied throne; the Duke of Marlborough, as Groom of the Stole, on a stool behind her. The Lords and Commons, who had arrived in procession, were arranged in the choir. The brave old Whig Bishop of Exeter, Sir Jonathan Trelawny ("And shall Trelawny die?"), preached the sermon. Guns at the Tower, on the river, and in St. James's Park, were fired at the Te Deum, and when the Queen started and returned. In 1704, the victory of Blenheim was celebrated; in 1705, the forcing of the French lines at Tirlemont; in 1706, the battle of Ramillies and Lord Peterborough's successes in Spain; in 1707, more triumphs; in 1708, the battle of Oudenarde; and last of all, in 1713, the Peace of Utrecht, when the Queen was unable to attend. On this last day the charity children of London, 4,000 in number, first attended outside the church.

St. Paul's was already, to all intents and purposes, completed. The dome was ringed with its golden gallery, and crowned with its glittering cross. In 1710, Wren's son and the body of Freemasons had laid the highest stone of the lantern of the cupola. But now commenced the bitterest mortifications of Wren's life. The commissioners had dwindled down to Dean Godolphin and six or seven civilians from Doctors' Commons. Wren's old friends were dead. His foes compelled him to pile the organ on the screen, though he had intended it to be under the north-west arch of the choir, where it was placed later. Wren wished to use mosaic for internal decoration; they pronounced it too costly, and they took the painting of the cupola out of Wren's hands, and gave it to Hogarth's father-in-law, Sir James Thornhill. They complained of wilful delay in the work, and accused Wren or his assistant of corruption; they also withheld part of his salary till the work was completed. Wren covered the cupola with lead, at a cost of £2,500; the committee were for copper, at £3,050. About the iron railing for the churchyard there was also wrangling. Wren wished a low fence, to leave the vestibule and the steps free and open. The commissioners thought Wren's design mean and weak, and chose the heavy and cumbrous iron-work, which spoilt the view of the west front, and was only removed in 1874.

The new organ, by Father Bernard Smith, which cost £2,000, was shorn of its full size by Wren, perhaps in vexation at its misplacement. The paltry statue of Queen Anne, in the churchyard, was by Bird, and cost £1,130, exclusive of the marble, which the Queen provided. The carvings in the choir, by Grinling Gibbons, cost £1,337 7s. 5d. On some of the exterior sculpture Cibber worked.

In 1718 a violent pamphlet appeared, written, it was supposed, by one of the commissioners. It accused Wren's head workmen of pilfering timber and cracking the bells. Wren proved the charges to be malicious and untrue. The commissioners now insisted on adding a stone balustrade all round St. Paul's, in spite of Wren's protests. He condemned the addition as "contrary to the principles of architecture, and as breaking into the harmony of the whole design;" but, he said, "ladies think nothing well without an edging."

The next year, the commissioners went a step further. Wren, then eighty-six years old, and in his forty-ninth year of office, was dismissed without apology from his post of Surveyor of Public Works. The German Court, hostile to all who had served the Stuarts, appointed in his place a poor pretender, named Benson. This charlatan—now only remembered by a line in the "Dunciad," which ridicules the singular vanity of a man who erected a monument to Milton in Westminster Abbey, and crowded the marble with his own titles—was afterwards dismissed from his surveyorship with ignominy, but had yet influence enough at Court to escape prosecution and obtain several valuable sinecures. Wren retired to his house at Hampton Court, and there sought consolation in philosophical and religious studies. Once a year, says Horace Walpole, the good old man was carried to St. Paul's, to contemplate the glorious chef-d'œuvre of his genius. Steele, in the Tatler, refers to Wren's vexations, and attributes them to his modesty and bashfulness.

The total sum expended on the building of St. Paul's Cathedral, according to Dean Milman, was £736,752 2s. 3¼d.; a small residue from the coal duty was all that was left for future repairs. To this Dean Clark added about £500, part of the profits arising from an Essex estate, the gift of an old Saxon king, leased from the Dean and Chapter. The charge of the fabric was vested not in the Dean and Chapter, but in the Archbishop of Canterbury, the Bishop of London, and the Lord Mayor for the time being. These trustees elect the surveyor and audit the accounts.

On the accession of George I. (1715), the new king, princes, and princesses went in state to St. Paul's. Seventy years elapsed before an English king again entered Wren's cathedral. In April,

1789, George III. went thither to thank God for his temporary recovery from insanity. Queen Charlotte, the Prince of Wales, and the Duke of York were present, and both Houses of Parliament. Bishop Porteus preached the sermon, and 6,000 charity children joined in the service. In 1797 King George came again to attend a thanksgiving for Lord Duncan's and Lord Howe's naval victories; French, Spanish, and Dutch flags waved above the procession, and Sir Horatio Nelson was there among other heroes.

The first grave sunk in St. Paul's was fittingly that of Wren, its builder. He lies in the place of honour, the extreme east of the crypt. The black marble slab is railed in, and the light from a small window-grating falls upon the venerated name. Sir Christopher died in 1723, aged ninety-one. The fine inscription, " Si monumentum requiris, circumspice," written probably by his son, or by Mylne, the builder of Blackfriars Bridge, was formerly in front of the organ-gallery, but is now placed over the north-western entrance.

The clergy of St. Paul's were for a long time jealous of allowing any monument in the cathedral. Dean Newton wished for one, but that was afterwards erected in St. Mary-le-Bow. A better man than the vain, place-hunting dean was the first so honoured. The earliest statue admitted was that of the benevolent Howard, who had mitigated suffering and sorrow in all the prisons of Europe; he stands at the corner of the dome facing that half-stripped athlete, Dr. Johnson; and the two are generally taken by country visitors for St. Peter and St. Paul. He who with Goldsmith had wandered through the Abbey, wondering if one day their names might not be recorded there, found a grave in Westminster, and, thanks to Reynolds, the first place of honour. Sir Joshua himself, as one of our greatest painters, took the third place, that Hogarth should have occupied; and the fourth was awarded to that great Oriental scholar, Sir William Jones. The clerical opposition was now broken through, for the world felt that the Abbey was full enough, and that St. Paul's required adorning.

Henceforward St. Paul's was chiefly set apart for naval and military heroes whom the city could best appreciate, while the poets, great writers, and statesmen were honoured in the Abbey, and laid among the old historic dead. From the beginning our sculptors resorted to pagan emblems and pagan allegorical figures; the result is that St. Paul's resembles a Pantheon of the Lower Empire, and is a hospital of third-rate art. The first naval conqueror so honoured was Rodney; Rossi received £6,000 for his cold and clumsy design:

Lord Howe's statue followed; and next that of Lord Duncan, the hero of Camperdown. It is a simple statue by Westmacott, with a seaman and his wife and child on the pedestal. For Lord St. Vincent Bailey produced a colossal statue and the usual scribbling, History and a trumpeting Victory.

Then came Nelson's brothers in arms—men of lesser mark; but the nation was grateful, and the Government was anxious to justify its wars by its victories. St. Paul's was growing less particular, and now opened its arms to the best men it could get. Many of Nelson's captains preceded him on the red road to death—Westcott, who fell at Aboukir; Mosse and Riou, who fell before Copenhagen, a far from stainless victory. Riou was the brave man whom Campbell immortalised in his fiery " Battle of the Baltic." Riou lies

" Full many a fathom deep,
By thy wild and stormy steep,
Elsinore."

Then at last, in 1806, came a hero worthy, indeed, of such a building—Nelson himself. At what a moment had Nelson expired!—at the close of a victory that had annihilated the fleets of France and Spain, and secured to Britain the empire of the seas. The whole nation that day shed tears of " pride and of sorrow." The Prince of Wales and all his brothers led the procession of nearly 8,000 soldiers, the chief mourner being Admiral Parker, whose name is connected with the Mutiny of the Nore. Nelson's coffin was formed out of a mast of the *L'Orient*—a vessel blown up at the battle of the Nile—presented to Nelson by his friend, the captain of the *Swiftsure*. The sarcophagus, singularly enough, had been designed by Michael Angelo's contemporary, Torreguiano, for Wolsey, in the days of his most insatiable pride, and had remained ever since in Wolsey's chapel at Windsor; Nelson's flag was to have been placed over the coffin, but as it was about to be lowered, the sailors who had borne it, as if by an irresistible impulse, stepped forward and tore it in pieces, for relics. Dean Milman, who, as a youth, was present, says, "I heard, or fancied I heard, the low wail of the sailors who encircled the remains of their admiral." Nelson's trusty companion, Lord Collingwood, who led the vanguard at Trafalgar, sleeps near his old captain, and Lord Northesk, who led the rear-guard, is buried opposite. A brass plate on the pavement under the dome marks the spot of Nelson's tomb. The monument to Nelson, inconveniently placed at the opening of the choir, is by one of our greatest sculptors—Flaxman. It is hardly worthy of the occasion, and the figures on the pedestal are puerile. Lord

Lyons is the last admiral whose monument has been erected in St. Paul's.

The military heroes have been contributed by various wars, just and unjust, successful and the reverse. There is that tough old veteran, Lord Heathfield, who drove off two angry nations from the scorched rock of Gibraltar ; Sir Isaac Brock, who fell near Niagara ; Sir Ralph Abercromby, who perished in Egypt ; and Sir John Moore, who played so well a losing game at Corunna. Hosts of Wellington's soldiers lie in St. Paul's—brave men, who

15,000 persons were present. The impressive funeral procession, with the representatives of the various regiments, and the solemn bursts of the "Dead March in Saul" at measured intervals, can never be forgotten by those who were present. The pall was borne by the general officers who had fought by the side of Wellington, and the cathedral was illuminated for the occasion. The service was read by Dean Milman, who had been, as we have before mentioned, a spectator of Nelson's funeral. So perfectly adapted for sound is St. Paul's, that

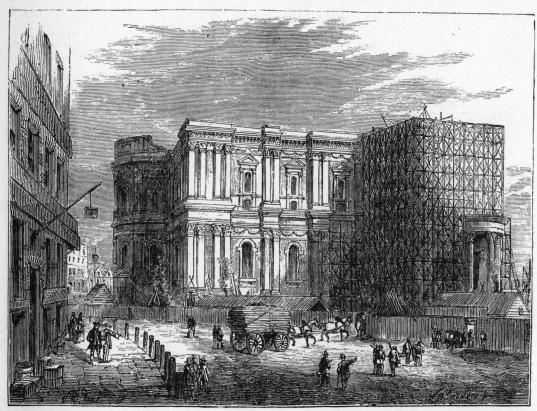

THE REBUILDING OF ST. PAUL'S. FROM AN ORIGINAL DRAWING IN THE POSSESSION OF J. G. CRACE, ESQ.

sacrificed their lives at Talavera, Vimiera, Ciudad Rodrigo, Salamanca, Vittoria, and Bayonne. Nor has our proud and just nation disdained to honour even equally gallant men who were defeated. There are monuments in St. Paul's to the vanquished at Bergen-op-Zoom, New Orleans, and Baltimore.

That climax of victory, Waterloo, brought Ponsonby and Picton to St. Paul's. Picton lies in the vestibule of the Wellington chapel. Thirty-seven years after Waterloo, in the fulness of his years, Wellington was deservedly honoured by a tomb in St. Paul's. It was impossible to lay him beside Nelson, so the eastern chapel of the crypt was appropriated for his sarcophagus. From 12,000 to

though the walls were muffled with black cloth, the Dean's voice could be heard distinctly, even up in the western gallery. A monument to the "iron Duke," consisting of a recumbent effigy surmounted by a canopy adorned with military trophies, from the designs of the late Mr. Stevens, was completed in 1878.

After Nelson and Wellington, the lesser names seem to dwindle down. Yet among the great, pure, and good, we may mention, there are some Crimean memorials. There also is the monument of Cornwallis, that good Governor-General of India ; those of the two Napiers, the historian and the conqueror of Scinde, true knights both ; that of Elphinstone, who twice refused the dignity of Governor-General of India ; and that of the saviour of our Indian empire, Sir Henry Lawrence. Nor should we forget the monuments of two Indian bishops—the scholarly Middleton, and the excellent and lovable Heber. There is an unsatisfactory monument in such a place, is the historian Hallam, a calm, sometimes cold, but always impartial writer.

In the crypt near Wren lie many of our most celebrated English artists. Sir Joshua Reynolds died in 1792. His pall was borne by peers, and upwards of a hundred carriages followed his hearse.

THE CHOIR OF ST. PAUL'S BEFORE THE REMOVAL OF THE SCREEN, *from an engraving published in* 1754.

statue of Turner, by Bailey ; and monuments to Dr. Babington, a London physician, and Sir Astley Cooper, the great surgeon. The ambitious monument to Viscount Melbourne, the Queen's first prime minister, by Baron Marochetti, stands in one of the alcoves of the nave ; great gates of black marble represent the entrance to a tomb, guarded by two angels of white marble at the portals. More worthy than the gay Melbourne of the honour of a

Near him lies his successor as president, West, the Quaker painter ; courtly Lawrence ; Barry, whom Reynolds detested ; rough, clever Opie ; Dance ; and eccentric Fuseli. In this goodly company, also, sleeps a greater than all of these—Joseph Mallord William Turner, the first landscape painter of the world. He had requested, when dying, to be buried as near to his old master, Reynolds, as possible. It is said that Turner, soured with the world, had threatened to make his shroud out of his grand picture of "The Building of Carthage." In this spot also rest Robert Mylne and Charles Robert Cockerell, the eminent architects, Sir Edwin Landseer, George Cruikshank, and Dean Milman.

Only one robbery has occurred in modern times in St. Paul's. In December, 1810, the plate repository of the cathedral was broken open by thieves, with the connivance of, as is supposed, some official, and 1,761 ounces of plate, valued at above £2,000, were stolen. The thieves broke open nine doors to get at the treasure, which was never afterwards heard of. The spoil included the chased silver-gilt covers of the large (1640) Bible, chalices, plates, tankards, and candlesticks.

The cathedral, left colourless and blank by Wren, has never yet been finished. The Protestant choir remains in one corner, like a dry, shrivelled nut in a large shell. Like the proud snail in the fable, that took possession of the lobster-shell and starved there, we remained for more than a century complacently content with our unfurnished house. At length our tardy zeal awoke. In 1858 the Bishop of London wrote to the Dean and Chapter, urging a series of Sunday evening services, for the benefit of the floating masses of Londoners. Dean Milman replied, at once warming to the proposal, and suggesting also the decoration and completion of St. Paul's. The earnest appeal for "the noblest church, in its style, of Christian Europe, the masterpiece of Wren, the glory and pride of London," was at once responded to. A committee of the leading merchants and bankers was formed, including those great authorities, Sir Charles Barry, Mr. Cockerell, Mr. Tite, and Mr. Penrose. They at once resolved to gladden the eye with colour, without disturbing the solemn and harmonious simplicity. Paintings, mosaics, marble and gilding were requisite; the dome was to be relieved of Thornhill's lifeless *grisailles;* and above all, stained-glass windows were pronounced indispensable.

The dome had originally been filled by Thornhill with eight scenes from the life of St. Paul. He received for them the not very munificent but quite adequate sum of 40s. per square yard. They soon began to show symptoms of decay, and Mr. Parris, the painter, invented an apparatus by which they could easily be repaired, but no funds could then be found; yet when the paintings fell off in flakes, much money and labour was expended on the restoration, which has now proved useless. Mr. Penrose has shown that so ignorant was Sir James of perspective, that his painted architecture has actually the effect of making Wren's thirty-two pilasters seem to lean forward.

Much has already been done in St. Paul's. Two out of the eight large spandrel pictures round the dome are already executed. There are eventually to be four evangelists and four major prophets. Above the gilt rails of the whispering gallery an inscription on a mosaic and gold ground has been placed. A marble memorial pulpit has been put up. The screen has been removed, and the organ, greatly enlarged and improved, has been divided into two parts, which have been placed on either side of the choir, above the stalls; the dome is lighted with gas; the golden gallery, ball, and cross have been re-gilt. Ten stained-glass windows have been inserted, and among the donors have been the Drapers' and Goldsmiths' Companies; there are also memorial windows to the late Bishop Blomfield, W. Cotton, Esq., and Dean Mansel. The Grocers', Merchant Taylors', Goldsmiths', Mercers, and Fishmongers' Companies have generously gilt the vaults of the choir and the arches adjoining the dome. Some fifty or more windows still require stained glass. The wall panels are to be in various places adorned with inlaid marbles. It is not intended that St. Paul's should try to rival St. Peter's at Rome in exuberance of ornament, but it still requires a good deal of clothing. The great army of sable martyrs in marble have been at last washed white, and the fire-engines might now advantageously be used upon the exterior.

A few figures about the dimensions of St. Paul's will not be uninteresting. The cathedral is 2,292 feet in circumference, and the height from the nave pavement to the top of the cross is 365 feet. The height of St. Peter's at Rome being 432 feet, St. Paul's could stand inside St. Peter's. The western towers are 220 feet high. From east to west, St. Paul's is 500 feet long, while St. Peter's is 669 feet. The cupola is considered by many as more graceful than that of St. Peter's, "though in its connection with the church by an order higher than that below it there is a violation of the laws of the art." The external appearance of St. Paul's rivals, if not excels, that of St. Peter's, but the inside is much inferior. The double portico of St. Paul's has been greatly censured. The commissioners insisted on twelve columns, as emblematical of the twelve apostles, and Wren could not obtain stones of sufficient size; but, as Mr. Gwilt observes, it would have been better to have had joined pillars rather than a Composite heaped on a Corinthian portico. In the tympanum is the Conversion of St. Paul, sculptured in high relief by Bird; on the apex is a colossal figure of St. Paul, and on the right and left are St. Peter and St.

James. Over the southern portico is sculptured the Phœnix; over the north are the royal arms and regalia, while on each side stand on guard five statues of the apostles. The ascent to the whispering gallery is by 260 steps, to the outer and highest golden gallery 560 steps, and to the ball 616 steps. The outer golden gallery is at the summit of the dome. The inner golden gallery is at the base of the lantern. Through this the ascent is by ladders to the small dome, immediately below the inverted consoles which support the ball and cross. Ascending through the cross iron-work in the centre, you look into the dark ball, which is said to weigh 5,600 pounds; thence to the cross, which weighs 3,360 pounds, and is 30 feet high. In 1821-2 Mr. Cockerell removed for a time the ball and cross.

From the haunches of the dome, says Mr. Gwilt, 200 feet above the pavement of the church, another cone of brickwork commences, 85 feet high and 94 feet in diameter at the bottom. This cone is pierced with apertures, as well for the purpose of diminishing its weight as for distributing the light between it and the outer dome. At the top it is gathered into a dome in the form of a hyperboloid, pierced near the vertex with an aperture 12 feet in diameter. The top of this cone is 285 feet from the pavement, and carries a lantern 55 feet high, terminating in a dome whereon a ball and (Aveline) cross is raised. The last-named cone is provided with corbels, sufficient in number to receive the hammer-beams of the external dome, which is of oak, and its base 220 feet from the pavement, its summit being level with the top of the cone. In form it is nearly hemispherical, and generated by radii 57 feet in length, whose centres are in a horizontal diameter passing through its base. The cone and the interior dome are restrained in their lateral thrust on the supports by four tiers of strong iron chains (weighing 95 cwt. 3 qrs. 23 lbs.), placed in grooves prepared for their reception, and run with lead. The lowest of these is inserted in masonry round their common base, and the other three at different heights on the exterior of the cone. Over the intersection of the nave and transepts for the external work, and for a height of 25 feet above the roof of the church, a cylindrical wall rises, whose diameter is 146 feet. Between it and the lower conical wall is a space, but at intervals they are connected by cross-walls. This cylinder is quite plain, but perforated by two courses of rectangular apertures. On it stands a peristyle of thirty columns of the Corinthian order, 40 feet high, including bases and capitals, with a plain entablature crowned by a balustrade. In this peristyle every fourth intercolumniation is filled up

solid, with a niche, and connection is provided between it and the wall of the lower cone. Vertically over the base of that cone, above the peristyle, rises another cylindrical wall, appearing above the balustrade. It is ornamented with pilasters, between which are two tiers of rectangular windows. From this wall the external dome springs. The lantern receives no support from it. It is merely ornamental, differing entirely, in that respect, from the dome of St. Peter's.

In 1822 Mr. Horner passed the summer in the lantern, sketching the metropolis; he afterwards erected an observatory several feet higher than the cross, and made sketches for a panorama on a surface of 1,680 feet of drawing paper. From these sheets was painted a panorama of London and its environs, first exhibited at the Colosseum, in Regent's Park, in 1829. The view from St. Paul's extends for twenty miles round. On the south the horizon is bounded by Leith Hill. In high winds the scaffold used to creak and whistle like a ship labouring in a storm, and once the observatory was torn from its lashings and turned partly over on the edge of the platform. The sight and sounds of awaking London are said to have much impressed the artist.

On entering the cathedral, says Mr. Horner, at three in the morning, the stillness which then prevailed in the streets of this populous city, contrasted with their midday bustle, was only surpassed by the more solemn and sepulchral stillness of the cathedral itself. But not less impressive was the development at that early hour of the immense scene from its lofty summit, whence was frequently beheld " the forest of London," without any indication of animated existence. It was interesting to mark the gradual symptoms of returning life, until the rising sun vivified the whole into activity, bustle, and business. On one occasion Mr. Horner passed the night in the observatory, for the purpose of meeting the first glimpse of day; but the cold was so intense as to preclude any wish to repeat the experiment.

Mr. Horner, in his narrative, mentions a narrow escape of Mr. Gwyn, while engaged in measuring the top of the dome in order to make a sectional drawing of the cathedral. While absorbed in his work Mr. Gwyn slipped down the globular surface of the dome till his foot was stopped by a projecting lump of lead. In this awful situation, like a man hanging to the moon, he remained till one of his assistants providentially saw and rescued him.

The following was, if possible, an even narrower escape :—When Sir James Thornhill was painting the cupola of St. Paul's Cathedral, a gentleman of his acquaintance was one day with him on the scaffolding, which, though wide, was not railed; he had just finished the head of one of the apostles, and running back, as is usual with painters, to observe the effect, had almost reached the extremity; the gentleman, seeing his danger, and not having time for words, snatched up a large brush and smeared the face. Sir James ran hastily forward, crying out, "Bless my soul, what have you done?" "I have only saved your life!" responded his friend.

Sir James Thornhill was the son of a reduced Dorsetshire gentleman. His uncle, the well-known physician, Dr. Sydenham, helped to educate him. He travelled abroad to see the works of the old masters, and on his return Queen Anne appointed him to paint the dome of St. Paul's. He was considered to have executed the work, in the eight panels, "in a noble manner." "He afterwards," says Pilkington, "executed several public works—painting, at Hampton Court, the Queen and Prince George of Denmark, allegorically; and in the chapel of All Souls, Oxford, the portrait of the founder, over the altar, the ceiling, and figures between the windows. His masterpiece is the refectory and saloon at Greenwich Hospital. He was knighted by George II. He died May 4, 1734, leaving a son, John, who became serjeant-painter to the king, and a daughter, who married Hogarth. He was a well-made and pleasant man, and sat in Parliament for some years."

The cathedral was artificially secured from lightning, according to the suggestion of the Royal Society, in 1769. The seven iron scrolls supporting the ball and cross are connected with other rods (used merely as conductors), which unite them with several large bars descending obliquely to the stone-work of the lantern, and connected by an iron ring with four other iron bars to the lead covering of the great cupola, a distance of forty-eight feet; thence the communication is continued by the rain-water pipes, which pass into the earth, thus completing the entire communication from the cross to the ground, partly through iron and partly through lead. On the clock-tower a bar of iron connects the pine-apple on the top with the iron staircase, and thence with the lead on the roof of the church. The bell-tower is similarly protected. By these means the metal used in the building is made available as conductors, the metal employed merely for that purpose being exceedingly small in quantity.

In 1841 the exterior of the dome was repaired by workmen resting upon a shifting iron frame. In 1848 a scaffold and observatory, as shown on page 258, were raised round the cross, and in three months some four thousand observations were made for a new trigonometrical survey of London.

Harting, in his "Birds of Middlesex," mentions the peregrine falcons of St. Paul's. "A pair of these birds," he says, "for many years frequented the top of St. Paul's, where it was supposed they had a nest; and a gentleman with whom I am acquainted has assured me that a friend of his once saw a peregrine strike down a pigeon in London, his attention having been first attracted by seeing a crowd of persons gazing upwards at the hawk as it sailed in circles over the houses." A pair of hawks frequenting the buildings at Westminster Abbey is referred to in "Annals of an Eventful Life," by Sir George Dasent.

A few nooks and corners of the cathedral have still escaped us. The library in the gallery over the southern aisle was formed by Bishop Compton, and consists of some 7,000 volumes, including some manuscripts from old St. Paul's. The room contains some loosely hung flowers, exquisitely carved in wood by Grinling Gibbons, and the floor is composed of 2,300 pieces of oak, inlaid without nails or pegs. At the end of the gallery is a geometrical staircase of 110 steps, which was constructed by Wren to furnish a private access to the library. In crossing thence to the northern gallery, we gain a fine view of the entire vista of the cathedral. What was once the Trophy-room —so called from its having contained Wren's first model for the re-building of the cathedral, and some old tattered flags—has since been used as a practising-room for the choir, and for meetings of the clergy, lay-helpers, &c. A staircase from the southern gallery leads to the south-western campanile tower, in which is the clock-room. The clock, which cost £300, was made by Langley Bradley in 1708. The minute-hands are 9 feet 8 inches long, and weigh 75 pounds each. The pendulum is 16 feet long, and the bob weighs 180 pounds, and yet is suspended by a spring no thicker than a shilling. The clock goes eight days, and strikes the hours on the great bell, the clapper of which weighs 180 pounds. Below the great bell are two smaller bells, on which the clock strikes the quarters. In the northern tower is the bell that tolls for prayers. Mr. E. B. Denison pronounced the St. Paul's bell, although the smallest, as by far the best of the four large bells of England— York, Lincoln, and Oxford being the other three.

The great bell of St. Paul's (about five tons) has a diameter of nine feet, and weighs 11,474 pounds. It was cast from the metal of Great Tom (Ton), a bell that once hung in a clock tower opposite

Westminster Hall. It was given away in 1698 by William III., and bought for St. Paul's for £385 17s. 6d. It was re-cast in 1716. The key-note (tonic) or sound of this bell is A flat—perhaps A natural—of the old pitch. It is never tolled but at the death or funeral of any of the Royal Family, the Bishop of London, the Dean, or the Lord Mayor, should he die during his mayoralty.

In 1878 a fine peal of bells was hung in the campanile tower, at the north-western corner of the cathedral. They were cast at the expense of the principal City Companies, aided by a gift from Lady Burdett-Coutts. The bells are twelve in number, and are inscribed with the names of the several Companies who gave them, also the date of their casting, together with appropriate legends.

Before the time of the present St. Paul's, and as long ago as the reign of Henry VII., there is on record a well-attested story of a young girl who, going to confess, was importuned by the monk then on his turn there for the purpose of confession in the building; and quickly escaping from him up the stairs of the great clock tower, raised the clapper or hammer of the bell of the clock, just as it had finished striking twelve, and, by means of the roof, eluded her assailant and got away. On accusing him, as soon as she reached her friends and home, she called attention to the fact of the clock having struck thirteen that time; and on those in the immediate neighbourhood of the cathedral being asked if so unusual a thing had been heard, they said it was so. This proved the story, and the monk was degraded.

And here we may insert a curious story of a monomaniac whose madness was associated with St. Paul's. Dr. Pritchard, in an essay on "Somnambulism and Animal Magnetism," in the "Cyclopædia of Medicine," gives the following remarkable case of ecstasis :—

A gentleman about thirty-five years of age, of active habits and good constitution, living in the neighbourhood of London, had complained for about five weeks of a slight headache. He was feverish, inattentive to his occupation, and negligent of his family. He had been cupped, and taken some purgative medicine, when he was visited by Dr. Arnould, of Camberwell. By that gentleman's advice, he was sent to a private asylum, where he remained about two years. His delusions very gradually subsided, and he was afterwards restored to his family. The account which he gave of himself was, almost *verbatim*, as follows :—One afternoon in the month of May, feeling himself a little unsettled, and not inclined to business, he thought he would take a walk into the City to amuse his mind; and having strolled into St. Paul's Churchyard, he stopped at the shop-window of Carrington and Bowles, and looked at the pictures, among which was one of the cathedral. He had not been long there before a short, grave-looking, elderly gentleman, dressed in dark brown clothes, came up and began to examine the prints, and, occasionally casting a glance at him, very soon entered into conversation with him; and, praising the view of St. Paul's which was exhibited at the window, told him many anecdotes of Sir Christopher Wren, the architect, and asked him at the same time if he had ever ascended to the top of the dome. He replied in the negative. The stranger then inquired if he had dined, and proposed that they should go to an eating-house in the neighbourhood, and said that after dinner he would accompany him up St. Paul's. "It was a glorious afternoon for a view, and he was so familiar with the place that he could point out every object worthy of attention." The kindness of the old gentleman's manner induced him to comply with the invitation, and they went to a tavern in some dark alley, the name of which he did not know. They dined, and very soon left the table and ascended to the ball, just below the cross, which they entered alone. They had not been there many minutes when, while he was gazing on the extensive prospect, and delighted with the splendid scene below him, the grave gentleman pulled out from an inside coat-pocket something resembling a compass, having round the edges some curious figures. Then, having muttered some unintelligible words, he placed it in the centre of the ball. He felt a great trembling and a sort of horror come over him, which was increased by his companion asking him if he should like to see any friend at a distance, and to know what he was at that moment doing, for if so the latter could show him any such person. It happened that his father had been for a long time in bad health, and for some weeks past he had not visited him. A sudden thought came into his mind, so powerful that it overcame his terror, that he should like to see his father. He had no sooner expressed the wish than the exact person of his father was immediately presented to his sight in the mirror, reclining in his arm-chair and taking his afternoon sleep. Not having fully believed in the power of the stranger to make good his offer, he became overwhelmed with terror at the clearness and truth of the vision presented to him, and he entreated his mysterious companion that they might immediately descend, as he felt very ill. The request was complied with, and on parting under the portico of the northern entrance the stranger said to him, "Remember, you are the slave of the Man of the Mirror!" He returned in the evening to his home, he does not know exactly at what hour; there is no concealment from him, for all places are alike open to him; he sees us and he hears us now.' I asked him where this being was who saw and heard us. He replied, in a voice of deep agitation, 'Have I not told you that he lives in the ball below the cross on the top of St. Paul's, and

THE SCAFFOLDING AND OBSERVATORY ON ST. PAUL'S IN 1848 (*see page* 256).

felt himself unquiet, depressed, gloomy, apprehensive, and haunted with thoughts of the stranger. For the last three months he has been conscious of the power of the latter over him. Dr. Arnould adds :—"I inquired in what way his power was exercised. He cast on me a look of suspicion, mingled with confidence, took my arm, and after leading me through two or three rooms, and then into the garden, exclaimed, 'It is of no use; that he only comes down to take a walk in the churchyard and get his dinner at the house in the dark alley? Since that fatal interview with the necromancer,' he continued, 'for such I believe him to be, he is continually dragging me before him on his mirror, and he not only sees me every moment of the day, but he reads all my thoughts, and I have a dreadful consciousness that no action of my life is free from his inspection, and no place

ST. PAUL'S AND THE NEIGHBOURHOOD IN 1540.

From a Copy, in the possession of J. G. Crace, Esq., of the earliest known view of London, taken by Van der Wyngarde for Philip II. of Spain.

can afford me security from his power.' On my replying that the darkness of the night would afford him protection from these machinations, he said, 'I know what you mean, but you are quite mistaken. I have only told you of the mirror; but in some part of the building which we passed in coming away, he showed me what he called a great bell, and I heard sounds which came from it, and which went to it—sounds of laughter, and of anger, and of pain. There was a dreadful confusion of sounds, and as I listened, with wonder and affright, he said, ' This is my organ of hearing; this great bell is in communication with all other bells within the circle of hieroglyphics, by which every word spoken by those under my command is made audible to me.' Seeing me look surprised at him, he said, ' I have not yet told you all, for he practises his spells by hieroglyphics on walls and houses, and wields his power, like a detestable tyrant, as he is, over the minds of those whom he has enchanted, and who are the objects of his constant spite, within the circle of the hieroglyphics.' I asked him what these hieroglyphics were, and how he perceived them. He replied, 'Signs and symbols which you, in your ignorance of their true meaning, have taken for letters and words, and read, as you have thought, "Day and Martin's and Warren's blacking."' 'Oh! that is all nonsense!' 'They are only the mysterious characters which he traces to mark the boundary of his dominion, and by which he prevents all escape from his tremendous power. How have I toiled and laboured to get beyond the limit of his influence! Once I walked for three days and three nights, till I fell down under a wall, exhausted by fatigue, and dropped asleep; but on awakening I saw the dreadful signs before mine eyes, and I felt myself as completely under his infernal spells at the end as at the beginning of my journey.'"

It is probable that this gentleman had actually ascended to the top of St. Paul's, and that impressions there received, being afterwards renewed in his mind when in a state of vivid excitement, in a dream of ecstatic reverie, became so blended with the creations of fancy as to form one mysterious vision, in which the true and the imaginary were afterwards inseparable. In 1855 the fees for seeing St. Paul's completely were 4s. 4d. each person. In 1847 the mere twopences paid to see the forty monuments produced the four vergers the sum of £430 3s. 8d. These exorbitant fees originated in the "stairs'-foot money" started by Jennings, the carpenter, in 1707, as a fund for the injured during the building of the cathedral. The fees now for viewing the entire building amount to 2s. 6d.

The staff of the cathedral consists of the dean, the precentor, the chancellor, the treasurer, the five archdeacons of London, Middlesex, Essex, Colchester, and St. Albans, thirty major canons or prebendaries (four of whom are resident), twelve minor canons, and six vicars-choral, besides the choristers. One of the vicars-choral officiates as organist, and three of the minor canons hold the appointments of sub-dean, librarian, and succentor, or under-precentor.

Three of the most celebrated men connected with St. Paul's in the present century have been Milman, Sydney Smith, and Barham (the author of "Ingoldsby Legends"). Smith and Barham both died in 1845; Dean Milman followed in 1858.

Of Sydney Smith's connection with St. Paul's we have many interesting records. One of the first things Lord Grey said on entering Downing Street, to a relation who was with him, was, "Now I shall be able to do something for Sydney Smith," and shortly after he was appointed by the Premier to a prebendal stall at St. Paul's, in exchange for the one he held at Bristol.

Mr. Cockerell, the architect, and superintendent of St. Paul's Cathedral, in a letter printed in Lady Holland's "Memoir of Sydney Smith," describes the *gesta* of the witty canon; how his early communications with himself (Mr. C.) and all the officers of the chapter were extremely unpleasant; but when the canon had investigated the matter, and there had been "a little collision," nothing could be more candid and kind than his subsequent treatment. He examined the prices of all the materials used in the repairs of the cathedral—as Portland stone, putty, and white lead; every item was taxed, payments were examined, and nothing new could be undertaken without his survey and personal superintendence. He surveyed the pinnacles and heights of the sacred edifice; and once, when it was feared he might stick fast in a narrow opening of the western towers, he declared that "if there were six inches of space there would be room enough for him." The insurance of the magnificent cathedral, Mr. Cockerell tells us, engaged his early attention; and the fabric was speedily and effectually insured in some of the most substantial offices in London. Not satisfied with this security, he advised the introduction of the mains of the New River into the lower parts of the fabric, and cisterns and movable engines in the roof; and quite justifiable was his joke, that "he would reproduce the Deluge in our cathedral."

He had also the library heated by a stove, so as to be more comfortable to the studious; and the bindings of the books were repaired. Lastly, Mr.

Smith materially assisted the progress of a suit in Chancery, by the successful result of which a considerable addition was made to the fabric fund.

It is very gratifying to read these circumstantial records of the practical qualities of Mr. Sydney Smith, as applied to the preservation of our magnificent metropolitan cathedral.

Before we leave Mr. Smith we may record an odd story of Lady B. calling the vergers "virgins." She asked Mr. Smith, one day, if it was true that he walked down St. Paul's with three virgins holding silver pokers before him. He shook his head and looked very grave, and bade her come and see. "Some enemy of the Church," he said, "some Dissenter, had clearly been misleading her."

Let us recapitulate a few of the English poets who have made special allusions to St. Paul's in their writings. Denham says of the restoration of St. Paul's, began by Charles I. :—

> "First salutes the place,
> Crowned with that sacred pile, so vast, so high,
> That whether 'tis a part of earth or sky
> Uncertain seems, and may be thought a proud
> Aspiring mountain or descending cloud.
> Paul's, the late theme of such a muse, whose flight
> Has bravely reached and soared above thy height,
> Now shalt thou stand, though sword, or time, or fire,
> Or zeal more fierce than they, thy fall conspire;
> Secure, while thee the best of poets sings,
> Preserved from ruin by the best of kings."

Byron, in the Tenth Canto of "Don Juan," treats St. Paul's contemptuously—sneering, as was his affectation, at everything, human or divine :—

> "A mighty mass of brick, and smoke, and shipping,
>   Dirty and dusky, but as wide as eye
> Could reach, with here and there a sail just skipping
>   In sight, then lost amidst the forestry
> Of masts; a wilderness of steeples peeping
>   On tiptoe through their sea-coal canopy;
> A huge, dim cupola, like a foolscap crown
> On a fool's head—and there is London Town!"

Among other English poets who have sung of St. Paul's, we must not forget Tom Hood, with his delightfully absurd ode, written on the cross, and full of most wise folly :—

> "The man that pays his pence and goes
>   Up to thy lofty cross, St. Paul's,
> Looks over London's naked nose,
>   Women and men;
>   The world is all beneath his ken;
>   He sits above the ball,
>   He seems on Mount Olympus' top,
> Among the gods, by Jupiter! and lets drop
>   His eyes from the empyreal clouds
>   On mortal crowds.
>
> "Seen from these skies,
> How small those emmets in our eyes!

> Some carry little sticks, and one
>   His eggs, to warm them in the sun;
>   Dear, what a hustle
>   And bustle!
> And there's my aunt! I know her by her waist,
>   So long and thin,
>   And so pinch'd in,
>   Just in the pismire taste.

> "Oh, what are men! Beings so small
>   That, should I fall,
>   Upon their little heads, I must
>   Crush them by hundreds into dust.

> "And what is life and all its ages!
>   There's seven stages!
> Turnham Green! Chelsea! Putney! Fulham!
>   Brentford and Kew!
>   And Tooting, too!
> And, oh, what very little nags to pull 'em!
> Yet each would seem a horse indeed,
>   If here at Paul's tip-top we'd got 'em!
> Although, like Cinderella's breed,
>   They're mice at bottom.
> Then let me not despise a horse,
> Though he looks small from Paul's high cross;
> Since he would be, as near the sky,
>   Fourteen hands high.

> "What is this world with London in its lap?
>   Mogg's map.
> The Thames that ebbs and flows in its broad channel?
>   A *tidy* kennel!
> The bridges stretching from its banks?
>   Stone planks.
> Oh, me! Hence could I read an admonition
>   To mad Ambition!
> But that he would not listen to my call,
> Though I should stand upon the cross, and *ball!*"

We can hardly close our account of St. Paul's without referring to that most beautiful and touching of all London sights, the anniversary of the charity schools on the first Thursday in June. About 8,000 children are generally present, ranged in a vast amphitheatre under the dome. Blake, the true but unrecognised predecessor of Wordsworth, has written an exquisite little poem on the scene, and well it deserves it. Such nosegays of little rosy faces can be seen on no other day. Very grand and overwhelming are the beadles of St. Mary Axe and St. Margaret Moses on this tremendous morning, and no young ensign ever bore his colours prouder than do these good-natured dignitaries their maces, staves, and ponderous badges. In endless ranks pour in the children, clothed in all sorts of quaint dresses. Boys in the knee-breeches of Hogarth's school-days, bearing glittering pewter badges on their coats; girls in blue and orange, with quaint little mob-caps white as snow, and long white gloves covering all their little arms. See, at a given signal of an extraordinary fugleman, how they all rise; at another signal how they hustle down. Then at last, when the "Old Hundredth" begins, all the little voices unite as the blending of many waters. Such fresh, happy voices, singing with such innocent, heedful tenderness as would bring tears to the eyes of even stony-hearted old Malthus, bring to the most irreligious thoughts of Him who bade little children come to Him, and would not have them repulsed.

Blake's poem begins—

" 'Twas on a Holy Thursday, their innocent faces clean,
Came children walking two and two, in red and blue and green;
Grey-headed beadles walked before, with wands as white as snow,
Till into the high dome of Paul's they like Thames' waters flow.

"Oh, what a multitude they seemed, those flowers of London town;
Seated in companies they were, with radiance all their own;

The hum of multitudes was there, but multitudes of lambs,
Thousands of little boys and girls, raising their innocent hands.

"Now like a mighty wind they raise to heaven the voice of song,
Or like harmonious thunderings the seats of heaven among;
Beneath them sit the aged men, wise guardians of the poor;
Then cherish pity, lest you drive an angel from your door."

In 1878-9 the grounds north, south, and east of the Cathedral were laid out as ornamental gardens, with grass-plats and gravel walks; the iron railing which encloses those three sides being at the same time lowered by reducing the height of the wall upon which it stands. These alterations laid bare some fragments of the foundations of the chapter-house, and of St. Faith's on the south of the nave, and also of "Paul's Cross" at the north-east corner of the churchyard. These improvements were effected solely at the cost of the Corporation of London, and the grounds were thrown open to the public in September, 1879.

CHAPTER XXII.

ST. PAUL'S CHURCHYARD.

St. Paul's Churchyard and Literature—Queen Anne's Statue—Execution of a Jesuit in St. Paul's Churchyard—Miracle of the "Face in the Straw"—Wilkinson's Story—Newbery the Bookseller—Paul's Chain—"Cocker"—Chapter House of St. Paul's—St. Paul's Coffee House—Child's Coffee House and the Clergy—Garrick's Club at the "Queen's Arms," and the Company there—"Sir Benjamin" Figgins—Johnson the Bookseller—Hunter and his Guests—Fuseli—Bonnycastle—Kinnaird—Musical Associations of the Churchyard—Jeremiah Clark and his Works—Handel at Meares' Shop—Young the Violin-maker—The "Castle" Concerts—An Old Advertisement—Wren at the "Goose and Gridiron"—St. Paul's School—Famous Paulines—Pepys visiting his Old School—Milton at St. Paul's.

THE shape of St. Paul's Churchyard has been compared to that of a bow and a string. The south side is the bow, the north the string. The booksellers overflowing from Fleet Street mustered strong here, till the Fire scared them off to Little Britain, from whence they regurgitated to the Row. At the sign of the "White Greyhound" the first editions of Shakespeare's "Venus and Adonis" and "The Rape of Lucrece," the first-fruits of a great harvest, were published by John Harrison. At the "Flower de Luce" and the "Crown" appeared the *Merry Wives of Windsor;* at the "Green Dragon," in the same locality, the *Merchant of Venice;* at the "Fox," *Richard II.;* at the "Angel," *Richard III.;* at the "Gun," *Titus Andronicus;* and at the "Red Bull," that masterpiece, *King Lear.* So that in this area near the Row the great poet must have paced with his first proofs in his doublet-pocket, wondering whether he should ever rival Spenser, or become immortal, like Chaucer. Here he must have come smiling over

Falstaff's perils, and here have walked with the ripened certainty of greatness and of fame stirring at his heart.

The ground-plot of the Cathedral is 2 acres 16 perches 70 feet. The western area of the churchyard marks the site of St. Gregory's Church. On the mean statue of Queen Anne a scurrilous epigram was once written by some ribald Jacobite, who spoke of the queen—

"With her face to the brandy-shop and her back to the church."

The precinct wall of St. Paul's first ran from Ave Maria Lane eastward along Paternoster Row to the old Exchange, Cheapside, and then southwards to Carter Lane, at the end of which it turned to Ludgate Archway. In the reign of Edward II. the Dean and Chapter, finding the precinct a resort of thieves and courtesans, rebuilt and purified it. Within, at the north-west corner, stood the bishop's palace, beyond which, eastward, was Pardon Churchyard and Becket Chapel, rebuilt with a stately cloister in the reign of Henry V. On the walls of this cloister, pulled down by the greedy Protector Somerset (Edward VI.), was painted one of those grim Dances of Death which Holbein at last carried to perfection. The cloister was full of monuments, and above was a library. In an enclosure east of this stood the College of Minor Canons; and at Canon Alley, east, was a burial chapel called the Charnel, from whence Somerset sent cart-loads of bones to Finsbury Fields. East of Canon Alley stood Paul's Cross, where open-air sermons were preached to the citizens, and often to the reigning monarch. East of it rose St. Paul's School and a belfry tower, in which hung the famous Jesus bells, won at dice by Sir Giles Partridge from that Ahab of England, Henry VIII. On the south side stood the Dean and Chapter's garden, dormitory, refectory, kitchen, slaughterhouse, and brewery. These eventually yielded to a cloister, near which, abutting on the cathedral wall, stood the chapter-house and the Church of St. Gregory. Westward were the houses of the residentiaries; and the deanery, according to Milman, an excellent authority, stood on its present site. The precinct had six gates—the first and chief in Ludgate Street; the second in Paul's Alley, leading to Paternoster Row; the third in Canon Alley, leading to the north door; the fourth, a little gate leading to Cheapside; the fifth, the Augustine gate, leading to Watling Street; the sixth, on the south side, by Paul's Chain. On the south tower of the west front was the Lollard's Tower, a bishop's prison for ecclesiastical offenders.

The 2,500 railings of the churchyard and the seven ornamental gates, weighing altogether two hundred tons, were cast at Brightling, Sussex, and cost 6d. a pound; the whole cost £11,202 0s. 6d.

In 1606 St. Paul's Churchyard was the scene of the execution of Father Garnet, one of the Gunpowder Plot conspirators—the only execution, as far as we know, that ever desecrated that spot. It is very doubtful, after all, whether Garnet was cognizant that the plot was really to be carried out, though he may have strongly suspected some dangerous and deadly conspiracy, and the Roman Catholics were prepared to see miracles wrought at his death.

On the 3rd day of May, 1606 (to condense Dr. Abbott's account), Garnet was drawn upon a hurdle, according to the usual practice, to his place of execution. The Recorder of London, the Dean of St. Paul's, and the Dean of Winchester were present, by command of the King— the former in the King's name, and the two latter in the name of God and Christ, to assist Garnet with such advice as suited the condition of a dying man. As soon as he had ascended the scaffold, which was much elevated in order that the people might behold the spectacle, Garnet saluted the Recorder somewhat familiarly, who told him that "it was expected from him that he should publicly deliver his real opinion respecting the conspiracy and treason; that it was now of no use to dissemble, as all was clearly and manifestly proved; but that if, in the true spirit of repentance, he was willing to satisfy the Christian world by declaring his hearty compunction, he might freely state what he pleased." The deans then told him that they were present on that occasion by authority, in order to suggest to him such matters as might be useful for his soul; that they desired to do this without offence, and exhorted him to prepare and settle himself for another world, and to commence his reconciliation with God by a sincere and saving repentance. To this exhortation Garnet replied "that he had already done so, and that he had before satisfied himself in this respect." The clergymen then suggested "that he would do well to declare his mind to the people." Then Garnet said to those near him, "I always disapproved of tumults and seditions against the king, and if this crime of the powder treason had been completed I should have abhorred it with my whole soul and conscience." They then advised him to declare as much to the people. "I am very weak," said he, "and my voice fails me. If I should speak to the people, I cannot make them hear me; it is impossible that they should hear me." Then said Mr. Recorder, "Mr. Garnet, if you will come with me, I will take care that they shall hear you," and, going before him, led him to the western end of the scaffold. He still hesitated to address the people, but the Recorder urged him to speak his mind freely, promising to repeat his words aloud to the multitude. Garnet then addressed the crowd as follows:—"My good fellow-citizens,—I am come hither, on the morrow of the invention of the Holy Cross, to see an end of all my pains and troubles in this world. I here declare before you all that I consider the late treason and conspiracy against the State to be cruel and detestable; and, for my part, all designs and endeavours against the king were ever misliked by me; and if this attempt had been perfected, as it was designed, I think it would have been altogether damnable; and I pray for all prosperity to the king, the queen, and the royal family." Here he paused, and the Recorder reminded him to ask pardon of the King for that which he had attempted. "I do so," said Garnet, "as far as I have sinned against him—namely, in that I did not reveal that whereof I had a general knowledge from Mr. Catesby, but not otherwise." Then said the Dean of Winchester, "Mr. Garnet, I pray you deal clearly in the matter : you were certainly privy to the whole business." "God forbid !" said Garnet ; "I never understood anything of the design of blowing up the Parliament House." "Nay," responded the Dean of Winchester, "it is manifest that all the particulars were known to you, and

tessing a sin, but by way of conference and consultation ; and that Greenaway and Catesby both came to confer with him upon that business, and that as often as he saw Greenaway he would ask him about that business because it troubled him. "Most certainly," said Garnet ; "I did so in order to prevent it, for I always misliked it." Then said the Dean, "You only withheld your approbation until the Pope had given his opinion." "But I was well persuaded," said Garnet, "that the

THE LIBRARY OF ST. PAUL'S (*see page* 256).

you have declared under your own hand that Greenaway told you all the circumstances in Essex." "That," said Garnet, "was in secret confession, which I could by no means reveal." Then said the Dean, "You have yourself, Mr. Garnet, almost acknowledged that this was only a pretence, for you have openly confessed that Greenaway told you not in a confession, but by way of a confession, and that he came of purpose to you with the design of making a confession ; but you answered that it was not necessary you should know the full extent of his knowledge." The dean further reminded him that he had affirmed under his own hand that this was not told him by way of con-

Pope would never approve the design." "Your intention," said the Dean of Winchester, "was clear from those two breves which you received from Rome for the exclusion of the King." "That," said Garnet, "was before the King came in." "But if you knew nothing of the particulars of the business," said the Dean, "why did you send Baynham to inform the Pope ? for this also you have confessed in your examinations." Garnet replied, "I have already answered to all these matters on my trial, and I acknowledge everything that is contained in my written confessions."

Then, turning his discourse again to the people, at the instance of the Recorder, he proceeded to

the same effect as before, declaring "that he wholly misliked that cruel and inhuman design, and that he had never sanctioned or approved of any such attempts against the King and State, and that this project, if it had succeeded, would have been in his mind most damnable."

Having thus spoken, he raised his hands, and made the sign of the cross upon his forehead and

The "face in the straw," to which allusion was made a few pages back, was a miracle said to have been performed at Garnet's death. The original fabricator of the story was one John Wilkinson, a young Roman Catholic, who at the time of Garnet's trial was about to commence his studies at the Jesuits' College at St. Omer's. Some time after his arrival there, Wilkinson was

spica Wilkinsoni.   Spica Jesuitica.

"THE FACE IN THE STRAW."—FROM ABBOT'S "ANTHOLOGIA," 1613 (*see page* 266).

breast, saying, "*In nomine Patris, Filii, et Spiritus Sancti! Jesus Maria! Maria, mater gratiæ! Mater misericordiæ! Tu me ab hoste protege, et hora mortis suscipe!*" Then he said, "*In manus tuas, Domine, commendo spiritum meum, quia tu redemisti me, Domine, Deus veritatis!*" Then, again crossing himself, he said, "*Per crucis hoc signum fugiat procul omne malignum! Infige crucem tuam, Domine, in corde meo;*" and again, "*Jesus Maria! Maria, mater gratiæ!*" In the midst of these prayers the ladder was drawn away, and, by the express command of the King, he remained hanging from the gallows until he was quite dead.

attacked by a dangerous disease, from which there was no hope of his recovery; and while in this state he gave utterance to the story, which Endæmon-Joannes relates in his own words, as follows:—"The day before Father Garnet's execution my mind was suddenly impressed (as by some external impulse) with a strong desire to witness his death, and bring home with me some relic of him. I had at that time conceived so certain a persuasion that my design would be gratified, that I did not for a moment doubt that I should witness some immediate testimony from God in favour of the innocence of his saint; though as often as the idea occurred to my mind, I endeavoured to drive it away, that I might not vainly appear to tempt Providence by looking for a miracle where it was not necessarily to be expected. Early the next morning I betook myself to the place of execution, and, arriving there before any other person, stationed myself close to the scaffold, though I was afterwards somewhat forced from my position as the crowd increased." Having then described the details of the execution, he proceeds thus :—"Garnet's limbs having been divided into four parts, and placed, together with the head, in a basket, in order that they might be exhibited, according to law, in some conspicuous place, the crowd began to disperse. I then again approached close to the scaffold, and stood between the cart and place of execution ; and as I lingered in that situation, still burning with the desire of bearing away some relic, that miraculous ear of straw, since so highly celebrated, came, I know not how, into my hand. A considerable quantity of dry straw had been thrown with Garnet's head and quarters into the basket, but whether this ear came into my hand from the scaffold or from the basket I cannot venture to affirm ; this only I can truly say, that a straw of this kind was thrown towards me before it had touched the ground. This straw I afterwards delivered to Mrs. N——, a matron of singular Catholic piety, who inclosed it in a bottle, which being rather shorter than the straw, it became slightly bent. A few days afterwards Mrs. N—— showed the straw in a bottle to a certain noble person, her intimate acquaintance, who, looking at it attentively, at length said, 'I can see nothing in it but a man's face.' Mrs. N—— and myself being astonished at this unexpected exclamation, again and again examined the ear of the straw, and distinctly perceived in it a human countenance, which others also, coming in as casual spectators, or expressly called by us as witnesses, likewise beheld at that time. This is, as God knoweth, the true history of Father Garnet's straw." The engraving upon the preceding page is taken from Abbot's "Anthologia," published in 1613, in which a full account of the "miracle" is given.

At 65, St. Paul's Churchyard, north-west corner, lived Goldsmith's kind friend and employer, Mr. John Newbery, that good-natured man with the red-pimpled face, who, as the philanthropic bookseller, figures pleasantly in the "Vicar of Wakefield ;" always in haste to be gone, he was ever on business of the utmost importance, and was at that time actually compiling materials for the history of one Thomas Trip. "The friend of all mankind," Dr. Primrose calls him. "The

honestest man in the nation," as Goldsmith said of him in a doggerel riddle which he wrote. Newbery's nephew printed the "Vicar of Wakefield " for Goldsmith, and the elder Newbery published the "Traveller," the corner-stone of Goldsmith's fame. It was the elder Newbery who unearthed the poet at his miserable lodgings in Green Arbour Court, and employed him to write his "Citizens of the World," at a guinea each, for his daily newspaper, the *Public Ledger* (1760). The Newberies seem to have been worthy, prudent tradesmen, constantly vexed and irritated at Goldsmith's extravagance, carelessness, and ceaseless cry for money ; and so it went on till the hare-brained, delightful fellow died, when Francis Newbery wrote a violent defence of the fever medicine, an excess of which had killed Goldsmith.

The office of the Registrar of the High Court of Admiralty occupied the site of the old cathedral bakehouse. Paul's Chain is so called from a chain that used to be drawn across the carriage-way of the churchyard, to preserve silence during divine service. The northern barrier of St. Paul's is of wood. Opposite the Chain, at the time of the Restoration, lived that king of writing and arithmetic masters, the man whose name has grown into a proverb—Edward Cocker—who wrote "The Pen's Transcendancy," an extraordinary proof of true eye and clever hand.

In the Chapter House of St. Paul's, which Mr. Peter Cunningham not too severely calls "a shabby, dingy-looking building," on the north side of the churchyard, was performed the unjust ceremony of degrading Samuel Johnson, the chaplain to William Lord Russell, the martyr of the party of liberty. The divines present, in compassion, and with a prescient eye for the future, purposely omitted to strip off his cassock, which rendered the ceremony imperfect, and afterwards saved the worthy man his benefice.

St. Paul's Coffee House stood at the corner of the archway of Doctors' Commons, on the site of "Paul's Brew House" and the "Paul's Head" tavern. Here, in 1721, the books of the great collector, Dr. Rawlinson, were sold, "after dinner ;" and they sold well.

Child's Coffee House, in St. Paul's Churchyard, was a quiet place, much frequented by the clergy of Queen Anne's reign, and by proctors from Doctors' Commons. Addison used to look in there, to smoke a pipe and listen, behind his paper, to the conversation. In the *Spectator*, No. 609, he smiles at a country gentleman who mistook all persons in scarves for doctors of divinity. This was at a time when clergymen always wore their black gowns in public. "Only a scarf of the first magnitude," he says, "entitles one to the appellation of 'doctor' from the landlady and the boy at 'Child's.'"

"Child's" was the resort of Dr. Mead, and other professional men of eminence. The Fellows of the Royal Society came here. Whiston relates that Sir Hans Sloane, Dr. Halley, and he were once at "Child's," when Dr. Halley asked him (Whiston) why he was not a member of the Royal Society? Whiston answered, "Because they durst not choose a heretic." Upon which Dr. Halley said, if Sir Hans Sloane would propose him, he (Dr. Halley) would second it, which was done accordingly.

Garrick, who kept up his interest with different coteries, carefully cultivated the City men, by attending a club held at the "Queen's Arms" tavern, in St. Paul's Churchyard. Here he used to meet Mr. Sharpe, a surgeon; Mr. Paterson, the City Solicitor; Mr. Draper, a bookseller, and Mr. Clutterbuck, a mercer; and these quiet cool men were his standing council in theatrical affairs, and his gauge of the city taste. They were none of them drinkers, and in order to make a reckoning, called only for French wine. Here Dr. Johnson started a City club, and was particular the members should not be "patriotic." Boswell, who went with him to the "Queen's Arms" club, found the members "very sensible, well-behaved men." Brasbridge, the silversmith of Fleet Street, who wrote his memoirs, has described a sixpenny card club held here at a later date. Among the members was that generous and hospitable man, Henry Baldwin, who, under the auspices of Garrick, the elder Colman, and Bonnell Thornton, started the *St. James's Chronicle*, the most popular evening paper of the day.

"I belonged," says Brasbridge, "to a sixpenny card club, at the 'Queen's Arms,' in St. Paul's Churchyard; it consisted of about twenty members, of whom I am the sole survivor. Among them was Mr. Goodwin, of St. Paul's Churchyard, a woollen draper, whose constant salutation, when he first came down-stairs in the morning, was to his shop, in these words, 'Good morrow, Mr. Shop; you'll take care of me, Mr. Shop, and I'll take care of you.' Another was Mr. Curtis, a respectable stationer, who from very small beginnings left his son £90,000 in one line, besides an estate of near £300 a year."

"The 'Free and Easy under the Rose' was another society which I frequented. It was founded sixty years ago, at the 'Queen's Arms,' in St. Paul's Churchyard, and was afterwards removed to the 'Horn' tavern. It was originally kept by Bates, who was never so happy as when standing behind a chair with a napkin under his arm; but arriving at the dignity of alderman, tucking in his callipash and calipee himself, instead of handing it round to the company, soon did his business. My excellent friend Briskett, the Marshal of the High Court of Admiralty, was president of this society for many years, and I was constantly in attendance as his vice. It consisted of some thousand members, and I never heard of any one of them that ever incurred any serious punishment. Our great fault was sitting too late; in this respect, according to the principle of Franklin, that 'time is money,' we were most unwary spendthrifts; in other instances, our conduct was orderly and correct."

One of the members in Brasbridge's time was Mr. Hawkins, a worthy but ill-educated spatterdash maker, of Chancery Lane, who daily murdered the king's English. He called an invalid an "individual," and said our troops in America had been "*manured*" to hardship. Another oddity was a Mr. Darwin, a Radical, who one night brought to the club-room a caricature of the head of George III. in a basket; and whom Brasbridge nearly frightened out of his wits by pretending to send one of the waiters for the City Marshal. Darwin was the great chum of Mr. Figgins, a wax-chandler in the Poultry; and as they always entered the room together, Brasbridge gave them the nickname of "Liver and Gizzard." Miss Boydell, when her uncle was Lord Mayor, conferred sham knighthood on Figgins, with a tap of her fan, and he was henceforward known as "Sir Benjamin."

The Churchyard publisher of Cowper's first volume of poems, "Table Talk," and also of "The Task," was a very worthy, liberal man — Joseph Johnson, who also published the "Olney Hymns" for Newton, the scientific writings of the persecuted Priestley, and the smooth, vapid verses of Darwin. Johnson encouraged Fuseli to paint a Milton Gallery, for an edition of the poet to be edited by Cowper. Johnson was imprisoned nine months in the King's Bench, for selling the political writings of Gilbert Wakefield. He, however, bore the oppression of the majority philosophically, and rented the marshal's house, where he gave dinners to his distinguished literary friends.

"Another set of my acquaintances," writes Leigh Hunt in his Autobiography, "used to assemble on Fridays at the hospitable table of Mr. Hunter, the bookseller, in St. Paul's Churchyard. They were the survivors of the literary party that were accustomed to dine with his predecessor, Mr. Johnson. The most regular were Fuseli and Bonnycastle. Now and then Godwin was present; oftener Mr. Kinnaird, the magistrate, a great lover of Horace.

"Fuseli was a small man, with energetic features and a white head of hair. Our host's daughter, then a little girl, used to call him the white-headed lion. He combed his hair up from the forehead, and as his whiskers were large his face was set in a kind of hairy frame, which, in addition to the fierceness of his look, really gave him an aspect of that sort. Otherwise his features were rather sharp than round. He would have looked much like an old military officer if his face, besides its real energy, had not affected more. There was the same defect in it as in his pictures. Conscious of not having all the strength he wished, he endeavoured to make up for it by violence and pretension. He carried this so far as to look fiercer than usual when he sat for his picture. His friend and engraver, Mr. Houghton, drew an admirable likeness of him in this state of dignified extravagance. He is sitting back in his chair, leaning on his hand, but looking ready to pounce withal. His notion of repose was like that of Pistol.

"A student reading in a garden is all over intensity of muscle, and the quiet tea-table scene in Cowper he has turned into a preposterous conspiracy of huge men and women, all bent on showing their thews and postures, with dresses as fantastic as their minds. One gentleman, of the existence of whose trousers you are not aware till you see the terminating line at the ankle, is sitting and looking grim on a sofa, with his hat on and no waistcoat.

"Fuseli was lively and interesting in conversation, but not without his usual faults of violence and pretension. Nor was he always as decorous as an old man ought to be, especially one whose turn of mind is not of the lighter and more pleasurable cast. The licences he took were coarse, and had not sufficient regard to his company. Certainly they went a great deal beyond his friend Armstrong, to whose account, I believe, Fuseli's passion for swearing was laid. The poet condescended to be a great swearer, and Fuseli thought it energetic to swear like him. His friendship with Bonnycastle had something childlike and agreeable in it. They came and went away together for years, like a couple of old schoolboys. They also like boys rallied one another, and sometimes made a singular display of it—Fuseli, at least, for it was he who was the aggressor.

"Bonnycastle was a good fellow. He was a tall, gaunt, long-headed man, with large features and spectacles, and a deep internal voice, with a twang of rusticity in it; and he goggled over his plate like a horse. I often thought that a bag of corn would have hung well on him. His laugh was equine, and showed his teeth upwards at the sides. Wordsworth, who notices similar mysterious manifestations on the part of donkeys, would have thought it ominous. Bonnycastle was extremely fond of quoting Shakespeare and telling stories, and if the *Edinburgh Review* had just come out, would have given us all the jokes in it. He had once a hypochondriacal disorder of long duration, and he told us that he should never forget the comfortable sensation given him one night during this disorder by his knocking a landlord that was insolent to him down the man's staircase. On the strength of this piece of energy (having first ascertained that the offender was not killed) he went to bed, and had a sleep of unusual soundness.

"It was delightful one day to hear him speak with complacency of a translation which had appeared in Arabic, and which began by saying, on the part of the translator, that it pleased God, for the advancement of human knowledge, to raise us up a Bonnycastle.

"Kinnaird, the magistrate, was a sanguine man, under the middle height, with a fine lamping black eye, lively to the last, and a body that 'had increased, was increasing, and ought to have been diminished,' which is by no means what he thought of the prerogative. Next to his bottle, he was fond of his Horace, and, in the intervals of business at the police office, would enjoy both in his arm-chair. Between the vulgar calls of this kind of magistracy and the perusal of the urbane Horace there must have been a quota of contradiction, which the bottle, perhaps, was required to render quite palatable."

Mr. Charles Knight's pleasant book, "Shadows of the Old Booksellers," reminds us also of another of the great Churchyard booksellers, John Rivington and Sons, at the "Bible and Crown." They published, in 1737, an early sermon by Whitefield, before he left the Church, and were booksellers to the Society for Promoting Christian Knowledge; and to this shop country clergymen invariably went to buy their theology, or to publish their own sermons.

In St. Paul's Churchyard, says Sir John Hawkins, in his "History of Music," were formerly many shops where music and musical instruments were sold, for which, at this time, no better reason can be given than that the service at the Cathedral drew together, twice a day, all the lovers of music in London—not to mention that the choirmen were wont to assemble there, and were met by their friends and acquaintances.

Jeremiah Clark, a composer of sacred music, who shot himself in his house in St. Paul's Churchyard, was educated in the Royal Chapel, under Dr. Blow, who entertained so great a friendship for him as to resign in his favour his place of Master of the Children and Almoner of St. Paul's, Clark being appointed his successor, in 1693, and shortly afterwards he became organist of the cathedral. "In July, 1700," says Sir John Hawkins, "he and his fellow pupils were appointed Gentlemen Extraordinary of the Royal Chapel; and in 1704 they were jointly admitted to the place of organist thereof, in the room of Mr. Francis Piggot. Clark had the misfortune to entertain a hopeless passion for a very beautiful lady, in a station of life far above him; his despair of success threw him into a deep melancholy; in short, he grew weary of his life, and on the first day of December, 1707, shot himself. He was determined upon this method of putting an end to his life by an event which, strange as it may seem, is attested by the late Mr. Samuel Weeley, one of the lay-vicars of St. Paul's, who was very intimate with him, and had heard him relate it. Being at the house of a friend in the country, he took an abrupt resolution to return to London; this friend having observed in his behaviour marks of great dejection, furnished him with a horse and a servant. Riding along the road, a fit of melancholy seized him, upon which he alighted, and giving the servant his horse to hold, went into a field, in a corner whereof was a pond, and also trees, and began a debate with himself whether he should then end his days by hanging or drowning. Not being able to resolve on either, he thought of making what he looked upon as chance the umpire, and drew out of his pocket a piece of money, and tossing it into the air, it came down on its edge, and stuck in the clay. Though the determination answered not his wish, it was far from ambiguous, as it seemed to forbid both methods of destruction, and would have given unspeakable comfort to a mind less disordered than his was. Being thus interrupted in his purpose, he returned, and mounting his horse, rode on to London, and in a short time after shot himself. He dwelt in a house in St. Paul's Churchyard, situate on the place where the Chapter-house now stands. Old Mr. Reading was passing by at the instant the pistol went off, and entering the house, found his friend in the agonies of death.

"The compositions of Clark are few. His anthems are remarkably pathetic, at the same time that they preserve the dignity and majesty of the church style. The most celebrated of them are 'I will love thee,' printed in the second book of the 'Harmonia Sacra;' 'Bow down thine ear,' and 'Praise the Lord, O Jerusalem.'

"The only works of Clark published by himself are lessons for the harpsichord and sundry songs, which are to be found in the collections of that day, particularly in the 'Pills to Purge Melancholy,' but they are there printed without the basses. He also composed for D'Urfey's comedy of 'The Fond Husband, or the Plotting Sisters,' that sweet ballad air, 'The bonny grey-eyed Morn,' which Mr. Gay has introduced into 'The Beggar's Opera,' and is sung to the words, ''Tis woman that seduces all mankind.'"

"Matheson, of Hamburg," says Hawkins, "had sent over to England, in order to their being published here, two collections of lessons for the harpsichord, and they were accordingly engraved on copper, and printed for Richard Meares, in St. Paul's Churchyard, and published in the year 1714. Handel was at this time in London, and in the afternoon was used to frequent St. Paul's Church for the sake of hearing the service, and of playing on the organ after it was over; from whence he and some of the gentlemen of the choir would frequently adjourn to the 'Queen's Arms' tavern, in St. Paul's Churchyard, where was a harpsichord. It happened one afternoon, when they were thus met together, Mr. Weeley, a gentleman of the choir, came in and informed them that Mr. Mattheson's lessons were then to be had at Mr. Meares's shop; upon which Mr. Handel ordered them immediately to be sent for, and upon their being brought, played them all over without rising from the instrument."

"There dwelt," says Sir John Hawkins, "at the west corner of London House Yard, in St. Paul's Churchyard, at the sign of the 'Dolphin and Crown,' one John Young, a maker of violins and other musical instruments. This man had a son, whose Christian name was Talbot, who had been brought up with Greene in St. Paul's choir, and had attained to great proficiency on the violin, as Greene had on the harpsichord. The merits of the two Youngs, father and son, are celebrated in the following quibbling verses, which were set to music in the form of a catch, printed in the pleasant 'Musical Companion,' published in 1726:—

"'You scrapers that want a good fiddle well strung,
    You must go to the man that is old while he's young;
    But if this same fiddle you fain would play bold,
    You must go to his son, who'll be young when he's old.
    There's old Young and young Young, both men of renown,
    Old sells and young plays the best fiddle in town.
    Young and old live together, and may they live long,
    Young to play an old fiddle, old to sell a new song.'

"This young man, Talbot Young, together with

FROM CHAPTER COURT TO CHEAPSIDE.

FROM PAUL'S CHAIN TO WATLING STREET.

ST. PAUL'S CHURCHYARD IN 1820.
(*From Views by Horner, in Mr. Crace's Collection.*)

Greene and several persons, had weekly meetings at his father's house, for practice of music. The fame of this performance spread far and wide; and in a few winters the resort of gentlemen performers was greater than the house would admit of; a small subscription was set on foot, and they re-

"The 'Castle' concerts continuing to flourish for many years, auditors as well as performers were admitted subscribers, and tickets were delivered out to the members in rotation for the admission of ladies. Their fund enabling them, they hired second-rate singers from the operas, and many

OLD ST. PAUL'S SCHOOL (*see page 272*).

moved to the 'Queen's Head' tavern, in Paternoster Row. Here they were joined by Mr. Woolaston and his friends, and also by a Mr. Franckville, a fine performer on the viol de Gamba. And after a few winters, being grown rich enough to hire additional performers, they removed, in the year 1724, to the 'Castle,' in Paternoster Row, which was adorned with a picture of Mr. Young, painted by Woolaston.

young persons of professions and trades that depended upon a numerous acquaintance, were induced by motives of interest to become members of the 'Castle' concert.

"Mr. Young continued to perform in this society till the declining state of his health obliged him to quit it; after which time Prospero Castrucci and other eminent performers in succession continued to lead the band. About the year 1744, at the instance of an alderman of London, now deservedly forgotten, the subscription was raised from two guineas to five, for the purpose of performing oratorios. From the 'Castle' this society removed to Haberdashers' Hall, where they continued for fifteen or sixteen years; from thence they removed to the 'King's Arms,' in Cornhill."

A curious old advertisement of 1681 relates to St. Paul's Alley:—"Whereas the yearly meeting of the name of Adam hath of late, through the deficiency of the last stewards, been neglected, these are to give notice to all gentlemen and others that are of that name that at William Adam's, commonly called the 'Northern Ale-house,' in St. Paul's Alley, in St. Paul's Churchyard, there will be a weekly meeting, every Monday night, of our namesakes, between the hours of six and eight of the clock in the evening, in order to choose stewards to revive our antient and annual feast."—*Domestic Intelligence*, 1681.

During the building of St. Paul's, Wren was the zealous Master of the St. Paul's Freemason's Lodge, which assembled at the "Goose and Gridiron," one of the most ancient lodges in London. He presided regularly at its meetings for upwards of eighteen years. He presented the lodge with three beautifully carved mahogany candlesticks, and the trowel and mallet which he used in laying the first stone of the great cathedral in 1675. In 1688 Wren was elected Grand Master of the order, and he nominated his old fellow-workers at St. Paul's, Cibber, the sculptor, and Strong, the master mason, Grand Wardens. In Queen Anne's reign there were 129 lodges—eighty-six in London, thirty-six in provincial cities, and seven abroad. Many of the oldest lodges in London are in the neighbourhood of St. Paul's.

"At the 'Apple Tree' Tavern," writes Mr. Jacob Larwood, in his "History of Inn and Tavern Signs," "in Charles Street, Covent Garden, in 1716, four of the leading London Freemasons' lodges, considering themselves neglected by Sir Christopher Wren, met and chose a Grand Master, *pro tem.*, until they should be able to place a noble brother at the head, which they did the year following, electing the Duke of Montague. Sir Christopher had been chosen in 1698. The three lodges that joined with the 'Apple Tree' lodge used to meet respectively at the 'Goose and Gridiron,' St. Paul's Churchyard; the 'Crown,' Parker's Lane; and at the 'Rummer and Grapes' Tavern, Westminster. The 'Goose and Gridiron' occurs at Woodhall, Lincolnshire, and in a few other localities. It is said to owe its origin to the following circumstances:—The 'Mitre' was a celebrated music-house

in London House Yard, at the north-west end of St. Paul's. When it ceased to be a music-house, the succeeding landlord, to ridicule its former destiny, chose for his sign a goose striking the bars of a gridiron with his foot, in ridicule of the 'Swan and Harp,' a common sign for the early music-houses. Such an origin does the *Tatler* give; but it may also be a vernacular reading of the coat of arms of the Company of Musicians, suspended probably at the door of the 'Mitre' when it was a music-house. These arms are a swan with his wings expanded, within a double tressure, counter, flory, argent. This double tressure might have suggested a gridiron to unsophisticated passers-by.

"The celebrated 'Mitre,' near the west end of St. Paul's, was the first music-house in London. The name of the master was Robert Herbert, *alias* Farges. Like many brother publicans, he was, besides being a lover of music, also a collector of natural curiosities, as appears by his 'Catalogue of many natural rarities, collected with great industrie, cost, and thirty years' travel into foreign countries, collected by Robert Herbert, *alias* Farges, gent., and sworn servant to his Majesty; to be seen at the place called the Music-house, *at the Mitre*, near the west end of S. Paul's Church, 1664.' This collection, or, at least, a great part of it, was bought by Sir Hans Sloane. It is conjectured that the 'Mitre' was situated in London House Yard, at the north-west end of St. Paul's, on the spot where afterwards stood the house known by the sign of the 'Goose and Gridiron.'"

St. Paul's School, known to cathedral visitors chiefly by that murky, barred-in, purgatorial playground opposite the east end of Wren's great edifice, is of considerable antiquity, for it was re-founded in 1512 by that zealous patron of learning, and friend of Erasmus, Dean Colet. This liberal-minded man was the eldest of twenty-two children, all of whom he survived. His father was a City mercer, who was twice Lord Mayor of London. Colet became Dean of St. Paul's in 1505, and soon afterwards, as Latimer tells us, narrowly escaped burning for his opposition to image-worship. Having no near relatives, Colet, in 1509, began to found St. Paul's School, adapted to receive 153 poor boys, the number of fishes taken by Peter in the miraculous draught. The building is said to have cost £4,500, and was endowed with lands in Buckinghamshire estimated by Stow, in 1598, as of the yearly value of £120 or better, and now worth £12,000, with a certainty of rising.

No children were to be admitted into the school but such as could say their catechism, and read and write competently. Each child was required to pay fourpence on his first admission to the school, which sum was to be given to the "poor scholar" who swept the school and kept the seats clean. The hours of study were to be from seven till eleven in the morning, and from one to five in the afternoon, with prayers in the morning, at noon, and in the evening. It was expressly stipulated that the pupils should never use tallow candles, but only wax, and those "at the cost of their friends." The most remarkable statute of the school is that by which the scholars were bound on Christmas-day to attend at St. Paul's Church and hear the child-bishop sermon, and after be at the high mass, and each of them offer one penny to the child-bishop. When Dean Colet was asked why he had left his foundation in trust to laymen (the Mercers' Company), as tenants of his father, rather than to an ecclesiastical foundation, he answered, "that there was no absolute certainty in human affairs, but, for his part, he found less corruption in such a body of citizens than in any other order or degree of mankind."

Erasmus, after describing the foundation and the school, which he calls "a magnificent structure, to which were attached two dwelling-houses for the masters," proceeds to say, "He divided the school into four chambers. The first—namely, the porch and entrance—in which the chaplain teaches, where no child is to be admitted who cannot read and write; the second apartment is for those who are taught by the under-master; the third is for the boys of the upper form, taught by the high master. These two parts of the school are divided by a curtain, to be drawn at will. Over the head-master's chair is an image of the boy Jesus, a beautiful work, in the gesture of teaching, whom all the scholars, going and departing, salute with a hymn. There is a representation of God the Father, also, saying, 'Hear ye him,' which words were written at my suggestion."

"The last apartment is a little chapel for divine service. In the whole school there are no corners or hiding-places; neither a dining nor a sleeping place. Each boy has his own place, one above another. Every class or form contains sixteen boys, and he that is at the head of a class has a little seat, by way of pre-eminence."

Erasmus, who took a great interest in St. Paul's School, drew up a grammar, and other elementary books of value, for his friend Colet, who had for one of his masters William Lily, "the model of grammarians." Colet's masters were always to be married men.

The school thus described shared in the Great Fire of 1666, and was rebuilt by the Mercers' Company in 1670. This second structure was superseded by the present edifice, designed and erected by George Smith, Esq., the architect of the Mercers' Company. It has the advantage of two additional masters' houses, and a large cloister for a playground underneath the school.

On occasions of the sovereigns of England, or other royal or distinguished persons, going in state through the City, a balcony is erected in front of this building, whence addresses from the school are presented to the illustrious visitors by the head boys. The origin of this right or custom of the Paulines is not known, but it is of some antiquity. Addresses were so presented to Charles V. and Henry VIII., in 1522; to Queen Elizabeth, 1558; and to Queen Victoria, when the Royal Exchange was opened, in 1844. Her Majesty, however, preferred to receive the address at the next levée; and this precedent was followed when the multitudes of London rushed to welcome the Prince of Wales and Princess Alexandra, in 1863.

The ancient school-room was on a level with the street, the modern one is built over the cloister. It is a finely-proportioned apartment, and has several new class-rooms adjoining, erected upon a plan proposed by Dr. Kynaston, the late head-master. At the south end of this noble room, above the master's chair, is a bust of the founder by Roubiliac. Over the seat is inscribed, "Intendas animum studiis et rebus honestis," and over the entrance to the room is the quaint and appropriate injunction found at Winchester and other public schools—"Disce, doce, aut discede."

St. Paul's School has an excellent library immediately adjoining the school-room, to which the eighth class have access out of school-hours, the six seniors occupying places in it in school-time.

In 1602 the masters' stipends were enlarged, and the surplus money set apart for college exhibitions. The head master receives £900 a year, the second master £400. The education is entirely gratuitous. The presentations to the school are in the gift of the Master of the Mercers' Company, which company has undoubtedly much limited Dean Colet's generous intentions. The school is rich in prizes and exhibitions. The latest chronicler of the Paulines says:—

"Few public schools can claim to have educated more men who figure prominently in English history than St. Paul's School. Sir Edward North, founder of the noble family of that name; Sir William Paget, who from being the son of a serjeant-at-mace became privy councillor to four successive sovereigns, and acquired the title now held by his descendant, the owner of Beaudesert; and John

Leland, the celebrated archæologist; William Whitaker, one of the earliest and most prominent chaplains of the Reformation; William Camden, antiquarian and herald; the immortal John Milton; Samuel Pepys; Robert Nelson, author of the 'Companion to the Festivals and Fasts of the Church of England;' Dr. Benjamin Calamy; Sir John Trevor, Master of the Rolls and Speaker of the House of Commons; John, the great Duke of Marlborough; Halley, the great astronomer; the gallant but unfortunate Major André; Sir Philip Francis; Sir Charles Wetherell; Sir Frederick Pollock, the late Lord Chief Baron; Lord Chancellor Truro; and the distinguished Greek Professor at Oxford, Benjamin Jowett."

Pepys seems to have been very fond of his old school. In 1659, he goes on Apposition Day to hear his brother John deliver his speech, which he had corrected; and on another occasion, meeting his old second master, Crumbun—a dogmatic old pedagogue, as he calls him—at a bookseller's in the Churchyard, he gives the school a fine copy of Stephens' "Thesaurus." In 1661, going to the Mercers' Hall in the Lord Admiral's coach, we find him expressing pleasure at going in state to the place where as a boy he had himself humbly pleaded for an exhibition to St. Paul's School.

According to Dugdale, an ancient cathedral school existed at St. Paul's. Bishop Balmeis (Henry I.) bestowed on it "the house of Durandus, near the Bell Tower;" and no one could keep a school in London without the licence of the master of Paul's, except the masters of St. Mary-le-Bow and St. Martin's-le-Grand.

The old laws of Dean Colet, containing many curious provisions and restrictions, among other things forbad cock-fighting "and other pageantry" in the school. It was ordered that the second master and chaplain were to reside in Old Change. There was a bust of good Dean Colet over the head-master's throne. Strype, speaking of the original dedication of the school to the child Jesus, says, "but the saint robbed his Master of the title." In early days there used to be great war between the "Paul's pigeons," as they were called, and the boys of St. Anthony's Free School, Threadneedle Street, whom the Paulines nicknamed "Anthony's pigs." The Anthony's boys were great carriers off of prizes for logic and grammar.

A new scheme having lately been passed for its future government, the school is about to be transferred to a site between Hammersmith and Kensington, and will soon become a thing of the past in connection with St. Paul's Churchyard.

CHAPTER XXIII.

PATERNOSTER ROW.

Its Successions of Traders—The House of Longman—Goldsmith at Fault—Tarleton, Actor, Host, and Wit—Ordinaries around St. Paul's: their Rules and Customs—The "Castle"—"Dolly's"—The "Chapter" and its Frequenters—Chatterton and Goldsmith—Dr. Buchan and his Prescriptions—Dr. Gower—Dr. Fordyce—The "Wittinagemot" at the "Chapter"—The "Printing Conger"—Mrs. Turner, the Poisoner—The Church of St. Michael "ad Bladum"—The Boy in Panier Alley.

PATERNOSTER ROW, that crowded defile north of the Cathedral, lying between the old Grey Friars and the Blackfriars, was once entirely ecclesiastical in its character, and, according to Stow, was so called from the stationers and text-writers who dwelt there and sold religious and educational books, alphabets, paternosters, aves, creeds, and graces. It then became famous for its spurriers, and afterwards for eminent mercers, silkmen, and lacemen; so that the coaches of the "quality" often blocked up the whole street. After the fire these trades mostly removed to Bedford Street, King Street, and Henrietta Street, Covent Garden. In 1720 (says Strype) there were stationers and booksellers who came here in Queen Anne's reign from Little Britain, and a good many tire-women, who sold commodes, top-knots, and other dressings for the female head. By degrees, however, learning ousted vanity, chattering died into studious silence, and the despots of literature ruled supreme. Many a groan has gone up from authors in this gloomy thoroughfare.

One only, and that the most ancient, of the Paternoster Row book-firms, will our space permit us to chronicle. The house of Longman is part and parcel of the Row. The first Longman, born in Bristol in 1699, was the son of a soap and sugar merchant. Apprenticed in London, he purchased, about 1724, the business of Mr. Taylor, the publisher of "Robinson Crusoe," for £2,282 9s. 6d., and his first venture was the works of Boyle. This patriarch died in 1755, and was succeeded by a nephew, Thomas Longman, who ventured much trade in America and "the plantations." He was succeeded by his son, Mr. T. L. Longman, a plain man of the old citizen style, who took as partner Mr. Owen Rees, a Bristol bookseller, a man of industry and acumen.

Before the close of the eighteenth century the house of Longman and Rees had become one of the largest in the City, both as publishers and book-merchants. When there was talk of an additional paper-duty, the ministers consulted, according to West, the new firm, and on their protest desisted; a reverse course, according to the same authority, would have checked operations on the part of that one firm alone of £100,000. Before the opening of the nineteenth century they had become possessed of some new and valuable copyrights—notably, the "Grammar" of Lindley Murray, of New York. This was in 1799.

The "lake poets" proved a valuable acquisition. Wordsworth came first to them, then Coleridge, and lastly Southey. In 1802 the Longmans commenced the issue of Rees' "Cyclopædia," reconstructed from the old Chambers', and about the same time the *Annual Review*, edited by Aikin, which for the nine years of its existence Southey and Taylor of Norwich mainly supported. The catalogue of the firm for 1803 is divided into no less than twenty-two classes. Among their books we note Paley's "Natural Theology," Sharon Turner's "Anglo-Saxon History," Adolphus's "History of King George III.," Pinkerton's "Geography," Fosbrooke's "British Monachism," Cowper's "Homer," Gifford's "Juvenal," Sotheby's "Oberon," and novels and romances not a few. At this time Mr. Longman used to have Saturday evening receptions in Paternoster Row.

Sir Walter Scott's "Guy Mannering," "The Monastery," and "The Abbot," were published by Longmans. "Lalla Rookh," by Tom Moore, was published by them, and they gave £3,000 for it.

In 1811 Mr. Brown, who had entered the house as an apprentice in 1792, and was the son of an old servant, became partner. Then came in Mr. Orme, a faithful clerk of the house—for the house required several heads, the old book trade alone being an important department. In 1826, when Constable of Edinburgh came down in the commercial crash, and brought poor Sir Walter Scott to the ground with him, the Longman firm succeeded to the *Edinburgh Review*, which is still their property. Mr. Green became a partner in 1824, and in 1856 Mr. Roberts was admitted. In 1829 the firm ventured on the publication of Lardner's "Cyclopædia," to which Scott, Tom Moore, Mackintosh, &c., contributed, and which

ended in 1846 with the 133rd volume. Messrs. Longman published Macaulay's "History of England," and the cheque for £20,000 which they paid him on account of it is historical.

Thomas Norton Longman resided for many years at Mount Grove, Hampstead, where he entertained many wits and scholars. He died there in 1842, leaving £200,000 personalty. In 1830 Mr. Thomas Longman entered the firm as a partner, and Mr. William Longman in 1836. "Longman, Green, Longman, and Roberts" became the style of the publishing house, the founder of which had commenced business on that spot 150 years before.

In 1773, a year before Goldsmith's death, Dr. Kenrick, a vulgar satirist of the day, wrote an anonymous letter in an evening paper called *The London Packet*, sneering at the poet's vanity, and calling "The Traveller" a flimsy poem, denying the "Deserted Village" genius, fancy, or fire, and calling "She Stoops to Conquer" the merest pantomime. Goldsmith's Irish blood fired at an allusion to Miss Horneck and his supposed rejection by her. Supposing Evans, of Paternoster Row, to be the editor of the *Packet*, Goldsmith resolved to chastise him. Evans, a brutal fellow, who turned his son out in the streets and separated from his wife because she took her son's part, denied all knowledge of the matter. As he turned his back to look for the libel, Goldsmith struck him sharply across the shoulders. Evans, a sturdy, hot Welshman, returned the blow with interest, and in the scuffle a lamp overhead was broken and covered the combatants with fish-oil. Dr. Kenrick then stepped from an adjoining room, interposed between the combatants, and sent poor Goldsmith home, bruised and disfigured, in a coach. Evans subsequently indicted Goldsmith for the assault, but the affair was compromised by Goldsmith paying £50 towards a Welsh charity. The friend who accompanied Goldsmith to this chivalrous but unsuccessful attack is said to have been Captain Horneck, but it seems more probable that it was Captain Higgins, an Irish friend mentioned in "The Haunch of Venison."

Near the site of the present Dolly's Chop House stood the "Castle," an ordinary kept by Shakespeare's friend and fellow actor, Richard Tarleton, the low comedian of Queen Elizabeth's reign. It was this humorous, ugly actor who no doubt suggested to the great manager many of his jesters, fools, and simpletons, and we know that the tag songs—such as that at the end of *All's Well that Ends Well*, "When that I was a little tiny boy"—were expressly written for Tarleton, and were danced by that comedian to the tune of a pipe and a tabor which he himself played. The part which Tarleton had to play as host and wit is well shown in his "Book of Jests:"—

"Tarleton keeping an ordinary in Paternoster Row, and sitting with gentlemen to make them merry, would approve mustard standing before them to have wit. 'How so?' saies one. 'It is like a witty scold meeting another scold, knowing that scold will scold, begins to scold first. So,' says he, 'the mustard being lickt up, and knowing that you will bite it, begins to bite you first.' 'I'll try that,' saies a gull by, and the mustard so tickled him that his eyes watered. 'How now?' saies Tarleton; 'does my jest savour?' 'I,' saies the gull, 'and bite too.' 'If you had had better wit,' saies Tarleton, 'you would have bit first; so, then, conclude with me, that dumbe unfeeling mustard hath more wit than a talking, unfeeling foole, as you are.' Some were pleased, and some were not; but all Tarleton's care was taken, for his resolution was ever, before he talkt any jest, to measure his opponent."

A modern antiquary has with great care culled from the "Gull's Horn Book" and other sources a sketch of the sort of company that might be met with at such an ordinary. It was the custom for men of fashion in the reign of Elizabeth and James to pace in St. Paul's till dinner-time, and after the ordinary again till the hour when the theatres opened. The author of "Shakespeare's England" says:—

"There were ordinaries of all ranks, the *table-d'hôte* being the almost universal mode of dining among those who were visitors to London during the season, or term-time, as it was then called. There was the twelvepenny ordinary, where you might meet justices of the peace and young knights; and the threepenny ordinary, which was frequented by poor lieutenants and thrifty attorneys. At the

RICHARD TARLETON, THE ACTOR (*copied from an old wood engraving*).

one the rules of high society were maintained, and the large silver salt-cellar indicated the rank of the guests. At the other the diners were silent and unsociable, or the conversation, if any, was so full of 'amercements and feoffments' that a mere countryman would have thought the people were conjuring.

"If a gallant entered the ordinary at about half-past eleven, or even a little earlier, he would find the room full of fashion-mongers, waiting for the meat to be served. There are men of all classes: titled men, who live cheap that they may spend more at Court; stingy men, who want to save the charges of house-keeping; courtiers, who come there for society and news; adventurers, who have no home; Templars, who dine there daily; and men about town, who dine at whatever place is nearest to their hunger. Lords, citizens, concealed Papists, spies, prodigal 'prentices, precisians, aldermen, foreigners, officers, and country gentlemen, all are here. Some have come on foot, some on horseback, and some in those new caroches the poets laugh at."

"The well-bred courtier, on entering the room, saluted those of his acquaintances who were in winter gathered round the fire, in summer round the window, first throwing his cloak to his page and hanging up his hat and sword. The parvenu would single out a friend, and walk up and down uneasily with the scorn and carelessness of a gentleman usher, laughing rudely and nervously, or obtruding himself into groups of gentlemen gathered round a wit or poet. Quarrelsome men paced about fretfully, fingering their sword-hilts and maintaining as sour a face as that Puritan moping in a corner, pent up by a group of young swaggerers, who are disputing over a card at gleek—vain men!—not caring whether it was Paul's, the Tennis Court, or the play-house, *published* their clothes, and talked as loud as they could, in order to appear at ease, and laughed over the Water Poet's last epigram or the last pamphlet of Marprelate. The soldiers bragged of nothing but of their employment in Ireland and the Low Countries—how they helped Drake to burn St. Domingo, or grave Maurice to hold out Breda. Tom Coryatt, or such weak-pated travellers, would babble of the Rialto and Prester John, and exhibit specimens of unicorns' horns or palm-leaves from the river Nilus. The implied that you had nearly finished dinner. The more unabashable, rapid adventurer, though but a beggarly captain, would often attack the capon while his neighbour, the knight, was still encumbered with his stewed beef; and when the justice of the peace opposite, who has just pledged him in sack, is knuckle-deep in the goose, he falls stoutly on the long-billed game; while at supper, if one of the college of critics, our gallant praised the last play or put his approving stamp upon the new poem.

DOLLY'S COFFEE-HOUSE (*see page 278*).

courtier talked of the fair lady who gave him the glove which he wore in his hat as a favour; the poet of the last satire of Marston or Ben Jonson, or volunteered to read a trifle thrown off of late by 'Faith, a learned gentleman, a very worthy friend,' though if we were to enquire, this varlet poet might turn out, after all, to be the mere decoy duck of the hostess, paid to draw gulls and fools thither. The mere dullard sat silent, playing with his glove or discussing at what apothecary's the best tobacco was to be bought.

"The dishes seemed to have been served up at these hot luncheons or early dinners in much the same order as at the present day—meat, poultry, game, and pastry. 'To be at your woodcocks'

"Primero and a 'pair' of cards followed the wine. Here the practised player learnt to lose with endurance, and neither to tear the cards nor crush the dice with his heel. Perhaps the jest may be true, and that men sometimes played till they sold even their beards to cram tennis-balls or stuff cushions. The patron often paid for the wine or disbursed for the whole dinner. Then the drawer came round with his wooden knife, and scraped off the crusts and crumbs, or cleared off the parings of fruit and cheese into his basket. The torn cards were thrown into the fire, the guests rose, rapiers were re-hung, and belts buckled on. The post news was heard, and the reckonings paid. The French lackey and Irish footboy led out the hobby horses, and some rode off to the play, others to the river-stairs to take a pair of oars to the Surrey side."

The "Castle," where Tarleton had so often talked of Shakespeare and his wit, perished in the Great Fire ; but was afterwards rebuilt, and here "The Castle Society of Music" gave their performances," no doubt aided by many of the St. Paul's Choir. Part of the old premises were subsequently (says Mr. Timbs) the Oxford Bible Warehouse, destroyed by fire in 1822, and since rebuilt. "Dolly's Tavern," which stood near the "Castle," derived its name from Dolly, an old cook of the establishment, whose portrait Gainsborough painted. Bonnell Thornton mentions the beefsteaks and gill ale at "Dolly's." The coffee-room, with its projecting fire-place, is as old as Queen Anne. The head of that queen is painted on a window at "Dolly's," and the entrance in Queen's Head Passage is christened from this painting.

The old taverns of London are to be found in the strangest nooks and corners, hiding away behind shops, or secreting themselves up alleys. Unlike the Paris café, which delights in the free sunshine of the boulevard, and displays its harmless revellers to the passers-by, the London tavern aims at cosiness, quiet, and privacy. It partitions and curtains-off its guests as if they were conspirators and the wine they drank was forbidden by the law. Of such taverns the "Chapter" is a good example.

The "Chapter Coffee House," at the corner of Chapter House Court, was in the last century famous for its punch, its pamphlets, and its newspapers. As lawyers and authors frequented the Fleet Street taverns, so booksellers haunted the "Chapter." Bonnell Thornton, in the Connoisseur, Jan., 1754, says :—"The conversation here naturally turns upon the newest publications, but their criticisms are somewhat singular. When they say a good book, they do not mean to praise the style or sentiment, but the quick and extensive sale of it. That book is best which sells most."

In 1770 Chatterton, in one of those apparently hopeful letters which he wrote home while in reality his proud heart was breaking, says :—"I am quite familiar at the 'Chapter Coffee House,' and know all the geniuses there." He desires a friend to send him whatever he has published, to be left at the "Chapter." So, again, writing from the King's Bench, he says a gentleman whom he met at the "Chapter" had promised to introduce him as a travelling tutor to the young Duke of Northumberland ; "but, alas ! I spoke no tongue but my own."

Perhaps that very day Chatterton came, half starved, and listened with eager ears to great authors talking. Oliver Goldsmith dined there, with Lloyd, that reckless friend of still more reckless Churchill, and some Grub Street cronies, and had to pay for the lot, Lloyd having quite forgotten the important fact that he was moneyless. Goldsmith's favourite seat at the "Chapter" became a seat of honour, and was long pointed out to visitors. Leather tokens of the coffee-house are still in existence.

Mrs. Gaskell has sketched the "Chapter" in 1848, with its low heavy-beamed ceilings, wainscoted rooms, and its broad, dark, shallow staircase. She describes it as formerly frequented by university men, country clergymen, and country booksellers, who, friendless in London, liked to hear the literary chat. Few persons slept there, and in a long, low, dingy room up-stairs the periodical meetings of "the trade" were held. "The high, narrow windows looked into the gloomy Row." Nothing of motion or of change could be seen in the grim, dark houses opposite, so near and close, although the whole width of the Row was between. The mighty roar of London ran round like the sound of an unseen ocean, yet every footfall on the pavement below might be heard distinctly in that unfrequented street.

The frequenters of the "Chapter Coffee House" (1797—1805) have been carefully described by Sir Richard Phillips. Alexander Stevens, editor of the "Annual Biography and Obituary," was one of the choice spirits who met nightly in the "Wittenagemot," as it was called, or the northeast corner box in the coffee-room. The neighbours, who dropped in directly the morning papers arrived, and before they were dried by the waiter, were called the "Wet Paper Club," and another set intercepted the wet evening papers. Dr. Buchan, author of that murderous book, "Domestic Medicine," which teaches a man how to kill himself and family cheaply, generally acted as moderator. He was a handsome, white-haired man, a Tory, a good-humoured companion, and a bon vivant. If any one began to complain, or appear hypochondriacal, he used to say—

"Now let me prescribe for you, without a fee. Here, John, bring a glass of punch for Mr. ——, unless he likes brandy and water better. Now, take that, sir, and I'll warrant you'll soon be well. You're a peg too low ; you want stimulus ; and if one glass won't do, call for a second."

Dr. Gower, the urbane and able physician of the Middlesex Hospital, was another frequent visitor, as also that great eater and worker, Dr. Fordyce, whose balance no potations could disturb.

Fordyce had fashionable practice, and brought rare news and much sound information on general subjects. He came to the "Chapter" from his wine, stayed about an hour, and sipped a glass of brandy and water. He then took another glass at the "London Coffee House," and a third at the "Oxford," then wound home to his house in Essex Street, Strand. The three doctors seldom agreed on medical subjects, and laughed loudly at each other's theories. They all, however, agreed in regarding the "Chapter" punch as an infallible and safe remedy for all ills.

The standing men in the box were Hammond and Murray. Hammond, a Coventry manufacturer, had scarcely missed an evening at the "Chapter" for forty-five years. His strictures on the events of the day were thought severe but able, and as a friend of liberty he had argued all through the times of Wilkes and the French and American wars. His Socratic arguments were very amusing. Mr. Murray, the great referee of the Wittenagemot, was a Scotch minister, who generally sat at the "Chapter" reading papers from 9 a.m. to 9 p.m. He was known to have read straight through every morning and evening paper published in London for thirty years. His memory was so good that he was always appealed to for dates and matters of fact, but his mind was not remarkable for general lucidity. Other friends of Stevens's were Dr. Birdmore, the Master of the Charterhouse, who abounded in anecdote; Walker, the rhetorician and dictionary-maker, a most intelligent man, with a fine enunciation; and Dr. Towers, a political writer, who over his half-pint of Lisbon grew sarcastic and lively. Also a grumbling man named Dobson, who between asthmatic paroxysms vented his spleen on all sides. Dobson was an author and paradox-monger, but so devoid of principle that he was deserted by all his friends, and would have died from want, if Dr. Garthshore had not placed him as a patient in an empty fever hospital. Robinson, "the king of booksellers," and his sensible brother John were also frequenters of the "Chapter," as well as Joseph Johnson, the friend of Priestley, Paine, Cowper, and Fuseli, from St. Paul's Churchyard. Phillips, the speculative bookseller, then commencing his *Monthly Magazine*, came to the "Chapter" to look out for recruits, and with his pockets well lined with guineas to enlist them. He used to describe all the odd characters at this coffee-house, from the glutton in politics, who waited at daylight for the morning papers, to the moping and disconsolate bachelor, who sat till the fire was raked out by the sleepy waiter at half-past twelve at night. These strange figures succeeded each other regularly, like the figures in a magic lantern.

Alexander Chalmers, editor of many works, enlivened the Wittenagemot by many sallies of wit and humour. He took great pains not to be mistaken for a namesake of his, who, he used to say, carried "the leaden mace." Other *habitués* were the two Parrys, of the *Courier* and *Jacobite* papers, and Captain Skinner, a man of elegant manners, who represented England in the absurd procession of all nations, devised by that German revolutionary fanatic, Anacharsis Clootz, in Paris in 1793. Baker, an ex-Spitalfields manufacturer, a great talker and eater, joined the coterie regularly, till he shot himself at his lodgings in Kirby Street. It was discovered that his only meal in the day had been the nightly supper at the "Chapter," at the fixed price of a shilling, with a supplementary pint of porter. When the shilling could no longer be found for the supper, he killed himself.

Among other members of these pleasant coteries were Lowndes, the electrician; Dr. Busby, the musician; Cooke, the well-bred writer of conversation; and Macfarlane, the author of "The History of George III.," who was eventually killed by a blow from the pole of a coach during an election procession of Sir Francis Burdett at Brentford. Another celebrity was a young man named Wilson, called Langton, from his stories of the *haut ton*. He ran up a score of £40, and then disappeared, to the vexation of Mrs. Brown, the landlady, who would willingly have welcomed him, even though he never paid, as a means of amusing and detaining customers. Waithman, the Common Councilman and Alderman, was always clear-headed and agreeable. There was also Mr. Paterson, a long-headed, speculative North Briton, who had taught Pitt mathematics. But such coteries are like empires; they have their rise and their fall. Dr. Buchan died; some pert young sparks offended the Nestor, Hammond, who gave up the place, after forty-five years' attendance, and before 1820 the "Chapter" grew silent and dull.

The fourth edition of the well-known "Antient and Modern Geography," says Nicholls, was published by an association of respectable booksellers, who about the year 1719 entered into an especial partnership, for the purpose of printing some expensive works, and styled themselves "the Printing Conger." The term "Conger" was supposed to have been at first applied to them invidiously, alluding to the conger eel, which is said to swallow the smaller fry; or it may possibly have been taken from *congeries*. The "Conger" met at the "Chapter."

The "Chapter" closed as a coffee-house in 1854, and was altered into a tavern.

One tragic memory, and one alone, as far as we know, attaches to Paternoster Row. It was here, in the reign of James I., that Mrs. Anne Turner lived, at whose house the poisoning of Sir Thomas Overbury was planned. It was here that Viscount Rochester met the infamous Countess of Essex; and it was Overbury's violent opposition to this shameful intrigue that led to his death from arsenic and diamond-dust, administered in the Tower by Weston, a servant of Mrs. Turner's, who received £180 for his trouble. Rochester and the Countess were disgraced, but their lives were spared. The Earl of Northampton, an accomplice of the countess, died before Overbury succumbed to his three months of torture.

"Mrs. Turner," says Sir Simonds d'Ewes, had "first brought up that vain and foolish use of yellow starch, coming herself to her trial in a yellow band and cuffs; and therefore, when she was afterwards executed at Tyburn, the hangman had his band and cuffs of the same colour, which made many after that day, of either sex, to forbear the use of that coloured starch, till at last it grew generally to be detested and disused."

In a curious old print of West Chepe, date 1585, in the vestry-room of St. Vedast's, Foster Lane, we see St. Michael's Church on the north side of Paternoster Row. It is a plain building, with a low square tower and pointed-headed windows. It was chiefly remarkable as the burial-place of that indefatigable antiquary, John Leland. This laborious man, educated at St. Paul's School, was one of the earliest Greek scholars in England, and one of the deepest students of Welsh and Saxon. Henry VIII. made him one of his chaplains, bestowed on him several benefices, and gave him a roving commission to visit the ruins of England and Wales and inspect the records of collegiate and cathedral libraries. He spent six years in this search, and collected a vast mass of material, then retired to his house in the parish of St. Michael-le-Quern to note and arrange his treasures. His mind, however, broke down under the load: he became insane, and died in that dreadful darkness of the soul, 1552. His great work, "The Itinerary of Great Britain," was not published till after his death. His large collections relating to London antiquities were, unfortunately for us, lost. The old church of "St. Michael ad Bladum," says Strype, "or 'at the Corn' (corruptly called the 'Quern') was so called because in place thereof was some time a corn-market, stretching up west to the shambles. It seemeth that this church was first builded about

the reign of Edward III. Thomas Newton, first parson there, was buried in the quire, in the year 1361, which was the 35th of Edward III. At the east end of this church stood an old cross called the Old Cross in West-cheap, which was taken down in the 13th Richard II.; since the which time the said parish church was also taken down, but new builded and enlarged in the year 1430; the 8th Henry VI., William Eastfield, mayor, and the commonalty, granting of the common soil of the City three foot and a half in breadth on the north part, and four foot in breadth towards the east, for the inlarging thereof. This church was repaired, and with all things either for use or beauty, richly supplied and furnished, at the sole cost and charge of the parishioners, in 1617. This church was burnt down in the Great Fire, and remains unbuilt, and laid into the street, but the conduit which was formerly at the east end of the church still remains. The parish is united to St. Vedast, Foster Lane. At the east end of this church, in place of the old cross, is now a water-conduit placed. William Eastfield, maior, the 9th Henry VI., at the request of divers common councels, granted it so to be. Whereupon, in the 19th of the said Henry, 1,000 marks was granted by a common councel towards the works of this conduit, and the reparation of others. This is called the Little Conduit in West Cheap, by Paul's Gate. At the west end of this parish church is a small passage for people on foot, thorow the same church; and west from the same church, some distance, is another passage out of Paternoster Row, and is called (of such a sign) Panyer Alley, which cometh out into the north, over against St. Martin's Lane.

'When you have sought the city round,
Yet still this is the highest ground.
August 27, 1688.'

This is writ upon a stone raised, about the middle of this Panier Alley, having the figure of a panier, with a boy sitting upon it, with a bunch of grapes, as it seems to be, held between his naked foot and hand, in token, perhaps, of plenty."

At the end of a somewhat long Latin epitaph to Marcus Erington in this church occurred the following lines:—

"Vita bonos, sed pœna malos, æterna capessit,
Vitæ bonis, sed pœna malis, per secula crescit.
His mors, his vita, perpetuatur ita."

John Bankes, mercer and squire, who was interred here, had a long epitaph, adorned with the following verses:—

"Imbalmed in pious arts, wrapt in a shroud
Of white, innocuous charity, who vowed,
Having enough, the world should understand
No need of money might escape his hand;

Bankes here is laid asleepe—this place did breed him—
A precedent to all that shall succeed him.
Note both his life and immitable end;
Not he th' unrighteous mammon made his friend;
Expressing by his talents' rich increase
Service that gain'd him praise and lasting peace.
Much was to him committed, much he gave,
Ent'ring his treasure there whence all shall have
Returne with use : what to the poore is given

Claims a just promise of reward in heaven.
Even such a banke *Bankes* left behind at last,
Riches stor'd up, which age nor time can waste."

On part of the site of the church of this parish, after the fire of London in 1666, was erected a conduit for supplying the neighbourhood with water ; but the same being found unnecessary, it was, with others, pulled down in 1727.

CHAPTER XXIV.

BAYNARD'S CASTLE AND DOCTORS' COMMONS.

Baron Fitzwalter and King John—The Duties of the Chief Bannerer of London—An Old-fashioned Punishment for Treason—Shakespearian Allusions to Baynard's Castle—Doctors' Commons and its Five Courts—The Court of Probate Act, 1857—The Court of Arches—The Will Office—Business of the Court—Prerogative Court—Faculty Office—Lord Stowell, the Admiralty Judge—Stories of Him—His Marriage—Sir Herbert Jenner Fust—The Court "Rising"—Dr. Lushington—Marriage Licences—Old Weller and the "Touters"—Doctors' Commons at the Present Day.

WE have already made passing mention of Baynard's Castle, the grim fortress near Blackfriars Bridge, immediately below St. Paul's, where, for several centuries after the Conquest, Norman barons held their state, and behind its stone ramparts maintained their petty sovereignty.

This castle took its name from Ralph Baynard, one of those greedy and warlike Normans who came over with the Conqueror, who bestowed on him many marks of favour, among others the substantial gift of the barony of Little Dunmow, in Essex. This chieftain built the castle, which derived its name from him, and, dying in the reign of Rufus, the castle descended to his grandson, Henry Baynard, who in 1111, however, forfeited it to the Crown for taking part with Helias, Earl of Mayne, who endeavoured to wrest his Norman possessions from Henry I. The angry king bestowed the barony and castle of Baynard, with all its honours, on Robert Fitzgerald, son of Gilbert, Earl of Clare, his steward and cup-bearer. Robert's son, Walter, adhered to William de Longchamp, Bishop of Ely, against John, Earl of Moreton, brother of Richard Cœur de Lion. He, however, kept tight hold of the river-side castle, which duly descended to Robert, his son, who in 1213 became castellan and standard-bearer of the city, On this same banneret, in the midst of his pride and prosperity, there fell a great sorrow. The licentious tyrant, John, who spared none who crossed his passions, fell in love with Matilda, Fitz-Walter's fair daughter, and finding neither father nor daughter compliant to his will, John accused the castellan of abetting the discontented barons, and attempted his arrest. But the river-side fortress was convenient for escape, and Fitz-Walter flew to France. Tradition says that in 1214 King John invaded France, but that after a time a truce was made between the two nations for five years. There was a river, or arm of the sea, flowing between the French and English tents, and across this flood an English knight, hungry for a fight, called out to the soldiers of the Fleur de Lis to come over and try a joust or two with him. At once Robert Fitz-Walter, with his visor down, ferried over alone with his barbed horse, and mounted ready for the fray. At the first course he struck John's knight so fiercely with his great spear, that both man and steed came rolling in a clashing heap to the ground. Never was spear better broken ; and when the squires had gathered up their discomfited master, and the supposed French knight had recrossed the ferry, King John, who delighted in a well-ridden course, cried out, with his usual oath, "By God's sooth, he were a king indeed who had such a knight !" Then the friends of the banished man seized their opportunity, and came running to the usurper, and knelt down and said, " O king, he is your knight ; it was Robert Fitz-Walter who ran that joust." Whereupon John, who could be generous when he could gain anything by it, sent the next day for the good knight, and restored him to his favour, allowed him to rebuild Baynard's Castle, which had been demolished by royal order, and made him, moreover, governor of the Castle of Hertford.

But Fitz-Walter could not forget the grave of his daughter, still green at Dunmow (for Matilda, indomitable in her chastity, had been poisoned by a messenger of John's, who sprinkled a deadly powder over a poached egg—at least, so the legend runs), and soon placed himself at the head of those brave barons who the next year forced the tyrant to sign Magna Charta at Runnymede. He was afterwards chosen general of the barons' army, to keep John to his word, and styled "Marshal of the Army of God and of the Church." He then, not having received knocks enough in England, joined the Crusaders, and was present at the great siege of Damietta. In 1216 (the first year of Henry III.) Fitz-Walter again appears to the front, watchful of English liberty, for his Castle of Hertford having been delivered to Louis of France, the dangerous ally of the barons, he required of the French to leave the same, "because the keeping thereof did by ancient right and title pertain to him." On which Louis, says Stow, prematurely showing his claws, replied scornfully "that Englishmen were not worthy to have such holds in keeping, because they did betray their own lord;" but Louis not long after left England rather suddenly, accelerated no doubt by certain movements of Fitz-Walter and his brother barons.

Fitz-Walter dying, and being buried at Dunmow, the scene of his joys and sorrows, was succeeded

THE FIGURE IN PANIER ALLEY (see page 280).

by his son Walter, who was summoned to Chester in the forty-third year of Henry III., to repel the fierce and half-savage Welsh from the English frontier. After Walter's death the barony of Baynard was in the wardship of Henry III. during the minority of Robert Fitz-Walter, who in 1303 claimed his right as castellan and banner-bearer of the City of London before John Blandon, or Blount, Mayor of London. The old formularies on which Fitz-Walter founded his claims are quoted by Stow from an old record which is singularly quaint and picturesque. The chief clauses run thus:—

"The said Robert and his heirs are and ought to be chief bannerets of London in fee, for the chastiliary which he and his ancestors had by Castle Baynard in the said city. In time of war the said Robert and his heirs ought to serve the city in manner as followeth—that is, the said Robert ought to come, he being the twentieth man of arms, on horseback, covered with cloth or armour, unto the great west door of St. Paul's, with his banner displayed before him, and when he is so come, mounted and apparelled, the mayor, with his aldermen and sheriffs armed with their arms, shall come out of the said church with a banner in his hand, all on foot, which banner shall be gules, the image of St. Paul gold, the face, hands, feet, and sword of silver; and as soon as the earl seeth the mayor come on foot out of the church, bearing such a banner, he shall alight from his horse and salute the mayor, saying unto him, 'Sir mayor, I am come to do my service which I owe to the city.' And the mayor and aldermen shall reply, 'We give to you as our banneret of fee in this city the banner of this city, to bear and govern, to the honour of this city to your power;' and the earl, taking the banner in his hands, shall go on foot out of the gate; and the mayor and his company following to the door, shall bring a horse to the said Robert, value twenty pounds, which horse shall be saddled with a saddle of the arms of the said earl, and shall be covered with sindals of the said arms. Also, they shall present him a purse of twenty pounds, delivering it to his chamberlain, for his charges that day."

The record goes on to say that when Robert is mounted on his £20 horse, banner in hand, he shall require the mayor to appoint a City Marshal (we have all seen him with his cocked hat and subdued commander-in-chief manner), "and the commons shall then assemble under the banner of St. Paul, Robert bearing the banner to Aldgate, and then delivering it up to some fit person. And if the army have to go out of the city, Robert shall choose two sage persons out of every ward to keep the city in the absence of the army." And these guardians were to be chosen in the priory of the Trinity, near Aldgate. And for every town or castle which the Lord of London besieged, if the

of the mayor or sheriff, was to be tried in the court of the said Robert.

"If any, therefore, be taken in his sokemanry, he must have his stocks and imprisonment in his soken, and he shall be brought before the mayor and judgment given him, but it must not be published till he come into the court of the said earl, and in his liberty; and if he have deserved death by treason, he is to be tied to a post in the Thames, at a good wharf, where boats are fastened,

THE CHURCH OF ST. MICHAEL AD BLADUM (*see page* 280).

siege continued a whole year, the said Robert was to receive for every siege, of the commonalty, one hundred shillings and no more. These were Robert Fitz-Walter's rights in times of war; in times of peace his rights were also clearly defined. His sok or ward in the City began at a wall of St. Paul's canonry, which led down by the brewhouse of St. Paul's to the river Thames, and so to the side of a wall, which was in the water coming down from Fleet Bridge. The ward went on by London Wall, behind the house of the Black Friars, to Ludgate, and it included all the parish of St. Andrew. Any of his sokemen indicted at the Guildhall of any offence not touching the body

two ebbings and two flowings of the water (!) And if he be condemned for a common theft, he ought to be led to the elms, and there suffer his judgment as other thieves. And so the said earl hath honour, that he holdeth a great franchise within the city, that the mayor must do him right; and when he holdeth a great council, he ought to call the said Robert, who should be sworn thereof, against all people, saving the king and his heirs. And when he cometh to the hustings at Guildhall, the mayor ought to rise against him, and sit down near him, so long as he remaineth, all judgments being given by his mouth, according to the records of the said Guildhall; and the waifes that come while he stayeth, he ought to give them to the town bailiff, or to whom he will, by the counsel of the mayor."

This old record seems to us especially quaint and picturesque. The right of banner-bearer to the City of London was evidently a privilege not to be despised by even the proudest Norman baron, however numerous were his men-at-arms, however thick the forest of lances that followed at his back. At the gates of many a refractory Essex or Hertford-shire castle, no doubt, the Fitz-Walters flaunted that great banner, that was emblazoned with the image of St. Paul, with golden face and silver feet; and the horse valued at £20, and the pouch with twenty golden pieces, must by no means have lessened the zeal and pride of the City castellan as he led on his trusty archers, or urged forward the half-stripped, sinewy men, who toiled at the cata-pult, or bent down the mighty springs of the terrible mangonel. Many a time through Aldgate must the castellan have passed with glittering armour and flaunting plume, eager to earn his hundred shillings by the siege of a rebellious town.

Then Robert was knighted by Edward I., and the family continued in high honour and reputa-tion through many troubles and public calamities. In the reign of Henry VI., when the male branch died out, Anne, the heiress, married into the Rat-cliffe family, who revived the title of Fitz-Walter.

It is not known how this castle came to the Crown, but certain it is that on its being consumed by fire in 1428 (Henry VI.), it was rebuilt by Hum-phrey, the good duke of Gloucester. On his death it was made a royal residence by Henry VI., and by him granted to the Duke of York, his luckless rival, who lodged here with his factious retainers during the lulls in the wars of York and Lancaster. In the year 1460, the Earl of March, lodging in Castle Baynard, was informed that his army and the Earl of Warwick had declared that Henry VI. was no longer worthy to reign, and had chosen him for their king. The earl coquetted, as usurpers often do, with these offers of the crown, declaring his insufficiency for so great a charge, till yielding to the exhortations of the Archbishop of Canterbury and the Bishop of Exeter, he at last consented. On the next day he went to St. Paul's in procession, to hear the *Te Deum*, and was then conveyed in state to West-minster, and there, in the Hall, invested with the sceptre by the confessor.

At Baynard's Castle, too, that cruel usurper, Richard III., practised the same arts as his pre-decessor. Shakespeare, who has darkened Richard almost to caricature, has left him the greatest wretch existing in fiction. At Baynard's Castle

our great poet makes Richard receive his accom-plice Buckingham, who had come from the Guild-hall with the Lord Mayor and aldermen to press him to accept the crown; Richard is found by the credulous citizens with a book of prayer in his hand, standing between two bishops. This man, who was already planning the murder of Hastings and the two princes in the Tower, affected religious scruples, and with well-feigned reluctance accepted "the golden yoke of sovereignty."

Thus at Baynard's Castle begins that darker part of the Crookback's career, which led on by crime after crime to the desperate struggle at Bosworth, when, after slaying his rival's standard-bearer, Richard was beaten down by swords and axes, and his crown struck off into a hawthorn bush. The defaced corpse of the usurper, stripped and gory, was, as the old chroniclers tell us, thrown over a horse and carried by a faithful herald to be buried at Leicester. It is in vain that modern writers try to prove that Richard was gentle and accomplished, that this murder attributed to him was profitless and impossible; his name will still remain in history blackened and accursed by charges that the great poet has turned into truth, and which, indeed, are difficult to refute. That Richard might have become a great, and wise, and powerful king, is possible; but that he hesitated to commit crimes to clear his way to the throne, which had so long been struggled for by the Houses of York and Lancaster, truth forbids us for a moment to doubt. He seems to have been one of those dark, wily natures that do not trust even their most intimate accomplices, and to have worked in such darkness that only the angels know what blows he struck, or what murders he planned. One thing is certain, that Henry, Clarence, Hastings, and the princes died in terribly quick succession, and at most con-venient moments.

Henry VIII. expended large sums in turning Baynard's Castle from a fortress into a palace. He frequently lodged there in burly majesty, and entertained there the King of Castile, who was driven to England by a tempest. The castle then became the property of the Pembroke family, and here, in July, 1553, the council was held in which it was resolved to proclaim Mary Queen of England, which was at once done at the Cheapside Cross by sound of trumpet.

Queen Elizabeth, who delighted to honour her special favourites, once supped at Baynard's Castle with the earl, and afterwards went on the river to show herself to her loyal subjects. It is particu-larly mentioned that the queen returned to her palace at ten o'clock.

The Earls of Shrewsbury afterwards occupied the castle, and resided there till it was burnt in the Great Fire. On its site stand the Carron works and the wharf of the Castle Baynard Copper Company.

Adjoining Baynard's Castle once stood a tower built by King Edward II., and bestowed by him on William de Ross, for a rose yearly, paid in lieu of all other services. The tower was in later times called "the Legates' Tower." Westward of this stood Montfichet Castle, and eastward of Baynard's Castle the Tower Royal and the Tower of London, so that the Thames was well guarded from Ludgate to the citadel. All round this neighbourhood, in the Middle Ages, great families clustered. There was Beaumont Inn, near Paul's Wharf, which, on the attainder of Lord Bardolf, Edward IV. bestowed on his favourite, Lord Hastings, whose death Richard III. (as we have seen) planned at his very door. It was afterwards Huntingdon House. Near Trigg Stairs the Abbot of Chertsey had a mansion, afterwards the residence of Lord Sandys. West of Paul's Wharf (Henry VI.) was Scroope's Inn, and near that a house belonging to the Abbey of Fescamp, given by Edward III. to Sir Thomas Burley. In Carter Lane was the mansion of the Priors of Okeborne, in Wiltshire, and not far from the present Puddle Dock was the great mansion of the Lords of Berkley, where, in the reign of Henry VI., the king-making Earl of Warwick kept tremendous state, with a thousand swords ready to fly out if he even raised a finger.

And now, leaving barons, usurpers, and plotters, we come to the Dean's Court archway of Doctors' Commons, the portal so long guarded by touters for licences, men in white aprons, who looked half like confectioners, and half like disbanded watermen. Here was the college of Doctors of Law, provided for the ecclesiastical lawyers in the early part of Queen Elizabeth's reign by Master Henry Harvey, Master of Trinity Hall, Cambridge, Prebendary of Ely, and Dean of the Arches; according to Sir George Howes, "a reverend, learned, and good man." The house had been inhabited by Lord Mountjoy, and Dr. Harvey obtained a lease of it for one hundred years of the Dean and Chapter of St. Paul's, for the annual rent of five marks. Before this the civilians and canonists had lodged in a small inconvenient house in Paternoster Row, afterwards the "Queen's Head Tavern." Cardinal Wolsey, always magnificent in his schemes, had planned a "fair college of stone" for the ecclesiastical lawyers, the plan of which Sir Robert Cotton possessed. In this college, in 1631, says

Buc, the Master of the Revels, lived in commons with the Judge of the High Court of Admiralty, being a doctor of civil law, the Dean of the Arches, the Judges of the Court of Delegates, the Vicar-General, and the Master or Custos of the Prerogative Court of Canterbury.

Doctors' Commons, says Strype, "consists of five courts—three appertaining to the see of Canterbury, one to the see of London, and one to the Lords Commissioners of the Admiralties." The functions of these several courts he thus defines :—

"Here are the courts kept for the practice of civil or ecclesiastical causes. Several offices are also here kept; as the Registry of the Archbishop of Canterbury, and the Registry of the Bishop of London.

"The causes whereof the civil and ecclesiastical law take cognisance are those that follow, as they are enumerated in the 'Present State of England :'— Blasphemy, apostacy from Christianity, heresy, schism, ordinations, institutions of clerks to benefices, celebration of Divine service, matrimony, divorces, bastardy, tythes, oblations, obventions, mortuaries, dilapidations, reparation of churches, probate of wills, administrations, simony, incests, fornications, adulteries, solicitation of chastity ; pensions, procurations, commutation of penance, right of pews, and other such like, reducible to those matters.

"The courts belonging to the civil and ecclesiastical laws are divers.

"First, the Court of *Arches*, which is the highest court belonging to the Archbishop of Canterbury. It was a court formerly kept in Bow Church in Cheapside ; and the church and tower thereof being arched, the court was from thence called *The Arches*, and so still is called. Hither are all appeals directed in ecclesiastical matters within the province of Canterbury. To this court belongs a judge who is called *The Dean of the Arches*, so styled because he hath a jurisdiction over a deanery in London, consisting of thirteen parishes exempt from the jurisdiction of the Bishop of London. This court hath (besides this judge) a registrar or examiner, an actuary, a beadle or crier, and an apparitor ; besides advocates and procurators or proctors. These, after they be once admitted by warrant and commission directed from the Archbishop, and by the Dean of the Arches, may then (and not before) exercise as advocates and proctors there, and in any other courts.

"Secondly, the Court of *Audience*. This was a court likewise of the Archbishop's, which he used to hold in his own house, where he received causes, complaints, and appeals, and had learned civilians living with him, that were auditors of the said causes before the Archbishop gave sentence. This court was kept in later times in St. Paul's. The judge belonging to this court was stiled '*Causarum, negotiorumque Cantuarien, auditor officialis.*' It had also other officers, as the other courts.

"Thirdly, the next court for civil causes belonging to the Archbishop is the *Prerogative* Court, wherein wills and testaments are proved, and all administrations taken, which belongs to the Archbishop by his prerogative, that is, by a special pre-eminence that this see hath in certain causes above ordinary bishops within his province; this takes place where the deceased hath goods to the value of £5 out of the diocese, and being of the diocese of London, to the value of £10. If any contention, grow, touching any such wills or administrations, the causes are debated and decided in this court.

"Fourthly, the Court of *Faculties and Dispensations*, whereby a privilege or special power is granted to a person by favour and indulgence to do that which by law otherwise he could not: as, to marry, without banns first asked in the church three several Sundays or holy days; the son to succeed his father in his benefice; for one to have two or more benefices incompatible; for non-residence, and in other such like cases.

"Fifthly, the Court of *Admiralty*, which was erected in the reign of Edward III. This court belongs to the Lord High Admiral of England, a high officer that hath the government of the king's navy, and the hearing of all causes relating to merchants and mariners. He takes cognisance of the death or mayhem of any man committed in the great ships riding in great rivers, beneath the bridges of the same next the sea. Also he hath power to arrest ships in great streams for the use of the king, or his wars. And in these things this court is concerned.

"To these I will add the Court of *Delegates;* to which high court appeals do lie from any of the former courts. This is the highest court for civil causes. It was established by an Act in the 25th Henry VIII., cap. 19, wherein it was enacted, 'That it should be lawful, for lack of justice at or in any of the Archbishop's courts, for the parties grieved to appeal to the King's Majesty in his Court of Chancery; and that, upon any such appeal, a commission under the Great Seal should be directed to such persons as should be named by the king's highness (like as in case of appeal from the Admiralty Court), to determine such appeals, and the cases concerning the same. And no further appeals to be had or made from the said commissioners for the same.' These commissioners are appointed judges only for that turn; and they are commonly of the spiritualty, or bishops; of the common law, as judges of Westminster Hall; as well as those of the civil law. And these are mixed one with another, according to the nature of the cause.

"Lastly, sometimes a Commission of *Review* is granted by the king under the Broad Seal, to consider and judge again what was decreed in the Court of Delegates. But this is but seldom, and upon great, and such as shall be judged just, causes by the Lord Keeper or High Chancellor. And this done purely by the king's prerogative, since by the Act for Delegates no further appeals were to be laid or made from those commissioners, as was mentioned before."

The Act 20 & 21 Vict., cap. 77, called "The Court of Probate Act, 1857," received the royal assent on the 25th of August, 1857. This is the great act which established the Court of Probate, and abolished the jurisdiction of the courts ecclesiastical.

The following, says Mr. Forster, are some of the benefits resulting from the reform of the Ecclesiastical Courts:—

That reform has reduced the depositaries for wills in this country from nearly 400 to 40.

It has brought complicated testamentary proceedings into a system governed by one vigilant court.

It has relieved the public anxiety respecting "the doom of English wills" by placing them in the custody of responsible men.

It has thrown open the courts of law to the entire legal profession.

It has given the public the right to prove wills or obtain letters of administration without professional assistance.

It has given to literary men an interesting field for research.

It has provided that which ancient Rome is said to have possessed, but which London did not possess—viz., a place of deposit for the wills of living persons.

It has extended the English favourite mode of trial—viz., trial by jury—by admitting jurors to try the validity of wills and questions of divorce.

It has made divorce not a matter of wealth but of justice: the wealthy and the poor alike now only require a clear case and "no collusion."

It has enabled the humblest wife to obtain a "protection order" for her property against an unprincipled husband.

It has afforded persons wanting to establish legitimacy, the validity of marriages, and the right to be deemed natural born subjects, the means of so doing.

Amongst its minor benefits it has enabled persons needing copies of wills which have been proved since January, 1858, in any part of the country, to obtain them from the principal registry of the Court of Probate in Doctors' Commons.

Sir Cresswell Cresswell was appointed Judge of the Probate Court at its commencement. He was likewise the first Judge of the Divorce Court.

The College property—the freehold portion, subject to a yearly rent-charge of £105, and to an annual payment of 5s. 4d., both payable to the Dean and Chapter of St. Paul's—was put up for sale by auction, in one lot, on November 28, 1862. The place was at once demolished, and the materials were sold, the site being utilised in forming the new thoroughfare from Blackfriars to the Mansion House : the roadway passes directly through what once was the College garden.

Chaucer, in his "Canterbury Tales," gives an unfavourable picture of the old sompnour (or apparitor to the Ecclesiastical Court) :—

> " A sompnour was ther with us in that place,
> Thad hadde a fire-red cherubimes face ;
> For sausefleme he was, with eyen narwe.
> As hote he was, and likerous as a sparwe,
> With scalled browes blake, and pilled berd ;
> Of his visage children were sore aferd.
> Ther n'as quiksilver, litarge, ne brimston,
> Boras, ceruse, ne oile of Tartre non,
> Ne oinement that wolde clense or bite,
> That him might helpen of his whelkes white,
> Ne of the nobbes sitting on his chekes.
> Wel loved he garlike, onions, and lekes,
> And for to drinke strong win as rede as blood.
> Than wold he speke, and crie as he were wood.
> And when that he wel dronken had the win,
> Than wold he speken no word but Latin.
> A fewe termes coude he, two or three,
> That he had lerned out of some decree ;
> No wonder is, he herd it all the day.
> And eke ye knowen wel, how that a jay
> Can clepen watte, as well as can the pope.
> But who so wolde in other thing him grope,
> Than hadde he spent all his philosophie,
> Ay, *Questio quid juris* wold he crie."

In 1585 there were but sixteen or seventeen doctors ; in 1694 that swarm had increased to forty-four. In 1595 there were but five proctors ; in 1694 there were forty-three. Yet even in Henry VIII.'s time the proctors were complained of, for being so numerous and clamorous that neither judges nor advocates could be heard. Cranmer, to remedy this evil, attempted to gradually reduce the number to ten, which was petitioned against as insufficient and tending to " delays and prolix suits."

" Doctors' Commons," says Defoe, " was a name very well known in Holland, Denmark, and Sweden, because all ships that were taken during the last wars, belonging to those nations, on suspicion of trading with France, were brought to trial here ; which occasioned that sarcastic saying abroad that we have often heard in conversation, that England was a fine country, but a man called Doctors' Commons was a devil, for there was no getting out of his clutches, let one's cause be never so good, without paying a great deal of money."

A writer in Knight's " London " (1843) gives a pleasant sketch of the Court of Arches in that year. The Common Hall, where the Court of Arches, the Prerogative Court, the Consistory Court, and the Admiralty Court all held their sittings, was a comfortable place, with dark polished wainscoting reaching high up the walls, while above hung the richly emblazoned arms of learned doctors dead and gone ; the fire burned cheerily in the central stove. The dresses of the unengaged advocates in scarlet and ermine, and of the proctors in ermine and black, were picturesque. The opposing advocates sat in high galleries, and the absence of prisoner's dock and jury-box—nay, even of a public—impressed the stranger with a sense of agreeable novelty.

Apropos of the Court of Arches once held in Bow Church. "The Commissary Court of Surrey," says Mr. Jeaffreson, in his "Book about the Clergy," "still holds sittings in the Church of St. Saviour's, Southwark ; and any of my London readers, who are at the small pains to visit that noble church during a sitting of the Commissary's Court, may ascertain for himself that, notwithstanding our reverence for consecrated places, we can still use them as chambers of justice. The court, of course, is a spiritual court, but the great, perhaps the greater, part of the business transacted at its sittings is of an essentially secular kind."

The nature of the business in the Court of Arches may be best shown by the brief summary given in the report for three years—1827, 1828, and 1829. There were 21 matrimonial cases ; 1 of defamation ; 4 of brawling ; 5 church-smiting ; 1 church-rate ; 1 legacy ; 1 tithes ; 4 correction. Of these 17 were appeals from the courts, and 21 original suits.

The cases in the Court of Arches were often very trivial. "There was a case," says Dr. Nicholls, "in which the cause had originally commenced in the Archdeacon's Court at Totnes, and thence there had been an appeal to the Court at Exeter, thence to the Arches, and thence to the Delegates ; after all, the issue having been simply, which of two persons had the right of hanging his hat on a particular peg." The other is of a sadder cast, and calculated to arouse a just indignation. Our authority is Mr. T. W. Sweet (Report on Eccles. Courts), who states : " In one instance, many years since, a suit was instituted which I thought produced a great deal of inconvenience and distress. It was the case of a person of the name of Russell, whose wife was supposed to have had her character impugned at Yarmouth by a Mr. Bentham. He had no remedy at law for the attack upon the lady's character, and a suit for defamation was instituted in the Commons. It was supposed the suit would be attended with very little expense, but I believe in the end it greatly contributed to ruin the party who instituted it; I think he said his proctor's bill would be £700. It went through several courts, and ultimately, I believe (according to the decision or agreement), each party paid his

lying entirely within the diocese where he died, probate or proof of the will is made, or administration taken out, before the bishop or ordinary of that diocese; but if there were goods and chattels only to the amount of £5 (except in the diocese of London, where the amount is £10) —in legal parlance, *bona notabilia*—within any other

THE PREROGATIVE OFFICE, DOCTORS' COMMONS, 1860 (*see page* 293).

own costs." It appears from the evidence subsequently given by the proctor, that he very humanely declined pressing him for payment, and never was paid; and yet the case, through the continued anxiety and loss of time incurred for six or seven years (for the suit lasted that time), mainly contributed, it appears, to the party's ruin.

As the law once stood, says a writer in Knight's "London," if a person died possessed of property

diocese, and which is generally the case, then the jurisdiction lies in the Prerogative Court of the Archbishop of the province—that is, either at York or at Doctors' Commons; the latter, we need hardly say, being the Court of the Archbishop of Canterbury. The two Prerogative Courts therefore engross the great proportion of the business of this kind through the country, for although the Ecclesiastical Courts have no power over the bequests of or succession to unmixed real property, if such were left, cases of that nature seldom or never occur. And, as between the two provinces, not only is that of Canterbury much more important and extensive, but since the introduction of the funding system, and the extensive diffusion of such property, nearly all wills of importance belonging even to the Province of York are also proved in Doctors' Commons, on account of the rule of the Bank of England to

to 30,000. In the same year extracts were taken from wills in 6,414 cases.

On the south side is the entry to the Prerogative Court, and at No. 10 the Faculty Office. On the east side are the offices of the Vicar-General and the Bishop of London, for the issuing of marriage licences. Down till about 1867 the Admiralty Court and the Probate Court were both at Doctors' Commons, but have since been re-

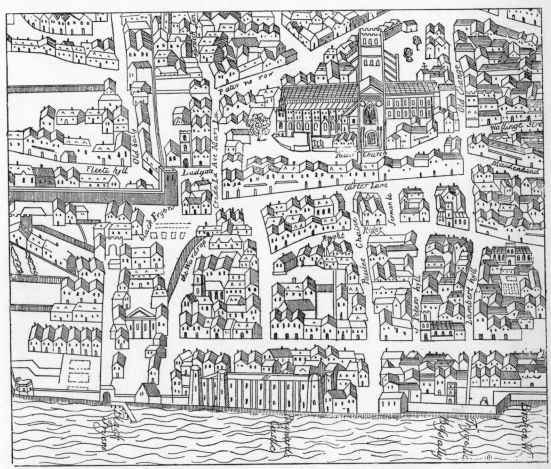

ST. PAUL'S AND NEIGHBOURHOOD. (*From Aggas' Plan*, 1563.)

acknowledge no probate of wills but from thence. To this cause, amongst others, may be attributed the striking fact that the business of this court between the three years ending with 1789 and the three years ending with 1829 had been doubled. Of the vast number of persons affected, or at least interested in this business, evidence might be found not only in the crowded rooms, but also in the statement given in the report of the Select Committee on the Admiralty and other Courts of Doctors' Commons in 1833, where it appears that in one year (1829) the number of searches amounted

moved to Somerset House. The office for proving wills and taking out letters of administration, however, still remains here. The great Admiralty judge of the early part of this century was Dr. Johnson's friend, Lord Stowell, the brother of Lord Eldon.

According to Sir Herbert Jenner Fust, Lord Stowell's decisions during the war have since formed a code of international law almost universally recognised. In one year alone (1806) he pronounced 2,206 decrees. Lord Stowell (then Dr. Scott) was made Advocate-General in Doctors' Commons in 1788, and Vicar-General or official principal for the

Archbishop of Canterbury. Soon after he became Master of the Faculties, and in 1798 was nominated Judge of the High Court of Admiralty, the highest dignity of the Doctors' Commons Courts. During the great French war, it is said Dr. Scott sometimes received as much as £1,000 a case for fees and perquisites in a prize cause. He left at his death personal property exceeding £200,000. He used to say that he admired above all other investments "the sweet simplicity of the Three per Cents.," and when purchasing estate after estate, observed "he liked plenty of elbow-room."

"It was," says Warton, "by visiting Sir Robert Chambers, when a fellow of University College, Oxford, that Johnson became acquainted with Lord Stowell; and when Chambers went to India, Lord Stowell, as he expressed it to me, seemed to succeed to his place in Johnson's friendship."

"Sir William Scott (Lord Stowell)," says Boswell, "told me that when he complained of a headache in the post-chaise, as they were travelling together to Scotland, Johnson treated him in a rough manner—'At your age, sir, I had no headache.'

"Mr. Scott's amiable manners and attachment to our Socrates," says Boswell in Edinburgh, "at once united me to him. He told me that before I came in the doctor had unluckily had a bad specimen of Scottish cleanliness. He then drank no fermented liquor. He asked to have his lemonade made sweeter; upon which the waiter, with his greasy fingers, lifted a lump of sugar and put it into it. The doctor, in indignation, threw it out. Scott said he was afraid he would have knocked the waiter down."

Again Boswell says:—"We dined together with Mr. Scott, now Sir William Scott, his Majesty's Advocate-General, at his chambers in the Temple—nobody else there. The company being so small, Johnson was not in such high spirits as he had been the preceding day, and for a considerable time little was said. At last he burst forth—'Subordination is sadly broken down in this age. No man, now, has the same authority which his father had—except a gaoler. No master has it over his servants; it is diminished in our colleges; nay, in our grammar schools.'"

"Sir William Scott informs me that on the death of the late Lord Lichfield, who was Chancellor of the University of Oxford, he said to Johnson, 'What a pity it is, sir, that you did not follow the profession of the law! You might have been Lord Chancellor of Great Britain, and attained to the dignity of the peerage; and now that the title of Lichfield, your native city, is extinct, you might have had it.' Johnson upon this seemed much agitated, and in an angry tone exclaimed, 'Why will you vex me by suggesting this when it is too late?'"

The strange marriage of Lord Stowell and the Marchioness of Sligo has been excellently described by Mr. Jeaffreson in his "Book of Lawyers."

"On April 10, 1813," says our author, "the decorous Sir William Scott, and Louisa Catherine, widow of John, Marquis of Sligo, and daughter of Admiral Lord Howe, were united in the bonds of holy wedlock, to the infinite amusement of the world of fashion, and to the speedy humiliation of the bridegroom. So incensed was Lord Eldon at his brother's folly that he refused to appear at the wedding; and certainly the chancellor's displeasure was not without reason, for the notorious absurdity of the affair brought ridicule on the whole of the Scott family connection. The happy couple met for the first time in the Old Bailey, when Sir William Scott and Lord Ellenborough presided at the trial of the marchioness's son, the young Marquis of Sligo, who had incurred the anger of the law by luring into his yacht, in Mediterranean waters, two of the king's seamen. Throughout the hearing of that *cause célèbre*, the Marchioness sat in the fetid court of the Old Bailey, in the hope that her presence might rouse amongst the jury or in the bench feelings favourable to her son. This hope was disappointed. The verdict having been given against the young peer, he was ordered to pay a fine of £5,000, and undergo four months' incarceration in Newgate, and—worse than fine and imprisonment — was compelled to listen to a parental address, from Sir William Scott, on the duties and responsibilities of men of high station. Either under the influence of sincere admiration for the judge, or impelled by desire of vengeance on the man who had presumed to lecture her son in a court of justice, the marchioness wrote a few hasty words of thanks to Sir William Scott, for his salutary exhortation to her boy. She even went so far as to say that she wished the erring marquis could always have so wise a counsellor at his side. This communication was made upon a slip of paper, which the writer sent to the judge by an usher of the court. Sir William read the note as he sat on the bench, and having looked towards the fair scribe, he received from her a glance and a smile that were fruitful of much misery to him. Within four months the courteous Sir William Scott was tied fast to a beautiful, shrill, voluble termagant, who exercised marvellous ingenuity in rendering him wretched and contemptible. Reared in a stately school of old-world politeness, the unhappy man was a model of decorum and urbanity. He took reasonable pride in the perfection of his tone and manner, and the marchioness—whose malice did not lack cleverness—was never more happy than when she was gravely expostulating with him, in the presence of numerous auditors, on his lamentable want of style and gentlemanlike bearing. It is said that, like Coke and Holt under similar circumstances, Sir William preferred the quietude of his chambers to the society of an unruly wife, and that in the cellar of his inn he sought compensation for the indignities and sufferings which he endured at home."

"Sir William Scott," says Mr. Surtees, then "removed from Doctors' Commons to his wife's house in Grafton Street, and, ever economical in his domestic expenses, brought with him his own doorplate, and placed it under the pre-existing plate of Lady Sligo, instead of getting a new door-plate for them both. Immediately after the marriage, Mr. Jekyll, so well known in the earliest part of this century for his puns and humour, happening to observe the position of these plates, condoled with Sir William on having to 'knock under.' There was too much truth in the joke for it to be inwardly relished, and Sir William ordered the plates to be transposed. A few weeks later Jekyll accompanied his friend Scott as far as the door, when the latter observed, 'You see I don't knock under now.' 'Not now,' was the answer received by the antiquated bridegroom ; ' now you knock up.'"

There is a good story current of Lord Stowell in Newcastle, that, when advanced in age and rank, he visited the school of his boyhood. An old woman, whose business was to clean out and keep the key of the school-room, conducted him. She knew the name and station of the personage whom she accompanied. She naturally expected some recompense—half-a-crown perhaps—perhaps, since he was so great a man, five shillings. But he lingered over the books, and asked a thousand questions about the fate of his old school-fellows ; and as he talked her expectation rose—half-a-guinea —a guinea—nay, possibly (since she had been so long connected with the school in which the great man took so deep an interest) some little annuity ! He wished her good-bye kindly, called her a good woman, and slipped a piece of money into her hand—it was a sixpence !

"Lord Stowell," says Mr. Surtees, "was a great eater. As Lord Eldon had for his favourite dish liver and bacon, so his brother had a favourite quite as homely, with which his intimate friends, when he dined with them, would treat him. It was a rich pie, compounded of beef steaks and layers of oysters. Yet the feats which Lord Stowell performed with the knife and fork were eclipsed by those which he would afterwards display with the bottle, and two bottles of port formed with him no uncommon potation. By wine, however, he was never, in advanced life at any rate, seen to be affected. His mode of living suited and improved his constitution, and his strength long increased with his years.

At the western end of Holborn there was a room generally let for exhibitions. At the entrance Lord Stowell presented himself, eager to see the "green monster serpent," which had lately issued cards of invitation to the public. As he was pulling out his purse to pay for his admission, a sharp but honest north-country lad, whose business it was to take the money, recognised him as an old customer, and, knowing his name, thus addressed him : "We can't take your shilling, my lord ; 'tis t' old serpent, which you have seen six times before, in other colours ; but ye can go in and see her." He entered, saved his money, and enjoyed his seventh visit to the "real original old sea-sarpint."

Of Lord Stowell it has been said by Lord Brougham that "his vast superiority was apparent when, as from an eminence, he was called to survey the whole field of dispute, and to unravel the variegated facts, disentangle the intricate mazes, and array the conflicting reasons, which were calculated to distract or suspend men's judgment." And Brougham adds that "if ever the praise of being luminous could be bestowed upon human compositions, it was upon his."

It would be impossible with the space at our command to give anything like a tithe of the good stories of this celebrated judge. We must pass on to other famous men who have sat on the judicial bench in Doctors' Commons.

Of Sir Herbert Jenner Fust, one of the great ecclesiastical judges of modern times, Mr. Jeaffreson tells a good story :—

"In old Sir Herbert's later days it was no mere pleasantry, or bold figure of speech, to say that the court had risen, for he used to be lifted from his chair and carried bodily from the chamber of justice by two brawny footmen. Of course, as soon as the judge was about to be elevated by his bearers, the bar rose ; and, also as a matter of course, the bar continued to stand until the strong porters had conveyed their weighty and venerable burden along the platform behind one of the rows of advocates and out of sight. As the trio worked their laborious way along the platform, there seemed to be some danger that they might blunder and fall through one of the windows into the space behind the court ; and at a time when Sir Herbert and

Dr. —— were at open variance, that waspish advocate had, on one occasion, the bad taste to keep his seat at the rising of the court, and with characteristic malevolence of expression say to the footmen, 'Mind, my men, and take care of that judge of yours; or, by Jove, you'll pitch him out of the window.' It is needless to say that this brutal speech did not raise the speaker in the opinion of the hearers."

Dr. Lushington, who died in 1872, aged ninety-one, is another ecclesiastical judge deserving notice. He entered Parliament in 1807, and retired in 1841. He began his political career when the Portland Administration (Perceval, Castlereagh, and Canning) ruled, and was always a steadfast reformer through good and evil report. He was one of the counsel for Queen Caroline, and aided Brougham and Denman in the popular triumph. He worked hard against slavery and for Parliamentary reform, and had heard not only many of Sir Robert Peel and Lord John Russell's earliest speeches, but also those of Mr. Gladstone and Mr. Disraeli. "Though it seemed," says the *Daily News*, "a little incongruous that questions of faith and ritual in the Church, and those of seizures or accidents at sea, should be adjudicated on by the same person, it was always felt that his decisions were based on ample knowledge of the law and diligent attention to the special circumstances of the individual case. As Dean of Arches he was called to pronounce judgment in some of the most exciting ecclesiastical suits of modern times. When the first prosecutions were directed against the Ritualistic innovators, as they were then called, of St. Barnabas, both sides congratulated themselves that the judgment would be given by so venerable and experienced a judge; and perhaps the dissatisfaction of both sides with the judgment proved its justice. In the prosecution of the Rev. H. B. Wilson and Dr. Rowland Williams, Dr. Lushington again pronounced a judgment which, contrary to popular expectation, was reversed on appeal by the Judicial Committee of the Privy Council."

But how can we leave Doctors' Commons without remembering—as we see the touters for licences, who look like half pie-men, half watermen—Sam Weller's inimitable description of the trap into which his father fell?

"Paul's Church-yard, sir," says Sam to Jingle; "a low archway on the carriage-side; bookseller's at one corner, hot-el on the other, and two porters in the middle as touts for licences."

"Touts for licences!" said the gentleman.

"Touts for licences," replied Sam. "Two coves in white aprons, touches their hats when you walk in—'Licence, sir, licence?' Queer sort them, and their mas'rs, too, sir—Old Bailey proctors—and no mistake."

"What do they do?" inquired the gentleman.

"Do! *you*, sir! That ain't the worst on't, neither. They puts things into old gen'lm'n's heads as they never dreamed of. My father, sir, was a coachman, a widower he wos, and fat enough for anything—uncommon fat, to be sure. His missus dies, and leaves him four hundred pound. Down he goes to the Commons to see the lawyer, and draw the blunt—very smart—top-boots on—nosegay in his button-hole—broad-brimmed tile—green shawl—quite the gen'lm'n. Goes through the archway, thinking how he should inwest the money; up comes the touter, touches his hat—'Licence, sir, licence?' 'What's that?' says my father. 'Licence, sir,' says he. 'What licence,' says my father. 'Marriage licence,' says the touter. 'Dash my weskit,' says my father, 'I never thought o' that.' 'I thinks you want one, sir,' says the touter. My father pulls up and thinks a bit. 'No,' says he, 'damme, I'm too old, b'sides I'm a many sizes too large,' says he. 'Not a bit on it, sir,' says the touter. 'Think not?' says my father. 'I'm sure not,' says he; 'we married a gen'lm'n twice your size last Monday.' 'Did you, though?' said my father. 'To be sure we did,' says the touter, 'you're a babby to him—this way, sir—this way!' And sure enough my father walks arter him, like a tame monkey behind a horgan, into a little back office, vere a feller sat among dirty papers, and tin boxes, making believe he was busy. 'Pray take a seat, vile I makes out the affidavit, sir,' says the lawyer. 'Thankee, sir,' says my father, and down he sat, and stared with all his eyes, and his mouth wide open, at the names on the boxes. 'What's your name, sir?' says the lawyer. 'Tony Weller,' says my father. 'Parish?' says the lawyer. 'Belle Savage,' says my father; for he stopped there wen he drove up, and he know'd nothing about parishes, *he* didn't. 'And what's the lady's name?' says the lawyer. My father was struck all of a heap. 'Blessed if I know,' says he. 'Not know!' says the lawyer. 'No more nor you do,' says my father; 'can't I put that in arterwards?' 'Impossible!' says the lawyer. 'Wery well,' says my father, after he'd thought a moment, 'put down Mrs. Clarke.' 'What Clarke?' says the lawyer, dipping his pen in the ink. 'Susan Clarke, Markis o' Granby, Dorking,' says my father; 'she'll have me if I ask, I dessay—I never said nothing to her; but she'll have me, I know.' The licence was made out, and she *did* have him, and what's more she's got him now; and

I never had any of the four hundred pound, worse luck. Beg your pardon, sir," said Sam, when he had concluded, "but when I gets on this here grievance, I runs on like a new barrow with the wheel greased."

The college, rebuilt after the Great Fire, is described by Elmes as an old brick building in the Carolean style, the interior consisting of two quadrangles once occupied by the doctors, a hall for the hearing of causes, a spacious library, a refectory, and other useful apartments. The site of the proctors' offices is now occupied by the Cathedral Choir School, built in 1874. In 1867, when Doctors' Commons was deserted by the proctors, a clever London essayist sketched the ruins very graphically, while the Metropolitan Fire Brigade occupied the lawyers' deserted town :—

" A deserted justice-hall, with dirty mouldering walls, broken doors and windows, shattered floor, and crumbling ceiling. The dust and fog of long-forgotten causes lowering everywhere, making the small leaden-framed panes of glass opaque, the dark wainscot grey, coating the dark rafters with a heavy dingy fur, and lading the atmosphere with a close unwholesome smell. Time and neglect have made the once-white ceiling like a huge map, in which black and swollen rivers and tangled mountain ranges are struggling for pre-eminence. Melancholy, decay, and desolation are on all sides. The holy of holies, where the profane vulgar could not tread, but which was sacred to the venerable gowned figures who cozily took it in turns to dispense justice and to plead, is now open to any passer-by. Where the public were permitted to listen is bare and shabby as a well-plucked client. The inner door of long-discoloured baize flaps listlessly on its hinges, and the true law-court little entrance-box it half shuts in is a mere nest for spiders. A large red shaft, with the word 'broken' rudely scrawled on it in chalk, stands where the judgment-seat was formerly; long rows of ugly piping, like so many shiny dirty serpents, occupy the seats of honour round it; staring red vehicles, with odd brass fittings : buckets, helmets, axes, and old uniforms fill up the remainder of the space. A very few years ago this was the snuggest little law-nest in the world; now it is a hospital and store-room for the Metropolitan Fire Brigade. For we are in Doctors' Commons, and lawyers themselves will be startled to learn that the old Arches Court, the old Admiralty Court, the old Prerogative Court, the old Consistory Court, the old harbour for delegates, chancellors, vicars-general, commissaries, prothonotaries, cursitors, seal-keepers, serjeants-at-mace, doctors, deans, apparitors, proctors,

and what not, is being applied to such useful purposes now. Let the reader leave the bustle of St. Paul's Churchyard, and, turning under the archway where a noble army of white-aproned touters formerly stood, cross Knightrider Street and enter the Commons. The square itself is a memorial of the mutability of human affairs. Its big sombre houses are closed. The well-known names of the learned doctors who formerly practised in the adjacent courts are still on the doors, but have, in each instance, 'All letters and parcels to be addressed' Belgravia, or to one of the western inns of court, as their accompaniment. The one court in which ecclesiastical, testamentary, and maritime law was tried alternately, and which, as we have seen, is now ending its days shabbily, but usefully, is through the further archway to the left. Here the smack *Henry and Betsy* would bring its action for salvage against the schooner *Mary Jane;* here a favoured gentleman was occasionally ' admitted a proctor exercent by virtue of a rescript;' here, as we learnt with awe, proceedings for divorce were ' carried on in pœnam,' and 'the learned judge, without entering into the facts, declared himself quite satisfied with the evidence, and pronounced for the separation;' and here the Dean of Peculiars settled his differences with the eccentrics who, I presume, were under his charge, and to whom he owed his title."

Where the old Probate Court and the reading-room connected with the Will-Office once stood, a large building has been lately erected, in which will for the future be transacted the principal business of the Post-Office Savings' Banks. Such are the changes that take place in our Protean city!

The Prerogative Will Office, of which we shall have more to say when we reach Somerset House, contains many last wills and testaments of great interest. There is a will written in short-hand, and one on a bed-post; but what are these to that of Shakespeare, three folio sheets, and his signature to each sheet! Why he left only his best bed to his wife long puzzled the antiquaries, but has since been explained. There is (or rather was, for it has now gone to Paris) the will of Napoleon, abusing the "oligarch" Wellington, and leaving 10,000 francs to the French officer Cantello, who was accused of a desire to assassinate the " Iron Duke." There are also the wills of Vandyke the painter, who died close by ; of Inigo Jones, Ben Jonson's rival in the Court masques of James and Charles ; of Sir Isaac Newton, Dr. Johnson, good old Izaak Walton, and indeed of almost everybody who had property in the south.

HERALDS' COLLEGE. (*From an old Print.*)

CHAPTER XXV.

HERALDS' COLLEGE.

Early Homes of the Heralds—The Constitution of the Herald's College—Garter King at Arms—Clarencieux and Norroy—The Pursuivants—
Duties and Privileges of Heralds—Good, Bad, and Jovial Heralds—A Notable Norroy King at Arms—The Tragic End of Two Famous
Heralds—The College of Arms' Library.

TURNING from the black dome of St. Paul's, and the mean archway of Dean's Court, into a region of gorgeous blazonments, we come to that quiet and grave house, like an old nobleman's, that stands aside from the new street from the Embankment, like an aristocrat shrinking from a crowd. The original Heralds' College, Cold Harbour House, founded by Richard II., stood in Poultney Lane, but the heralds were turned out by Henry VII., who gave their mansion to Bishop Tunstal, whom he had driven from Durham Palace. The heralds then retired to Ronceval Priory, at Charing Cross, afterwards Northumberland Place. Queen Mary, however, in 1555, gave to Gilbert Dethick, Garter King of Arms, and the other heralds and pursuivants, their present college, formerly Derby

House, which had belonged to the first Earl of Derby, who married Lady Margaret, Countess of Richmond, mother to King Henry VII. The grant specified that there the heralds might dwell together, and "at meet times congregate, speak, confer, and agree among themselves, for the good government of the faculty."

The College of Arms, on the east side of St. Bennet's Hill, was swept away before the Great Fire; but all the records and books, except one or two, were preserved. The estimate for the rebuilding was only £5,000, but the City being drained of cash, it was attempted to raise the money by subscription; only £700, however, was so raised, the rest was paid from office fees, Sir William Dugdale building the north-west corner at his own charge,

THE LAST HERALDIC COURT. (*From an Old Picture in the Heralds' College; the Figures by Rowlandson, Architecture by Wesh.*)

and Sir Henry St. George, Clarencieux, giving £530. This handsome and dignified brick building, completed in 1683, is ornamented with Ionic pilasters, that support an angular pediment, and the "hollow arch of the gateway" was formerly considered a curiosity. The central wainscoted hall is where the Courts of Sessions were at one time held; to the left is the library and search-room, round the top of which runs a gallery; on either side are the apartments of the kings, heralds, and pursuivants.

"This corporation," we are told, "consists of thirteen members—viz., three kings at arms, six heralds at arms, and four pursuivants at arms; they are nominated by the Earl Marshal of England, as ministers subordinate to him in the execution of their offices, and hold their places patent during their good behaviour. They are thus distinguished:—

Kings at Arms.	Heralds.	Pursuivants.
Garter.	Somerset.	Rouge Dragon.
Clarencieux.	Richmond.	Blue Mantle.
Norroy.	Lancaster.	Portcullis.
	Windsor.	Rouge Croix.
	Chester.	
	York.	

"However ancient the offices of heralds may be, we have hardly any memory of their titles or names before Edward III. In his reign military glory and heraldry were in high esteem, and the patents of the King of Arms at this day refer to the reign of King Edward III. The king created the two provincials, by the titles of Clarencieux and Norroy; he instituted Windsor and Chester heralds, and Blue Mantle pursuivant, beside several others by foreign titles. From this time we find the officers of arms employed at home and abroad, both in military and civil affairs: military, with our kings and generals in the army, carrying defiances and making truces, or attending tilts, tournaments, and duels; as civil officers, in negotiations, and attending our ambassadors in foreign Courts; at home, waiting upon the king at Court and Parliament, and directing public ceremonies.

"In the fifth year of King Henry V. armorial bearings were put under regulations, and it was declared that no persons should bear coat arms that could not justify their right thereto by prescription or grant; and from this time they were communicated to persons as *insignia, gentilitia*, and hereditary marks of *noblesse*. About the same time, or soon after, this victorious prince instituted the office of Garter King of Arms; and at a Chapter of the Kings and Heralds, held at the siege of Rouen in Normandy, on the 5th of January, 1420, they formed themselves into a regular society,

with a common seal, receiving Garter as their chief.

"The office of Garter King at Arms was instituted for the service of the Most Noble Order of the Garter; and, for the dignity of that order, he was made sovereign within the office of arms, over all the other officers, subject to the Crown of England, by the name of Garter King at Arms of England. By the constitution of his office he must be a native of England, and a gentleman bearing arms. To him belongs the correction of arms, and all ensigns of arms, usurped or borne unjustly, and the power of granting arms to deserving persons, and supporters to the nobility and Knights of the Bath. It is likewise his office to go next before the sword in solemn processions, none interposing except the marshal; to administer the oath to all the officers of arms; to have a habit like the registrar of the order, baron's service in the Court, lodgings in Windsor Castle; to bear his white rod, with a banner of the ensigns of the order thereon, before the sovereign; also, when any lord shall enter the Parliament chamber, to assign him his place, according to his degree; to carry the ensigns of the order to foreign princes, and to do, or procure to be done, what the sovereign shall enjoin relating to the order, with other duties incident to his office of principal King of Arms. The other two kings are called Provincial kings, who have particular provinces assigned them, which together comprise the whole kingdom of England—that of Clarencieux comprehending all from the river Trent southwards; that of Norroy, or North Roy, all from the river Trent northward. These Kings at Arms are distinguished from each other by their respective badges, which they may wear at all times, either in a gold chain or a ribbon, Garters being blue, and the Provincials purple.

"The six heralds take place according to seniority in office. They are created with the same ceremonies as the kings, taking the oath of an herald, and are invested with a tabard of the Royal arms embroidered upon satin, not so rich as the kings', but better than the pursuivants', with a silver collar of SS.; they are esquires by creation.

"The four pursuivants are also created by the Duke of Norfolk, the Earl Marshal, when they take their oath of a pursuivant, and are invested with a tabard of the Royal arms upon damask. It is the duty of the heralds and pursuivants to attend on the public ceremonials, one of each class together by a monthly rotation.

"These heralds are the king's servants in ordinary, and therefore, in the vacancy of the office of Earl Marshal, have been sworn into their offices by the Lord Chamberlain. Their meetings are termed Chapters, which they hold the first Thursday in every month, or oftener if necessary, wherein all matters are determined by a majority of voices, each king having two voices."

One of the earliest instances of the holding an heraldic court was that in the time of Richard II., when the Scropes and Grosvenors had a dispute about the right to bear certain arms. John of Gaunt and Chaucer were witnesses on this occasion; the latter, who had served in France during the wars of Edward III., and had been taken prisoner, deposed to seeing a certain cognizance displayed during the campaign.

The system of heraldic visitations, when the pedigrees of the local gentry were tested, and the arms they bore approved or cancelled, originated in the reign of Henry VIII. The monasteries, with their tombs and tablets and brasses, and their excellent libraries, had been the great repositories of the provincial genealogies, more especially of the abbeys' founders and benefactors. These records were collected and used by the heralds, who thus as it were preserved and carried on the monastic genealogical traditions. These visitations were of great use to noble families in proving their pedigrees, and preventing disputes about property. The visitations continued till 1686 (James II.), but a few returns appear to have been made as late as 1704. Why they ceased in the reign of William of Orange is not known; perhaps the respect for feudal rank decreased as the new dynasty grew more powerful. The result of the cessation of these heraldic assizes, however, is that American gentlemen, whose Puritan ancestors left England during the persecutions of Charles II., are now unable to trace their descent, and the heraldic gap can never be filled up.

Three instances only of the degradation of knights are recorded in three centuries' records of the Court of Honour. The first was that of Sir Andrew Barclay, in 1322; the second, of Sir Ralph Grey, in 1464; and the third, of Sir Francis Michell, in 1621, the last knight being convicted of heinous offences and misdemeanors. On this last occasion the Knights' Marshals' men cut off the offender's sword, took off his spurs and flung them away, and broke his sword over his head, at the same time proclaiming him "an infamous arrant knave."

The Earl Marshal's office—sometimes called the Court of Honour—took cognizance of words supposed to reflect upon the nobility. Sir Richard Grenville was fined heavily for having said that the Duke of Suffolk was a base lord; and Sir George Markham in the enormous sum of £10,000, for saying, when he had horsewhipped the huntsman of Lord D'Arcy, that he would do the same to his master if he tried to justify his insolence. In 1622 the legality of the court was tried in the Star Chamber by a contumacious herald, who claimed arrears of fees, and to King James's delight the legality of the court was fully established. In 1646 Mr. Hyde (afterwards Lord Chancellor Clarendon) proposed to do away with the court, on account of vexatious causes multiplying, and very arbitrary authority being exercised. He particularly cited a case of great oppression, in which a rich citizen had been ruined in his estate and imprisoned, for merely calling an heraldic swan a goose. After the Restoration, says Mr. Planché, in Knight's "London," the Duke of Norfolk, hereditary Earl Marshal, hoping to re-establish the court, employed Dr. Plott, the learned but credulous historian of Staffordshire, to collect the materials for a history of the court, which, however, was never completed. The court, which had outlived its age, fell into desuetude, and the last cause heard concerning the right of bearing arms (Blount *versus* Blunt) was tried in the year 1720 (George I.). In the old arbitrary times the Earl Marshal's men have been known to stop the carriage of a *parvenu*, and by force deface his illegally assumed arms.

Heralds' fees in the Middle Ages were very high. At the coronation of Richard II. they received £100, and 100 marks at that of the queen. On royal birthdays and on great festivals they also required largess. The natural result of this was that, in the reign of Henry V., William Burgess, Garter King of Arms, was able to entertain the Emperor Sigismund in sumptuous state at his house at Kentish Town.

The escutcheons placed on the walls of the college—one bearing the legs of Man, and the other the eagle's claw of the House of Stanley—are not ancient, and were merely put up to heraldically mark the site of old Derby House.

In the Rev. Mark Noble's elaborate "History of the College of Arms" we find some curious stories of worthy and unworthy heralds. Among the evil spirits was Sir William Dethick, Garter King at Arms, who provoked Elizabeth by drawing out treasonable emblazonments for the Duke of Norfolk, and James I. by hinting doubts, as it is supposed, against the right of the Stuarts to the crown. He was at length displaced. He seems to have been an arrogant, proud, stormy man, who used at public ceremonials to buffet the heralds and pursuivants who blundered or offended him. He was buried at St. Paul's, in 1612, near the grave of Edward III.'s herald, Sir Pain Roet, Guienne King at Arms, and Chaucer's father-in-law. Another black sheep was Cook, Clarencieux King at Arms in the reign of Queen Elizabeth, who was accused of granting arms to any one for a large fee, and of stealing forty or fifty heraldic books from the college library. There was also Ralph Brooke, York Herald in the same reign, a malicious and ignorant man, who attempted to confute some of Camden's genealogies in the "Britannia." He broke open and stole some muniments from the office, and finally, for two felonies, was burnt in the hand at Newgate.

To such rascals we must oppose men of talent and scholarship like the great Camden. This grave and learned antiquary was the son of a painter in the Old Bailey, and, as second master of Westminster School, became known to the wisest and most learned men of London, Ben Jonson honouring him as a father, and Burleigh, Bacon, and Lord Brooke regarding him as a friend. His "Britannia" is invaluable, and his "Annals of Elizabeth" are full of the heroic and soaring spirit of that great age. Camden's house, at Chislehurst, was afterwards the seat of Lord Camden, and in it died the Emperor Napoleon III. of France.

Sir William Le Neve (Charles I.), Clarencieux, was another most learned herald. He is said to have read the king's proclamation at Edgehill with great marks of fear. His estate was sequestered by the Parliament, and he afterwards went mad from loyal and private grief and vexation. In Charles II.'s reign we find the famous antiquary, Elias Ashmole, Windsor Herald for several years. He was the son of a Lichfield saddler, and was brought up as a chorister-boy. That impostor, Lilly, calls him the "greatest virtuoso and curioso" that was ever known or read of in England; for he excelled in music, botany, chemistry, heraldry, astrology, and antiquities. His "History of the Order of the Garter" formed no doubt part of his studies at the College of Arms.

In the same reign as Ashmole, that great and laborious antiquary, Sir William Dugdale, was Garter King of Arms. In early life he became acquainted with Spelman, an antiquary as profound as himself, and with the same mediæval power of work. He fought for King Charles in the Civil Wars. His great work was the "Monasticon Anglicanum," in three volumes folio, which disgusted the Puritans and delighted the Catholics. His "History of Warwickshire" was considered a model of county histories. His "Baronage of England"

contained many errors. In his visitations he was very severe in defacing fictitious arms.

Francis Sandford, first Rouge Dragon Pursuivant, and then Lancaster Herald under Charles II., published an excellent "Genealogical History of England," and curious accounts of the funeral of General Monk and of the coronation of James II. He was so attached to James that he resigned his office at the Revolution, and died, true to the last, old, poor, and neglected, somewhere in Bloomsbury, in 1693.

Sir John Vanbrugh, the witty dramatist, for building Castle Howard, was made Clarencieux King of Arms, to the great indignation of the heralds, whose pedantry he ridiculed. He afterwards sold his place for £2,000, avowing ignorance of his profession and his constant neglect of his official duties.

In the same reign, to Peter Le Neve (Norroy) we are indebted for the careful preservation of the invaluable "Paxton Letters," of the reigns of Henry VI., Edward IV., and Richard III., purchased and afterwards published by Sir John Fenn.

Another eminent herald was John Anstis, created Garter in 1718 (George I.), after being imprisoned as a Jacobite. He wrote learned works on the Orders of the Garter and the Bath, and left behind him valuable materials in MS. for the "History of the College of Arms," now preserved in the library.

Francis Grose, that roundabout, jovial friend of Burns, was Richmond Herald for many years, but he resigned his appointment in 1763, to become Adjutant and Paymaster of the Hampshire Militia. Grose was the son of a Swiss jeweller, who had settled in London. His "Views of Antiquities in England and Wales" helped to restore a taste for Gothic art. He died in 1791.

Of Oldys, that eccentric antiquary, who was Norroy King at Arms in the reign of George II.—the Duke of Norfolk having appointed him from the pleasure he felt at the perusal of his "Life of Sir Walter Raleigh"—Grose gives an amusing account :—

"William Oldys, Norroy King at Arms," says Grose, "author of the 'Life of Sir Walter Raleigh' and of several others in the 'Biographia Britannica,' was natural son of a Dr. Oldys, in the Commons, who kept his mother very privately, and probably very meanly, as when he dined at a tavern he used to beg leave to send home part of the remains of any fish or fowl for his *cat*, which cat was afterwards found out to be Mr. Oldys' mother. His parents dying when he was very young, he soon squandered away his small patrimony, when he became first an attendant in Lord Oxford's library and afterwards librarian. He was a little mean-looking man, of a vulgar address, and, when I knew him, rarely sober in the afternoon, never after supper. His favourite liquor was porter, with a glass of gin between each pot. Dr. Ducarrel told me he used to stint Oldys to three pots of beer whenever he visited him. Oldys seemed to have little classical learning, and knew nothing of the sciences; but for index-reading, title-pages, and the knowledge of scarce English books and editions, he had no equal. This he had probably picked up in Lord Oxford's service, after whose death he was obliged to write for the booksellers for a subsistence. Amongst many other publications, chiefly in the biographical line, he wrote the 'Life of Sir Walter Raleigh,' which got him much reputation. The Duke of Norfolk, in particular, was so pleased with it that he resolved to provide for him, and accordingly gave him the patent of Norroy King at Arms, then vacant. The patronage of that duke occasioned a suspicion of his being a Papist, though I really think without reason; this for a while retarded his appointment. It was underhand propagated by the heralds, who were vexed at having a stranger put in upon them. He was a man of great good-nature, honour, and integrity, particularly in his character as an historian. Nothing, I firmly believe, would ever have biassed him to insert any fact in his writings he did not believe, or to suppress any he did. Of this delicacy he gave an instance at a time when he was in great distress. After the publication of his 'Life of Sir Walter Raleigh,' some booksellers, thinking his name would sell a piece they were publishing, offered him a considerable sum to father it, which he refused with the greatest indignation. He was much addicted to low company; most of his evenings he spent at the 'Bell' in the Old Bailey, a house within the liberties of the Fleet, frequented by persons whom he jocularly called *rulers*, from their being confined to the rules or limits of that prison. From this house a watchman, whom he kept regularly in pay, used to lead him home before twelve o'clock, in order to save sixpence paid to the porter of the Heralds' office, by all those who came home after that time; sometimes, and not unfrequently, two were necessary. He could not resist the temptation of liquor, even when he was to officiate on solemn occasions; for at the burial of the Princess Caroline he was so intoxicated that he could scarcely walk, but reeled about with a crown 'coronet' on a cushion, to the great scandal of his brethren. His method of composing was somewhat singular. He had a number of small parchment bags inscribed with the names of the persons whose lives he intended to write; into these bags he put every circumstance and anecdote he could collect, and from thence drew up his history. By his excesses he was kept poor, so that he was frequently in distress; and at his death, which happened about five on Wednesday morning, April 15th, 1761, he left little more than was sufficient to bury him. Dr. Taylor, the oculist, son of the famous doctor of that name and profession, claimed administration at the Commons, on account of his being *nullius filius*—Anglicè, a bastard. He was buried the 19th following, in the north aisle of the Church of St. Benet, Paul's Wharf, towards the upper end of the aisle. He was about seventy-two years old. Amongst his works is a preface to Izaak Walton's 'Angler.'"

The following pretty anacreontic, on a fly drinking out of his cup of ale, which is doubtless well known, is from the pen of Oldys :—

> "Busy, curious, thirsty fly,
> Drink with me, and drink as I;
> Freely welcome to my cup,
> Couldst thou sip and sip it up.
> Make the most of life you may;
> Life is short, and wears away.

> "Both alike are mine and thine,
> Hastening quick to their decline;
> Thine's a summer, mine no more,
> Though repeated to threescore;
> Threescore summers, when they're gone,
> Will appear as short as one."

The Rev. Mark Noble comments upon Grose's text by saying that this story of the crown must be incorrect, as the coronet at the funeral of a princess is always carried by Clarencieux, and not by Norroy.

In 1794, two eminent heralds, Benjamin Pingo, York Herald, and John Charles Brooke, Somerset Herald, were crushed to death in a crowd at the side door of the Haymarket Theatre. Mr. Brooke had died standing, and was found as if asleep, and with colour still in his cheeks.

Edmund Lodge, Lancaster Herald, who died in 1839, is chiefly known for his interesting series of "Portraits of Illustrious British Personages," accompanied by excellent biographical memoirs, and for his invaluable "Peerage."

During the Middle Ages heralds were employed to bear letters, defiances, and treaties to foreign princes and persons in authority; to proclaim war, and bear offers of marriage, &c.; and after battles to catalogue the dead, and note their rank by the heraldic bearings on their banners, shields, and tabards. In later times they were allowed to correct false crests, arms, and cognizances, and register noble descents in their archives. They conferred arms on those who proved themselves able to maintain the state of a gentleman, they marshalled great or rich men's funerals, arranged armorial bearings for tombs and stained-glass windows, and laid down the laws of precedence at state ceremonials. Arms, it appears from Mr. Planché, were sold to the "new rich" as early as the reign of King Henry VIII., who wished to make a new race of gentry, in order to lessen the power of the old nobles. The fees varied then from £6 13s. 6d. to £5.

In the old times the heralds' messengers were able:—A book of emblazonment executed for Prince Arthur, the brother of Henry VIII., who died young, and whose widow Henry married ; the Warwick Roll, a series of figures of all the Earls of Warwick from the Conquest to the reign of Richard III., executed by Rouse, a celebrated antiquary of Warwick, at the close of the fifteenth century ; and a tournament roll of Henry VIII., in which that stalwart monarch is depicted in regal state, with all the "pomp, pride, and circumstance of glorious (mimic) war." In the gallery over the library are to be seen the sword and dagger which belonged to the unfortunate James of Scotland,

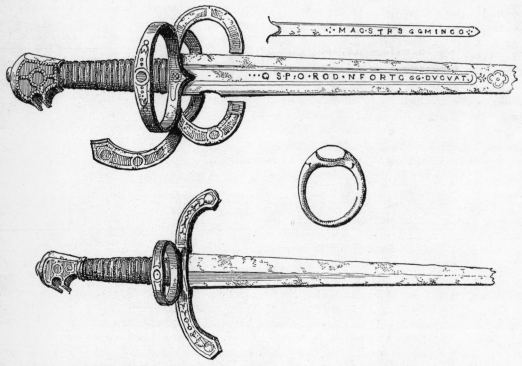

SWORD, DAGGER, AND RING OF KING JAMES OF SCOTLAND. (*Preserved in the Heralds' College.*)

called knights caligate. After seven years' service they became knight-riders, our modern Queen's messengers ; after seven years more they became pursuivants, and then heralds. In later times, says Mr. Planché, the herald's honourable office was transferred to nominees of the Tory nobility, discarded valets, butlers, or sons of upper servants. Mr. Canning, when Premier, very properly put a stop to this system, and appointed to this post none but young and intelligent men of manners and education.

Among the many curious volumes of genealogy in the library of the College of Arms—volumes which have been the result of centuries of research and patient study—the following are chiefly notice-

that chivalrous king who died fighting to the last on the hill at Flodden. The sword-hilt has been enamelled, and still shows traces of gilding which has once been red-wet with the Southron's blood ; and the dagger is a strong and serviceable weapon, as no doubt many an English archer and billman that day felt. The heralds also show the plain turquoise ring which tradition says the French queen sent James, begging him to ride a foray in England. Copies of it have been made by the London jewellers. These trophies are heirlooms of the house of Howard, whose bend argent, to use the words of Mr. Planché, "received the honourable augmentation of the Scottish lion, in testimony of the prowess displayed by the gallant soldier who commanded the English forces on that memorable occasion." Here are also to be seen a portrait of Talbot, Earl of Shrewsbury, the great warrior, from his tomb in Old St. Paul's; a curious pedigree of the Saxon kings from Adam, illustrated with many beautiful drawings in pen and ink, about the

Lodge derived his well-known "Illustrations of British History;" notes, &c., made by Glover, Vincent, Philpot, and Dugdale; a volume in the handwriting of the venerable Camden ("Clarencieux"); and the collections of Sir Edward Walker, Secretary at War, *temp.* Charles I.

LINACRE'S HOUSE. *From a Print in the " Gold-headed Cane" (see page* 303).

period of Henry VIII., representing the Creation, Adam and Eve in Paradise, the building of Babel, the rebuilding of the Temple, &c. &c.; MSS., consisting chiefly of heralds' visitations, records of grants of arms and royal licences; records of modern pedigrees (*i.e.*, since the discontinuance of the visitations in 1687); a most valuable collection of official funeral certificates; a portion of the Arundel MSS.; the Shrewsbury or Cecil papers, from which

The Wardrobe, a house long belonging to the Government, in the Blackfriars, was built by Sir John Beauchamp (died 1359), whose tomb in Old St. Paul's was usually taken for the tomb of the good Duke Humphrey. Beauchamp's executors sold it to Edward III., and it was subsequently converted into the office of the Master of the Wardrobe, and the repository for the royal clothes. When Stow drew up his "Survey," Sir John Fortescue was lodged in the house as Master of the Wardrobe. What a royal ragfair this place must have been for rummaging antiquaries, equal to twenty Madame Tussaud's and all the ragged regiments of Westminster Abbey put together!

"There were also kept," says Fuller, "in this place the ancient clothes of our English kings, which they wore on great festivals; so that this Wardrobe was in effect a library for antiquaries, therein to read the mode and fashion of garments in all ages. These King James in the beginning of his reign gave to the Earl of Dunbar, by whom they were sold, re-sold, and re-re-re-sold at as many hands almost as Briareus had, some gaining vast estates thereby." (Fuller's "Worthies.")

We mentioned before that Shakespeare in his will left to his favourite daughter, Susannah, the Warwickshire doctor's wife, a house near the Wardrobe; but the exact words of the document may be worth quoting:—

"I gyve, will, bequeath," says the poet, "and devise unto my daughter, Susannah Hall, all that messuage or tenement, with the appurtenances, wherein one John Robinson dwelleth, situat, lying, and being in the Blackfriars in London, nere the Wardrobe."

After the Great Fire the Wardrobe was removed, first to the Savoy, and afterwards to Buckingham Street, in the Strand. The last master was Ralph, Duke of Montague, on whose death, in 1709, the office, says Cunningham, was, "I believe, abolished."

Swan Alley, near the Wardrobe, reminds us of the Beauchamps, for the swan was the cognizance of the Beauchamp family, long distinguished residents in this part of London.

In the Council Register of the 18th of August, 1618, there may be seen "A List of Buildings and Foundations since 1615." It is therein said that Edward Alleyn, Esq., dwelling at Dulwich (the well-known player and founder of Dulwich College), had built six tenements of timber upon new foundations, within two years past, in Swan Alley, near the Wardrobe."

In Great Carter Lane stood the old Bell Inn, whence, in 1598, Richard Quyney directs a letter "To my loving good friend and countryman, Mr. Wm. Shackespeare, deliver thees"—the only letter addressed to Shakespeare known to exist. The original was in the possession of Mr. R. B. Wheeler, of Stratford-upon-Avon.

Stow mixes up the old houses near Doctors' Commons with Rosamond's Bower at Woodstock. "Upon Paul's Wharf Hill," he says, "within a great gate, next to the Doctors' Commons, were many fair tenements, which, in their leases made from the Dean and Chapter, went by the name of *Camera Dianæ*—*i.e.*, Diana's Chamber, so denominated from a spacious building that in the time of Henry II. stood where they were. In this Camera, an arched and vaulted structure, full of intricate ways and windings, this Henry II. (as some time he did at Woodstock) kept, or was supposed to have kept, that jewel of his heart, Fair *Rosamond*, she whom there he called *Rosamundi*, and here by the name of Diana; and from hence had this house that title.

"For a long time there remained some evident testifications of tedious turnings and windings, as also of a passage underground from this house to Castle Baynard; which was, no doubt, the king's way from thence to his Camera Dianæ, or the chamber of his brightest Diana.

"St. Anne's, within the precinct of the Blackfriars, was pulled down with the Friars Church by Sir Thomas Cawarden, Master of the Revels; but in the reign of Queen Mary, he being forced to find a church to the inhabitants, allowed them a lodging chamber above a stair, which since that time, to wit in the year 1597, fell down, and was again, by collection therefore made, new built and enlarged in the same year."

The parish register records the burials of Isaac Oliver, the miniature painter (1617), Dick Robinson, the player (1647), Nat. Field, the poet and player (1632–3), William Faithorn, the engraver (1691); and there are the following interesting entries relating to Vandyck, who lived and died in this parish, leaving a sum of money in his will to its poor:—

"Jasper Lanfranch, a Dutchman, from Sir Anthony Vandikes, buried 14th February, 1638."

"Martin Ashent, Sir Anthony Vandike's man, buried 12th March, 1638."

"Justinia, daughter to Sir Anthony Vandyke and his lady, baptised 9th December, 1641."

The child was baptised on the very day her illustrious father died.

A portion of the old burying-ground is still to be seen in Church-entry, Ireland Yard.

"In this parish of St. Benet's, in Thames Street," says Stow, "stood Le Neve Inn, belonging formerly to John de Mountague, Earl of Salisbury, and after to Sir John Beauchamp, Kt., granted to Sir Thomas Erpingham, Kt., of Erpingham in Norfolk, and Warden of the Cinque Ports, Knight of the Garter. By the south end of Adle Street, almost against Puddle Wharf, there is one antient building of stone and timber, builded by the Lords of Berkeley, and therefore called Berkeley's Inn. This house is now all in ruin, and letten out in several tenements; yet the arms of the Lord Berkeley remain in the stone-work of an arched gate; and is between a chevron, crosses ten, three, three, and four."

Richard Beauchamp, Earl of Warwick, was lodged in this house, then called Berkeley's Inn, in the parish of St. Andrew, in the reign of Henry VI.

St. Andrew's Wardrobe Church is situated upon rising ground, on the east side of Puddle-Dock Hill, in the ward of Castle Baynard. The advowson of this church was anciently in the noble family of Fitzwalter, to which it probably came by virtue of the office of Constable of the Castle of London, that is, Baynard's Castle. That it is not of a modern foundation is evident by its having had Robert Marsh for its rector, before the year 1322. This church was anciently denominated "St. Andrew juxta Baynard's Castle," from its vicinity to that palace.

"Knightrider Street was so called," says Stow "(as is supposed), from knights riding thence through the street west to Creed Lane, and so out at Ludgate towards Smithfield, when they went there to tourney, joust, or otherwise to show acti-vities before the king and states of the realm."

Linacre's house in Knightrider Street was given by him to the College of Physicians, and was used as their place of meeting till the early part of the seventeenth century.

In his student days Linacre had been patronised by Lorenzo de Medicis, and at Florence, under Demetrius Chalcondylas, who had fled from Con-stantinople when it was taken by the Turks, he acquired a perfect knowledge of the Greek language. He studied eloquence at Bologna, under Politian, one of the most eloquent Latinists in Europe, and while he was at Rome devoted himself to medicine and the study of natural philosophy, under Her-molaus Barbarus. Linacre was the first English-man who read Aristotle and Galen in the original Greek. On his return to England, having taken the degree of M.D. at Oxford, he gave lectures in physic, and taught the Greek language in that university. His reputation soon became so high that King Henry VII. called him to court, and entrusted him with the care of the health and edu-cation of his son, Prince Arthur. To show the extent of his acquirements, we may mention that he instructed Princess Katharine in the Italian lan-guage, and that he published a work on mathe-matics, which he dedicated to his pupil, Prince Arthur.

His treatise on grammar was warmly praised by Melancthon. This great doctor was successively physician to Henry VII., Henry VIII., Edward VI., and the Princess Mary. He established lectures on physic (says Dr. Macmichael, in his amusing book, "The Gold-headed Cane"), and towards the close of his life he founded the Royal College of Physicians, holding the office of President for seven years. Linacre was a friend of Lily, the grammarian, and was consulted by Erasmus. The College of Physicians first met in 1518 at Linacre's house (now called the Stone House), Knightrider Street, and which still belongs to the society. Between the two centre windows of the first floor are the arms of the college, granted 1546—a hand proper, vested argent, issuing out of clouds, and feeling a pulse; in base, a pomegranate between five demi fleurs-de-lis border-ing the edge of the escutcheon. In front of the build-ing was a library, and there were early donations of books, globes, mathematical instruments, minerals, &c. Dissections were first permitted by Queen Elizabeth, in 1564. As soon as the first lec-tures were founded, in 1583, a spacious anatomical theatre was built adjoining Linacre's house, and here the great Dr. Harvey gave his first course of lectures; but about the time of the accession of Charles I. the College removed to a house of the Dean and Chapter of St. Paul's, at the bottom of Amen Corner, where they planted a botanical garden and built an anatomical theatre. During the civil wars the Parliament levied £5 a week on the College. Eventually sold by the Puritans, the house and gardens were purchased by Dr. Harvey and given to the society. The great Harvey built a museum and library at his own expense, which were opened in 1653, and Harvey, then nearly eighty, relinquished his office of Pro-fessor of Anatomy and Surgery. The garden at this time extended as far west as the Old Bailey, and as far south as St. Martin's Church. Harvey's gift consisted of a convocation room and a library, to which Selden contributed some Oriental MS., Elias Ashmole many valuable volumes, the Marquis of Dorchester £100; and Sir Theodore Mayerne, physician to four kings—viz., Henry IV. of France, James I., Charles I., and Charles II.—left his library. The old library was turned into a lecture and reception room, for such visitors as Charles II., who in 1665 attended here the anatomical præ-lections of Dr. Ent, whom he knighted on the occasion. This building was destroyed by the Great Fire, from which only 112 folio books were saved. The College never rebuilt its premises, and on the site were erected the houses of three residentiaries of St. Paul's. Shortly after a piece of ground was purchased in Warwick Lane, and the new building opened in 1674. A similar grant to that of Linacre's was that of Dr. Lettsom, who in the year 1773 gave the house and library in Bolt Court, which was at one time occupied by the Medical Society of London.

The view of Linacre's House, in Knightrider Street, which we give on page 301, is taken from a print in the "Gold-headed Cane," an amusing work to which we have already referred.

CHAPTER XXVI.

CHEAPSIDE—INTRODUCTORY AND HISTORICAL.

Ancient Reminiscences of Cheapside—Stormy Days therein—The Westchepe Market—Something about the Pillory—The Cheapside Conduits—The Goldsmiths' Monopoly—Cheapside Market—Gossip anent Cheapside by Mr. Pepys—A Saxon Rienzi—Anti-Free-Trade Riots in Cheapside—Arrest of the Rioters—A Royal Pardon—Jane Shore.

WHAT a wealth and dignity there is about Cheapside; what restless life and energy ; with what vigorous pulsation life beats to and fro in that great commercial artery ! How pleasantly on a summer morning that last of the Mohicans, the green plane-tree now deserted by the rooks, at the corner of Wood Street, flutters its leaves ! How fast the crowded omnibuses dash past with their loads of young Greshams and future rulers of Lombard Street ! How grandly Bow steeple bears itself, rising proudly in the sunshine ! How the great webs of gold chains sparkle in the jeweller's windows ! How modern everything looks ! And yet only a short time since some workmen at a foundation in Cheapside, twenty-five feet below the surface, came upon traces of primeval inhabitants in the shape of a deer's skull, with antlers, and the skull of a wolf, struck down, perhaps, more than a thousand years ago, by the bronze axe of some British savage. So the world rolls on: the times change, and we change with them.

The engraving which we give on page 307 is from one of the most ancient representations extant of Cheapside. It shows the street decked out in holiday attire for the procession of the wicked old queen-mother, Marie de Medici, on her way to visit her son-in-law, Charles I., and her wilful daughter, Henrietta Maria.

The City records, explored with such unflagging interest by Mr. Riley in his "Memorials of London," furnish us with some interesting gleanings relating to Cheapside. In the old letter books in the Guildhall—the Black Book, Red Book, and White Book—we see it in storm and calm, observe the vigilant and jealous honesty of the guilds, and become witnesses again to the bloody frays, cruel punishments, and even the petty disputes of the middle-age craftsmen, when Cheapside was one glittering row of goldsmiths' shops, and the very heart of the wealth of London. The records culled so carefully by Mr. Riley are brief but pregnant;

they give us facts uncoloured by the historian, and highly suggestive glimpses of strange modes of life in wild and picturesque eras of our civilisation. Let us take the most striking *seriatim*.

In 1273 the candle-makers seem to have taken a fancy to Cheapside, where the horrible fumes of that necessary but most offensive trade soon excited the ire of the rich citizens, who at last expelled seventeen of the craft from their sheds in Chepe. In the third year of Edward II. it was ordered and commanded on the king's behalf, that "no man or woman should be so bold as henceforward to hold common market for merchandise in Chepe, or any other highway within the City, except Cornhill, after the hour of nones " (probably about three p.m.) ; and the same year it was forbidden, under pain of imprisonment, to scour pots in the roadway of Chepe, to the hindrance of folks who were passing ; so that we may conclude that in the London of Edward II. there was a good deal of that out-door work which the traveller still sees in the back streets of Continental towns.

Holocausts of spurious goods were not uncommon in Cheapside. In 1311 (Edward II.) we find that at the request of the hatters and haberdashers, search had been made for traders selling " bad and cheating hats," that is, of false and dishonest workmanship, made of a mixture of wool and flocks. The result was the seizure of forty grey and white hats, and fifteen black, which were publicly burnt in the street of Chepe. What a burning such a search would lead to in our less scrupulous days ! Why, the pile would reach half way up St. Paul's. Illegal nets had been burnt opposite Friday Street in the previous reign. After the hats came a burning of fish panniers defective in measure ; while in the reign of Edward III. some false chopins (wine measures) were destroyed. This was rough justice, but still the seizures seem to have been far fewer than they would be in our boastful epoch.

There was a generous lavishness about the royalty of the Middle Ages, however great a fool or scoundrel the monarch might be. Thus we read that on the safe delivery of Queen Isabel (wife of Edward II.), in 1312, of a son, afterwards Edward III., the Conduit in Chepe, for one day, ran with nothing but wine for all those who chose to drink there; and at the cross, hard by the church of St. Michael in West Chepe, there was a pavilion extended in the middle of the street, in which was set a tun of wine for all passers-by to drink of.

The mediæval guilds, useful as they were in keeping trades honest (Heaven knows they need supervision enough now !) still gave rise to jealousies and feuds. The sturdy craftsmen of those days, inured to arms, flew to the sword as the quickest arbitrator, and preferred clubs and bills to Chancery courts and Common Pleas. The stones of Chepe were often crimsoned with the blood of these angry disputants. Thus, in 1327, under Edward III., the saddlers and the joiners and bit-makers came to blows. In May of that year armed parties of these rival trades fought right and left in Cheapside and Cripplegate. The whole city ran to the windows in alarm, and several workmen were killed and many mortally wounded, to the great scandal of the City, and the peril of many quiet people. The conflict at last became so serious that the mayor, aldermen, and sheriffs had to interpose, and the dispute came to be finally settled at a great discussion of the three trades at the Guildhall, with what result the record does not state.

In this same reign of Edward III. the excessive length of the tavern signs or "ale-stakes," as they were then called, was complained of by persons riding in Cheapside. All the taverners of the City were therefore summoned to the Guildhall, and warned that no sign or bush (hence the proverb, "Good wine needs no bush") should henceforward extend over the king's highway beyond the length of seven feet, under pain of a fine of forty pence to the chamber of the Guildhall.

In 1340 (Edward III.) two more guilds fell to quarrelling. This time it was the pelterers (furriers) and fishmongers, who seem to have tanned each other's hides with considerable zeal. It came at last to this, that the portly mayor and sheriffs had to venture out among the sword-blades, cudgels, and whistling volleys of stones, but at first with little avail, for the combatants were too hot. They soon arrested some scaly and fluffy misdoers, it is true; but then came a wild rush, and the noisy combatants were rescued; and, most audacious of all, one Thomas, son of John Hansard, fishmonger, with sword drawn (terrible to relate !), seized the mayor by his august throat, and tried to lop him on the neck; and one brawny rascal, John le Brewere, a porter, desperately wounded one of the City serjeants: so that here, as the fishmongers would have observed, "there was a pretty kettle of fish." For striking a mayor blood for blood was the only expiation, and Thomas and John were at once tried at the Guildhall, found guilty on their own confession, and beheaded in Chepe; upon hearing which Edward III. wrote to the mayor, and complimented him on his display of energy on this occasion.

Chaucer speaks of the restless 'prentices of Chepe under Edward III. :—

> "A prentis dwelled whilom in our citee—
> At every bridale would he sing and hoppe;
> He loved bet the taverne than the shoppe—
> For when ther eny riding was in Chepe
> Out of the shoppe thider wold he lepe,
> And til that he had all the sight ysein,
> And danced wel, he wold not come agen."
>
> (*The Coke's Tale.*)

In the luxurious reign of Richard II. the guilds were again vigilant, and set fire to a number of caps that had been oiled with rank grease, and that had been frilled by the feet and not by the hand, "so being false and made to deceive the commonalty." In this same reign (1393), when the air was growing dark with coming mischief, an ordinance was passed prohibiting secret huckstering of stolen and bad goods by night "in the common hostels," instead of the two appointed markets held every feast-day, by daylight only, in "Westchepe" and Cornhill. The Westchepe market was held by day between St. Lawrence Lane and a house called "the Cage," between the first and second bell, and special provision was made that at these markets no crowd should obstruct the shops adjacent to the open-air market. To close the said markets the "bedel of the ward" was to ring a bell (probably, says Mr. Riley, the bell on the Tun, at Cornhill) twice—first, an hour before sunset, and another final one half an hour later. Another civic edict relating to markets occurs in 1379, under Richard II., when the stands for stalls at the High Cross of Chepe were let by the mayor and chamberlain at 13s. 4d. each. At the same time the stalls round the brokers' cross, at the north door of St. Paul's, erected by the Earl of Gloucester in the reign of Henry III., were let at 10s. and 6s. 8d. each. The stationers, or vendors of small wares, on the taking down of the Cross in 1390, probably retired to Paternoster Row.

The punishment of the pillory, either in Cheapside or Cornhill, the "Letter Book" does not say which, was freely used in the Middle Ages for scandal-mongers, dishonest traders, and forgers; and very deterring the shameful exposure must have been to even the most brazen offender. Thus, in the reign of Richard II., we find John le Strattone, for obtaining thirteen marks by means of a forged letter, was led through Chepe with trumpets and pipes to the pillory on "Cornhalle" for one hour, on two successive days.

For the sake of classification we may here mention a few earlier instances of the same ignominious punishment. In 1372, under Edward III., Nicholas Mollere, a smith's servant, for spreading a lying report that foreign merchants were to be allowed the same rights as freemen of the City, was set in the pillory for one hour, with a whetstone hung round his neck. In the same heroic reign Thomas Lanbye, a chapman, for selling rims of base metal for cups, pretending them to be silvergilt, was put in the pillory for two hours; while in 1382, under Richard II., we find Roger Clerk, of Wandsworth, for pretending to cure a poor woman of fever by a talisman wrapped in cloth of gold, was ridden through the City to the music of trumpets and pipes; and the same year a cook in Bread Street, for selling stale slices of cooked conger, was put in the pillory for an hour, and the said fish burned under his rascally nose.

Sometimes, however, the punishment awarded to these civic offenders consisted in less disgraceful penance, as, for instance, in the reign of Richard II., a man named Highton, who had assaulted a worshipful alderman, was sentenced to lose his hand; but the man being a servant of the king, was begged off by certain lords, on condition of his walking through Chepe and Fleet Street, carrying a lighted wax candle of three pounds' weight to St. Dunstan's Church, where he was to offer it on the altar.

In 1591, when Elizabeth sent her brave but rash young favourite, Essex, with 3,500 men, to help Henry IV. to besiege Rouen, two fanatics named Coppinger and Ardington, the former calling himself a prophet of mercy and the latter a prophet of vengeance, proclaimed their missions in Cheapside, and were at once laid by the heels. But the old public punishment still continued, for in 1,600, the year before the execution of Essex, we read that "Mrs. Fowler's case was decided" by sentencing that lady to be whipped in Bridewell; while a Captain Hermes was sent to the pillory, his brother was fined £100 and imprisoned, and Gascone, a soldier, was sentenced to ride to the Cheapside pillory with his face to the horse's tail,

to be there branded in the face, and afterwards imprisoned for life.

In 1578, when Elizabeth was coquetting with Anjou and the French marriage, we find in one of those careful lists of the Papists of London kept by her subtle councillors, a Mr. Loe, vintner, of the "Mitre," Cheapside, who married a sister of Bishop Bonner. In 1587, the year before the defeat of the Armada, and when Leicester's army was still in Holland, doing little, and the very month that Sir William Stanley and 13,000 Englishmen surrendered Deventer to the Prince of Parma, we find the Council writing to the Lord Mayor about a mutiny, requiring him "to see that the soldiers levied in the City for service in the Low Countries, who had mutinied against Captain Sampson, be punished with some severe and extraordinary correction: to be tied to carts and flogged through Cheapside to Tower Hill, then to be set upon a pillory, and each to have one ear cut off."

In the reign of James I. the same ignominious and severe punishment continued; for in 1611 one Floyd, we know not for what offence, was fined £5,000, sentenced to be whipped to the pillories of Westminster and Cheapside, to be branded in the face, and then imprisoned in Newgate.

To return to our historical sequence. In 1388 (Richard II.) it was ordered that every person selling fish taken east of London Bridge should sell the same at the Cornhill market; while all Thames fish caught west of the bridge were to be sold near the conduit in Chepe, and nowhere else, under pain of forfeiture of the fish.

The eleventh year of Richard II. brought a real improvement to the growing city, for certain "substantial men of the ward of Farringdon Within" were then allowed to build a new water-conduit near the church of St. Michael le Quern, in Westchepe, to be supplied by the great pipe opposite St. Thomas of Accon, providing the great conduit should not be injured; and on this occasion the Earl of Gloucester's broken cross at St. Paul's was removed.

Early in the reign of Henry V. complaints were made by the poor that the brewers, who rented the fountains and chief upper pipe of the Cheapside conduit, drew also from the smaller pipe below, and the brewers were warned that for every future offence they would be fined 6s. 8d. In the fourth year of this chivalrous monarch a "hostiller" named Benedict Wolman, under-marshal of the Marshalsea, was condemned to death for a conspiracy to bring a man named Thomas Ward, *alias* Trumpington, from Scotland, and to pass him off as Richard II.

ANCIENT VIEW OF CHEAPSIDE.

(From La Serre's "Entrée de la Reyne Mère du Roy," showing the Procession of Mary de Medicis.)

Wolman was drawn through Cornhill and Cheapside to the gallows at Tyburn, where he was "hanged and beheaded."

Lydgate, that dull Suffolk monk, who followed Chaucer, though at a great distance, has, in his ballad of "Lackpenny," described Chepe in the reign of Henry VI. The hero of the poem says—

> "Then to the Chepe I gan me drawn,
> 　Where much people I saw for to stand;
> One offered me velvet, silk, and lawn;
> 　Another he taketh me by the hand,
> 　'Here is Paris thread, the finest in the land.'
> I never was used to such things indeed,
> And, wanting money, I might not speed."

In 1622 the traders of the Goldsmiths' Company began to complain that alien traders were creeping into and alloying the special haunts of the trade, Goldsmiths' Row and Lombard Street; and that 183 foreign goldsmiths were selling counterfeit jewels, engrossing the business and impoverishing its members.

City improvements were carried with a high hand in the reign of Charles I., who, determined to clear Cheapside of all but goldsmiths, in order to make the eastern approach to St. Paul's grander, committed to the Fleet some of the alien traders who refused to leave Cheapside. This unfortunate monarch seems to have carried out even his smaller measures in a despotic and unjustifiable manner, as we see from an entry in the State Papers, October 2, 1634. It is a petition of William Bankes, a Cheapside tavern-keeper, and deposes:—

"Petition of William Bankes to the king. Not fully twelve months since, petitioner having obtained a licence under the Great Seal to draw wine and vent it at his house in Cheapside, and being scarce entered into his trade, it pleased his Majesty, taking into consideration the great disorders that grew by the numerous taverns within London, to stop so growing an evil by a total suppression of victuallers in Cheapside, &c., by which petitioner is much decayed in his fortune. Beseeches his Majesty to grant him (he not being of the Company of Vintners in London, but authorised merely by his Majesty) leave to victual and retail meat, it being a thing much desired by noblemen and gentlemen of the best rank and others (for the which, if they please, they may also contract beforehand, as the custom is in other countries), there being no other place fit for them to eat in the City."

The foolish determination to make Cheapside more glittering and showy seems again to have struck the weak despot, and an order of the Council, November 16, went forth that—"Whereas in Goldsmith's Row, in Cheapside and Lombard Street, divers shops are held by persons of other trades, whereby that uniform show which was an ornament to those places and a lustre to the City is now greatly diminished," all the shops in Goldsmith's Row are to be occupied by none but goldsmiths; and all the goldsmiths who keep shops in other parts of the City are to resort thither, or to Lombard Street or Cheapside."

The next year we find a tradesman who had been expelled from Goldsmiths' Row praying bitterly to be allowed to stay a year longer, as he cannot find a residence, the removal of houses in Cheapside, Lombard Street, and St. Paul's Churchyard having rendered shops scarce.

In 1637 the king returns again to the charge, and determines to carry out his tyrannical whim by the following order of the Council :—"The Council threaten the Lord Mayor and aldermen with imprisonment, if they do not forthwith enforce the king's command that all shops should be shut up in Cheapside and Lombard Street that were not goldsmiths' shops." The Council "had learned that there were still twenty-four houses and shops that were not inhabited by goldsmiths, but in some of them were one Grove and Widow Hill, stationers; one Sanders, a drugster; Medcalfe, a cook; Renatus Edwards, a girdler; John Dover, a milliner; and Brown, a bandseller."

In 1664 we discover from a letter of the Dutch ambassador, Van Goch, to the States-General, that a great fire in Cheapside, "the principal street of the City," had burned six houses. In this reign the Cheapside market seems to have given great vexation to the Cheapside tradesmen. In 1665 there is a State Paper to this effect :—

"The inquest of Cheap, Cripplegate, Cordwainer, Bread Street, and Farringdon Within wards, to the Lord Mayor and Court of Aldermen of London. In spite of orders to the contrary, the abuses of Cheapside Market continue, and the streets are so pestered and encroached on that the passages are blocked up and trade decays. Request redress by fining those who allow stalls before their doors except at market times, or by appointing special persons to see to the matter, and disfranchise those who disobey; the offenders are 'marvellous obstinate and refractory to all good orders,' and not to be dealt with by common law."

Pepys, in his inimitable "Diary," gives us two interesting glimpses of Cheapside; one of the fermenting times immediately preceding the Restoration; the other a few years later, showing the effervescing spirit of the London 'prentices of the time of Charles II. :—

" 1659.—Coming home, heard that in Cheapside there had been but a little before a gibbet set up, and the picture of Huson hung upon it in the middle of the street. (John Hewson, who had been a shoemaker, became a colonel in the Parliament army, and sat in judgment on the king. He escaped hanging by flight, and died in 1662 at Amsterdam.)

" 1664.—So home, and in Cheapside, both coming and going, it was full of apprentices, who have been here all this day, and have done violence, I think, to the master of the boys that were put in the pillory yesterday. But Lord! to see how the trained-bands are raised upon this, the drums beating everywhere as if an enemy were upon them—so much is this city subject to be put into a disarray upon very small occasions. But it was pleasant to hear the boys, and particularly one very little one, that I demanded the business of. He told me that that had never been done in the City since it was a city—two 'prentices put in the pillory, and that it ought not to be so."

Cheapside has been the scene of two great riots, which were threatening enough to render them historically important. The one was in the reign of Richard I., the other in that of Henry VIII. The first of these, a violent protest against Norman oppression, was no doubt fomented, if not originated, by the down-trodden Saxons. It began thus :—On the return of Richard from his captivity in Germany, and before his fiery retaliation on France, a London citizen named William with the Long Beard, *alias* Fitzosbert, a deformed man, but of great courage and zeal for the poor, sought the king, and appealing to his better nature, laid before him a detail of great oppressions and outrages wrought by the Mayor and rich aldermen of the city, to burden the humbler citizens and relieve themselves, especially at "the hoistings" when any taxes or tollage were to be levied. Fitzosbert, encouraged at gaining the king's ear, and hoping too much from the generous but rapacious Norman soldier, grew bolder, openly defended the causes of oppressed men, and thus drew round him daily great crowds of the poor.

"Many gentlemen of honour," says Holinshed, "sore hated him for his presumptious attempts to the hindering of their purposes ; but he had such comfort of the king that he little paused for their malice, but kept on his intent, till the king, being advertised of the assemblies which he made, commanded him to cease from such doings, that the people might fall again to their sciences and occupations, which they had for the most part left off at the instigation of this William with the Long Beard, which he nourished of purpose, to seem the more grave and manlike, and also, as it were, in despite of them which counterfeited the Normans (that were for the most part shaven), and because he would resemble the ancient usage of the English nation. The king's commandment in restraint of people's resort unto him was well kept for a time, but it was not long before they began to follow him again as they had done before. Then he took upon him to make unto them certain speeches. By these and such persuasions and means as he used, he had gotten two and fifty thousand persons ready to have taken his part."

How far this English Rienzi intended to obtain redress by force we cannot clearly discover ; but he does not seem to have been a man who would have stopped at anything to obtain justice for the oppressed—and that the Normans were oppressors, till they became real Englishmen, there can be no doubt. The rich citizens and the Norman nobles, who had clamped the City fast with fortresses, soon barred out Longbeard from the king's chamber. The Archbishop of Canterbury especially, who ruled the City, called together the rich citizens, excited their fears, and with true priestly craft persuaded them to give sure pledges that no outbreak should take place, although he denied all belief in the possibility of such an event. The citizens, overcome by his oily and false words, willingly gave their pledges, and were from that time in the archbishop's power. The wily prelate then, finding the great demagogue was still followed by dangerous and threatening crowds, appointed two burgesses and other spies to watch Fitzosbert, and, when it was possible, to apprehend him.

These men at a convenient time set upon Fitzosbert, to bind and carry him off; but Longbeard was a hero at heart and full of ready courage. Snatching up an axe, he defended himself manfully, slew one of the archbishop's emissaries, and flew at once for sanctuary into the Church of St. Mary Bow. Barring the doors and retreating to the tower, he and some trusty friends turned it into a small fortress, till at last his enemies, gathering thicker round him and setting the steeple on fire, forced Longbeard and a woman whom he loved, and who had followed him there, into the open street.

As the deserted demagogue was dragged forth through the fire and smoke, still loth to yield, a son of the burgess whom he had stricken dead ran forward and stabbed him in the side. The wounded man was quickly overpowered ; for the citizens, afraid to forfeit their pledges, did not come to his aid as he had expected, and he was hurried to the Tower, where the expectant archbishop sat ready to condemn him. We can imagine what that drum-head trial would be like. Longbeard was at once condemned, and with nine of his adherents, scorched and smoking from the fire, was sentenced to be hung on a gibbet at the Smithfield Elms. For all this, the fermentation did not soon subside; the people too late remembered how Fitzosbert had pleaded for their rights, and braved king, prelate, and baron; and they loudly exclaimed against the archbishop for breaking sanctuary, and putting to death a man who had only defended himself against assassins, and was innocent of other crimes. The love for the dead man, indeed, at last rose to such a height that the rumour ran that miracles were wrought by even touching the chains by which he had been bound in the Tower. He became for a time a saint to the poorer and more suffering subjects of the Normans, and the place where he was beheaded in Smithfield was visited as a spot of special holiness.

But this riot of Longbeard was but the threatening of a storm. A tempest longer and more terrible broke over Cheapside on " Evil May Day," in the reign of Henry VIII. Its origin was the jealousy of the Lombards and other foreign money-lenders and craftsmen entertained by the artisans and 'prentices of London. Its actual cause was the seduction of a citizen's wife by a Lombard named Francis de Bard, of Lombard Street. The loss of the wife might have been borne, but the wife took with her, at the Italian's solicitation, a box of her husband's plate. The husband demanding first his wife and then his plate, was flatly refused both. The injured man tried the case at the Guildhall, but was foiled by the intriguing foreigner, who then had the incomparable rascality to arrest the poor man for his wife's board.

" This abuse," says Holinshed, "was much hated; so that the same and manie other oppressions done by the Lombards increased such a malice in the Englishmen's hearts, that at the last it burst out. For amongst others that sore grudged these matters was a broker in London, called John Lincolne, that busied himself so farre in the matter, that about Palme Sundie, in the eighth yeare of the King's reign, he came to one Doctor Henry Standish with these words: 'Sir, I understand that you shall preach at the Sanctuarie, Spittle, on Mondaie in Easter Weeke, and so it is, that Englishmen, both merchants and others, are undowne, for strangers have more liberty in this land than Englishmen, which is against all reason, and also against the commonweal of the realm. I beseech you, therefore, to declare this in your sermon, and in soe doing you shall deserve great thanks of

my Lord Maior and of all his brethren;' and herewith he offered unto the said Doctor Standish a bill containing this matter more at large. . . Dr. Standish refused to have anything to do with the matter, and John Lincolne went to Dr. Bell, a chanon of the same Spittle, that was appointed likewise to preach upon the Tuesday in Easter Weeke, whome he perswaded to read his said bill in the pulpit."

This bill complained vehemently of the poverty of London artificers, who were starving, while the foreigners swarmed everywhere; also that the English merchants were impoverished by foreigners, who imported all silks, cloth of gold, wine, and iron, so that people scarcely cared even to buy of an Englishman. Moreover, the writer declared that foreigners had grown so numerous that, on a Sunday in the previous Lent, he had seen 600 strangers shooting together at the popinjay. He also insisted on the fact of the foreigners banding in fraternities, and clubbing together so large a fund, that they could overpower even the City of London.

Lincoln, having won over Dr. Bell to read the complaint, went round and told every one he knew that shortly they would have news; and excited the 'prentices and artificers to expect some speedy rising against the foreign merchants and workmen. In due time the sermon was preached, and Dr. Bell drew a strong picture of the riches and indolence of the foreigners, and the struggling and poverty of English craftsmen.

The train was ready, and on such occasions the devil is never far away with the spark. The Sunday after the sermon, Francis de Bard, the aforesaid Lombard, and other foreign merchants, happened to be in the King's Gallery at Greenwich Palace, and were laughing and boasting over Bard's intrigue with the citizen's wife. Sir Thomas Palmer, to whom they spoke, said, " Sirs, you have too much favour in England;" and one William Bolt, a merchant, added, "Well, you Lombards, you rejoice now; but, by the masse, we will one day have a fling at you, come when it will." And that saying the other merchants affirmed. This tale was reported about London.

The attack soon came. "On the 28th of April, 1513," says Holinshed, "some young citizens picked quarrels with the strangers, insulting them in various ways, in the streets; upon which certain of the said citizens were sent to prison. Then suddenly rose a secret rumour, and no one could tell how it began, that on May-day next the City would rise against the foreigners, and slay them; insomuch that several of the strangers fled from the City. This rumour reached the King's Council, and

Cardinal Wolsey sent for the Mayor, to ask him what he knew of it; upon which the Mayor told him that peace should be kept. The Cardinal told him to take pains that it should be. The Mayor came from the Cardinal's at four in the afternoon of May-day eve, and in all haste sent for his brethren to the Guildhall; yet it was almost seven before they met. It was at last decided, with the consent of the Cardinal, that instead of a strong watch being set, which might irritate, all citizens should be warned to keep their servants within doors on the dreaded day. The Recorder and Sir Thomas More, of the King's Privy Council, came to the Guildhall, at a quarter to nine a.m., and desired the aldermen to send to every ward, forbidding citizens' servants to go out from seven p.m. that day to nine a.m. of the next day.

"After this command had been given," says the chronicler, "in the evening, as Sir John Mundie, an alderman, came from his ward, and found two young men in Chepe, playing at the bucklers, and a great many others looking on, for the command was then scarce known, he commanded them to leave off; and when one of them asked why, he would have had him to the counter. Then all the young 'prentices resisted the alderman, taking the young fellow from him, and crying ''Prentices and Clubs.' Then out of every door came clubs and weapons. The alderman fled, and was in great danger. Then more people arose out of every quarter, and forth came serving men, watermen, courtiers, and others; so that by eleven o'clock there were in Chepe six or seven hundred; and out of Paul's Churchyard came 300, which knew not of the other. So out of all places they gathered, and broke up the counters, and took out the prisoners that the Mayor had committed for hurting the strangers; and went to Newgate, and took out Studleie and Petit, committed thither for that cause.

"The Mayor and Sheriff made proclamation, but no heed was paid to them. Herewith being gathered in plumps, they ran through St. Nicholas' shambles, and at St. Martin's Gate there met with them Sir Thomas More, and others, desiring them to goe to their lodgings; and as they were thus intreating, and had almost persuaded the people to depart, they within St. Martin's threw out stones, bats, and hot water, so that they hurt divers honest persons that were there with Sir Thomas More: insomuch as at length one Nicholas Downes, a sergeant of arms, being there with the said Sir Thomas More, and sore hurt amongst others, cried 'Down with them!' and then all the misruled persons ran to the doors and windows of the houses round Saint Martin's, and spoiled all that they found.

"After that they ran headlong into Cornhill, and there likewise spoiled divers houses of the French men that dwelled within the gate of Master Newton's house, called Queene Gate. This Master Newton was a Picard borne, and reputed to be a great favourer of Frenchmen in their occupiengs and trades, contrary to the laws of the Citie. If the people had found him, they had surelie have stricken off his head; but when they found him not, the watermen and certain young preests that were there, fell to rifling, and some ran to Blanch-apelton, and broke up the strangers' houses and spoiled them. Thus from ten or eleven of the clock these riotous people continued their outrageous doings, till about three of the clock, at what time they began to withdraw, and went to their places of resort; and by the way they were taken by the Maior and the heads of the Citie, and sent some of them to the Tower, some to Newgate, some to the counters, to the number of 300.

"Manie fled, and speciallie the watermen and preests and serving men, but the 'prentices were caught by the backs, and had to prison. In the meantime, whilst the hottest of this ruffling lasted, the Cardinall was advertised thereof by Sir Thomas Parre; whereon the Cardinall strengthened his house with men and ordnance. Sir Thomas Parre rode in all haste to Richmond, where the King lay, and informed him of the matter; who incontinentlie sent forth hastilie to London, to understand the state of the Citie, and was truely advertised how the riot had ceased, and manie of the misdoers apprehended. The Lieutenant of the Tower, Sir Roger Cholmeleie (no great friend to the Citie), in a frantike furie, during the time of this uprore, shot off certaine pieces of ordinance against the Citie, and though they did no great harm, yet he won much evil will for his hastie doing, because men thought he did it of malice, rather than of any discretion.

"About five o'clock, the Earls of Shrewsbury and Surrey, Thomas Dockerin, Lord of Saint John's, and George Neville, Lord of Abergavenny, came to London with such force as they could gather in haste, and so did the Innes of Court. Then were the prisoners examined, and the sermon of Dr. Bell brought to remembrance, and he sent to the Tower. Herewith was a Commission of Oyer and Determiner, directed to the Duke of Norfolk and other lords, to the Lord Mayor of London, and the aldermen, and to all the justices of England, for punishment of this insurrection. (The Citie thought the Duke bare them a grudge for a lewd preest of

BEGINNING OF THE RIOT IN CHEAPSIDE. (see page 311).

his that the yeare before was slaine in Chepe, insomuch that he then, in his fury, said, 'I pray God I may once have the citizens in my power!' And likewise the Duke thought that they bare him no good will; wherefore he came into the Citie with prisoners were brought through the street, tied in ropes, some men, and some lads of thirteen years of age. Among them were divers not of the City, some priests, some husbandmen and labourers. The whole number amounted unto two hundred, three

CHEAPSIDE CROSS, AS IT APPEARED IN 1547.
(*Showing part of the Procession of Edward VI. to his Coronation, from a Painting of the Time.*)

thirteen hundred men, in harnesse, to keepe the oier and determiner.)

"At the time of the examination the streets were filled with harnessed men, who spake very opprobrious words to the citizens, which the latter, although two hundred to one, bore patiently. The inquiry was held at the house of Sir John Fineux, Lord Chief Justice of England, neare to St. Bride's, in Fleet Street.

"When the lords were met at the Guildhall, the score, and eighteen persons. Eventually, thirteen were found guilty, and adjudged to be hanged, drawn, and quartered. Eleven pairs of gallows were set up in various places where the offences had been committed, as at Aldgate, Blanchappleton, Gratious Street, Leaden Hall, and before every Counter. One also at Newgate, St. Martin's, at Aldersgate, and Bishopsgate. Then were the prisoners that were judged brought to those places of execution, and executed in the most rigorous manner in the presence of the Lord Edward Howard, son to the Duke of Norfolke, a knight marshal, who showed no mercie, but extreme crueltie to the poore yonglings in their execution; and likewise the duke's servants spake many opprobrious words. On Thursday, May the 7th, was Lincolne, Shirwin, and two brethren called Bets, and diverse other persons, adjudged to die; and Lincolne said, 'My lords, I meant well, for if you knew the mischiefe that is insued in this realme by strangers, you would remedie it. And many times I have complained, and then I was called a busie fellow; now, our Lord have mercie on me!' They were laid on hurdels and drawne to the Standard in Cheape, and first was John Lincolne executed; and as the others had the ropes about their neckes, there came a commandment from the king to respit the execution. Then the people cried, 'God save the king!' and so was the oier and terminer deferred till another daie, and the prisoners sent againe to ward. The armed men departed out of London, and all things set in quiet.

"On the 11th of May, the king being at Greenwich, the Recorder of London and several aldermen sought his presence to ask pardon for the late riot, and to beg for mercy for the prisoners; which petition the king sternly refused, saying that although it might be that the substantial citizens did not actually take part in the riot, it was evident, from their supineness in putting it down, that they 'winked at the matter.'

"On Thursday, the 22nd of May, the king, attended by the cardinal and many great lords, sat in person in judgment in Westminster Hall, the mayor, aldermen, and all the chief men of the City being present in their best livery. The king commanded that all the prisoners should be brought forth, so that in came the poore yonglings and old false knaves, bound in ropes, all along one after another in their shirts, and everie one a halter about his necke, to the number of now foure hundred men and eleven women; and when all were come before the king's presence, the cardinall sore laid to the maior and commonaltie their negligence; and to the prisoners he declared that they had deserved death for their offense. Then all the prisoners together cried, 'Mercie, gratious lord, mercie!' Herewith the lords altogither besought his grace of mercie, at whose sute the king pardoned them all. Then the cardinal gave unto them a good exhortation, to the great gladnesse of the hearers.

"Now when the generall pardon was pronounced all the prisoners shouted at once, and altogither cast up their halters into the hall roofe, so that the king might perceive they were none of the discreetest sort. Here is to be noticed that diverse offendors that were not taken, hearing that the king was inclined to mercie, came well apparelled to Westminster, and suddenlie stripped them into their shirts with halters, and came in among the prisoners, willinglie to be partakers of the king's pardon; by which dooing it was well known that one John Gelson, yeoman of the Crowne, was the first that began to spoile, and exhorted others to doe the same; and because he fled and was not taken, he came in with a rope among the other prisoners, and so had his pardon. This companie was after called the 'black-wagon.' Then were all the gallows within the Citie taken downe, and many a good prayer said for the king."

Jane Shore, that beautiful but frail woman, who married a goldsmith in Lombard Street, and was the mistress of Edward IV., was the daughter of a merchant in Cheapside. Drayton describes her minutely from a picture extant in Elizabeth's time, but now lost.

"Her stature," says the poet, "was meane; her haire of a dark yellow; her face round and full; her eye gray, delicate harmony being between each part's proportion and each proportion's colour; her body fat, white, and smooth; her countenance cheerful, and like to her condition. The picture I have seen of her was such as she rose out of her bed in the morning, having nothing on but a rich mantle cast under one arme over her shoulder, and sitting on a chair on which her naked arm did lie. Shore, a young man of right goodly person, wealth, and behaviour, abandoned her after the king had made her his concubine. Richard III., causing her to do open penance in St. Paul's Churchyard, *commanded that no man should relieve her*, which the tyrant did not so much for his hatred to sinne, but that, by making his brother's life odious, he might cover his horrible treasons the more cunningly."

An old ballad quaintly describes her supposed death, following an entirely erroneous tradition:—

" My gowns, beset with pearl and gold,
Were turn'd to simple garments old;
My chains and gems, and golden rings,
To filthy rags and loathsome things.

" Thus was I scorned of maid and wife,
For leading such a wicked life;
Both sucking babes and children small,
Did make their pastime at my fall.

" I could not get one bit of bread,
Whereby my hunger might be fed,
Nor drink, but such as channels yield,
Or stinking ditches in the field.

" Thus weary of my life, at lengthe
  I yielded up my vital strength,
  Within a ditch of loathsome scent,
  Where carrion dogs did much frequent ;

" The which now, since my dying daye,
  Is Shoreditch call'd, as writers saye ;*
  Which is a witness of my sinne,
  For being concubine to a king."

Sir Thomas More, however, distinctly mentions Jane Shore being alive in the reign of Henry VIII., and seems to imply that he had himself seen her. "He (Richard III.) caused," says More, "the Bishop of London to put her to an open penance, going before the cross in procession upon a Sunday, with a taper in her hand ; in which she went in countenance and face demure, so womanly, and albeit she were out of all array save her kirtle only, yet went she so fair and lovely, namely while the wondering of the people cast a comely red in her cheeks (of which she before had most miss), that her great shame was her much praise among those who were more amorous of her body than curious of her soul ; and many good folk, also, who hated her living, and were glad to see sin corrected, yet pitied they more her penance than rejoiced therein, when they considered that the Protector procured it more of a corrupt intent than any virtuous intention.

" Proper she was, and fair ; nothing in her body that you would have changed, but if you would, have wished her somewhat higher. Thus say they who knew her in her youth ; albeit some who now see her (for yet she liveth) deem her never to have been well-visaged ; whose judgment seemeth to me to be somewhat like as though men should guess the beauty of one long departed by her scalp taken out of the charnel-house. For now is she old, lean, withered, and dried up—nothing left but shrivelled skin and hard bone. And yet, being even such, whoso well advise her visage, might guess and devine which parts, how filled, would make it a fair face.

" Yet delighted men not so much in her beauty as in her pleasant behaviour. For a proper wit had she, and could both read well and write, merry in company, ready and quick of answer, neither mute nor full of babble, sometimes taunting without displeasure, and not without disport."

CHAPTER XXVII.

CHEAPSIDE SHOWS AND PAGEANTS.

A Tournament in Cheapside—The Queen in Danger—The Street in Holiday Attire—The Earliest Civic Show on record—The Water Processions— A Lord Mayor's Show in Queen Elizabeth's Reign—Gossip about Lord Mayors' Shows—Splendid Pageants—Royal Visitors at Lord Mayor's Shows—A Grand Banquet in Guildhall—George III. and the Lord Mayor's Show—The Lord Mayor's State Coach—The Men in Armour—Sir Claudius Hunter and Elliston—Stow and the Midsummer Watch.

WE do not hear much in the old chronicles of tournaments and shivered spears in Cheapside, but of gorgeous pageants much. On coronation days and days when our kings rode from the Tower to Westminster, or from Castle Baynard eastward, Cheapside blossomed at once with flags and banners, rich tapestry hung from every window, and the very gutters ran with wine, so loyal and generous were the citizens of those early days. Costume was bright and splendid in the Middle Ages, and heraldry kept alive the habit of contrasting and mingling colours. Citizens were wealthy, and, moreover, lavish of their wealth.

In these processions and pageants, Cheapside was always the very centre of the show. There velvets and silks trailed ; there jewels shone ; there spearheads and axe-heads glittered ; there breastplates and steel caps gleamed ; there proud horses fretted ; there bells clashed ; there the mob clamoured ; there proud, warlike, and beautiful faces showed, uncapped and unveiled, to the seething, jostling people ; and there mayor and aldermen grew hottest, bowed most, and puffed out with fullest dignity.

In order to celebrate the birth of the heir of England, the Black Prince, in 1330, a great tournament was proclaimed in London. Philippa and all the female nobility were invited to be present. Thirteen knights were engaged on each side, and the tournament was held in Cheapside, between Wood Street and Queen Street ; the highway was covered with sand, to prevent the horses' feet from slipping, and a grand temporary wooden tower was erected, for the accommodation of the Queen and her ladies. But scarcely had this fair company entered the tower, when the scaffolding suddenly gave way, and all present fell to the ground with the Queen. Though no one was injured, all were terribly frightened, and great confusion ensued.

* But it had this name long before, being so called from its being a common *sewer* (vulgarly called *shore*) or drain. (See Stow.)

When the young king saw the peril of his wife, he flew into a tempest of rage, and vowed that the careless carpenters who had constructed the building should instantly be put to death. Whether he would thus far have stretched the prerogative of an English sovereign can never be known (says Miss Strickland), for his angelic partner, scarcely recovered from the terror of her fall, threw herself on her knees before the incensed king, and so effectually pleaded for the pardon of the poor men, that Edward became pacified, and forgave them.

When the young princess, Anne of Bohemia, the first wife of the royal prodigal, Richard II., entered London, a castle with towers was erected at the upper end of Cheapside. On the wooden battlements stood fair maidens, who blew gold leaf on the King, Queen, and retinue, so that the air seemed filled with golden butterflies. This pretty device was much admired. The maidens also threw showers of counterfeit gold coins before the horses' feet of the royal cavalcade, while the two sides of the tower ran fountains of red wine.

On the great occasion when this same Anne, who had by this time supped full of troubles, and by whose entreaties the proud, reckless young king, who had, as it were, excommunicated the City and now forgave it, came again into Chepe, red and white wine poured in fountains from a tower opposite the Great Conduit. The King and Queen were served from golden cups, and at the same place an angel flew down in a cloud, and presented costly golden circlets to Richard and his young wife.

Two days before the opening of Parliament, in 1423, Katherine of Valois, widow of Henry V., entered the city in a chair of state, with her child sitting on her knee. When they arrived at the west door of St. Paul's Cathedral, the Duke Protector lifted the infant king from his chair and set him on his feet, and, with the Duke of Exeter, led him between them up the stairs going into the choir; then, having knelt at the altar for a time, the child was borne into the churchyard, there set upon a fair courser, and so conveyed through Cheapside to his own manor of Kennington.

Time went on, and the weak young king married the fair amazon of France, the revengeful and resolute Margaret of Anjou. At the marriage pageant maidens acted, at the Cheapside conduit, a play representing the five wise and five foolish virgins. Years after, the corpse of the same king passed along the same street; but no huzzas, no rejoicing now. It was on the day after the restoration of Edward IV., when people dared not speak above a breath of what might be happening in the Tower, that the corpse of Henry VI. was borne through Cheapside to St. Paul's, barefaced, on a bier, so that all might see it, though it was surrounded by more brown bills and glaives than torches.

By-and-by, after the fierce retribution of Bosworth, came the Tudors, culminating and ending with Elizabeth.

As Elizabeth of York (Henry VII.'s consort) went from the Tower to Westminster to be crowned, the citizens hung velvets and cloth of gold from the windows in Chepe, and stationed children, dressed like angels, to sing praises to the Queen as she passed by. When the Queen's corpse was conveyed from the Tower, where she died, in Cheapside were stationed thirty-seven virgins, the number corresponding with the Queen's age, all dressed in white, wearing chaplets of white and green, and bearing lighted tapers.

As Anne Boleyn, during her short felicity, proceeded from the Tower to Westminster, on the eve of her coronation, the conduit of Cheapside ran, at one end white wine, and at the other red. At Cheapside Cross stood all the aldermen, from amongst whom advanced Master Walter, the City Recorder, who presented the Queen with a purse, containing a thousand marks of gold, which she very thankfully accepted, with many goodly words. At the Little Conduit of Cheapside was a rich pageant, full of melody and song, where Pallas, Venus, and Juno gave the Queen an apple of gold, divided into three compartments, typifying wisdom, riches, and felicity.

When Queen Elizabeth, young, happy and regal, proceeded through the City the day before her coronation, as she passed through Cheapside, she smiled; and being asked the reason, she replied, "Because I have just heard one say in the crowd, 'I remember old King Harry the Eighth.'" When she came to the grand allegory of Time and Truth, at the Little Conduit, in Cheapside, she asked, who an old man was that sat with his scythe and hour-glass. She was told "Time." "Time?" she repeated; "and Time has brought me here!"

In this pageant she spied that Truth held a Bible, in English, ready for presentation to her; and she bade Sir John Perrot (the knight nearest to her, who held up her canopy, and a kinsman, afterwards beheaded) to step forward and receive it for her; but she was informed such was not the regular manner of presentation, for it was to be let down into her chariot by a silken string. She therefore told Sir John Perrot to stay; and at the proper crisis, some verses being recited by Truth, the book descended, "and the Queen received it in both her hands, kissed it, clasped it to her bosom, and thanked the City for this present, esteemed above all others. She promised to read it diligently, to the great comfort of the bystanders." All the houses in Cheapside were dressed with banners and streamers, and the richest carpets, stuffs, and cloth of gold tapestried the streets. At the upper end of Chepe, the Recorder presented the Queen, from the City, with a handsome crimson satin purse, containing a thousand marks in gold, which she most graciously pocketed. There were trumpeters at the Standard in Chepe, and the City waits stood at the porch of St. Peter's, Cornhill. The City companies stretched in rows from Fenchurch Street to the Little Conduit in Chepe, behind rails, which were hung with cloth.

On an occasion when James I. and his wife visited the City, at the Conduit, Cheapside, there was a grand display of tapestry, gold cloth, and silks; and before the structure "a handsome apprentice was appointed, whose part it was to walk backwards and forwards, as if outside a shop, in his flat cap and usual dress, addressing the passengers with his usual cry for custom of, 'What d'ye lack, gentles? What will you buy? silks, satins, or taff—taf—fetas?' He then broke into premeditated verse:—

" ' But stay, bold tongue ! I stand at giddy gaze !
　Be dim, mine eyes ! What gallant train are here,
　That strikes minds mute, puts good wits in a maze?
　Oh ! 'tis our King, royal King James, I say !
　Pass on in peace, and happy be thy way ;
　Live long on earth, and England's sceptre sway.' "

Henrietta Maria, that pretty, wilful queen of Charles I., accompanied by the Duke of Buckingham and Bassompierre, the French ambassador, went to what the latter calls *Shipside*, to view the Lord Mayor's procession. She also came to a masquerade at the Temple, in the costume of a City lady. Mistress Bassett, the great lace-woman of Cheapside, went foremost of the Court party at the Temple carnival, and led the Queen by the hand.

But what are royal processions to the Lord Mayor's Show?

The earliest civic show on record, writes Mr. Fairholt, who made a specialty of this subject, took place in 1236, on the passage of Henry III. and Eleanor of Provence through the City to Westminster. They were escorted by the mayor, aldermen, and 360 mounted citizens, apparelled in robes of embroidered silk, and each carrying in their hands a cup of gold or silver, in token of the privilege claimed by the City for the lord mayor to officiate as chief butler at the king's coronation. On the return of Edward I. from the Holy Land the citizens, in the wildness of their loyalty, threw, it is said, handfuls of gold and silver out of window to the crowd. It was on the return of the same

king from his Scotch victories that the earliest known City pageant took place. Each guild had its show. The Fishmongers had gilt salmon and sturgeon, drawn by eight horses, and six-and-forty knights riding sea-horses, followed by St. Magnus (it was St. Magnus' day), with 1,000 horsemen.

Mr. Fairholt proved from papers still preserved by the Grocers' Company that water processions took place at least nineteen years earlier than the usual date (1453) set down for their commencement. Sir John Norman is mentioned by the City poet as the first Lord Mayor that rowed to Westminster. He had silver oars, and so delighted the London watermen that they wrote a ballad about him, of which two lines only still exist—

" Row thy boat, Norman,
　Row to thy leman."

In the troublous reign of Henry VI. the Goldsmiths made a special stand for their privileges on Lord Mayor's day. They complained loudly that they had always ridden with the mayor to Westminster and back, and that on their return to Chepe they sit on horseback "above the Cross afore the Goldsmiths' Row ; but that on the morrow of the Apostles Simon and Jude, when they came to their stations, they found the Butchers had forestalled them, who would not budge for all the prayers of the wardens of the Goldsmiths, and hence had arisen great variance and strife." The two guilds submitted to the Lord Mayor's arbitration, whereupon the Mayor ruled that the Goldsmiths should retain possession of their ancient stand.

The first Lord Mayor's pageant described by the old chroniclers is that when Anne Boleyn "came from Greenwich to Westminster on her coronation day, and the Mayor went to serve her as chief butler, according to ancient custom." Hall expressly says that the water procession on that occasion resembled that of Lord Mayor's Day. The Mayor's barge, covered with red cloth (blue except at royal ceremonies), was garnished with goodly banners and streamers, and the sides hung with emblazoned targets. In the barge were "shalms, shagbushes, and divers other instruments, which continually made goodly harmony." Fifty barges, filled with the various Companies, followed, marshalled and kept in order by three light wherries with officers. Before the Mayor's barge came another barge, full of ordnance and containing a huge dragon (emblematic of the Rouge Dragon in the Tudor arms), which vomited wild fire ; and round about it stood terrible monsters and savages, also vomiting fire, discharging squibs, and making "hideous noises." By the side of the Mayor's barge was the bachelors' barge, in which were trumpeters and other musicians. The decks of the Mayor's barge, and the sail-yards, and top-castles were hung with flags and rich cloth of gold and silver. At the head and stern were two great banners, with the royal arms in beaten gold. The sides of the and about the mount sat virgins, "singing and playing sweetly." The Mayor's company, the Haberdashers, came first, then the Mercers, then the Grocers, and so on, the barges being garnished with banners and hung with arras and rich carpets. In 1566–7 the water procession was very costly,

THE LORD MAYOR'S PROCESSION. *From Hogarth's "Industrious Apprentice."* (*See page* 323.)

barge were hung with flags and banners of the Haberdashers' and Merchant Adventurers' Companies, the Lord Mayor, Sir Stephen Peacock, being a haberdasher. On the outside of the barge shone three dozen illuminated royal escutcheons. On the left hand of this barge came another boat, in which was a pageant. A white falcon, crowned, stood upon a mount, on a golden rock, environed with white and red roses (Anne Boleyn's device),

and seven hundred pounds of gunpowder were burned. This is the first show of which a detailed account exists, and it is to be found recorded in the books of the Ironmongers' Company.

A curious and exact description of a Lord Mayor's procession in Elizabeth's reign, written by William Smith, a London haberdasher, in 1575, is still extant. The day after St. Simon and Jude the Mayor went by water to Westminster, attended

BOW CHURCH AND CHEAPSIDE IN 1750.
(*From a Print in Mr. Crace's Collection.*)

by the barges of all the companies, duly marshalled and hung with emblazoned shields. On their return they landed at Paul's Wharf, where they took horse, " and in great pomp passed through the great street of the city called Cheapside." The road was cleared by beadles and men dressed as devils, and wild men, whose clubs discharged squibs. First came two great standards, bearing the arms of the City and of the Lord Mayor's company ; then two drums, a flute, and an ensign of the City, followed by seventy or eighty poor men, two by two, in blue gowns with red sleeves, each one bearing a pike and a target, with the arms of the Lord Mayor's company. These were succeeded by two more banners, a set of hautboys playing; after these came wyfflers, or clearers of the way, in velvet coats and gold chains, and with white staves in their hands. After the pageant itself paced six- teen trumpeters, more wyfflers to clear the way, and after them the bachelors—sixty, eighty, or one hundred—of the Lord Mayor's company, in long gowns, with crimson satin hoods. These bachelors were to wait on the Mayor. Then followed twelve more trumpeters and the drums and flutes of the City, an ensign of the Mayor's company, the City waits in blue gowns, red sleeves, and silver chains; then the honourable livery, in long robes, each with his hood, half black, half red, on his left shoulder. After them came sheriffs' officers and Mayor's officers, the common serjeant, and the chamberlain. Before the Mayor went the sword- bearer in his cap of honour, the sword, in a sheath set with pearls, in his right hand ; while on his left came the common cryer, with the great gilt club and a mace on his shoulder. The Mayor wore a long scarlet gown, with black velvet hood and rich gold collar about his neck ; and with him rode that fallen dignitary, the ex-Mayor. Then followed all the aldermen, in scarlet gowns and black velvet tippets, those that had been mayors wearing gold chains. The two sheriffs came last of all, in scarlet gowns and gold chains. About one thou- sand persons sat down to dinner at Guildhall—a feast which cost the Mayor and the two sheriffs £400, whereof the Mayor disbursed £200. Im- mediately after dinner they went to evening prayer at St. Paul's, the poor men aforementioned carrying torches and targets. The dinner still continues to be eaten, but the service at St. Paul's, as interfering with digestion, was abandoned after the Great Fire. In the evening farewell speeches were made to the Lord Mayor by allegorical per- sonages, and painted posts were set up at his door.

One of the most gorgeous Lord Mayor's shows was that of the year 1616, devised by Anthony Munday, one of the great band of Shakesperean dramatists, who wrote plays in partnership with Drayton. The drawings for the pageant are still in the possession of the Fishmongers' Company. The new mayor was John Leman, a member of that body, knighted during his mayoralty. The first pageant represented a buss, or Dutch fishing-boat, on wheels. The fishermen in it were busy drawing up nets full of live fish and throwing them to the people. On the mast and at the head of the boat were the insignia of the company—St. Peter's keys and two arms supporting a crown. The second pageant was a gigantic crowned dolphin, ridden by Arion. The third pageant was the king of the Moors riding on a golden leopard, and scattering gold and silver freely round him. He was attended by six tributary kings in gilt armour on horseback, each carrying a dart and gold and silver ingots. This pageant was in honour of the Fishmongers' brethren the Goldsmiths. The fourth pageant was the usual pictorial pun on the Lord Mayor's name and crest. The car bore a large lemon-tree full of golden fruit, with a pelican in her nest feeding her young proper. At the top of the tree sat five children, representing the five senses. The boys were dressed as women, each with her emblem— Seeing, by an eagle ; Hearing, by a hart ; Touch, by a spider ; Tasting, by an ape ; and Smelling, by a dog. The fifth pageant was Sir William Wal- worth's bower, which was hung with the shields of all lord mayors who had been Fishmongers. Upon a tomb within the bower was laid the effigy in knightly armour of Sir William, the slayer of Wat Tyler. Five mounted knights attended the car, and a mounted man-at-arms bore Wat Tyler's head upon a dagger. In attendance were six trumpeters and twenty-four halberdiers, arrayed in light blue silk, emblazoned with the Fishmongers' arms on the breast and Walworth's on the back. Then followed an angel with golden wings and crown, riding on horseback, who, on the Lord Mayor's approach, with a golden rod awoke Sir William from his long sleep, and the two then became speakers in the interlude.

The great central pageant was a triumphal car drawn by two mermen and two mermaids. In the highest place sat a guardian angel defending the crown of Richard II., who sat just below her. Under the king sat female personifications of the royal virtues, Truth, Virtue, Honour, Temperance, Fortitude, Zeal, Equity, Conscience, beating down Treason and Mutiny, the two last being enacted " by burly men." In a seat corresponding with the king's sat Justice, and below her Authority, Law, Vigilance, Peace, Plenty, and Discipline.

Shirley, the dramatist of the reign of Charles I., has described the Show in his "Contention for Honour and Riches." Clod, a sturdy countryman, exclaims, "I am plain Clod; I care not a beanstalk for the best *what lack you* on you all. No, not the next day after Simon and Jude, when you go a-feasting to Westminster with your galley-foist and your pot-guns, to the very terror of the paper whales; when you land in shoals, and make the understanders in Cheapside wonder to see ships swim on men's shoulders; when the fencers flourish and make the king's liege people fall down and worship the devil and St. Dunstan; when your whifflers are hanged in chains, and Hercules Club spits fire about the pageants, though the poor children catch cold that shone like painted cloth, and are only kept alive with sugar-plums; with whom, when the word is given, you march to Guildhall, with every man his spoon in his pocket, where you look upon the giants, and feed like Saracens, till you have no stomach to go to St. Paul's in the afternoon. I have seen your processions, and heard your lions and camels make speeches, instead of grace before and after dinner. I have heard songs, too, or something like 'em; but the porters have had all the burden, who were kept sober at the City charge two days before, to keep time and tune with their feet; for, brag what you will of your charge, all your pomp lies upon their back." In "Honoria and Memoria," 1652, Shirley has again repeated this humorous and graphic description of the land and water pageants of the good citizens of the day; he has, however, abridged the general detail, and added some degree of indelicacy to his satire. He alludes to the wild men that cleared the way, and their fireworks, in these words: "I am not afeard of your green Robin Hoods, that fright with fiery club your pitiful spectators, that take pains to be stifled, and adore the wolves and camels of your company."

Pepys, always curious, always chatty, has, of course, several notices of Lord Mayors' shows; for instance:—

"Oct. 29th, 1660 (Restoration year).— I up early, it being my Lord Mayor's day (Sir Richard Browne), and neglecting my office, I went to the Wardrobe, where I met my Lady Sandwich and all the children; and after drinking of some strange and incomparably good clarett of Mr. Remball's, he and Mr. Townsend did take us, and set the young lords at one Mr. Nevill's, a draper in Paul's Churchyard; and my lady and my Lady Pickering and I to one Mr. Isaacson's, a linendraper at the 'Key,' in Cheapside, where there was a company of fine ladies, and we were very civilly treated, and had a very good place to see the pageants, which were many, and I believe good for such kind of things, but in themselves but poor and absurd. The show being done, we got to Paul's with much ado, and went on foot with my Lady Pickering to her lodging, which was a poor one in Blackfryars, where she never invited me to go in at all, which methought was very strange. Lady Davis is now come to our next lodgings, and she locked up the lead's door from me, which puts me in great disquiet.

"Oct. 29, 1663.—Up, it being Lord Mayor's Day (Sir Anthony Bateman). This morning was brought home my new velvet cloak—that is, lined with velvet, a good cloth the outside—the first that ever I had in my life, and I pray God it may not be too soon that I begin to wear it. I thought it better to go without it because of the crowde, and so I did not wear it. At noon I went to Guildhall, and, meeting with Mr. Proby, Sir R. Ford's son, and Lieutenant-Colonel Baron, a City commander, we went up and down to see the tables, where under every salt there was a bill of fare, and at the end of the table the persons proper for the table. Many were the tables, but none in the hall but the mayor's and the lords of the privy council that had napkins or knives, which was very strange. We went into the buttry, and there stayed and talked, and then into the hall again, and there wine was offered and they drunk, I only drinking some hypocras, which do not break my vowe, it being, to the best of my present judgment, only a mixed compound drink, and not any wine. If I am mistaken, God forgive me! But I do hope and think I am not. By-and-by met with Creed, and we with the others went within the several courts, and there saw the tables prepared for the ladies, and judges, and bishops—all great signs of a great dining to come. By-and-by, about one o'clock, before the Lord Mayor come, came into the hall, from the room where they were first led into, the Chancellor, Archbishopp before him, with the Lords of the Council, and other bishopps, and they to dinner. Anon comes the Lord Mayor, who went up to the lords, and then to the other tables, to bid wellcome; and so all to dinner. I sat near Proby, Baron, and Creed, at the merchant strangers' table, where ten good dishes to a messe, with plenty of wine of all sorts, of which I drank none; but it was very unpleasing that we had no napkins nor change of trenchers, and drunk out of earthen pitchers and wooden dishes. It happened that after the lords had half dined, came the French ambassador up to the lords' table, where he was to have sat; he would not sit down nor dine with the Lord Mayor, who was not yet come, nor have a table to himself, which was offered, but, in a discontent, went away again. After I had dined, I and Creed rose and went up and down the house, and up to the ladies' room, and there stayed gazing upon them. But though there were many and fine, both young and old, yet I could not discern one handsome face there, which was very strange. I expected musique, but there was none, but only trumpets and drums, which displeased me. The dinner, it seems, is made by the mayor and two sheriffs for the time being, the Lord Mayor paying one half, and they the other; and the whole, Proby says, is reckoned to come to about seven or eight hundred at most. Being wearied with looking at a company of ugly women, Creed and I went away, and took coach, and through Cheapside, and there saw the pageants, which were very silly. The Queene mends apace, they say, but yet talks idle still."

In 1672 "London Triumphant, or the City in Jollity and Splendour," was the title of Jordan's pageant for Sir Robert Hanson, of the Grocers' Company. The Mayor, just against Bow Church, was saluted by three pageants; on the two side stages were placed two griffins (the supporters of the Grocers' arms), upon which were seated two negroes, Victory and Gladness attending; while in the centre or principal stage behind reigned Apollo, surrounded by Fame, Peace, Justice, Aurora, Flora, and Ceres. The god addressed the Mayor in a very high-flown strain of compliment, saying—

> "With Oriental eyes I come to see,
> And gratulate this great solemnitie.
> It hath been often said, so often done,
> That all men will worship the rising sun.
> (*He rises.*)
> Such are the blessings of his beams. But now
> The rising sun, my lord, doth worship you."
> (*Apollo bows politely to the Lord Mayor.*)

Next was displayed a wilderness, with Moors planting and labouring, attended by three pipers and several kitchen musicians that played upon tongs, gridirons, keys, "and other such like confused musick." Above all, upon a mound, sat America, "a proper masculine woman, with a tawny face," who delivered a lengthy speech, which concluded the exhibition for that day.

In 1676 the pageant in Cheapside, which dignified Sir Thomas Davies' accession as Lord Mayor, was "a Scythian chariot of triumph," in which sat a fierce Tamburlain, of terrible aspect and morose disposition, who was, however, very civil

and complimentary upon the present occasion. He was attended by Discipline, bearing the king's banner, Conduct that of the Mayor, Courage that of the City, while Victory displayed the flag of the Drapers' Company. The lions of the Drapers' arms drew the car, led by "Asian captive princes, in royal robes and crowns of gold, and ridden by two negro princes." The third pageant was "Fortune's Bower," in which the goddess sat with Prosperity, Gladness, Peace, Plenty, Honour, and Riches. A lamb stood in front, on which rode a boy, "holding the banner of the Virgin." The fourth pageant was a kind of "chase," full of shepherds and others preparing cloth, dancing, tumbling, and curvetting, being intended to represent confusion.

In the show of 1672 two giants, Gogmagog and Corineus, fifteen feet high, whose ancestors were probably destroyed in the Great Fire, appeared in two chariots, "merry, happy, and taking tobacco, to the great admiration and delight of all the spectators." Their predecessors are spoken of by Marston, the dramatist, Stow, and Bishop Corbet. In 1708 (says Mr. Fairholt) the present Guildhall giants were carved by Richard Saunders. In 1837 Alderman Lucas exhibited two wickerwork copies of Gog and Magog, fourteen feet high, their faces on a level with the first-floor windows of Cheapside, and these monstrosities delighted the crowd.

In 1701 (William III.) Sir William Gore, mercer, being Lord Mayor, displayed at his pageant the famous "maiden chariot" of the Mercers' Company. It was drawn by nine white horses, ridden by nine allegorical personages—four representing the four quarters of the world, the other five the retinue of Fame—and all sounding remorselessly on silver trumpets. Fourteen pages, &c., attended the horses, while twenty lictors in silver helmets and forty attendants cleared a way for the procession. The royal virgin in the chariot was attended by Truth and Mercy, besides kettle-drummers and trumpeters. The quaintest thing was that at the Guildhall banquet the virgin, surrounded by all her ladies and pages, dined in state at a separate table.

The last Lord Mayor's pageant of the old school was in 1702, under Anne, when Sir Samuel Dashwood, vintner, entertained Her Majesty at the Guildhall. Poor Elkanah Settle (Pope's butt) wrote the *libretto*, in hopes to revive a festival then "almost dropping into oblivion." On his return from Westminster, the Mayor was met at the Blackfriars Stairs by St. Martin, patron of the Vintners, in rich armour and riding a white steed. The generous saint was attended by twenty dancing satyrs, with tambourines; ten halberdiers, with rustic music; and ten Roman lictors. At St.

Paul's Churchyard the saint made a stand, and, drawing his sword, cut off half his crimson scarf, and gave it to some beggars and cripples who importuned him for charity. The pageants were fanciful enough, and poor Settle must have cudgelled his dull brains well for it. The first was an Indian galleon crowded by Bacchanals wreathed with vines. On the deck of the grape-hung vessel sat Bacchus himself, "properly drest." The second pageant was the chariot of Ariadne, drawn by panthers. Then came St. Martin, as a bishop in a temple, and next followed "the Vintage," an eight-arched structure, with termini of satyrs and ornamented with vines. Within was a bar, with a beautiful person keeping it, with drawers (waiters), and gentlemen sitting drinking round a tavern table. On seeing the Lord Mayor, the bar-keeper called to the drawers—

> " Where are your eyes and ears ?
> See there what honourable *gent* appears !
> Augusta's great Prætorian lord—but hold !
> Give me a goblet of true Orient mould.
> And with," &c.

In 1727, the first year of the reign of King George II., the king, queen, and royal family having received a humble invitation from the City to dine at Guildhall, their Majesties, the Princess Royal, and her Royal Highness the Princess Carolina, came into Cheapside about three o'clock in the afternoon, attended by the great officers of the court and a numerous train of the nobility and gentry in their coaches, the streets being lined from Temple Bar by the militia of London, and the balconies adorned with tapestry. Their Majesties and the princesses saw the Lord Mayor's procession from a balcony near Bow Church. Hogarth has introduced a later royal visitor—Frederick, Prince of Wales—in a Cheapside balcony, hung with tapestry, in his " Industrious and Idle Apprentices" (plate xii.). A train-band man in the crowd is firing off a musket to express his delight.

Sir Samuel Fludyer, Lord Mayor of London in the year 1761, the year of the marriage of good King George III., appears to have done things with thoroughness. In a contemporary chronicle we find a very sprightly narrative of Sir Samuel's Lord Mayor's show, in which the king and queen, with "the rest of the royal family," participated—their Majesties, indeed, not getting home from the Guildhall ball until two in the morning. Our sight-seer was an early riser. He found the morning foggy, as is common to this day in London about the 9th of November; but soon the fog cleared away, and the day was brilliantly fine—an exception, he notes, to what had already, in his time,

become proverbial, that the Lord Mayor's day is almost invariably a bad one. He took boat on the Thames, that he might accompany the procession of state barges on their way to Westminster. He reports "the silent highway" as being quite covered with boats and gilded barges. The barge of the Skinners' Company was distinguished by the outlandish dresses of strange-spotted skins and painted hides worn by the rowers. The barge belonging to the Stationers' Company, after having passed through one of the narrow arches of Westminster Bridge, and tacked about to do honour to the Lord Mayor's landing, touched at Lambeth and took on board, from the archbishop's palace, a hamper of claret—the annual tribute of theology to learning. The tipple must have been good, for our chronicler tells us that it was "constantly reserved for the future regalement of the master, wardens, and court of assistants, and not suffered to be shared by the common crew of liverymen." He did not care to witness the familiar ceremony of swearing in the Lord Mayor in Westminster Hall, but made the best of his way to the Temple Stairs, where it was the custom of the Lord Mayor to land on the conclusion of the aquatic portion of the pageant. There he found some of the City companies already landed, and drawn up in order in Temple Lane, between two rows of the train-bands, " who kept excellent discipline." Other of the companies were wiser in their generation ; they did not land prematurely to cool their heels in Temple Lane, while the royal procession was passing along the Strand, but remained on board their barges regaling themselves comfortably. The Lord Mayor encountered good Samaritans in the shape of the master and benchers of the Temple, who invited him to come on shore and lunch with them in the Temple Hall.

Every house from Temple Bar to Guildhall was crowded from top to bottom, and many had scaffoldings besides ; carpets and rich hangings were hung out on the fronts all the way along ; and our friend notes that the citizens were not mercenary, but "generously accommodated their friends and customers gratis, and entertained them in the most elegant manner, so that though their shops were shut, they might be said to have kept open house."

The royal procession, which set out from St. James's Palace at noon, did not reach Cheapside until near four, when in the short November day it must have been getting dark. Our sight-seer, as the royal family passed his window, counted between twenty and thirty coaches-and-six belonging to them and to their attendants, besides those of the foreign ambassadors, officers of state, and the principal nobility. There preceded their Majesties the Duke of Cumberland, Princess Amelia, the Duke of York, in a new state coach; the Princes William Henry and Frederic, the Princess Dowager of Wales, and the Princesses Augusta and Caroline in one coach, preceded by twelve footmen with black caps, followed by guards and a grand retinue. The king and queen were in separate coaches, and had separate retinues. Our friend in the window of the "Queen's Arms" was in luck's way. From a booth at the eastern end of the churchyard the children of Christ's

and the balconies waved their hats, and the ladies their handkerchiefs."

The Lord Mayor's state coach was drawn by six beautiful iron-grey horses, gorgeously caparisoned, and the Companies made a grand appearance. Even a century ago, however, degeneracy had set in. Our sight-seer complains that the Armourers' and Braziers', the Skinners' and Fishmongers' Companies were the only companies that had on the occasion anything like the pageantry exhibited of old. The Armourers sported an archer riding erect in his car, having his bow in his left hand, and his quiver and arrows hanging behind his left shoulder;

FIGURES OF GOG AND MAGOG SET UP IN GUILDHALL AFTER THE FIRE.

Hospital paid their public respects to their Majesties, the senior scholar of the grammar-school reciting a lengthy and loyal address, after which the boys chanted "God Save the King." At last the royal family reached the house of Mr. Barclay, the Quaker, from the balcony of which, hung with crimson silk damask, they were to see, with what daylight remained, the civic procession that presently followed; but in the interval came Mr. Pitt, in his chariot, accompanied by Earl Temple. The great commoner was then in the zenith of his popularity; and our sight-seer narrates how, "at every step, the mob clung about every part of the vehicle, hung upon the wheels, hugged his footmen, and even kissed his horses. There was a universal huzza, and the gentlemen at the windows

also a man in complete armour. The Skinners were distinguished by seven of their company being dressed in fur, having their skins painted in the form of Indian princes. The pageant of the Fishmongers consisted of a statue of St. Peter finely gilt, a dolphin, two mermaids, and a couple of sea-horses; all of whom duly passed before Georgius Rex as he leaned over the balcony with Queen Charlotte by his side.

Our chronicler understood well the strategic movements indispensable to the zealous sight-seer. As soon as the Lord Mayor's procession had passed him, he "posted along the back lanes, to avoid the crowd," and reached the Guildhall in advance of the Lord Mayor. He had procured a ticket for the banquet through the interest of a friend, who

THE ROYAL BANQUET IN GUILDHALL. *From a Contemporary Print.* (*See page 326.*)

was one of the committee for managing the entertainment, and also a "mazarine." It is explained that this was a kind of nickname given to the common councilmen, on account of their wearing mazarine blue silk gowns. He learned that the doors of the hall had been first opened at nine in the morning for the admission of ladies into the galleries, who were the friends of the committee men, and who got the best places; and subsequently at twelve for the general reception of all who had a right to come in. What a terrible spell of waiting those fortunate unfortunates comprising the earliest batch must have had! The galleries presented a very brilliant show; and among the company below were all the officers of state, the principal nobility, and the foreign ambassadors. The Lord Mayor arrived at half-past six, and the sheriffs went straight to Mr. Barclay's to conduct the royal family to the hall. The passage from the hall-gate to steps leading to the King's Bench was lined by "mazarines" with candles in their hands, by aldermen in their red gowns, and gentlemen pensioners with their axes in their hands. At the bottom of the steps stood the Lord Mayor and the Lady Mayoress, with the entertainment committee, to receive the members of the royal family as they arrived. The princes and princesses, as they successively came in, waited in the body of the hall until their Majesties' entrance. On their arrival being announced, the Lord Mayor and the Lady Mayoress, as the chronicler puts it, advanced to the great door of the hall; and at their Majesties' entrance, the Lord Mayor presented the City sword, which being returned, he carried before the King, the Queen following, with the Lady Mayoress behind her. "The music had struck up, but was drowned in the acclamations of the company; in short, all was life and joy; even the giants, Gog and Magog, seemed to be almost animated." The King, at all events, was more than almost animated; he volubly praised the splendour of the scene, and was very gracious to the Lord Mayor on the way to the council chamber, followed by the royal family and the reception committee. This room reached, the Recorder delivered the inevitable addresses, and the wives and daughters of the aldermen were presented. These ladies had the honour of being saluted by his Majesty, and of kissing the Queen's hand, then the sheriffs were knighted, as also was the brother of the Lord Mayor.

After half an hour's stay in the council chamber, the royal party returned into the hall, and were conducted to the upper end of it, called the hustings, where a table was provided for them, at which they sat by themselves. There had been, it seems, a knotty little question of etiquette. The ladies-in-waiting on the Queen had claimed the right of custom to dine at the same table with her Majesty, but this was disallowed; so they dined at the table of the Lady Mayoress in the Court of King's Bench. The royal table "was set off with a variety of emblematic ornaments, beyond description elegant," and a superb canopy was placed over their Majesties' heads at the upper end. For the Lord Mayor, aldermen, and their ladies, there was a table on the lower hustings. The privy councillors, ministers of state, and great nobles dined at a table on the right of this; the foreign ministers at one on the left. For the mazarines and the general company there were eight tables laid out in the body of the hall, while the judges, serjeants, and other legal celebrities, dined in the old council chamber, and the attendants of the distinguished visitors were regaled in the Court of Common Pleas.

George and his consort must have found a fine appetite between noon and nine o'clock, the hour at which the dinner was served. The aldermen on the committee acted as waiters at the royal table. The Lord Mayor stood behind the King, "in quality of chief butler, while the Lady Mayoress waited on Her Majesty" in the same capacity, but soon after seats were taken they were graciously sent to their places. The dinner consisted of three courses, besides the dessert, and the purveyors were Messrs. Horton and Birch, the same house which in the present day supplies most of the civic banquets. The illustration which we give on the previous page is from an old print of the period representing this celebrated festival, and is interesting not merely on account of the scene which it depicts, but also as a view of Guildhall at that period.

The bill of fare at the royal table on this occasion is extant, and as it is worth a little study on the part of modern epicures, we give it here at full length for their benefit:—

FIRST SERVICE.

Venison, turtle soups, fish of every sort, viz., dorys, mullets, turbots, tench, soles, &c., nine dishes.

SECOND SERVICE.

A fine roast, ortolans, teals, quails, ruffs, knotts, peachicks, snipes, partridges, pheasants, &c., nine dishes.

THIRD SERVICE.

Vegetables and made dishes, green peas, green morelles, green truffles, cardoons, artichokes, ducks' tongues, fat livers, &c., eleven dishes.

FOURTH SERVICE.

Curious ornaments in pastry and makes, jellies, blomonges, in variety of shapes, figures, and colours, nine dishes.

In all, not including the dessert, there were placed on the tables four hundred and fourteen dishes, hot and cold. Wine was varied and copious. In the language of the chronicler, " champagne, burgundy, and other valuable wines were to be had everywhere, and nothing was so scarce as water." When the second course was being laid on, the toasts began. The common crier, standing before the royal table, demanded silence, then proclaimed aloud that their Majesties drank to the health and prosperity of the Lord Mayor, aldermen, and common council of the City of London. Then the common crier, in the name of the civic dignitaries, gave the toast of health, long life, and prosperity to their most gracious Majesties. After dinner there was no tarrying over the wine-cup. The royal party retired at once to the council chamber, " where they had their tea." What became of the rest of the company is not mentioned, but clearly the Guildhall could have been no place for them. That was summarily occupied by an army of carpenters. The tables were struck and carried out. The hustings, where the great folks had dined, and the floor of which had been covered with rich carpeting, was covered afresh, and the whole hall rapidly got ready for the ball, with which the festivities were to conclude. On the return of their majesties, and as soon as they were seated under the canopy, the ball was opened by the Duke of York and the Lady Mayoress. It does not appear that the royal couple took the floor, but " other minuets succeeded by the younger branches of the royal family with ladies of distinction."

About midnight His Majesty, beginning probably to get sleepy with all this derangement of his ordinarily methodical way of living, signified his desire to take his departure; but things are not always possible even when kings are in question. Such was the hurry and confusion outside—at least, that is the reason assigned by the chronicler—that there was great delay in fetching up the royal carriages to the Guildhall door. It is more than probable that the coachmen were all drunk, not excepting the state coachman himself. Their Majesties waited half an hour before their coach could be brought up, and perhaps, after all the interchange of civilities, went away in bad temper. The Princess Dowager of Wales did so, for she waited some time in the temporary passage, " nor could she be prevailed on to retire into the hall." There was no procession on the return from the City. The royal people returned home as they best might, and according as their carriages came to hand. But we are told that on the return journey,

past midnight as it was, the crowd in some places was quite as great as it had been in the daytime, and that Mr. Pitt was vociferously cheered all the way to his own door. The King and Queen did not get home to St. James's till two o'clock in the morning; and it is a confirmation of the suggestion that the coachman must have been drunk, that in turning under the gate one of the glasses of their coach was broken by the roof of the sentry-box. As for the festive people left behind in the Guildhall, they kept the ball up till three o'clock, and we are told that " the whole was concluded with the utmost regularity and decorum." Indeed, Sir Samuel Fludyer's Lord Mayor's day appears to have been a triumphant success. His Majesty himself, we are told, was pleased to declare " that to be elegantly entertained he must come into the City." The foreign ministers in general expressed their wonder, and one of them politely said in French, that this entertainment was only fit for one king to give to another.

One of the Barclays has left a pleasant account of this visit of George III. to the City to see the Lord Mayor's Show :—" The Queen's clothes," says the lady, " which were as rich as gold, silver, and silk could make them, was a suit from which fell a train supported by a little page in scarlet and silver. The lustre of her stomacher was inconceivable. The King I think a very personable man. All the princes followed the King's example in complimenting each of us with a kiss. The Queen was upstairs three times, and my little darling, with Patty Barclay and Priscilla Bell, were introduced to her. I was present, and not a little anxious, on account of my girl, who kissed the Queen's hand with so much grace, that I thought the Princess Dowager would have smothered her with kisses. Such a report of her was made to the King, that Miss was sent for, and afforded him great amusement by saying, ' that she loved the king, though she must not love fine things, and her grandpapa would not allow her to make a curtsey.' Her sweet face made such an impression on the Duke of York, that I rejoiced she was only five instead of fifteen. When he first met her, he tried to persuade Miss to let him introduce her to the Queen, but she would by no means consent, till I informed her he was a prince, upon which her little female heart relented, and she gave him her hand—a true copy of the sex. The King never sat down, nor did he taste anything during the whole time. Her Majesty drank tea, which was brought her on a silver waiter by brother John, who delivered it to the lady in waiting, and she presented it kneeling. The leave they took of us was such as we might expect from our equals—full of apologies for our trouble for their entertainment, which they were so anxious to have explained, that the Queen came up to us as we stood on one side of the door, and had every word interpreted. My brothers had the honour of assisting the Queen into her coach. Some of us sat up to see them return, and the King and Queen took especial notice of us as they passed. The King ordered twenty-four of his guard to be placed opposite our door all night, lest any of the canopy should be pulled down by the mob, in which " (the canopy, it is to be presumed) "there were 100 yards of silk damask."

"From the above particulars we learn," says Dr. Doran, " that it was customary for our sovereigns to do honour to industry long before the period of the Great Exhibition year, which is erroneously supposed to be the opening of an era when a sort of fraternisation took place between commerce and the Crown. Under the old reign, too, the honour took a homely, but not an undignified, and if still a ceremonious, yet a hearty shape. It may be questioned, if Royalty were to pay a visit to the family of the present Mr. Barclay, whether the monarch would celebrate the brief sojourn by kissing all the daughters of ' Barclay and Perkins.' He might do many things not half so pleasant."

The most important feature of the modern show, says Mr. Fairholt very truly, is the splendidly carved and gilt coach in which the Lord Mayor rides ; and the paintings that decorate it may be considered as the relics of the ancient pageants that gave us the living representatives of the virtues and attributes of the chief magistrate here delineated. Cipriani was the artist who executed this series of paintings, in 1757 ; and they exhibit upon the panel of the right door, Fame presenting the Mayor to the genius of the City ; on the left door, the same genius, attended by Britannia, who points with her spear to a shield, inscribed " Henry Fitz-Alwin, 1109." On each side of the doors are painted Truth, with her mirror ; Temperance, holding a bridle ; Justice, and Fortitude. The front panel exhibits Faith and Hope, pointing to St. Paul's ; the back panel Charity, two female figures, typical of Plenty and Riches, casting money and fruits into her lap— while a wrecked sailor and sinking ship fill up the background. By the kind permission of the Lord Mayor we are enabled to give a representation of the ponderous old vehicle, which is still the centre of attraction every 9th of November.

The carved work of the coach is elaborate and beautiful, consisting of Cupids supporting the City arms, &c. The roof was formerly ornamented in the centre with carved work, representing four boys supporting baskets of fruit, &c. These were damaged by coming into collision with an archway leading into Blackwall Hall, about fifty years ago ; some of the figures were knocked off, and the group was entirely removed in consequence. This splendid coach was paid for by a subscription of £60 from each of the junior aldermen, and such as had not passed the civic chair—its total cost being £1,065 3s. Subsequently each alderman, when sworn into office, contributed that sum to keep it in repair ; for which purpose, also, each Lord Mayor gave £100, which was allowed to him in case the cost of the repairs during his mayoralty rendered it requisite. This arrangement was not, however, complied with for many years ; after which the whole expense fell upon the Lord Mayor, and in one year it exceeded £300. This outlay being considered an unjust tax upon the mayor for the time being, the amount over £100 was repaid to him, and the coach became the property of the corporation, the expenses ever since being paid by the Committee for General Purposes. Even so early as twenty years after its construction it was found necessary to repair the coach at an expense of £335 ; and the average expense of the repairs during seven years of the present century is said to have been as much as £115. Hone justly observes, "All that remains of the Lord Mayor's Show to remind the curiously-informed of its ancient character, is the first part of the procession. These are the poor men of the company to which the Lord Mayor belongs, habited in long gowns and close caps of the company's colour, bearing shields on their arms, but without javelins. So many of these lead the show as there are years in the Lord Mayor's age."

Of a later show "Aleph" gives a pleasant account. " I was about nine years old," he says, "when from a window on Ludgate Hill I watched the ponderous mayor's coach, grand and wide, with six footmen standing on the footboard, rejoicing in bouquets as big as their heads and canes four feet high, dragged slowly up the hill by a team of be-ribboned horses, which, as they snorted along, seemed to be fully conscious of the precious freight in the rear. Cinderella's carriage never could boast so goodly a driver ; his full face, of a dusky or purple red, swelled out on each side like the breast of a pouting pigeon ; his three-cornered hat was almost hidden by wide gold lace ; the flowers in his vest were full-blown and jolly, like himself ; his horsewhip covered with blue ribbons, rising and falling at intervals merely for form—such horses were not made to be flogged. Coachee's box was rather a throne than a seat. Then a dozen gorgeous walking footmen on either hand; grave marshalmen, treading gingerly, as if they had corns; and City officers in scarlet, playing at soldiers, but looking anything but soldierly; two trumpeters before and behind, blowing an occasional blast. . . .

"How that old coach swayed to and fro, with its dignified elderly gentlemen and rubicund Lord Mayor, rejoicing in countless turtle feeds—for, reader, it was Sir William Curtis! . . .

"As the ark of copper, plate glass, and enamel crept slowly up the incline, a luckless sweeper-boy (in those days such dwarfed lads were forced to climb chimneys) sidled up to one of the fore horses, and sought to detach a pink bow from his mane. The creature felt his honours diminishing, and turned to snap at the blackee. The sweep screamed, the horse neighed, the mob shouted, and Sir William turned on his pivot cushion to learn what the noise meant; and thus we were enabled to gaze on a Lord Mayor's face. In sooth he was a goodly gentleman, burly, and with three fingers' depth of fat on his portly person, yet every feature evinced kindliness and benevolence of no common order."

The men in armour were from time immemorial important features in the show, and the subjects of many a jest. Hogarth introduces them in one of his series, "Industry and Idleness," and *Punch* has cast many a missile at those disconsolate warriors, who all but perished under their weight of armour, degenerate race that we are !

The suits of burnished mail, though generally understood to be kindly lent for the occasion by the custodian of the Tower armoury, seem now and then to have been borrowed from the playhouse, possibly for the reason that the imitation accoutrements were more showy and superb than the real.

This was at any rate the case (says Mr. Dutton Cook) in 1812, when Sir Claudius Hunter was Lord Mayor, and Mr. Elliston was manager of the Surrey Theatre. A melodramatic play was in preparation, and for this special object the manager had provided, at some considerable outlay, two magnificent suits of brass and steel armour of the fourteenth century, expressly manufactured for him by Mr. Marriott of Fleet Street. No expense had been spared in rendering this harness as complete and splendid as could be. Forthwith Sir Claudius applied to Elliston for the loan of the new armour to enhance the glories of the civic pageant. The request was acceded to with the proviso that the suit of steel could only be lent in the event of the ensuing 9th of November proving free from

damp and fog. No such condition, however, was annexed to the loan of the brass armour; and it was understood that Mr. John Kemble had kindly undertaken to furnish the helmets of the knights with costly plumes, and personally to superintend the arrangement of these decorations. Altogether, it would seem that the mayor stood much indebted to the managers, who, willing to oblige, yet felt that their courtesy was deserving of some sort of public recognition. At least this was Elliston's view of the matter, who read with chagrin sundry newspaper paragraphs, announcing that at the approaching inauguration of Sir Claudius some of the royal armour from the Tower would be exhibited, but ignoring altogether the loan of the matchless suits of steel and brass from the Surrey Theatre. The manager was mortified; he could be generous, but he knew the worth of an advertisement. He expostulated with the future mayor. Sir Claudius replied that he did not desire to conceal the transaction, but rather than it should go forth to the world that so high a functionary as an alderman of London had made a request to a theatrical manager, he thought it advisable to inform the public that Mr. Elliston had offered the use of his property for the procession of the 9th. This was hardly a fair way of stating the case, but at length the following paragraph, drawn up by Elliston, was agreed upon for publication in the newspapers :— "We understand that Mr. Elliston has lent to the Lord Mayor elect the two magnificent suits of armour, one of steel and the other of brass, manufactured by Marriott of Fleet Street, and which cost not less than £600. These very curious specimens of the revival of an art supposed to have been lost will be displayed in the Lord Mayor's procession, and afterwards in Guildhall, with some of the royal armour in the Tower." It would seem also, according to another authority, that the wearers of the armour were members of the Surrey company.

On the 9th Elliston was absent from London, but he received from one left in charge of his interests a particular account of the proceedings of the day :—

"The unhandsome conduct of the Lord Mayor has occasioned me much trouble, and will give you equal displeasure. In the first place, your paragraph never would have appeared at all had I not interfered in the matter; secondly, cropped-tailed hacks had been procured without housings, so that I was compelled to obtain two trumpeters' horses from the Horse Guards, long-tailed animals, and richly caparisoned; thirdly, the helmets which had been delivered at Mr. Kemble's house were not returned until twelve o'clock on the day of action, with three miserable feathers in each, which appeared to have been plucked from the draggle tail of a hunted cock; this I also remedied by sending off at the last moment to the first plumassier for the hire of proper feathers, and the helmets were ultimately decorated with fourteen superb plumes; fourthly, the Lord Mayor's officer, who rode in Henry V. armour, jealous of our stately aspect, attempted to seize one of our horses, on which your rider made as gallant a retort as ever knight in armour could have done, and the assailer was completely foiled."

This was bad enough, but in addition to this

practicable to him. His comrade in brass made light of these objections, gladly took the proffered cup into his gauntleted hands, and "drank the red wine through the helmet barred," as though he had been one of the famous knights of Branksome Tower. It was soon apparent that the man in brass was intoxicated. He became obstreperous; he began to reel and stumble, accoutred as he was, to the hazard of his own bones and to the great dismay of bystanders. It was felt that his fall might entail disaster upon many. Attempts were made to remove him, when he assumed a pugilistic attitude, and resolutely declined to quit the hall. Nor was it possible to enlist against him the ser-

THE LORD MAYOR'S COACH.

the narrator makes further revelation of the behind-the-scenes secrets of a civic pageant sixty years ago. On the arrival of the procession it was found that no accommodation had been arranged for "Mr. Elliston's men," nor were any refreshments proffered them. "For seven hours they were kept within Guildhall, where they seem to have been considered as much removed from the necessities of the flesh as Gog and Magog above their heads."· At length the compassion, or perhaps the sense of humour, of certain of the diners was moved by the forlorn situation of the knights in armour, and bumpers of wine were tendered them. The man in steel discreetly declined this hospitable offer, alleging that after so long a fast he feared the wine would affect him injuriously. It was whispered that his harness imprisoned him so completely that eating and drinking were alike im-

vices of his brother warrior. The man in steel sided with the man in brass, and the two heroes thus formed a powerful coalition, which was only overcome at last by the onset of numbers. The scene altogether was of a most scandalous, if comical, description. It was some time past midnight when Mr. Marriot, the armourer, arrived at Guildhall, and at length succeeded in releasing the two half-dead warriors from their coats of mail.

After all, these famous suits of armour never returned to the wardrobe of the Surrey Theatre, or gleamed upon its stage. From Guildhall they were taken to Mr. Marriott's workshop. This, with all its contents, was accidentally consumed by fire. But the armourer's trade had taught him chivalry. At his own expense, although he had lost some three thousand pounds by the fire, he provided Elliston with new suits of armour in lieu of those that had been destroyed. To his outlay the Lord Mayor and the City authorities contributed—nothing ! although but for the procession of the 9th of November the armour had never been in peril.

The most splendid sight that ever glorified mediæval Cheapside was the Midsummer Marching Watch, a grand City display, the description of which makes even the brown pages of old Stow glow with light and colour, seeming to rouse in the old London chronicler recollections of his youth.

Chamber of London. Besides the which lights, every constable in London, in number more than 240, had his cresset ; the charge of every cresset was in light two shillings four pence ; and every cresset had two men, one to bear or hold it, another to bear a bag with light, and to serve it ; so that the poor men pertaining to the cressets taking wages, besides that every one had a strawen hat, with a badge painted, and his breakfast, amounted in number to almost 2,000. The Marching Watch

THE DEMOLITION OF CHEAPSIDE CROSS. *From an old Print.* (*See page* 334.)

" Besides the standing watches," says Stow, " all in bright harness, in every ward and street in the City and suburbs, there was also a Marching Watch, that passed through the principal streets thereof ; to wit, from the Little Conduit, by Paul's Gate, through West Cheap by the *Stocks*, through Cornhill, by Leaden Hall, to Aldgate ; then back down Fenchurch Street, by Grasse Church, about Grasse Church Conduit, and up Grasse Church Street into Cornhill, and through into West Cheap again, and so broke up. The whole way ordered for this Marching Watch extended to 3,200 taylors' yards of assize. For the furniture whereof, with lights, there were appointed 700 cressets, 500 of them being found by the Companies, the other 200 by the

contained in number about 2,000 men, part of them being old soldiers, of skill to be captains, lieutenants, serjeants, corporals, &c. ; whifflers, drummers and fifes, standard and ensign bearers, demi-launces on great horses, gunners with hand-guns, or half hakes, archers in coats of white fustian, signed on the breast and back with the arms of the City, their bows bent in their hands, with sheafs of arrows by their side ; pikemen, in bright corslets, burganets, &c. ; halbards, the like ; the billmen in Almain rivets and aprons of mail, in great number.

" This Midsummer Watch was thus accustomed yearly, time out of mind, until the year 1539, the 31st of Henry VIII. ; in which year, on the 8th of

May, a great muster was made by the citizens at the *Mile's End*, all in bright harness, with coats of white silk or cloth, and chains of gold, in three great battels, to the number of 15,000; which passed through London to Westminster, and so through the Sanctuary and round about the Park of St. James, and returned home through Oldborn.

"King Henry, then considering the great charges of the citizens for the furniture of this unusual muster, forbad the Marching Watch provided for at midsummer for that year; which being once laid down, was not raised again till the year 1548, the second of Edward the Sixth, Sir John Gresham then being Maior, who caused the Marching Watch, both on the eve of Saint John Baptist, and of Saint Peter the Apostle, to be revived and set forth, in as comely order as it had been accustomed.

"In the months of June and July, on the vigil of festival days, and on the same festival days in the evenings, after the sun-setting, there were usually made bonefires in the streets, every man bestowing wood or labour towards them. The wealthier sort, also, before their doors, near to the said bonefires, would set out tables on the vigils, furnished with sweet bread and good drink; and on the festival days, with meat and drink, plentifully; whereunto they would invite their neighbours and passengers also, to sit and be merry with them in great familiarity, praising God for his benefits bestowed on them. These were called Bonefires, as well of good amity amongst neighbours, that being before at controversie, were there by the labours of others reconciled, and made of bitter enemies loving friends; as also for the virtue that a great fire hath to purge the infection of the air. On the vigil of Saint John Baptist, and on Saint Peter and Paul, the apostles, every man's door being shadowed with green birch, long fennel, St. John's wort, orpin, white lillies, and such-like, garnished upon with beautiful flowers, had also lamps of glass, with oyl burning in them all the night. Some hung out branches of iron, curiously wrought, containing hundreds of lamps, lighted at once, which made a goodly show, namely, in New Fish Street, Thames Street, &c."

CHAPTER XXVIII.

CHEAPSIDE: CENTRAL.

Grim Chronicles of Cheapside—Cheapside Cross—Puritanical Intolerance—The Old London Conduits—Mediæval Water-carriers—The Church of St. Mary-le-Bow—"Murder will out"—The "Sound of Bow Bells"—Sir Christopher Wren's Bow Church—Remains of the Old Church—The Seldam—Interesting Houses in Cheapside and their Memories—Goldsmiths' Row—The "Nag's Head" and the Self-consecrated Bishops—Keats' House—Saddler's Hall—A Prince Disguised—Blackmore, the Poet—Alderman Boydell, the Printseller—His Edition of Shakespeare—"Puck"—The Lottery—Death and Burial.

THE Cheapside Standard, opposite Honey Lane, was also a fountain, and was rebuilt in the reign of Henry VI. In the year 1293, under Edward I., three men had their right hands stricken off here for rescuing a prisoner arrested by an officer of the City. In Edward III.'s reign two fishmongers, for aiding a riot, were beheaded at the Standard. Here also, in the reign of Richard II., Wat Tyler, that unfortunate reformer, beheaded Richard Lions, a rich merchant. When Henry IV. usurped the throne, very beneficially for the nation, it was at the Standard in Chepe that he caused Richard II.'s blank charters to be burned. In the reign of Henry VI. Jack Cade, a man who seems to have aimed at removing real evils, beheaded the Lord Say, as readers of Shakespeare's historical plays will remember; and in 1461 John Davy had his offending hand cut off at the Standard for having struck a man before the judges at Westminster.

Cheapside Cross, one of the nine crosses erected by Edward I., that soldier king, to mark the resting-places of the body of his beloved queen, Eleanor of Castile, on its way from Lincoln to Westminster Abbey, stood in the middle of the road facing Wood Street. It was built in 1290 by Master Michael, a mason, of Canterbury. From an old painting at Cowdray, in Sussex, representing the procession of Edward VI. from the Tower to Westminster, an engraving of which we have given on page 313, we gather that the cross was both stately and graceful. It consisted of three octangular compartments, each supported by eight slender columns. The basement story was probably twenty feet high; the second, ten; the third, six. In the first niche stood the effigy of probably a contemporaneous pope; round the base of the second were four apostles, each with a ·nimbus round his head; and above them sat the Virgin, with the infant Jesus in her arms. The highest niche was occupied by four standing figures, while crowning all rose a cross surmounted by the emblematic dove. The whole was rich with highly-finished ornament.

Fox, the martyrologist, says the cross was erected on what was then an open spot of Cheapside. Some writers assert that a statue of Queen Eleanor first stood on the spot, but this is very much doubted. The cross was rebuilt in 1441, and combined with a drinking-fountain. The work was a long time about, as the full design was not carried to completion till the first year of Henry VII. This second erection was, in fact, a sort of a timber-shed surrounding the old cross, and covered with gilded lead. It was, we are told, re-gilt on the visit of the Emperor Charles V. On the accession of Edward VI., that child of promise, the cross was altered and beautified.

The generations came and went. The 'prentice who had played round the cross as a newly-girdled lad sat again on its steps as a rich citizen, in robes and chain. The shaven priest who stopped to mutter a prayer to the half-defaced Virgin in the votive niche gave place to his successor in the Geneva gown, and still the cross stood, a memory of death, that spares neither king nor subject. But in Elizabeth's time, in their horror of image-worship, the Puritans, foaming at the mouth at every outward and visible sign of the old religion, took great exception at "the idolatrous cross of Chepe." Violent protest was soon made. In the night of June 21st, 1581, an attack was made on the lower tier of images—*i.e.*, the Resurrection, Virgin, Christ, and Edward the Confessor, all which were miserably mutilated. The Virgin was "robbed of her son, and the arms broken by which she stayed him on her knees, her whole body also haled by ropes and left ready to fall." The Queen offered a reward, but the offenders were not discovered. In 1595 the effigy of the Virgin was repaired, and afterwards "a newe sonne, mis-shapen (as borne out of time), all naked, was laid in her arms; the other images continuing broken as before." Soon an attempt was made to pull down the woodwork, and substitute a pyramid for the crucifix; the Virgin was superseded by the goddess Diana—"a woman (for the most part naked), and water, conveyed from the Thames, filtering from her naked breasts, but oftentimes dried up." Elizabeth, always a trimmer in these matters, was indignant at these fanatical doings; and thinking a plain cross, a symbol of the faith of our country, ought not to give scandal, she ordered one to be placed on the summit, and gilt. The Virgin also was restored; but twelve nights afterwards she was

again attacked, "her crown being plucked off, and almost her head, taking away her naked child, and stabbing her in the breast." Thus dishonoured the cross was left till the next year, 1600, when it was rebuilt, and the universities were consulted as to whether the crucifix should be restored. They all sanctioned it, except Dr. Abbot, afterwards Archbishop of Canterbury; but there was to be no dove. In a sermon of the period the following passage occurs:—"Oh! this cross is one of the jewels of the harlot of Rome, and is left and kept here as a love-token, and gives them hope that they shall enjoy it and us again." Yet the cross remained undisturbed for several years. At this period it was surrounded by a strong iron railing, and decorated in the most inoffensive manner. It consisted of only four stones. Superstitious images were superseded by grave effigies of apostles, kings, and prelates. The crucifix only of the original was retained. The cross itself was in bad taste, being half-Grecian, half-Gothic; the whole, architecturally, being much inferior to the former fabric.

The uneasy zeal of the Puritanical sects soon revived. On the night of January 24th, 1641, the cross was again defaced, and a sort of literary contention began. We have "The Resolution of those Contemners that will no Crosses;" "Articles of High Treason exhibited against Cheapside Cross;" "The Chimney-sweepers' Sad Complaint, and Humble Petition to the City of London for erecting a Neue Cross;" "A Dialogue between the Cross in Chepe and Charing Cross." Of these here is a specimen—

> *Anabaptist.* O! idol now,
> 　　　Down must thou!
> 　　　Brother Ball,
> 　　　Be sure it shall.
> *Brownist.* Helpe! Wren,
> 　　　Or we are undone men.
> 　　　I shall not fall,
> 　　　To ruin all.

Cheap Cross. I'm so crossed, I fear my utter destruction is at hand.

Charing Cross. Sister of Cheap, crosses are incident to us all, and our children. But what's the greatest cross that hath befallen you?

Cheap Cross. Nay, sister; if my cross were fallen, I should live at more heart's ease than I do.

Charing Cross. I believe it is the cross upon your head that hath brought you into this trouble, is it not?

These disputes were the precursors of its final destruction. In May, 1643, the Parliament deputed to the work Robert Harlow, who went with a troop of horse and two companies of foot, and executed his orders most completely. The official account says rejoicingly:—

"On the 2nd of May, 1643, the cross in Cheapside

was pulled down. At the fall of the top cross drums beat, trumpets blew, and multitudes of caps were thrown into the air, and a great shout of people with joy. The 2nd of May, the almanack says, was the invention of the cross, and the same day at night were the leaden popes burnt (they were not popes, but eminent English prelates) in the place where it stood, with ringing of bells and great acclamation, and no hurt at all done in these actions."

The 10th of the same month the " Book of Sports," a collection of ordinances allowing games on the Sunday, put forth by James I., was burnt by the hangman, where the Cross used to stand, and at the Exchange.

" Aleph " gives us the title of a curious tract, published the very day the Cross was destroyed :— " The Downfall of Dagon; or, the Taking Down of Cheapside Crosse; wherein is contained these principles : 1. The Crosse Sicke at Heart. 2. His Death and Funerall. 3. His Will, Legacies, In- ventory, and Epitaph. 4. Why it was removed. 5. The Money it will bring. 6. Noteworthy, that it was cast down on that day when it was first invented and set up."

It may be worth giving an extract or two :— " I am called the ' Citie Idoll;' the Brownists spit at me, and throw stones at me; others hide their eyes with their fingers; the Anabaptists wish me knockt in pieces, as I am like to be this day; the sisters of the fraternity will not come near me, but go about by Watling Street, and come in again by Soaper Lane, to buy their provisions of the market folks. . . . I feele the pangs of death, and shall never see the end of the merry month of May; my breath stops; my life is gone; I feel myself a-dying downwards."

Here are some of the bequests :—" I give my iron-work to those people which make good swords, at Hounslow; for I am all Spanish iron and steele to the back.

" I give my body and stones to those masons that cannot telle how to frame the like againe, to keepe by them for a patterne; for in time there will be more crosses in London than ever there was yet.

" I give my ground whereon I stood to be a free market-place.

"JASPER CROSSE, HIS EPITAPH.

" I look for no praise when I am dead,
For, going the right way, I never did tread ;
I was harde as an alderman's doore,
That's shut and stony-hearted to the poore.
I never gave alms, nor did anything
Was good, nor e'er said, God save the King.

I stood like a stock that was made of wood,
And yet the people would not say I was good ;
And if I tell them plaine, they're like to mee—
Like stone to all goodnesse. But now, reader, see
Me in the dust, for crosses must not stand,
There is too much cross tricks within the land ;
And, having so done never any good,
I leave my prayse for to be understood ;
For many women, after this my losse,
Will remember me, and still will be crosse—
Crosse tricks, crosse ways, and crosse vanities,
Believe the Crosse speaks truth, for here he lyes.

" I was built of lead, iron, and stone. Some say that divers of the crowns and sceptres are of silver, besides the rich gold that I was gilded with, which might have been filed and saved, yielding a good value. Some have offered four hundred, some five hundred; but they that bid most offer one thousand for it. I am to be taken down this very Tuesday; and I pray, good reader, take notice by the almanack, for the sign falls just at this time, to be in the feete, to showe that the crosse must be laide equall with the grounde, for our feete to tread on and what day it was demolished; that is, on the day when crosses were first invented and set up; and so I leave the rest to your con- sideration."

Howell, the letter-writer, lamenting the demoli- tion of so ancient and visible a monument, says that trumpets were blown all the while the crowbars and pickaxes were working. Archbishop Laud in his " Diary " notes that on May 1st the fanatical mob broke the stained-glass windows of his Lambeth chapel, and tore up the steps of his communion table.

" On Tuesday," this fanatic of another sort writes, " the cross in Cheapside was taken down to cleanse that great street of superstition." The amiable Evelyn notes in his " Diary " that he him- self saw " the furious and zelous people demolish that stately crosse in Cheapside." In July, 1645, two years afterwards, and in the middle of the Civil War, Whitelock (afterwards Oliver Cromwell's trimming minister) mentions a burning on the site of the Cheapside cross of crucifixes, Popish pictures, and books. Soon after the demolition of the cross, says Howell, a high square stone rest was " popped up in Cheapside, hard by the Standard," according to the legacy of Russell, a good-hearted porter. This " rest and be thankful " bore the following simple distich :—

" God bless thee, porter, who great pains doth take ;
Rest here, and welcome, when thy back doth ache."

There are four views of the old Cheapside cross extant—one at Cowdray, one in the Pepysian library, Cambridge. A third, engraved by Wilkinson, represents the procession of Mary de Medicis, on her way through Cheapside; and another, which we give on page 331, shows the demolition of the cross.

The old London conduits were pleasant gathering places for 'prentices, serving-men, and servant girls — open-air parliaments of chatter, scandal, love-making, and trade talk. Here all day repaired the professional water-carriers, rough, sturdy fellows, like Ben Jonson's Cob, who were hired to supply the houses of the rich goldsmiths of Chepe, and who, before Sir Hugh Middleton brought the New River to London, were indispensable to the citizen's very existence.

The Great Conduit of Cheapside stood in the middle of the east end of the street near its junction with the Poultry, while the Little Conduit was at the west end, facing Foster Lane and Old Change. Stow, that indefatigable stitcher together of old history, describes the larger conduit curtly as bringing sweet water "by pipes of lead underground from Tyburn (Paddington) for the service of the City." It was castellated with stone and cisterned in lead about 1285, under Edward I. and again new built and enlarged by Thomas Ham, a sheriff in 1479. Ned Ward, writing in 1700, in his lively, ribald way, describes Cheapside conduit (he does not say which) palisaded with chimney-sweepers' brooms and surrounded by sweeps probably waiting to be hired, so that "a countryman, seeing so many black attendants waiting at a stone hovel, took it to be one of Old Nick's tenements."

In the reign of Edward III. the supply of water for the City seems to have been derived chiefly from the river, the local conduits being probably insufficient. The carters, called "water-leders" in 24th Edward III., were ordered by the City to charge three-halfpence for taking a cart from Dowgate or Castle Baynard to Chepe, and five farthings if they stopped short of Chepe, while a sand-cart from Aldgate to Chepe Conduit was allowed to charge threepence.

The Church of St. Mary-le-Bow, the sound of whose mellow bells is supposed to be so dear to cockney ears, is the glory and crown of modern Cheapside. The music it casts forth into the troubled London air has a special magic of its own, and has a power to waken memories of the past. This *chef-d'œuvre* of Sir Christopher Wren, whose steeple—as graceful as it is stately—rises like a lighthouse above the roar and jostle of the human deluge below, stands on an ecclesiastical site of great antiquity. The old tradition is that here, as at St. Paul's and Westminster, was a Roman temple, but of that there is no proof whatever. The first Bow Church seems, however, to have been one of the earliest churches built by the conquerors of Harold; and here, no doubt, the sullen Saxons came to sneer at the masse chanted with a French accent. The first church was racked by storm and fire, was for a time turned into a fortress, was afterwards the scene of a murder, and last of all became one of our earliest ecclesiastical courts. Stow, usually very clear and unconfused, rather contradicts himself for once about the origin of the name of the church—"St. Mary de Arcubus or Bow." In one place he says it was so called because it was the first London church built on arches; and elsewhere, when out of sight of this assertion, he says that it took its name from certain stone arches supporting a lantern on the top of the tower. The first is more probably the true derivation, for St. Paul's could also boast its Saxon crypt. Bow Church is first mentioned in the reign of William the Conqueror, and it was probably built at that period.

There seems to have been nothing specially to disturb the fair building and its ministering priests till the reign of William Rufus, when in a tremendous storm that sent the monks to their knees, and shook the very saints from their niches over portal and arch, the roof of Bow Church was, by one great wrench of the wind, lifted off and wafted down like a mere dead leaf into the street. It does not say much for the state of the highway that four of the huge rafters, twenty-six feet long, were driven (so the chroniclers say) twenty-two feet into the ground.

In 1270 part of the steeple fell, and caused the death of several persons; so that the work of mediæval builders does not seem to have been always irreproachable.

In 1284, under Edward I., blood was shed, and the right of sanctuary violated, in Bow Church. One Duckett, a goldsmith, having in that warlike age wounded in some fray a person named Ralph Crepin, took refuge in this church, and slept in the steeple. While there, certain friends of Crepin entered during the night, and violating the sanctuary, first slew Duckett, and then so placed the body as to induce the belief that he had committed suicide. A verdict to this effect was accordingly returned at the inquisition, and the body was interred with the customary indignities. The real circumstances, however, being afterwards discovered, through the evidence of a boy, who, it appears, was with Duckett in his voluntary confinement, and had hid himself during the struggle, the murderers, among whom was a woman, were apprehended and

executed.   After this occurrence the church was
interdicted for a time, and the doors and windows
stopped with brambles.

The first we hear of the nightly ringing of Bow
bell at nine o'clock—a reminiscence, probably, of

the revival of an old and favourite usage.   The
rhymes are—

" Clarke of the Bow bell, with the yellow lockes,
    For thy late ringing, thy head shall have knockes."

To this the clerk replies—

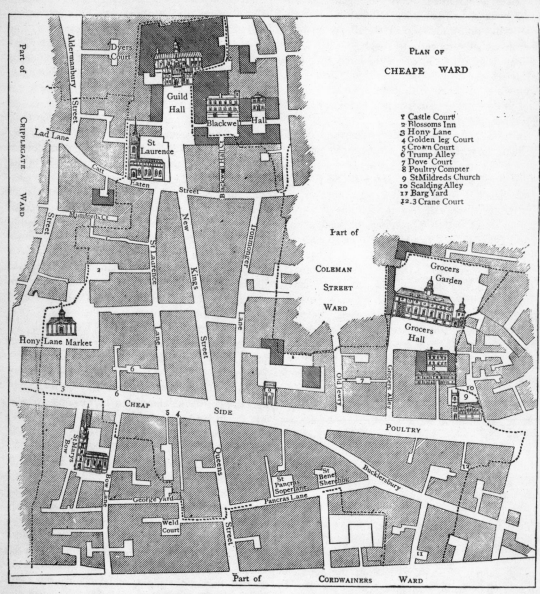

PLAN OF

CHEAPE WARD

1 Castle Court
2 Blossoms Inn
3 Hony Lane
4 Golden leg Court
5 Crown Court
6 Trump Alley
7 Dove Court
8 Poultry Compter
9 St Mildreds Church
10 Scalding Alley
11 Barg Yard
12-3 Crane Court

OLD MAP OF THE WARD OF CHEAP—ABOUT 1750.

the tyrannical Norman curfew, or signal for ex-
tinguishing the lights at eight p.m.—is in 1315
(Edward II.).   It was the go-to-bed bell of those
early days ; and two old couplets still exist, supposed
to be the complaint of the sleepy 'prentices of
Chepe and the obsequious reply of the Bow Church
clerk.   In the reign of Henry VI. the steeple was
completed, and the ringing of the bell was, perhaps,

" Children of Chepe, hold you all still,
    For you shall have Bow bell rung at your will."

In 1315 (Edward II.) William Copeland, church-
warden of Bow, gave a new bell to the church, or
had the old one re-cast.

In 1512 (Henry VIII.) the upper part of the
steeple was repaired, and the lanthorn and the
stone arches forming the open coronet of the tower

were finished with Caen stone. It was then proposed to glaze the five corner lanthorns and the top lanthorn, and light them up with torches or cressets at night, to serve as beacons for travellers on the northern roads to London; but the idea was never carried out.

By the Great Fire of 1666, the old church was destroyed; and in 1671 the present edifice was commenced by Sir C. Wren. After it was erected the parish was united to two others, Allhallows, Honey Lane, and St. Pancras, Soper Lane. As the right of presentation to the latter of them is also vested in the Archbishop of Canterbury, and that of the former in the Grocers' Company, the Archbishop nominates twice consecutively, and the Grocers' Company once. We learn from the "Parentalia," that the former church had been mean and low. On digging out the ground, a foundation was discovered sufficiently firm for the intended fabric, which, on further examination, the account states, appeared to be the walls and pavement of a temple, or church, of Roman workmanship, entirely buried under the level of the present street.

THE SEAL OF BOW CHURCH.
(See page 338.)

In reality, however (unless other remains were found below those since seen, which is not probable), this was nothing more than the crypt of the ancient Norman church, and it may still be examined in the vaults of the present building; for, as the account informs us, upon these walls was commenced the new church. The former building stood about forty feet southwards from Cheapside; and in order to bring the new steeple forward to the line of the street, the site of a house not yet rebuilt was purchased, and on it the excavations were commenced for the foundation of the tower. Here a Roman causeway was found, supposed to be the once northern boundary of the colony. The church was completed (chiefly at the expense of subscribers)

in 1680. A certain Dame Dyonis Williamson, of Hale's Hall, in the county of Norfolk, gave £2,000 towards the rebuilding. Of the monuments in the church, that to the memory of Dr. Newton Bishop of Bristol, and twenty-five years rector of Bow Church, is the most noticeable. In 1820 the spire was repaired by George Gwilt, architect, and the upper part of it taken down and rebuilt. There used to be a large building, called the Crown-sild, or shed, on the north side of the old church (now the site of houses in Cheapside), which was erected by Edward III., as a place from which the Royal Family might view tournaments and other entertainments thereafter occurring in Cheapside. Originally the King had nothing but a temporary wooden shed for the purpose; but this falling down, as already described (page 316), led to the erection of the Crown-sild.

"Without the north side of this church of St. Mary Bow," says Stow, "towards West Chepe, standeth one fair building of stone, called in record Seldam, a shed which greatly darkeneth the said church; for by means thereof all the windows and doors on that side are stopped up. King Edward caused this sild or shed to be made, and to be strongly built of stone, for himself, the queen, and other estates to stand in, there to behold the joustings and other shows at their pleasure. And this house for a long time after served for that use —viz., in the reigns of Edward III. and Richard II.; but in the year 1410 Henry IV. confirmed the said shed or building to Stephen Spilman, William Marchfield, and John Whateley, mercers, by the name of one New Seldam, shed, or building, with shops, cellars, and edifices whatsoever appertaining, called Crownside or Tamersilde, situate in the Mercery in West Chepe, and in the parish of St. Mary de Arcubus, in London, &c. Notwithstanding which grant the kings of England and other great estates, as well of foreign countries repairing to this realm, as inhabitants of the same, have usually repaired to this place, therein to behold the shows of this city passing through West Chepe—viz., the great watches accustomed in the night, on the even of St. John the Baptist and St. Peter at Midsummer, the example whereof were over long to recite, wherefore let it suffice briefly to touch one. In the year 1510, on St. John's even at night, King Henry VIII. came to this place, then called the King's Head in Chepe, in the livery of a yeoman of the guard, with a halbert on his shoulder, and there beholding the watch, departed privily when the watch was done, and was not known to any but whom it pleased him; but on St. Peter's night next following he and the queen came royally riding to the said place, and there with their nobles beheld the watch of the city, and returned in the morning."

The *Builder*, of 1845, gives a full account of the discovery of architectural remains beneath some houses in Bow Churchyard :—

"They are," says the *Builder*, "of a much later date than the celebrated Norman crypt at present existing under the church. Beneath the house No. 5 is a square vaulted chamber, twelve feet by seven feet three inches high, with a slightly pointed arch of ribbed masonry, similar to some of those of the Old London Bridge. There had been in the centre of the floor an excavation, which might have been formerly used as a bath, but which was now arched over and converted into a cesspool. Proceeding towards Cheapside, there appears to be a continuation of the vaulting beneath the houses Nos. 4 and 3. The arch of the vault here is plain and more pointed. The masonry appears, from an aperture near to the warehouse above, to be of considerable thickness. This crypt or vault is seven feet in height, from the floor to the crown of the arch, and is nine feet in width, and eighteen feet long. Beneath the house No. 4 is an outer vault. The entrance to both these vaults is by a depressed Tudor arch, with plain spandrils, six feet high, the thickness of the walls about four feet. In the thickness of the eastern wall of one of the vaults are cut triangular-headed niches, similar to those in which, in ancient ecclesiastical edifices, the basins containing the holy water, and sometimes lamps, were placed. These vaultings appear originally to have extended to Cheapside; for beneath a house there, in a direct line with these buildings and close to the street, is a massive stone wall. The arches of this crypt are of the low pointed form, which came into use in the sixteenth century.

There are no records of any monastery having existed on this spot, and it is difficult to conjecture what the building originally was. Mr. Chaffers thought it might be the remains of the *Crown-sild*, or shed, where our sovereigns resorted to view the joustings, shows, and great marching matches on the eves of great festivals."

The ancient silver parish seal of St. Mary-le-Bow, of which we give an engraving on page 337, representing the tower of the church as it existed before the Great Fire of 1666, is still in existence. It represents the old coronetted tower with great exactitude.

The first recorded rector of Bow Church was William D. Cilecester (1287, Edward I.) ; and the earliest known monument in the church was in memory of Sir John Coventry, Lord Mayor in 1425 (Henry VI.) The living is in the gift of the Archbishop of Canterbury and the Grocers' Company, the former having two turns, and the latter one.

Lovers of figures may like to know that the height of Bow steeple is 221 feet 8½ inches. The church altogether cost £7,388 8s. 7d.

It was in Bow parish, Maitland thinks, that John Hare, the rich mercer, lived, at the sign of the "Crown," in the reign of Henry VIII. He was a Suffolk man, made a large fortune, and left a considerable sum in charity—to poor prisoners, to the hospitals, the lazar-houses, and the alms-men of Whittington College—and thirty-five heavy gold mourning rings to special friends.

Edward IV., the same day he was proclaimed, dined at the palace at Paul's (that is, Baynard's Castle, near St. Paul's), in the City, and continued there till his army was ready to march in pursuit of King Henry ; during which stay in the City he caused Walter Walker, an eminent grocer in Cheapside, to be apprehended and tried for a few harmless words innocently spoken by him—viz., that he would make his son heir to the Crown, inoffensively meaning his own house, which had the crown for its sign ; for which imaginary crime he was beheaded in Smithfield, on the eighth day of this king's reign. This "Crown" was probably Hare's house.

The house No. 108, Cheapside, opposite Bow Church, was rebuilt after the Great Fire upon the sites of three ancient houses, called respectively the "Black Bull," leased to Daniel Waldo ; the "Cardinalle Hat," leased to Ann Stephens ; and the "Black Boy," leased to William Carpenter, by the Mercers' Company. In the library of the City of London there are MSS. from the Surveys of Wills, &c., after the Fire of London, giving a description of the property, as well as the names of the respective owners. It was subsequently leased to David Barclay, linendraper ; and has been visited by six reigning sovereigns, from Charles II. to George III., on civic festivities, and for witnessing the Lord Mayor's show. In this house Sir Edward Waldo was knighted by Charles II., and the Lord Mayor, in 1714, was created a baronet by George I. When the house was taken down in 1861, the fine old oak-panelled dining-room, with its elaborate carvings, was purchased entire, and removed to Wales. The purchaser has written an interesting description (privately printed) of the panelling, the royal visits, the Barclay family, and other interesting matters.

In 1861 there was sold, says Mr. Timbs, amongst the old materials of No. 108, the "fine old oak-panelling of a large dining-room, with chimney-piece and cornice to correspond, elaborately carved in fruit and foliage, in capital preservation, 750 feet superficial." These panels were purchased by Mr. Morris Charles Jones, of Gunrog, near Welshpool, in North Wales, for £72 10s. 3d., including commission and expenses of removal, being about 1s. 8d. per foot superficial. It has been conveyed from Cheapside to Gunrog. This room was the principal apartment of the house of Sir Edward Waldo, and stated, in a pamphlet by Mr. Jones, "to have been visited by six reigning sovereigns, from Charles II. to George III., on the occasion of civic festivities and for the purpose of witnessing the Lord Mayor's show." (See Mr. Jones's pamphlet, privately printed, 1864.) A contemporary (the *Builder*) doubts whether this carving can be the work of Gibbons ; " if so, it is a rare treasure, cheaply gained. But, except in St. Paul's, a Crown and ecclesiastical structure, be it remembered, not a corporate one, there is not a single example of Gibbons' art to be seen in the City of London proper."

Goldsmiths' Row, in Cheapside, between Old Change and Bucklersbury, was originally built by Thomas Wood, goldsmith and sheriff, in 1491 (Henry VII.). Stow, speaking of it, says : " It is a most beautiful frame of houses and shops, consisting of tenne faire dwellings, uniformly builded foure stories high, beautified towards the street with the Goldsmiths' arms, and likeness of Woodmen, in memorie of his name, riding on monstrous beasts, all richly painted and gilt." Maitland assures us " it was beautiful to behold the glorious appearance of goldsmith's shops, in the south row of Cheapside, which reached from the Old Change to Bucklersbury, exclusive of four shops."

The sign in stone of a nag's head upon the front of the old house, No. 39, indicates, it is supposed, the tavern at the corner of Friday Street, where, according to Roman Catholic scandal, the Protestant bishops, on Elizabeth's accession, consecrated each other in a very irregular manner.

Pennant thus relates the scandalous story :—" It was pretended by the adversaries of our religion, that a certain number of ecclesiastics, in their hurry to take possession of the vacant sees, assembled here, where they were to undergo the ceremony from Anthony Kitchen, *alias* Dunstan, Bishop of Llandaff, a sort of occasional conformist, who had taken the oaths of supremacy to Queen Elizabeth. Bonner, Bishop of London, then confined in prison, hearing of it, sent his chaplain to Kitchen, threatening him with excommunication in case he proceeded. The prelate, therefore, refused to perform the ceremony ; on which, say the Roman Catholics, Parker and the other candidates, rather than defer possession of their dioceses, determined to consecrate one another, which, says the story, they did without any sort of scruple, and Scory began with Parker, who instantly rose Archbishop of Canterbury. The simple refutation of this lying story may be read in Strype's ' Life of Archbishop Parker.' " The " Nag's Head Tavern " is shown in La Serre's print, " Entrée de la Reyne Mère du Roy," 1638, of which we gave a copy on page 307 of this work.

" The confirmation," says Strype, "was performed three days after the Queen's letters commissional above-said ; that is, on the 9th day of December, in the Church of St. Mary de Arcubus (*i.e.* Mary-le-Bow, in Cheapside), regularly, and according to the usual custom ; and then after this manner :— First, John Incent, public notary, appeared personally, and presented to the Right Reverend the Commissaries, appointed by the Queen, her said letters to them directed in that behalf ; humbly praying them to take upon them the execution of the said letters, and to proceed according to the contents thereof, in the said business of confirmation. And the said notary public publicly read the Queen's commissional letters. Then, out of the reverence and honour those bishops present (who were Barlow, Scory, Coverdale, and the suffragan of Bedford), bore to her Majesty, they took upon them the commission, and accordingly resolved to proceed according to the form, power, and effect of the said letters. Next, the notary exhibited his proxy for the Dean and Chapter of the Metropolitan Church, and made himself a party for them ; and, in the procuratorial name of the said Dean and Chapter, presented the venerable Mr. Nicolas Bullingham, LL.D., and placed him before the said commissioners; who then exhibited his proxy for the said elect of Canterbury, and made himself a party for him. Then the said notary exhibited the original citatory mandate, together with the certificate on the back side, concerning the execution of the same; and then required all and singular persons cited, to be publicly called. And consequently a threefold proclamation was made, of all and singular opposers, at the door of the parochial church aforesaid; and so as is customary in these cases.

"Then, at the desire of the said notary to go on in this business of confirmation, they, the commissioners, decreed so to do, as was more fully contained in a schedule read by Bishop Barlow, with the consent of his colleagues. It is too long to relate distinctly every formal proceeding in this business; only it may be necessary to add some few of the most material passages.

"Then followed the deposition of witnesses concerning the life and actions, learning and abilities of the said elect; his freedom, his legitimacy, his priesthood, and such like. One of the witnesses was John Baker, of thirty-nine years old, gent., who is said to sojourn for the present with the venerable Dr. Parker, and to be born in the parish of St. Clement's, in Norwich. He, among other things, witnessed, 'That the same reverend father was and is a prudent man, commended for his knowledge of sacred Scripture, and for his life and manners. That he was a freeman, and born in lawful matrimony; that he was in lawful age, and in priest's orders, and a faithful subject to the Queen;' and the said Baker, in giving the reason of his knowledge in this behalf, said, 'That he was the natural brother of the Lord Elect, and that they were born *ex unis parentibus*' (or rather, surely, *ex una parente*, *i.e.*, of one mother). William Tolwyn, M.A., aged seventy years, and rector of St. Anthony, London, was another witness, who had known the said elect thirty years, and knew his mother, and that he was still very well acquainted with him, and of his certain knowledge could testify all above said.

"The notary exhibited the process of the election by the Dean and Chapter; which the commissioners did take a diligent view of, and at last, in the conclusion of this affair, the commissioners decreed the said most reverend lord elected and presently confirmed, should receive his consecration; and committed to him the care, rule, and administration, both of the temporals and spirituals of the said archbishopric; and decreed him to be inducted into the real, actual, and corporal possession of the same archbishopric.

"After many years the old story is ventured again into the world, in a book printed at Douay, anno 1654, wherein they thus tell their tale. 'I know they (*i.e.*, the Protestants) have tried many ways, and feigned an old record (meaning the authentic register of Archbishop Parker) to prove their ordination from Catholic bishops. But it was false, as I have received from two certain witnesses. The former of them was Dr. Darbyshire, then Dean of St. Paul's (canon there, perhaps, but never dean), and nephew to Dr. Boner, Bishop of London; who almost sixty years since lived at Meux Port, then a holy, religious man (a Jesuit), very aged, but perfect in sense and memory, who, speaking what he knew, affirmed to myself and another with me, *that like good fellows they made themselves bishops at an inn, because they could get no true bishops to consecrate them*. My other witness was a gentleman of honour, worth, and credit, dead not many years since, whose father, a chief judge of this kingdom, visiting Archbishop Heath, saw a letter, sent from Bishop Boner out of the Marshalsea, by one of his chaplains, to the archbishop, read, while they sat at dinner together; wherein he merrily related the manner how these new bishops (because he had dissuaded Ogelthorp, Bishop of Carlisle, from doing it in his diocese) ordained one another at an inn, where they met together. And while others laughed at this new manner of consecrating bishops, the archbishop himself, gravely, and not without tears, expressed his grief to see such a ragged company of men come poor out of foreign parts, and appointed to succeed the old clergy.'

"Which forgery, when once invented, was so acceptable to the Romanists, that it was most confidently repeated again in an English book, printed at Antwerp, 1658, *permissione superiorum*, being a second edition, licensed by Gulielmo Bolognimo, where the author sets down his story in these words:—'The heretics who were named to succeed in the other bishops' sees, could not prevail with Llandaff (whom he calls a little before *an old simple man*) to consecrate them at the "Nag's Head," in Cheapside, where they appointed to meet him. And therefore they made use of Scory, who was never ordained bishop, though he bore the name in King Edward's reign. Kneeling before him, he laid the Bible upon their heads or shoulders, and bid them rise up and preach the word of God sincerely. 'This is,' added he, 'so evident a truth, that for the space of fifty years no Protestant durst contradict it.'"

"The form adopted at the confirmation of Archbishop Parker," writes Dr. Pusey in a letter dated

1865, quoted by Mr. Timbs, "was carefully framed on the old form used in the confirmations by Archbishop Chichele (which was the point for which I examined the registers in the Lambeth library). The words used in the consecration of the bishops confirmed by Chichele do not occur in the registers. The words used by the consecrators of Parker, 'Accipe Spiritum sanctum,' were read in the later pontificals, as in that of Exeter, Lacy's (Maskell's 'Monumenta Ritualia,' iii. 258). Roman Catholic writers admit *that* only is essential to consecration which the English service-book retained—prayer during the service, which should have reference to the office of bishop, and the imposition of hands. And, in fact, Cardinal Pole engaged to retain in their orders those who had been so ordained under Edward VI., and his act was confirmed by Paul IV." (Sanders, *De Schism. Angl.*, l. iii. 350.)

The house No. 73, Cheapside, shown in our illustration on page 343, was erected, from the design of Sir Christopher Wren, for Sir William Turner, Knight, who served the office of Lord Mayor in the year 1668–9, and here he kept his mayoralty.

At the "Queen's Arms Tavern," No. 71, Cheapside, the poet Keats once lived. The second floor of the house which stretches over the passage leading to this tavern was his lodging. Here, says Cunningham, he wrote his magnificent sonnet on Chapman's "Homer," and all the poems in his first little volume. Keats, the son of a liverystable keeper in Moorfields, was born in 1795, and died of consumption at Rome in 1821. He published his "Endymion" (the inspiration suggested from Lempriere alone) in 1818. We annex the glorious sonnet written within sound of Bow bells :—

ON FIRST LOOKING INTO CHAPMAN'S "HOMER."

"Much have I travell'd in the realms of gold,
    And many goodly states and kingdoms seen ;
    Round many western islands have I been,
Which bards, in fealty to Apollo, hold.
Oft of one wide expanse had I been told
    That deep-brow'd Homer ruled as his demesne ;
    Yet did I never breathe its pure serene
Till I heard Chapman speak out loud and bold ;
Then felt I like some watcher of the skies
    When a new planet swims into his ken ;
Or like stout Cortez when with eagle eyes
    He stared at the Pacific—and all his men
Look'd at each other with a wild surmise—
    Silent, upon a peak in Darien."

Behnes' poor bald statue of Sir Robert Peel, at the Paternoster Row end of Cheapside, was uncovered July 21st, 1855. The *Builder* at the time justly lamented that so much good metal was wasted. The statue is without thought—the head is set on the neck awkwardly, the pedestal is senseless, and the two double lamps at the side are mean and paltry.

Saddlers' Hall is close to Foster Lane, Cheapside. "Near unto this lane," says Strype, "but in Cheapside, is Saddlers' Hall—a pretty good building, seated at the upper end of a handsome alley, near to which is Half Moon Alley, which is but small, at the upper end of which is a tavern, which gives a passage into Foster Lane, and another into Gutter Lane."

"This appears," says Maitland, "to be a fraternity of great antiquity, by a convention agreed upon between them and the Dean and Chapter of St. Martin's-le-Grand, about the reign of Richard I., at which time I imagine it to have been an Adulterine Guild, seeing it was only incorporated by letters patent of Edward I., by the appellation of 'The Wardens, or Keepers and Commonalty of the Mystery or Art of Sadlers, London.' This company is governed by a prime and three other wardens, and eighteen assistants, with a livery of seventy members, whose fine on admission is ten pounds."

At the entrance is an ornamental door-case, and an iron gate, and it is a very complete building for the use of such a company. It is adorned with fretwork and wainscot, and the Company's arms are carved in stone over the gate next the street. The great hall is a handsome and spacious apartment, and contains, amongst other objects of interest, a full-length portrait of Frederick, Prince of Wales, who became Master of the Company.

In 1736 Frederick, Prince of Wales, the father of George III., being desirous of seeing the Lord Mayor's show privately, visited the City in disguise. At that time it was the custom for several of the City companies, particularly for those who had no barges, to have stands erected in the streets through which the Lord Mayor passed on his return from Westminster, in which the freemen of companies were accustomed to assemble. It happened that his Royal Highness was discovered by some of the Saddlers' Company, in consequence of which he was invited to their stand, which invitation he accepted, and the parties were so well pleased with each other that his Royal Highness was soon after chosen Master of the Company, a compliment which he also accepted. The City on that occasion formed a resolution to compliment his Royal Highness with the freedom of London, pursuant to which the Court of Lord Mayor and Aldermen attended the prince, on the 17th of

December, with the said freedom, of which the following is a copy :—

"The most high, most potent, and most illustrious Prince Frederick Lewis, Prince of Great Britain, Electoral Prince of Brunswick-Lunenburg, Prince of Wales, Duke of Cornwall, Duke of of the Saddlers, in the time of the Right Honourable Sir John Thompson, Knight, Lord Mayor, and John Bosworth, Esq., Chamberlain of the said City." In his "Industry and Idleness," Hogarth shows us the prince and princess on the balcony of Saddler's Hall.

BOW CHURCH, CHEAPSIDE. (*From a view taken about* 1750.)

Rothsay, Duke of Edinburgh, Marquis of the Isle of Ely, Earl of Eltham, Earl of Chester, Viscount Launceston, Baron of Renfrew, Baron of Snowdon, Lord of the Isles, Steward of Scotland, Knight of the most noble Order of the Garter, and one of his Majesty's most honourable Privy Council, of his mere grace and princely favour, did the most august City of London the honour to accept the freedom thereof, and was admitted of the Company

That dull poet, worthy Sir Richard Blackmore, whom Locke and Addison praised and Dryden ridiculed, lived either at Saddlers' Hall or just opposite. It was on this wearisome author of his day that Garth wrote these verses :—

"Unwieldy pedant, let thy awkward muse,
    With censures praise, with flatteries abuse.
  To lash, and not be felt, in thee's an art ;
    Thou ne'er mad'st any but thy schoolboys smart.

Then be advis'd, and scribble not agen ;
Thou'rt fashioned for a flail, and not a pen.
If B——l's immortal wit thou wouldst descry,
Pretend 'tis he that writ thy poetry.
Thy feeble satire ne'er can do him wrong ;
Thy poems and thy patients live not long."

verses in his carriage, as he drove to visit his patients, a feat to which Dryden alludes when he talks of Blackmore writing to the "rumbling of his carriage-wheels."

At No. 90, Cheapside lived Alderman Boydell,

NO. 73, CHEAPSIDE. *From an Old View.* (*See page* 341.)

And some other satirical verses on Sir Richard began thus :—

"'Twas kindly done of the good-natured cits,
To place before thy door a brace of tits."

Blackmore, who had been brought up as an attorney's clerk and schoolmaster, wrote most of his

engraver and printseller, a man who in his time did more for English art than all the English monarchs from the Conquest downwards. He was apprenticed, when more than twenty years old, to Mr. Tomson, engraver, and soon felt a desire to popularise and extend the art. His first funds he derived from the sale of a book of 152 humble prints, engraved by himself. With the profits he was enabled to pay the best engravers liberally, to make copies of the works of our best masters.

"The alderman assured me," says "Rainy Day Smith," "that when he commenced publishing, he etched small plates of landscapes, which he produced in plates of six, and sold for sixpence; and that as there were very few print-shops at that time in London, he prevailed upon the sellers of children's toys to allow his little books to be put in their windows. These shops he regularly visited every Saturday, to see if any had been sold, and to leave more. His most successful shop was the sign of the 'Cricket Bat,' in Duke's Court, St. Martin's Lane, where he found he had sold as many as came to five shillings and sixpence. With this success he was so pleased, that, wishing to invite the shopkeeper to continue in his interest, he laid out the money in a silver pencil-case; which article, after he had related the above anecdote, he took out of his pocket and assured me he never would part with. He then favoured me with the following history of Woollett's plate of the 'Niobe,' and, as it is interesting, I shall endeavour to relate it in Mr. Boydell's own words:—

"'When I got a little forward in the world,' said the venerable alderman, 'I took a whole shop, for at my commencement I kept only half a one. In the course of one year I imported numerous impressions of Vernet's celebrated "Storm," so admirably engraved by Lerpinière, for which I was obliged to pay in hard cash, as the French took none of our prints in return. Upon Mr. Woollett's expressing himself highly delighted with the "Storm," I was induced, knowing his ability as an engraver, to ask him if he thought he could produce a print of the same size which I could send over, so that in future I could avoid payment in money, and prove to the French nation that an Englishman could produce a print of equal merit; upon which he immediately declared that he should like much to try.

"'At this time the principal conversation among artists was upon Mr. Wilson's grand picture of "Niobe," which had just arrived from Rome. I therefore immediately applied to his Royal Highness the Duke of Gloucester, its owner, and procured permission for Woollett to engrave it. But before he ventured upon the task, I requested to know what idea he had as to the expense, and after some consideration, he said he thought he could engrave it for one hundred guineas. This sum, small as it may now appear, was to me,' observed the alderman, 'an unheard-of price, being con-

siderably more than I had given for any copper-plate. However, serious as the sum was, I bade him get to work, and he proceeded with all cheerfulness, for as he went on I advanced him money; and though he lost no time, I found that he had received nearly the whole amount before he had half finished his task. I frequently called upon him, and found him struggling with serious difficulties, with his wife and family, in an upper lodging in Green's Court, Castle Street, Leicester Square, for there he lived before he went into Green Street. However, I encouraged him by allowing him to draw on me to the extent of twenty-five pounds more; and at length that sum was paid, and I was unavoidably under the necessity of saying, "Mr. Woollett, I find we have made too close a bargain with each other. You have exerted yourself, and I fear I have gone beyond my strength, or, indeed, what I ought to have risked, as we neither of us can be aware of the success of the speculation. However, I am determined, whatever the event may be, to enable you to finish it to your wish—at least, to allow you to work upon it as long as another twenty-five pounds can extend, but there we must positively stop." The plate was finished; and, after taking very few proofs, I published the print at five shillings, and it succeeded so much beyond my expectations, that I immediately employed Mr. Woollett upon another engraving, from another picture by Wilson; and I am now thoroughly convinced that had I continued publishing subjects of this description, my fortune would have been increased tenfold.'"

"In the year 1786," says Knowles, in his "Life of Fuseli," "Mr. Alderman Boydell, at the suggestion of Mr. George Nicol, began to form his splendid collection of modern historical pictures, the subjects being from Shakespeare's plays, and which was called 'The Shakespeare Gallery.' This liberal and well-timed speculation gave great energy to this branch of the art, as well as employment to many of our best artists and engravers, and among the former to Fuseli, who executed eight large and one small picture for the gallery. The following were the subjects: 'Prospero,' 'Miranda,' 'Caliban,' and 'Ariel,' from the *Tempest;* 'Titania in raptures with Bottom, who wears the ass's head, attendant fairies, &c.;' 'Titania awaking, discovers Oberon at her side, Puck is removing the ass's head from Bottom' (*Midsummer Night's Dream*); 'Henry V. with the Conspirators' (*King Henry V.*); 'Lear dismissing Cordelia from his Court' (*King Lear*); 'Ghost of Hamlet's Father' (*Hamlet*); 'Falstaff and Doll' (*King Henry IV., Second Part*); 'Mac-

beth meeting the Witches on the Heath' (*Macbeth*);
'Robin Goodfellow' (*Midsummer Night's Dream*).
This gallery gave the public an opportunity of
judging of Fuseli's versatile powers.

"The stately majesty of the 'Ghost of Hamlet's
Father' contrasted with the expressive energy of
his son, and the sublimity brought about by the
light, shadow, and general tone, strike the mind
with awe. In the picture of 'Lear' is admirably
portrayed the stubborn rashness of the father, the
filial piety of the discarded daughter, and the
wicked determination of Regan and Goneril. The
fairy scenes in *Midsummer Night's Dream* amuse
the fancy, and show the vast inventive powers of
the painter; and 'Falstaff with Doll' is exquisitely
ludicrous.

"The example set by Boydell was a stimulus to
other speculators of a similar nature, and within a
few years appeared the Macklin and Woodmason
galleries; and it may be said with great truth that
Fuseli's pictures were among the most striking, if
not the best, in either collection."

"A.D. 1787," says Northcote, in his "Life of
Reynolds," "when Alderman Boydell projected the
scheme of his magnificent edition of the plays of
Shakespeare, accompanied with large prints from
pictures to be executed by English painters, it was
deemed to be absolutely necessary that something
of Sir Joshua's painting should be procured to grace
the collection; but, unexpectedly, Sir Joshua appeared to be rather shy in the business, as if he
thought it degrading himself to paint for a printseller, and he would not at first consent to be
employed in the work. George Stevens, the editor
of Shakespeare, now undertook to persuade him to
comply, and, taking a bank-bill of five hundred
pounds in his hand, he had an interview with Sir
Joshua, when, using all his eloquence in argument,
he, in the meantime, slipped the bank-bill into his
hand; he then soon found that his mode of reasoning
was not to be resisted, and a picture was promised.
Sir Joshua immediately commenced his studies,
and no less than three paintings were exhibited at
the Shakspeare Gallery, or at least taken from that
poet, the only ones, as has been very correctly said,
which Sir Joshua ever executed for his illustration,
with the exception of a head of 'King Lear' (done
indeed in 1783), and now in possession of the Marchioness of Thomond, and a portrait of the Hon.
Mrs. Tollemache, in the character of 'Miranda,' in
The Tempest, in which 'Prospero' and 'Caliban' are
introduced.

"One of these paintings for the Gallery was
'Puck,' or 'Robin Goodfellow,' as it has been
called, which, in point of expression and animation,
is unparalleled, and one of the happiest efforts of Sir
Joshua's pencil, though it has been said by some
cold critics not to be perfectly characteristic of the
merry wanderer of Shakespeare. 'Macbeth,' with
the witches and the caldron, was another, and for
this last Mr. Boydell paid him 1,000 guineas; but
who is now the possessor of it I know not.

"'Puck' was painted in 1789. Walpole depreciates
it as 'an ugly little imp (but with some character)
sitting on a mushroom half as big as a mile-stone.'
Mr. Nicholls, of the British Institution, related to Mr.
Cotton that the alderman and his grandfather were
with Sir Joshua when painting the death of Cardinal
Beaufort. Boydell was much taken with the portrait
of a naked child, and wished it could be brought
into the Shakspeare. Sir Joshua said it was painted
from a little child he found sitting on his steps in
Leicester Square. Nicholls' grandfather then said,
'Well, Mr. Alderman, it can very easily come into
the Shakspeare if Sir Joshua will kindly place him
upon a mushroom, give him fawn's ears, and make
a Puck of him.' Sir Joshua liked the notion, and
painted the picture accordingly.

"The morning of the day on which Sir Joshua's
'Puck' was to be sold, Lord Farnborough and
Davies, the painter, breakfasted with Mr. Rogers,
and went to the sale together. When the picture
was put up there was a general clapping of hands,
and yet it was knocked down to Mr. Rogers for
105 guineas. As he walked home from the sale,
a man carried 'Puck' before him, and so well was
the picture known that more than one person,
as they were going along the street, called out,
'There it is!' At Mr. Rogers' sale, in 1856, it
was purchased by Earl Fitzwilliam for 980 guineas.
The grown-up person of the sitter for 'Puck' was
in Messrs. Christie and Manson's room during
the sale, and stood next to Lord Fitzwilliam, who
is also a survivor of the sitters to Sir Joshua.
The merry boy, whom Sir Joshua found upon his
door-step, subsequently became a porter at Elliot's
brewery, in Pimlico."

In 1804, Alderman Boydell applied through his
friend, Sir John W. Anderson, to the House of
Commons, for leave to dispose of his paintings and
drawings by lottery. In his petition he described
himself, with modesty and pathos, as an old man of
eighty-five, anxious to free himself from debts which
now oppressed him, although he, with his brethren,
had expended upwards of £350,000 in promoting
the fine arts. Sixty years before he had begun to
benefit engraving by establishing a school of English
engravers. At that time the whole print commerce
of England consisted in importing a few foreign
prints (chiefly French) "to supply the cabinets of

the curious." In time he effected a total change in this branch of commerce, "very few prints being now imported, while the foreign market is principally supplied with prints from England." By degrees, the large sums received from the Continent for English plates encouraged him to attempt also an English school of pictorial painting, the want of such a school having been long a source of opprobrium among foreign writers on England. The Shakespeare Gallery was sufficient to convince the world that English genius only needed encouragement to obtain a facility, versatility, and independence of thought unknown to the Italian, Flemish, or French schools. That Gallery he had long hoped to have left to a generous public, but the recent Vandalic revolution in France had cut up his revenue by the roots, Flanders, Holland, and Germany being his chief marts. At the same time he acknowledged he had not been provident, his natural enthusiasm for promoting the fine arts having led him after each success to fly at once to some new artist with the whole gains of his former undertaking. He had too late seen his error, having increased his stock of copper-plates to such a heap that all the print-sellers in Europe (especially in these unfavourable times) could not purchase them. He therefore prayed for permission to create a lottery, the House having the assurance of the even tenor of a long life " that it would be fairly and honourably conducted."

The worthy man obtained leave for his lottery,

and died December 11, a few days after the last tickets were sold. He was buried with civic state in the Church of St. Olave, Jewry, the Lord Mayor, aldermen, and several artists attending. Boydell was very generous and charitable. He gave pictures to adorn the City Council Chamber, the Court Room of the Stationers' Company, and the dining-room of the Sessions House. He was also a generous benefactor to the Humane Society and the Literary Fund, and was for many years the President of both Societies. The Shakespeare Gallery finally fell by lottery to Mr. Tassie, the well-known medallist, who thrived to a good old age upon the profits of poor Boydell's too generous expenditure. This enterprising man was elected Alderman of Cheap Ward in 1782, Sheriff in 1785, and Lord Mayor in 1790. His death was occasioned by a cold, caught at the Old Bailey Sessions. His nephew, Josiah Boydell, engraved for him for forty years.

It was the regular custom of Mr. Alderman Boydell (says "Rainy Day" Smith), who was a very early riser, to repair at five o'clock immediately to the pump in Ironmonger Lane. There, after placing his wig upon the ball at the top, he used to sluice his head with its water. This well known and highly respected character was one of the last men who wore a three-cornered hat, commonly called the "Egham, Staines, and Windsor."

CHAPTER XXIX.

CHEAPSIDE TRIBUTARIES—SOUTH.

The King's Exchange—Friday Street and the Poet Chaucer—The Wednesday Club in Friday Street—William Paterson, Founder of the Bank of England—How Easy it is to Redeem the National Debt—St. Matthew's and St. Margaret Moses—Bread Street and the Bakers' Shops—St. Austin's, Watling Street—The Fraternity of St. Austin's—St. Mildred's, Bread Street—The Mitre Tavern—A Priestly Duel—Milton's Birth-place—The "Mermaid"—Sir Walter Raleigh and the Mermaid Club—Thomas Coryatt, the Traveller—Bow Lane—Queen Street—Soper's Lane—A Mercer Knight—St. Bennet Sherehog—Epitaphs in the Church of St. Thomas Apostle—A Charitable Merchant.

OLD 'CHANGE was formerly the old Exchange, so called from the King's Exchange, says Stow, there kept, which was for the receipt of bullion to be coined.

The King's Exchange was in Old Exchange, now Old 'Change, Cheapside. "It was here," says Tite, "that one of those ancient officers, known as the King's Exchanger, was placed, whose duty it was to attend to the supply of the mints with bullion, to distribute the new coinage, and to regulate the exchange of foreign coin. Of these officers there were anciently three—two in London, at the Tower and Old Exchange, and one in the city of Canter-

bury. Subsequently another was appointed, with an establishment in Lombard Street, the ancient rendezvous of the merchants; and it appears not improbable that Queen Elizabeth's intention was to have removed this functionary to what was pre-eminently designated by her ' The Royal Exchange,' and hence the reason for the change of the name of this edifice by Elizabeth."

"In the reign of Henry VII.," says Francis, in his "History of the Bank of England," "the Royal prerogative forbade English coins to be exported, and the Royal Exchange was alone entitled to give native money for foreign coin or bullion. During the reign of Henry VIII. the coin grew so debased as to be difficult to exchange, and the Goldsmiths quietly superseded the royal officer. In 1627 Charles I., ever on the watch for power, re-established the office, and in a pamphlet written by his orders, asserted that 'the prerogative had always been a flower of the Crown, and that the Goldsmiths had left off their proper trade and turned exchangers of plate and foreign coins for our English coins, although they had no right.' Charles entrusted the office of 'changer, exchanger, and ante-changer' to Henry Rich, first Earl of Holland, who soon deserted his cause for that of the Parliament. The office has not since been re-established."

No. 36, Old 'Change was formerly the "Three Morrice Dancers" public-house, with the three figures sculptured on a stone as the sign and an ornament (*temp*. James I.). The house was taken down about 1801. There is an etching of this very characteristic sign on stone.

The celebrated poet and enthusiast, Lord Herbert of Cherbury, lived, in the reign of James I., in a "house among gardens, near the old Exchange." At the beginning of the last century, the place was chiefly inhabited by American merchants; at this time it is principally inhabited by calico printers and Manchester warehousemen.

"Friday Street was so called," says Stow, "of fishmongers dwelling there, and serving Friday's Market." In the roll of the Scrope and Grosvenor heraldic controversy (Edward III.) the poet Chaucer is recorded as giving the following evidence connected with this street :—

"Geffray Chaucere, Esqueer, of the age of forty years, and moreover armed twenty-seven years for the side of Sir Richard Lescrop, sworn and examined, being asked if the arms, azyure, a bend or, belonged or ought to pertain to the said Sir Richard by right and heritage, said, Yes ; for he saw him so armed in Frannce, before the town of Petters, and Sir Henry Lescrop armed in the same arms with a white label and with banner; and the said Sir Richard armed in the entire arms azyure a bend or, and so during the whole expedition until the said Geaffray was taken. Being asked how he knew that the said arms belonged to the said Sir Richard, said that he had heard old knights and esquires say that they had had continual possession of the said arms; and that he had seen them displayed on banners, glass paintings, and vestments, and commonly called the arms of Scrope. Being asked whether he had ever heard of any interruption or challenge made by Sir Robert Grosvenor or his ancestors, said No ; but that he was once in Friday Street, London, and walking up the street he ob-

served a new sign hanging out with these arms thereon, and enquired what inn that was that had hung out these arms of Scrope ? And one answered him, saying, ' They are not hung out, Sir, for the arms of Scrope, nor painted there for those arms, but they are painted and put there by a Knight of the county of Chester, called Sir Robert Grosvernor.' And that was the first time he ever heard speak of Sir Robert Grosvernor or his ancestors, or of any one bearing the name of Grosvernor." This is really almost the only authentic scrap we possess of the facts of Chaucer's life.

The " White Horse," a tavern in Friday Street, makes a conspicuous figure in the " Merry Conceited Jests of George Peele," the poet and play-writer of Elizabeth's reign.

At the Wednesday Club in Friday Street, William Paterson, the founder of the Bank of England, and originator of the unfortunate Darien scheme, held his real or imaginary Wednesday club meetings, at which were discussed proposals for the union of England and Scotland, and the redemption of the National Debt. This remarkable financier was born at Lochnabar, in Dumfriesshire, in 1648, and died in 1719. The following extracts from Paterson's probably imaginary conversations are of interest :—

"And thus," says Paterson, "supposing the people of Scotland to be in number one million, and that as matters now stand their industry yields them only about five pounds per annum per head, as reckoned one with another, or five millions yearly in the whole, at this rate these five millions will by the union not only be advanced to six, but put in a way of further improvement ; and allowing £100,000 per annum were on this foot to be paid in additional taxes, yet there would still remain a yearly sum of about £900,000 towards subsisting the people more comfortably, and making provision against times of scarcity, and other accidents, to which, I understand, that country is very much exposed (1706)."

"And I remember complaints of this kind were very loud in the days of King Charles II.," said Mr. Brooks, "particularly that, though in his time the public taxes and impositions upon the people were doubled or trebled to what they formerly were, he nevertheless run at least a million in debt."

"If men were uneasy with public taxes and debts in the time of King Charles II.," said Mr. May, "because then doubled or trebled to what they had formerly been, how much more may they be so now, when taxed at least three times more, and the public debts increased from about one million, as you say they then were, to fifty millions or upwards?. . . . and yet France is in a way of being entirely out of debt in a year or two."

"At this rate," said Mr. May, "Great Britain may possibly be quite out of debt in four or five years, or less. But though it seems we have been at least as hasty in running into debt as those in France,

pay seems to have sprung up with Sir Nathaniel Gould, in 1725, when it was opposed.

St. Matthew's was situate on the west side of Friday Street. The patronage of it was in the Abbot and Convent of Westminster. This church, being destroyed by the Fire of London, in 1666,

THE DOOR OF SADDLERS' HALL (*see page* 341).

yet would I by no means advise us to run so hastily out; slower measures will be juster, and consequently better and surer."

Mr. Pitt's celebrated measure was based upon an opinion that money could be borrowed with advantage to pay the national debt. Paterson proposed to redeem it out of a surplus revenue, administered so skilfully as to lower the interest in the money market. The notion of *borrowing* to

was handsomely rebuilt, and the parish of St. Peter, Cheap, added to it by Act of Parliament. The following epitaph (1583) was in this church :—

"Anthony Cage entombed here doth rest,
　Whose wisdome still prevail'd the Commonweale ;
A man with God's good gifts so greatly blest,
　That few or none his doings may impale,
A man unto the widow and the poore,
　A comfort, and a succour evermore.
Three wives he had of credit and of fame ;

The first of them, Elizabeth that hight,
Who buried here, brought to this *Cage*, by name,
Seventeene young plants, to give his table light."

"At St. Margaret Moyses," says Stow, "was buried Mr. Buss (or Briss), a Skinner, one of the masters of the hospital. There attended all the masters of the hospital, with green staves in their hands, and all the Company in their liveries, with twenty clerks singing before. The sermon was preached by Mr. Jewel, afterwards Bishop of Salisbury; and therein he plainly affirmed there was no purgatory. Thence the Company retired to his house to dinner. This burial was *an.* 1559, Jan. 30."

records, that in the year 1302, which was the 30th of Edward I., the bakers of London were bound to sell no bread in their shops or houses, but in the market here; and that they should have four hall motes in the year, at four several terms, to determine of enormities belonging to the said company. Bread Street is now wholly inhabited by rich merchants, and divers fair inns be there, for good receipt of carriers and other travellers to the City. It appears in the will of Edward Stafford, Earl of Wylshire, dated the 22nd of March, 1498, and 14 Henry VII., that he lived in a house in Bread Street, in London, which belonged to the family of

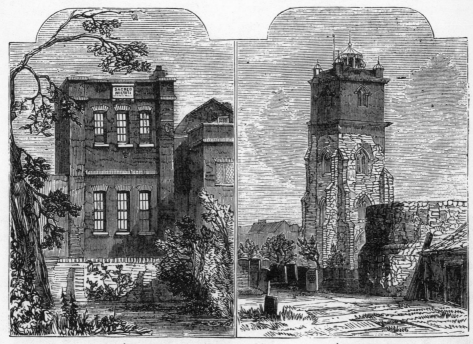

MILTON'S HOUSE.   (*See page* 350.)   MILTON'S BURIAL-PLACE.

The following epitaph (1569) is worth preserving:—

"Beati mortui qui in Domino moriuntur."—Apoc. 14.
    "To William Dane, that sometime was
        An ironmonger; where each degree
    He worthily (with praise) did passe.
        By Wisdom, Truth, and Heed, was he
    Advanc'd an Alderman to be;
        Then Sheriffe; that he, with justice prest,
    And cost, performed with the best.
        In almes frank, of conscience cleare;
    In grace with prince, to people glad;
        His vertuous wife, his faithful peere,
    MARGARET, this monument hath made;
        Meaning (through God) that as shee had
    With him (in house) long lived well;
        Even so in Tombes Blisse to dwell."

"Bread Street," says Stow, "is so called of bread there in old times then sold; for it appeareth by

Stafford, Duke of Bucks afterwards; he bequeathed all the stuff in that house to the Lord of Buckingham, for he died without issue."

The parish church of "St. Augustine, in Watheling Street" was destroyed by the Great Fire, but rebuilt in 1682. Stow informs us that here was a fraternity founded A.D. 1387, called the *Fraternity of St. Austin's*, in Watling Street, and other good people dwelling in the City. "They were, on the eve of St. Austin's, to meet at the said church, in the morning at high mass, and every brother to offer a penny. And after that to be ready, *al mangier ou al revele; i.e., to eat or to revel*, according to the ordinance of the master and wardens of the fraternity. They set up in the honour of God and St. Austin, one branch of six tapers in the said church, before the image of St. Austin; and also two torches, with the which if any of the said fraternity were commended to God, he might be carried to the earth. They were to meet at the vault at Paul's (perhaps St. Faith's), and to go thence to the Church of St. Austin's, and the priests and the clerks said *Placebo* and *Dirige*, and in matins, a mass of requiem at the high altar."

"There is a flat stone," says Stow, "in the south aisle of the church. It is laid over an Armenian merchant, of which foreign merchants there be divers that lodge and harbour in the Old 'Change in this parish."

St. Mildred's, in Bread Street, was repaired in 1628. "At the upper end of the chancel," says Strype, "is a fine window, full of cost and beauty, which being divided into five parts, carries in the first of them a very artful and curious representation of the Spaniard's Great Armado, and the battle in 1588; in the second, the monument of Queen Elizabeth; in the third, the Gunpowder Plot; in the fourth, the lamentable time of infection, 1625; and in the fifth and last, the view and lively portraiture of that worthy gentleman, Captain Nicolas Crispe, at whose sole cost (among other) this beautiful piece of work was erected, as also the figures of his vertuous wife and children, with the arms belonging to them." This church, burnt down in the Great Fire, was rebuilt subsequently.

St. Mildred was a Saxon lady, and daughter of Merwaldus, a West-Mercian prince, and brother to Penda, King of the Mercians, who, despising the pomps and vanities of this world, retired to a convent at Hale, in France, whence, returning to England, accompanied by seventy virgins, she was consecrated abbess of a new monastery in the Isle of Thanet, by Theodore, Archbishop of Canterbury, where she died abbess, A.D. 676.

On the east side of Bread Street stood the church of Allhallows. "On the south side of the chancel, in a little part of this church, called *The Salter's Chapel*," says Strype, "is a very fair window, with the portraiture or figure of him that gave it, very curiously wrought upon it. This church, ruined in the Great Fire, is built up again without any pillars, but very decent, and is a lightsome church."

"In the 22nd of Henry VIII., the 17th of August, two priests of this church fell at variance, that the one drew blood of the other, wherefore the same church was suspended, and no service sung or said therein for the space of one month after; the priests were committed to prison, and the 15th of October, being enjoined penance, they went at the head of a general procession, bare-footed and bare-legged, before the children, with beads and books in their hands, from Paul's, through Cheap, Cornhill," &c.

Among the epitaphs the following, given by Stow, is quaint :—

"To the sacred memory of that worthy and faithfull minister of Christ, Master Richard Stocke ; who after 32 yeeres spent in the ministry, wherein by his learned labours, joined with wisedome, and a most holy life, God's glory was much advanced, his Church edified, piety increased, and the true honour of a pastor's life maintained ; deceased April 20, 1626. Some of his loving parishioners have consecrated this monument of their never-dying love, Jan. 28, 1628.

"Thy lifelesse Trunke
(O Reverend Stocke),
Like Aaron's rod
Sprouts out againe ;
And after two
Full winters past,
Yields Blossomes
And ripe fruit amaine.
For why, this work of piety,
Performed by some of thy Flocke,
To thy dead corps and sacred urne,
Is but the fruit of this old Stocke."

The father of Milton, the poet, was a scrivener in Bread Street, living at the sign of "The Spread Eagle," the armorial ensign of his family. The first turning on the left hand, as you enter from Cheapside, was called "Black Spread Eagle Court," and not unlikely from the family ensign of the poet's father. Milton was born in this street (December 9, 1608), and baptised in the adjoining church of Allhallows, Bread Street, where the register of his baptism was preserved. Of the house in which he resided in later life, and the churchyard of St. Giles, Cripplegate, where he was buried, we give a view on page 349. Aubrey tells us that the house and chamber in which the poet was born were often visited by foreigners, even in the poet's lifetime. The house was destroyed in the Great Fire, and "Paradise Lost" was published after it. On the site of Allhallows Church large warehouses and offices have been erected. On one of these a tablet is placed, bearing this inscription : "Milton, born in Bread Street, 1608 ; baptised in Church of Allhallows, which stood here *ante* 1878."

There was a City prison formerly in Bread Street. "On the west side of Bread Street," says Stow, "amongst divers fair and large houses for merchants, and fair inns for passengers, had they one prison-house pertaining to the sheriffs of London, called the Compter, in Bread Street ; but in 1555 the prisoners were removed from thence to one other new Compter in Wood Street, provided by the City's purchase, and built for that purpose."

The "Mermaid" Tavern, in Cheapside, about the site of which there has been endless controversy, stood in Bread Street, with side entrances, as

Mr. Burn has shown, with admirable clearness, in Friday Street and Bread Street ; hence the disputes of antiquaries.

Mr. Burn, in his book on "Tokens," says, "The site of the 'Mermaid' is clearly defined, from the circumstance of W. R., a haberdasher of small wares, 'twixt Wood Street and Milk Street, adopting the sign, 'Over against the Mermaid Tavern in Cheapside.'" The tavern was destroyed in the Great Fire.

Here Sir Walter Raleigh is, by one of the traditions, said to have instituted "The Mermaid Club." Gifford, in his edition of "Ben Jonson," has thus described the club :—"About this time (1603) Jonson probably began to acquire that turn for conviviality for which he was afterwards noted. Sir Walter Raleigh, previously to his unfortunate engagement with the wretched Cobham and others, had instituted a meeting of *beaux esprits* at the 'Mermaid,' a celebrated tavern in Friday Street. Of this club, which combined more talent and genius than ever met together before or since, our author was a member, and here for many years he regularly repaired, with Shakespeare, Beaumont, Fletcher, Selden, Cotton, Carew, Martin, Donne, and many others, whose names, even at this distant period, call up a mingled feeling of reverence and respect." But this is doubted. A writer in the *Athenæum*, Sept. 16, 1865, states :—"The origin of the common tale of Raleigh founding the 'Mermaid Club,' of which Shakespeare is said to have been a member, has not been traced. Is it older than Gifford?" Again :—"Gifford's apparent invention of the 'Mermaid Club.' Prove to us that Raleigh founded the 'Mermaid Club,' that the wits attended it under his presidency, and you will have made a real contribution to our knowledge of Shakespeare's time, even if you fail to show that our poet was a member of that club." The tradition, it is thought, must be added to the long list of Shakespearian doubts.

But we nevertheless have a noble record left of the wit combats here in the celebrated epistle of Beaumont to Jonson :—

"Methinks the little wit I had is lost
Since I saw you ; for wit is like a rest
Held up at tennis, which men do the best
With the best gamesters. What things have we seen
Done at the 'Mermaid?' Heard words that have been
So nimble, and so full of subtle flame,
As if that every one from whence they came
Had meant to put his whole wit in a jest,
And had resolved to live a fool the rest
Of his dull life. Then, when there hath been thrown
Wit able enough to justify the town
For three days past—wit that might warrant be
For the whole city to talk foolishly
Till that were cancelled ; and when that was gone,

We left an air behind us, which alone
Was able to make the two next companies
Right witty ; though but downright fools, more wise."

"Many," says Fuller, "were the wit combats betwixt him (Shakespeare) and Ben Jonson, which two I behold like a Spanish great galleon and an English man-of-war. Master Jonson (like the former) was built far higher in learning, solid, but slow in his performances ; Shakespeare, with the English man-of-war, lesser in bulk, but lighter in sailing, could turn with all tides, and take advantage of all winds, by the quickness of his wit and invention."

These combats, one is willing to think, although without any evidence at all, took place at the "Mermaid" on such evenings as Beaumont so glowingly describes. But all we really know is that Beaumont and Ben Jonson met at the "Mermaid," and Shakespeare might have been of the company. Fuller, Mr. Charles Knight reminds us, was only eight years old when Shakespeare died.

John Rastell, the brother-in-law of Sir Thomas More, was a printer, living at the sign of the "Mermaid," in Cheapside. "The Pastyme of the People" (folio, 1529) is described as "breuly copyled and empryntyd in Chepesyde, at the sygne of the 'Mearemayd,' next to Pollys (Paul's) Gate." Stow also mentions this tavern :—"They" (Coppinger and Arthington, false prophets), says the historian, "had purposed to have gone with the like cry and proclamation, through other the chiefe parts of the Citie ; but the presse was so great, as that they were forced to goe into a taverne in Cheape, at the sign of the 'Mermayd,' the rather because a gentleman of his acquaintance plucked at Coppinger, whilst he was in the cart, and blamed him for his demeanour and speeches."

There was also a "Mermaid" in Cornhill.

In Bow Lane resided Thomas Coryat, an eccentric traveller of the reign of James I., and a butt of Ben Jonson and his brother wits. In 1608 Coryat took a journey on foot through France, Italy, Germany, &c., which lasted five months, during which he had travelled 1,975 miles, more than half upon one pair of shoes, which were only once mended, and on his return were hung up in the Church of Odcombe, in Somersetshire. He published his travels under this title, "Crudities hastily gobbled up in Five Months' Travels in France, Savoy, Italy, Rhetia, Helvetia, some parts of High Germany, and the Netherlands, 1611," 4to ; reprinted in 1776, 3 vols., 8vo. This work was ushered into the world by an "Odcombian banquet," consisting of near sixty copies of verses, made by the best poets of that time, which, if they did not make Coryat pass with the world for a man of great parts and learning, contributed not a little to the sale of his book. Among these poets were Ben Jonson, Sir John Harrington, Inigo Jones (the architect), Chapman, Donne, Drayton, and others.

Parsons, an excellent comedian, also resided in Bow Lane.

"A greater artist," says Dr. Doran, in "Her Majesty's Servants," "than Baddeley left the stage soon after him, in 1795, after three-and-thirty years of service, namely, Parsons, the original 'Crabtree' and 'Sir Fretful Plagiary,' 'Sir Christopher Curry,' 'Snarl' to Edwin's 'Sheepface,' and 'Lope Torry,' in *The Mountaineers*. . . . . His *forte* lay in old men, his pictures of whom, in all their characteristics, passions, infirmities, cunning, or imbecility, was perfect. When 'Sir Sampson Legand' says to 'Foresight,' 'Look up, old star-gazer! Now is he poring on the ground for a crooked pin, or an old horse-nail with the head towards him!'" we are told there could not be a finer illustration of the character which Congreve meant to represent than Parsons showed at the time in his face and attitude.

In Queen Street, on the south side of Cheapside, stood Ringed Hall, the house of the Earls of Cornwall, given by them, in Edward III.'s time, to the Abbot of Beaulieu, near Oxford. Henry VIII. gave it to Morgan Philip, *alias* Wolfe. Near it was "Ipres Inn," built by William of Ipres, in King Stephen's time, which continued in the same family in 1377.

Stow says of Soper Lane, now Queen Street: —"Soper Lane, which lane took that name, not of soap-making, as some have supposed, but of Alleyne le Sopar, in the ninth of Edward II."

"In this Soper's Lane," Strype informs us, "the pepperers anciently dwelt—wealthy tradesmen, who dealt in spices and drugs. Two of this trade were divers times mayors in the reign of Henry III., viz., Andrew Bocherel, and John de Gisorcio or Gisors. In the reign of King Edward II., *anno* 1315, they came to be governed by rules and orders, which are extant in one of the books of the chamber under this title, '*Ordinatio Piperarum de Soper's Lane.*'" Sir Baptist Hicks, Viscount Campden, of the time of James I., whose name is preserved in Hicks's Hall, and Campden Hill, Kensington, was a rich mercer, at the sign of the "White Bear," at Soper Lane end, in Cheapside. Strype says that "Sir Baptist was one of the first citizens that, after knighthood, kept their shops, and, being charged with it by some of the aldermen, he gave this answer, first—'That his servants kept the shop, though he had a regard to the special

credit thereof; and that he did not live altogether upon the interest, as most of the aldermen did, laying aside their trade after knighthood.'"

The parish church of St. Syth, or Bennet Shere-hog, or Shrog, "seemeth," says Stow, "to take that name from one Benedict Shorne, some time a citizen, and stock-fish monger, of London, a new builder, repairer, or benefactor thereof, in the reign of Edward II.; so that Shorne is but corruptly called Shrog, and more correctly Shorehog, or (as now) Sherehog." The following curious epitaph is preserved by Stow :—

"Here lieth buried the body of Ann, the wife of John Farrar, gentleman, and merchant adventurer of this city, daughter of William Shepheard, of Great Rowlright, in the county of Oxenford, Esqre. She departed this life the twelfth day of July, An. Dom. 1613, being then about the age of twenty-one yeeres.

"Here was a bud,
    Beginning for her May ;
Before her flower,
    Death took her hence away.
But for what cause ?
    That friends might joy the more ;
Where there hope is,
    She flourisheth now before.
She is not lost,
    But in those joyes remaine,
Where friends may see,
    And joy in her againe."

"In the Church of St. Pancras, Soper Lane, there do lie the remains," says Stow, "of Robert Packinton, merchant, slain with a gun, as he was going to morrow mass from his house in Cheape to St. Thomas of Acons, in the year 1536. The murderer was never discovered, but by his own confession, made when he came to the gallows at Banbury to be hanged for felony."

The following epitaph is also worth giving :—

"Here lies a Mary, mirror of her sex,
For all that best their souls or bodies decks.
Faith, form, or fame, the miracle of youth ;
For zeal and knowledge of the sacred truth.
For frequent reading of the Holy Writ,
For fervent prayer, and for practice fit.
For meditation full of use and art ;
For humbleness in habit and in heart.
For pious, prudent, peaceful, praiseful life ;
For all the duties of a Christian wife ;
For patient bearing seven dead-bearing throws ;
For one alive, which yet dead with her goes ;
From Travers, her dear spouse, her father, Hayes,
Lord maior, more honoured in her virtuous praise."

"The Church of St. Thomas Apostle stood where now the cemetery is," says Maitland, "in Queen Street. It was of great antiquity, as is manifest by the state thereof in the year 1181. The parish is united to the Church of St. Mary Alder-mary. There were five epitaphs in Greek and Latin to 'Katherine Killigrew.' The best is by Andrew Melvin."

"Of monuments of antiquity there were none left undefaced, except some arms in the windows, which were supposed to be the arms of John Barnes, mercer, Maior of London in the year 1371, a great builder thereof. A benefactor thereof was Sir William Littlesbury, alias *Horn* (for King Edward IV. so named him), because he was most excellent in a horn. He was a salter and merchant of the staple, mayor of London in 1487, and was buried in the church, having appointed, by his testament, the bells to be changed for four new ones of good tune and sound ; but that was not performed. He gave five hundred marks towards repairing of highways between London and Cambridge. His dwelling-house, with a garden and appurtenances in the said parish, he devised to be sold, and bestowed in charitable actions. His house, called the 'George,' in Bred Street, he gave to the salters ; they to find a priest in the said church, to have six pounds thirteen and fourpence the year. To every preacher at St. Paul's Cross, and at the Spittle, he left fourpence for ever ; to the prisoners of Newgate, Ludgate, from rotation to King's Bench, in victuals, ten shillings at Christmas, and ten shillings at Easter for ever," which legacies, however, it appears, were not carried out.

CHAPTER XXX.

CHEAPSIDE TRIBUTARIES, NORTH.

Goldsmiths' Hall—Its Early Days—Tailors and Goldsmiths at Loggerheads—The Goldsmiths' Company's Charters and Records—Their Great Annual Feast—They receive Queen Margaret of Anjou in State—A Curious Trial of Skill—Civic and State Duties—The Goldsmiths break up the Image of their Patron Saint—The Goldsmiths' Company's Assays—The Ancient Goldsmiths' Feasts—The Goldsmiths at Work— Goldsmiths' Hall at the Present Day—The Portraits—St. Leonard's Church—St. Vedast—Discovery of a Stone Coffin—Coachmakers' Hall.

IN Foster Lane, the first turning out of Cheapside northwards, our first visit must be paid to the Hall of the Goldsmiths, one of the richest, most ancient, and most practical of all the great City companies.

The original site of Goldsmiths' Hall belonged, in the reign of Edward II., to Sir Nicholas de Segrave, a Leicestershire knight, brother of Gilbert de Segrave, Bishop of London. The date of the Goldsmiths' first building is uncertain, but it is first mentioned in their records in 1366 (Edward III.). The second hall is supposed to have been built by Sir Drew Barentyn, in 1407 (Henry IV.). The Livery Hall had a bay window on the side next to Huggin Lane ; the roof was surmounted with a lantern and vane ; the reredos in the screen was surmounted by a silver-gilt statue of St. Dunstan ; and the Flemish tapestry represented the story of the patron saint of goldsmiths. Stow, writing in 1598, expresses doubt at the story that Bartholomew Read, goldsmith and mayor in 1502, gave a feast there to more than 100 persons, as the hall was too small for that purpose.

From 1641 till the Restoration, Goldsmiths' Hall served as the Exchequer of the Commonwealth. All the money obtained from the sequestration of Royalists' estates was here stored, and then disbursed for State purposes. The following is a description of the earlier hall :—

"The buildings," says Herbert, "were of a fine red brick, and surrounded a small square court, paved ; the front being ornamented with stone corners, wrought in rustic, and a large arched entrance, which exhibited a high pediment, supported on Doric columns, and open at the top, to give room for a shield of the Company's arms. The livery, or common hall, which was on the east side of the court, was a spacious and lofty apartment, paved with black and white marble, and very elegantly fitted up. The wainscoting was very handsome, and the ceiling and its appendages richly stuccoed—an enormous flower adorning the centre, and the City and Goldsmiths' arms, with various decorations, appearing in its other compartments. A richly-carved screen, with composite pillars, pilasters, &c. ; a balustrade, with vases, terminating in branches for lights (between which displayed the banners and flags used on public occasions) ; and a beaufet of considerable size, with white and gold ornaments, formed part of the embellishments of this splendid room."

"The balustrade of the staircase was elegantly carved, and the walls exhibited numerous reliefs of scrolls, flowers, and instruments of music. The court-room was another richly-wainscoted apartment, and the ceiling very grand, though, perhaps, somewhat overloaded with embellishments. The chimney-piece was of statuary marble, and very sumptuous."

The guild of Goldsmiths is of extreme antiquity, having been fined in 1180 (Henry II.) as adulterine, that is, established or carried on without the king's special licence; for in any matter where fines could be extorted, the Norman kings took a paternal interest in the doings of their patient subjects. In 1267 (Henry III.) the goldsmiths seem to have been infected with the pugnacious spirit of the age; for we come upon bands of goldsmiths and tailors fighting in London streets, from some guild jealousy;

The goldsmiths were incorporated into a permanent company in the prodigal reign of Richard II., and they no doubt drove a good business with that thriftless young Absalom, who, it is said wore golden bells on his sleeves and baldric. For ten marks—not a very tremendous consideration, though it was, no doubt, all he could get—Richard's

INTERIOR OF GOLDSMITHS' HALL (*see page* 362).

and 500 snippers of cloth meeting, by appointment, 500 hammerers of metal, and having a comfortable and steady fight. In the latter case many were killed on both sides, and the sheriff at last had to interpose with the City's *posse comitatus* and with bows, swords, and spears. The ringleaders were finally apprehended, and thirteen of them condemned and executed. In 1278 (Edward I.) many spurious goldsmiths were arrested for frauds in trade, three Englishmen were hung, and more than a dozen unfortunate Jews.

grandfather, that warlike and chivalrous monarch, Edward III., had already incorporated the Company, and given "the Mystery" of Goldsmiths the privilege of purchasing in mortmain an estate of £20 per annum, for the support of old and sick members; for these early guilds were benefit clubs as well as social companies, and jealous privileged monopolists; and Edward's grant gave the corporation the right to inspect, try, and regulate all gold and silver wares in any part of England, with the power to punish all offenders detected in

TRIAL OF THE PIX. (*See page 357.*)

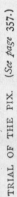

working adulterated gold and silver. Edward, in all, granted four charters to the Worshipful Company.

Henry IV., Henry V., and Edward IV. both granted and confirmed the liberties of the Company. The Goldsmiths' records commence in 5 Edward III., and furnish much curious information. In this reign all who were of Goldsmiths' Hall were required to have shops in Chepe, and to sell no silver or gold vessels except in Chepe or in the King's Exchange. The first charter complains loudly of counterfeit metal, of false bracelets, lockets, rings, and jewels, made and exported; and also of vessels of tin made and subtly silvered over.

The Company began humbly enough, and in their first year of incorporation (1335) fourteen apprentices only were bound, the fees for admission being 2s., and the pensions given to twelve persons coming to only £1 16s. In the year 1343 the number of apprentices rose to seventy-four; and in 1344 there were payments for licensing foreign workmen and non-freemen.

During the Middle Ages these City companies were very attentive to religious observances, and the Wardens' accounts show constant entries referring to such ceremonies. Their great annual feast was on St. Dunstan's Day (St. Dunstan being the patron saint of goldsmiths), and the books of expenses show the cost of masses sung for the Company by the chaplain, payments for ringing the bells at St. Paul's, for drinking obits at the Company's standard at St. Paul's, for lights kept burning at St. James's Hospital, and for chantries maintained at the churches of St. John Zachary (the Goldsmiths' parish church), St. Peter-le-Chepe, St. Matthew, Friday Street, St. Vedast, Foster Lane, and others.

About the reign of Henry VI. the records grow more interesting, and reflect more strongly the social life of the times they note. In 1443 we find the Company received a special letter from Henry VI., desiring them, as a craft which had at all times "notably acquitted themselves," more especially at the king's return from his coronation in Paris, to meet his queen, Margaret of Anjou, on her arrival, in company with the Mayor, aldermen, and the chief London crafts. On this occasion the goldsmiths wore "bawderykes of gold, short jagged scarlet hoods," and each past-Warden or renter had his follower clothed in white, with a black hood and black felt hat. In this reign John Chest, a goldsmith of Chepe, for slanderous words against the Company, was condemned to come to Goldsmiths' Hall, and on his knees ask all the Company "forgiveness for what he had myssayde," and was also forbidden to wear the livery of the Company

for a whole month. Later still, in this reign, a goldsmith named German Lyas, for selling a tablet of adulterated gold, was compelled to give to the fraternity a gilt cup, weighing twenty-four ounces, and to implore pardon on his knees. In 1458 (Henry VI.), a goldsmith was fined for giving a false return of broken gold to a servant of the Earl of Wiltshire, who had brought it to be sold.

In the fourth year of King Edward IV. a very curious trial of skill between the jealous English goldsmiths and their foreign rivals took place at the "Pope's Head" tavern (now Pope's Head Alley), Cornhill. The contending craftsmen had to engrave four puncheons of steel (the breadth of a penny sterling) with cat's heads and naked figures in high relief and low relief; Oliver Davy, the Englishman, won, and White Johnson, the Alicant goldsmith, lost his wager of a crown and a dinner to the Company. In this reign there were 137 native goldsmiths in London, and 41 foreigners— total, 178. The foreigners lived chiefly in Westminster, Southwark, St. Clement's Lane, Abchurch Lane, Brick Lane, and Bearbinder Lane.

In 1511 (Henry VIII.) the Company agreed to send twelve men to attend the City Night-watch, on the vigils of St. John Baptist, and St. Peter and Paul. The men were to be cleanly harnessed, to carry bows and arrows, and to be arrayed in jackets of white, with the City arms. In 1540 the Company sent six of their body to fetch in the new Queen, Anne of Cleves, "the Flemish mare," as her disappointed bridegroom called her. The six goldsmiths must have looked very gallant in their black velvet coats, gold chains, and velvet caps with brooches of gold; and their servants in plain russet coats. Sir Martin Bowes was the great goldsmith in this reign; he is the man whom Stow accused, when Lord Mayor, of rooting up all the gravestones and monuments in the Grey Friars, and selling them for £50. He left almshouses at Woolwich, and two houses in Lombard Street, to the Company.

In 1546 (same reign) the Company sent twenty-four men, by royal order, to the king's army. They were to be "honest, comely, and well-harnessed persons—four of them bowmen, and twelve billmen. They were arrayed in blue and red (after my Lord Norfolk's fashion), hats and hose red and blue, and with doublets of white fustian." This same year, the greedy despot Henry having discovered some slight inaccuracy in the assay, contrived to extort from the poor abject goldsmiths a mighty fine of 3,000 marks. The year this English Ahab died, the Goldsmiths resolved, in compliment to the Reformation, to break up the image of their patron saint, and also a great standing cup with an image of the same saint upon the top. Among the Company's plate there still exists a goodly cup given by Sir Martin Bowes, and which is said to be the same from which Queen Elizabeth drank at her coronation.

The government of the Company has been seen to have been vested in an alderman in the reign of Henry II., and in four wardens as early as 28 Edward I. The wardens were divided, at a later period, into a prime warden (always an alderman of London), a second warden, and two renter wardens. The clerk, under the name of "clerk-comptroller," is not mentioned till 1494; but a similar officer must have been established much earlier. Four auditors and two porters are named in the reign of Henry VI. The assayer, or as he is now called, assay warden (to whom were afterwards joined two assistants), is peculiar to the Goldsmiths.

The Company's assay of the coin, or trial of the pix, a curious proceeding of great solemnity, now takes place every year. "It is," says Herbert, in his "City Companies," "an investigation or inquiry into the purity and weight of the money coined, before the Lords of the Council, and is aided by the professional knowledge of a jury of the Goldsmiths' Company; and in a writ directed to the barons for that purpose (9 and 10 Edward I.) is spoken of as a well-known custom.

"The Wardens of the Goldsmiths' Company are summoned by precept from the Lord Chancellor to form a jury, of which their assay master is always one. This jury are sworn, receive a charge from the Lord Chancellor; then retire into the Court-room of the Duchy of Lancaster, where the pix (a small box, from the ancient name of which this ceremony is denominated), and which contains the coins to be examined, is delivered to them by the officers of the Mint. The indenture or authority under which the Mint Master has acted being read, the pix is opened, and the coins to be assayed being taken out, are inclosed in paper parcels, each under the seals of the Wardens, Master, and Comptrollers. From every 15 lbs. of silver, which are technically called 'journies,' two pieces at the least are taken at hazard for this trial; and each parcel being opened, and the contents being found correct with the indorsement, the coins are mixed together in wooden bowls, and afterwards weighed. From the whole of these moneys so mingled, the jury take a certain number of each species of coin, to the amount of 1 lb. weight, for the assay by fire; and the indented trial pieces of gold and silver, of the dates specified in the indenture, being pro-

duced by the proper officer, a sufficient quantity is cut from either of them for the purpose of comparing with it the pound weight of gold or silver by the usual methods of assay. The perfection or imperfection of these are certified by the jury, who deliver their verdict in writing to the Lord Chancellor, to be deposited amongst the papers of the Privy Council. If found accurate, the Mint Master receives his certificate, or, as it is called, *quietus*" (a legal word used by Shakespeare in Hamlet's great soliloquy). "The assaying of the precious metals, anciently called the 'touch,' with the marking or stamping, and the proving of the coin, at what is called the 'trial of the pix,' were privileges conferred on the Goldsmiths' Company by the statute 28 Edward I. They had for the former purpose an assay office more than 500 years ago, which is mentioned in their books. Their still retaining the same privilege makes the part of Goldsmiths' Hall, where this business is carried on, a busy scene during the hours of assaying. In the old statute all manner of vessels of gold and silver are expected to be of good and true alloy, namely, 'gold of a certain *touch*,' and silver of the sterling alloy; and no vessel is to depart out of the hands of the workman until it is assayed by the workers of the Goldsmiths' craft.

"The *Hall mark* shows where manufactured, as the *Leopard's head* for London. *Duty mark* is the head of the Sovereign, showing the duty is paid. *Date mark* is a letter of the alphabet, which varies every year; thus, the Goldsmiths' Company have used, from 1716 to 1755, Roman capital letters; 1756 to 1775, small Roman letters; 1776 to 1795, old English letters; 1796 to 1815, Roman capital letters, from A to U, omitting J; 1816 to 1835 small Roman letters a to u, omitting j; from 1836, old English letters. There are two qualities of gold and silver. The inferior is mostly in use. The quality marks for silver are Britannia, or the head of the reigning monarch; for gold, the lion passant, 22 or 18, which denotes that fine gold is 24-carat; 18 only 75 per cent. gold; sometimes rings are marked 22. The *manufacturer's mark* is the initials of the maker.

"The Company are allowed 1 per cent., and the fees for stamping are paid into the Inland Revenue Office. At Goldsmiths' Hall, in the years 1850 to 1863 inclusive, there were assayed and marked 85 22-carat watch-cases, 316,347 18-carat, 493 15-carat, 1550 12-carat, 448 9-carat, making a total of 318,923 cases, weighing 467,250 ounces 6 dwts. 18 grains. The Goldsmiths' Company append a note to this return, stating that they have no knowledge of the value of the cases assayed, except of the intrinsic value, as indicated by the weight and quality of the gold given in the return. The silver watch-cases assayed at the same establishment in the fourteen years, 1,139,704, the total weight being 2,302,192 ounces 19 dwts. In the year 1857 the largest number of cases were assayed out of the fourteen. The precise number in that year was 106,860, this being more than 10,000 above any year in the period named. In a subsequent year the number was only 77,608. A similar note with regard to value is appended to the return of silver cases as to the gold." There has been a complaint lately made that inferior jewellery is often tampered with after receiving the Hall mark.

An old book, probably Elizabethan, the "Touchstone for Goldsmith's Wares," observes, "That goldsmiths in the City and liberties, as to their particular trade, are under the Goldsmiths' Company's control, whether members or not, and ought to be of *their own company*, though, from mistake or design, many of them are free of others. For the wardens, being by their charters and the statutes appointed to survey, assay, and mark the silver-work, are to be chosen from members, such choice must sometimes fall upon them that are either of other trades, or not skilled in their curious art of making assays of gold and silver, and consequently unable to make a true report of the goodness thereof ; or else the necessary attendance thereon is too great a burden for the wardens. Therefore they (the wardens) have appointed an *assay master*, called by them their deputy warden, allowing him a considerable yearly salary, and who takes an oath for the due performance of his office. They have large steel puncheons and marks of different sizes, with the leopard's-head, crowned ; the *lion*, and a certain *letter*, which letter they change alphabetically every year, in order to know the year any particular work was assayed or marked, as well as the markers. These marks," he adds, "are every year new made, for the use of fresh wardens ; and although the assaying is referred to the assay master, yet the *touch-wardens* look to the striking of the marks." To acquaint the public the better with this business of the assay, the writer of the "Touchstone" has prefixed a frontispiece to his work, intended to represent the interior of an assay office (we should suppose that of the old Goldsmiths' Hall), and makes reference by numbers to the various objects shown—as, 1. The refining furnace ; 2. The test, with silver refining in it ; 3. The fining bellows ; 4. The man blowing or working them ; 5. The test-mould ; 6. A wind-hole to melt silver in, with bellows ; 7. A pair of organ bellows ; 8. A man

melting, or boiling, or nealing silver at them ; 9. A block, with a large anvil placed thereon ; 10. Three men forging plate ; 11. The fining and other goldsmith's tools ; 12. The assay furnace ; 13. The assay master making assays ; 14. This man putting the assays into the fire ; 15. The warden marking the plate on the anvil ; 16. His officer holding his plate for the marks ; and 17. Three goldsmiths' small workers at work. In the office are stated to be a sworn weigher to weigh and make entry of all silver-work brought in, and who re-weighs it to the owners when worked, reserving the ancient allowance for so doing, which is 4 grains out of every 1 lb. marked, for a re-assay yearly of all the silver works they have passed the preceding year. There are also, he says, a table, or tables, in columns, one whereof is of hardened lead, and the other of vellum or parchment (the lead columns having the worker's initials struck in them, and the other the owner's names) ; and the seeing that these marks are right, and plainly impressed on the gold and silver work, is one of the warden's peculiar duties. The manner of marking the assay is thus :—The assay master puts a small quantity of the silver upon trial in the fire, and then, taking it out again, he, with his exact scales *that will turn with the weight of the hundredth* part of a grain, computes and reports the goodness or badness of the gold and silver.

The allowance of four grains to the pound, Malcolm states to have been continued till after 1725 ; for gold watch-cases, from one to four, one shilling ; and all above, threepence each ; and in proportion for other articles of the same metal. "The assay office," he adds, "seems, however, to have been a losing concern with the Company, their receipts for six years, to 1725, being £1,615 13s. 11½d., and the payments, £2,074 3s. 8d."

The ancient goldsmiths seem to have wisely blended pleasure with profit, and to have feasted right royally : one of their dinner bills runs thus :—

EXPENSES OF ST. DUNSTAN'S FEAST.
1473 (12 *Edward IV.*).

	£	s.	d.
To eight minstrels in manner accustomed	2	13	8
Ten bonnets for ditto	0	6	8
Their dinner	0	3	4
Two hogsheads of wine	2	10	0
One barrel of Muscadell	0	6	6
Red wine, 17 qrts. and 3 galls.	0	11	10
Four barrels of good ale	0	17	4
Two ditto of 2dy half-penny	0	6	0
In spice bread	0	16	8
In other bread	0	10	10
In comfits and spice (36 articles)	5	17	6
Poultry, including 12 capons at 8d.	2	16	11
Pigeons at 1½d., and 12 more geese, at 7d. each.			

With "butchery," "fishmongery," and "miscellaneous articles," the total amount of the feast was £26 17s. 7d.

A supper bill which occurs in the 11th of Henry VIII. amounts to only £5 18s. 6d., and it enumerates the following among the provisions:— Bread, two bushels of meal, a kilderkin and a firkin of good ale, 12 capons, four dozen of chickens, four dishes of Surrey (sotterey) butter, 11 lbs. of suet, six marrow bones, a quarter of a sheep, 50 eggs, six dishes of sweet butter, 60 oranges, gooseberries, strawberries, 56 lbs. of cherries, 17 lbs. 10 oz. of sugar, cinnamon, ginger, cloves, and mace, saffron, rice flour, "raisins, currants," dates, white salt, bay salt, red vinegar, white vinegar, verjuice, the hire of pewter vessels, and various other articles.

In City pageants the Goldsmiths always held a conspicuous place. The following is an account of their pageant in jovial Lord Mayor Vyner's time (Charles II.):—

"First pageant. A large triumphal chariot of gold, richly set with divers inestimable and various coloured jewels, of dazzling splendour, adorned with sundry curious figures, fictitious stories, and delightful landscapes; one ascent of seats up to a throne, whereon a person of majestic aspect sitteth, the representer of Justice, hieroglyphically attired, in a long red robe, and on it a golden mantle fringed with silver; on her head a long dishevelled hair of flaxen colour, curiously curled, on which is a coronet of silver; in her left hand she advanceth a touchstone (the tryer of *Truth* and discoverer of *Falsehood*); in her right hand she holdeth up a golden balance, with silver scales, equi-ponderent, to weigh justly and impartially; her arms dependent on the heads of two *leopards*, which emblematically intimate *courage* and *constancy*. This chariot is drawn by two golden unicorns, in excellent carving work, with equal magnitude, to the left; on whose backs are mounted two raven-black negroes, attired according to the dress of India; on their heads, wreaths of divers coloured feathers; in their right hands they hold golden cups; in their left hands, two displayed banners, the one of the king's, the other of the Company's arms, all which represent the crest and the supporters of the ancient, famous, and worshipful Company of Goldsmiths.

"Trade pageant. On a very large pageant is a very rich seat of state, containing the representer of the Patron to the Goldsmiths' Company, Saint Dunstan, attired in a dress properly expressing his prelatical dignity, in a robe of fine white lawn, over which he weareth a cope or vest of costly bright cloth of gold, down to the ground; on his reverend grey head, a golden mitre, set with topaz, ruby, emerald, amethyst, and sapphire. In his left hand he holdeth a golden crozier, and in his right hand he useth a pair of goldsmith's tongs. Beneath these steps of ascension to his chair, in opposition to St. Dunstan, is properly painted a goldsmith's forge and furnace, with fire and gold in it, a workman blowing with the bellows. On his right and left hand, there is a large press of gold and silver plate, representing a shop of trade; and further in front, are several artificers at work on anvils with hammers, beating out plate fit for the forgery and formation of several vessels in gold and silver. There are likewise in the shop several wedges or ingots of gold and silver, and a step below St. Dunstan sitteth an assay-master, with his glass frame and balance, for trial of gold and silver, according to the standard. In another place there is also disgrossing, drawing, and flatting of gold and silver wire. There are also finers melting, smelting, fining, and parting gold and silver, both by fire and water; and in a march before this orfery, are divers miners in canvas breeches, red waistcoats, and red caps, bearing spades, pickaxes, twibills, and crows, for to sink shafts, and make adits. The Devil, also, appearing to St. Dunstan, is catched by the nose at a proper *qu*, which is given in his speech. When the speech is spoken, the great anvil is set forth, with a silversmith holding on it a plate of massive silver, and three other workmen at work, keeping excellent time in their orderly strokes upon the anvil."

The Goldsmiths in the Middle Ages seem to have been fond of dress. In a great procession of the London crafts to meet Richard II.'s fair young queen, Anne of Bohemia, all the mysteries of the City wore red and black liveries. The Goldsmiths had on the red of their dresses bars of silver-work and silver trefoils, and each of the seven score Goldsmiths, on the black part, wore fine knots of gold and silk, and on their worshipful heads red hats, powdered with silver trefoils. In Edward IV.'s reign, the Company's taste changed. The Liverymen wore violet and scarlet gowns like the Goldsmiths' sworn friends, the Fishmongers; while, under Henry VII., they wore violet gowns and black hoods. In Henry VIII.'s reign the hoods of the mutable Company went back again to violet and scarlet.

In 1456 (Henry VI.) the London citizens seem to have been rather severe with their apprentices; for we find William Hede, a goldsmith, accusing his apprentice of beating his mistress. The apprentice was brought to the kitchen of the Goldsmith's Hall, and there stripped naked, and beaten by his master till blood came. This punishment was inflicted in the presence of several

people.   The apprentice then asked his master's
forgiveness on his knees.

The Goldsmiths' searches for bad and defective
work were arbitrary enough, and made with great
formality.   "The wardens," say the ordinances,
"every quarter, once, or oftener, if need be, shall

also dressed, following.   Their mode of proceeding
is given in the following account, entitled "The
Manner and Order for Searches at Bartholomew
Fayre and Our Ladye Fayre" (Henry VIII.):—

"M^d.   The Bedell for the time beyng shall
walke upon Seynt Barthyllmewes Eve all alonge

EXTERIOR OF GOLDSMITHS' HALL (*see page* 361).

search in London, Southwark, and Westminster, that
all the goldsmiths there dwelling work true gold
and silver, according to the Act of Parliament,
and shall also make due search for their weights."

The manner of making this search, as elsewhere
detailed, seems to have resembled that of our
modern inquest, or annoyance juries; the Company's beadle, in full costume and with his insignia
of office, marching first; the wardens, in livery,
with their hoods; the Company's clerk, two renter
wardens, two brokers, porters, and other attendants,

Chepe, for to see what plaate ys in eu^{r}y mannys
deske and gyrdyll.   And so the sayd wardeyns for
to goo into Lumberd Streate, or into other places
there, where yt shall please theym.   And also the
clerk of the Fellyshyppe shall wayt uppon the seyd
wardeyns for to wryte eu^{r}y p^{r}cell of sylu^r stuffe
then distrayned by the sayd wardeyns.

"Also the sayd wardeyns been accustomed to
goo into Barth'u Fayre, upon the evyn or daye,
at theyr pleasure, in theyre lyuerey gownes and
hoodys, as they will appoint, and two of the livery,

ancient men, with them; the renters, the clerk, and the bedell, in their livery, with them; and the brokers to wait upon my masters the wardens, to see every hardware men show, for deceitful things, beads, gawds of beads, and other stuff; and then they to drink when they have done, where they please.

"Also the said wardens be accustomed at our Lady day, the Nativity, to walk and see the fair at Southwark, in like manner with their company, as is aforesaid, and to search there likewise."

Another order enjoins the two second wardens "to ride into Stourbrydge fair, with what officers they liked, and do the same."

Amongst other charges against the trade at this date, it is said "that dayly divers straungers and other gentils" complained and found themselves aggrieved, that they came to the shops of goldsmiths within the City of London, and without the City, and to their booths and fairs, markets, and other places, and there bought of them *old plate* new refreshed in gilding and burnishing; it appearing to all "such straungers and other gentils" that such old plate, so by them bought, was new, sufficient, and able; whereby all such were deceived, to the grete "dysslaunder and jeopardy of all the seyd crafte of goldsmythis."

ALTAR OF DIANA (*see page* 362).

In consequence of these complaints, it was ordained (15 Henry VII.) by all the said fellowship, that no goldsmith, within or without the City, should thenceforth put to sale such description of plate, in any of the places mentioned, without it had the mark of the "Lybardishede crowned." All plate put to sale contrary to these orders the wardens were empowered to break. They also had the power, at their discretion, to fine offenders for this and any other frauds in manufacturing. If any goldsmith attempted to prevent the wardens from breaking bad work, they could seize such work, and declare it forfeited, according to the Act of Parliament, appropriating the one half (as thereby

directed) to the king, and the other to the wardens breaking and making the seizure.

The present Goldsmiths' Hall was the design of Philip Hardwick, R.A. (1832–5), and boasts itself the most magnificent of the City halls. The old hall had been taken down in 1829, and the new hall was built without trenching on the funds set apart for charity. The style is Italian, of the seventeenth and eighteenth centuries. The building is 180 feet in front and 100 feet deep. The west or chief façade has six attached Corinthian columns, the whole height of the front supporting a rich Corinthian entablature and bold cornice; and the other three fronts are adorned with pilasters, which also terminate the angles. Some of the blocks in the column shafts weigh from ten to twelve tons each. The windows of the principal story, the echinus moulding of which is handsome, have bold and enriched pediments, and the centre windows are honoured by massive balustrade balconies. In the centre, above the first floor, are the Company's arms, festal emblems, rich garlands, and trophies. The entrance door is a rich specimen of cast work. Altogether, though rather jammed up behind the Post-office, this building is worthy of the powerful and wealthy company who make it their domicile.

The modern Renaissance style, it must be allowed, though less picturesque than the Gothic, is lighter, more stately, and more adapted for civic purposes.

The hall and staircase are much admired, and are not without grandeur. They were in 1871 entirely lined with costly marbles of different sorts and colours, and the result is very splendid. The staircase branches right and left, and ascends to a domed gallery. Leaving that respectable porter dozy but watchful in his beehive chair in the vestibule, we ascend the steps. On the square pedestals which ornament the balustrade of the first flight of stairs stand four graceful marble statuettes of the seasons, by Nixon. Spring is looking at a bird's-nest; Summer, wreathed with flowers, leads a lamb; Autumn carries sheaves of corn; and Winter presses his robe close against the wind. Between the double scagliola columns of the gallery are a group of statues; the bust of the sailor king, William IV., by Chantrey, is in a niche above. A door on the top of the staircase opens to the Livery hall; the room for the Court of Assistants is on the right of the northernmost corridor. The great banqueting-hall, 80 by 40 feet, and 35 feet high, has a range of Corinthian columns on either side. The five lofty, arched windows are filled with the armorial bearings of eminent goldsmiths of past times; and at the north end is a spacious alcove for the display of plate, which is lighted from above. On the side of the room is a large mirror, with busts of George III. and his worthy son, George IV. Between the columns are portraits of Queen Adelaide, by Sir Martin Archer Shee, and William IV. and Queen Victoria, by the Court painter, Sir George Hayter. The court-room has an elaborate stucco ceiling, with a glass chandelier, which tinkles when the scarlet mail-carts rush off from the yard below. In this room, beneath glass, is preserved the interesting little altar of Diana, found in digging the foundations of the new hall. Though greatly corroded, it has been of fine workmanship, and the outlines are full of grace. There are also some pictures of great merit and interest. First among them is Janssen's fine portrait of Sir Hugh Myddleton. He is dressed in black, and rests his hand upon a shell. This great benefactor of London left to the Goldsmiths' Company a share in his water-works, which is now worth more than £1,000 a year. Another portrait is that of Sir Thomas Vyner, that jovial Lord Mayor, who dragged Charles II. back for a second bottle. A third is a portrait (after Holbein) of Sir Martin Bowes, Lord Mayor in 1545 (Henry VIII.); and there is also a large picture, attributed to Giulio Romano, the only painter Shakespeare mentions in his plays. In the foreground is St. Dunstan, in rich robes and crozier in hand, while behind, the saint takes the Devil by the nose, much to the approval of flocks of angels above. The great white marble mantelpiece came from Canons, the seat of the Duke of Chandos; and the two large terminal busts are attributed to Roubiliac. The sumptuous drawing-room, adorned with crimson satin, white and gold, has immense mirrors, and a stucco ceiling, wrought with fruit, flowers, birds, and animals, with coats of arms blazoned on the four corners. The court dining-room displays on the marble chimney-piece two boys holding a wreath

encircling the portrait of Richard II., by whom the Goldsmiths were first incorporated. In the livery tea-room is a conversation piece, by Hudson (Reynolds' master), containing portraits of six Lord Mayors, all Goldsmiths. The Company's plate, as one might suppose, is very magnificent, and comprises a chandelier of chased gold, weighing 1,000 ounces; two superb old gold plates, having on them the arms of France quartered with those of England; and, last of all, there is the gold cup (attributed to Cellini) out of which Queen Elizabeth is said to have drank at her coronation, and which was bequeathed to the Company by Sir Martin Bowes. At the Great Exhibition of 1851 this spirited Company awarded £1,000 to the best artist in gold and silver plate, and at the same time resolved to spend £5,000 on plate of British manufacture.

From the Report of the Charity Commissioners it appears that the Goldsmiths' charitable funds, exclusive of gifts by Sir Martin Bowes, amount to £2,013 per annum.

Foster Lane was in old times chiefly inhabited by working goldsmiths.

"Dark Entry, Foster Lane," says Strype, "gives a passage into St. Martin's-le-Grand. On the north side of this entry was seated the parish church of St. Leonard, Foster Lane, which being consumed in the Fire of London, is not rebuilt, but the parish united to Christ Church; and the place where it stood is inclosed within a wall, and serveth as a burial-place for the inhabitants of the parish."

On the west side of Foster Lane stood the small parish church of St. Leonard's. This church, says Stow, was repaired and enlarged about the year 1631. A very fair window at the upper end of the chancel (1533) cost £500.

In this church were some curious monumental inscriptions. One of them, to the memory of Robert Trappis, goldsmith, bearing the date 1526, contained this epitaph:—

> " When the bels be merrily rung,
> And the masse devoutly sung,
> And the meate merrily eaten,
> Then shall Robert Trappis, his wife and
> children be forgotten."

On a stone, at the entering into the choir, was inscribed in Latin, " Under this marble rests the body of Humfred Barret, son of John Barret, gentleman, who died A.D. 1501." On a fair stone, in the chancel, nameless, was written:—

> "Live to Dye.
> "All flesh is grass, and needs must fade
> To earth again, whereof 'twas made."

St. Vedast, otherwise St. Foster, was a French saint, Bishop of Arras and Cambray in the reign of Clovis, who, according to the Rev. Alban Butler, performed many miracles on the blind and lame. Alaric had a great veneration for this saint.

In 1831, some workmen digging a drain discovered, ten or twelve feet below the level of Cheapside, and opposite No. 17, a curious stone coffin, now preserved in a vault, under a small brick grave, on the north side of St. Vedast's; whether Roman or Anglo-Saxon, it consists of a block of freestone, seven feet long and fifteen inches thick, hollowed out to receive a body, with a deeper cavity for the head and shoulders. When found, it contained a skeleton, and was covered with a flat stone. Several other stone coffins were found at the same time.

The interior of St. Foster is a melancholy instance of Louis Quatorze ornamentation. The church is divided by a range of Tuscan columns, and the ceiling is enriched with dusty wreaths of stucco flowers and fruit. The altar-piece consists of four Corinthian columns, carved in oak, and garnished with cherubim, palm-branches, &c. In the centre, above the entablature, is a group of well-executed winged figures, and beneath is a sculptured pelican. In 1838 Mr. Godwin spoke highly of the transparent blinds of this church, painted with various Scriptural subjects, as a substitute for stained glass.

"St. Vedast Church, in Foster Lane," says Maitland, "is on the east side, in the Ward of Farringdon Within, dedicated to St. Vedast, Bishop of Arras, in the province of Artois. The first time I find it mentioned in history is, that Walter de London was presented thereto in 1308. The patronage of the church was anciently in the Prior and Convent of Canterbury, till the year 1352, when, coming to the archbishop of that see, it has been in him and his successors ever since; and is one of the thirteen peculiars in this city belonging to that archiepiscopal city. This church was not entirely destroyed by the fire in 1666, but nothing left standing but the walls; the crazy steeple continued standing till the year 1694, when it was taken down and beautifully rebuilt at the charge of the united parishes. To this parish that of St. Michael Quern is united."

Among the odd monumental inscriptions in this church are the following :—

"Lord of thy infinite grace and Pittee
Have mercy on me Agnes, somtym the wyf
  Of William Milborne, Chamberlain of this citte,
Which toke my passage fro this wretched lyf,

The year of gras one thousand fyf hundryd and fyf,
The xii. day of July ; no longer was my spase,
  It plesy'd then my Lord to call me to his Grase ;
Now ye that are living, and see this picture,
  Pray for me here, whyle ye have tyme and spase,
That God of his goodnes wold me assure,
  In his everlasting mansion to have a plase.
        Obiit Anno 1505."

"Here lyeth interred the body of Christopher Wase, late citizen and goldsmith of London, aged 66 yeeres, and dyed the 22nd September, 1605 ; who had to wife Anne, the daughter of William Prettyman, and had by her three sons and three daughters.

"Reader, stay, and thou shalt know
    What he is, that here doth sleepe ;
  Lodged amidst the Stones below,
    Stones that oft are seen to weepe.
Gentle was his Birth and Breed,
    His carriage gentle, much contenting ;
  His word accorded with his Deed,
    Sweete his nature, soone relenting.
From above he seem'd protected,
    Father dead before his Birth.
  An orphane only, but neglected.
    Yet his Branches spread on Earth,
Earth that must his Bones containe,
    Sleeping, till *Christ's* Trumpe shall wake them,
  Joyning them to Soule againe,
    And to Blisse eternal take them.
It is not this rude and little Heap of Stones,
Can hold the Fame, although't containes the Bones ;
Light be the Earth, and hallowed for thy sake,
Resting in Peace, Peace that thou so oft didst make."

Coachmakers' Hall, in Noble Street, Foster Lane, originally built by the Scriveners' Company, was afterwards sold to the Coachmakers. Here the "Protestant Association" held its meetings, and here originated the dreadful riots of the year 1780. The Protestant Association was formed in February, 1778, in consequence of a bill brought into the House of Commons to repeal certain penalties and liabilities imposed upon Roman Catholics. When the bill was passed, a petition was framed for its repeal; and here, in this very hall (May 29, 1780), the following resolution was proposed and carried :—

"That the whole body of the Protestant Association do attend in St. George's Fields, on Friday next, at ten of the clock in the morning, to accompany Lord George Gordon to the House of Commons, on the delivery of the Protestant petition." His lordship, who was present on this occasion, remarked that "if less than 20,000 of his fellow-citizens attended him on that day, he would not present their petition."

Upwards of 50,000 "true Protestants" promptly answered the summons of the Association, and the Gordon riots commenced, to the six days' terror of the metropolis.

CHAPTER XXXI.
CHEAPSIDE TRIBUTARIES, NORTH :—WOOD STREET.

Wood Street—Pleasant Memories—St. Peter's in Chepe—St. Michael's and St. Mary Staining—St. Alban's, Wood Street—Some Quaint Epitaphs—
Wood Street Compter and the Hapless Prisoners therein—Wood Street Painful, Wood Street Cheerful—Thomas Ripley—The Anabaptist
Rising—A Remarkable Wine Cooper—St. John Zachary and St. Anne-in-the-Willows—Haberdashers' Hall—Something about the Mercers.

WOOD STREET runs from Cheapside to London Wall. Stow has two conjectures as to its name—first, that it was so called because the houses in it were built all of wood, contrary to Richard I.'s edict that London houses should be built of stone, to prevent fire ; secondly, that it was called after one Thomas Wood, sheriff in 1491 (Henry VII.), who dwelt in this street, was a benefactor to St. Peter in Chepe, and built "the beautiful row of houses over against Wood Street end."

At Cheapside Cross, which stood at the corner of Wood Street, all royal proclamations used to be read, even long after the cross was removed. Thus, in 1666, we find Charles II.'s declaration of war against Louis XIV. proclaimed by the officers at arms, serjeants at arms, trumpeters, &c., at Whitehall Gate, Temple Bar, the end of Chancery Lane, Wood Street, Cheapside, and the Royal Exchange. Huggin's Lane, in this street, derives its name, as Stow tells us, from a London citizen who dwelt here in the reign of Edward I., and was called Hugan in the Lane.

That pleasant tree at the left-hand corner of Wood Street, which has cheered many a weary business man with memories of the fresh green fields far away, was for long the residence of rooks, who built there. In 1845 two fresh nests were built, and one was lately visible ; but the birds deserted their noisy town residence several years ago. Probably, as the north of London was more built over, and such feeding-grounds as Belsize Park turned to brick and mortar, the birds found the fatigue of going miles in search of food for their young unbearable, and so migrated. Leigh Hunt, in one of his agreeable books, remarks that there are few districts in London where you will not find a tree. "A child was shown us," says Leigh Hunt, "who was said never to have beheld a tree but one in St. Paul's Churchyard, now gone. Whenever a tree was mentioned, it was this one; she had no conception of any other, not even of the remote tree in Cheapside." This famous tree marks the site of St. Peter in Chepe, a church destroyed by the Great Fire. The terms of the lease of the low houses at the west-end corner are said to forbid the erection of another storey or the removal of the tree. Whether this restriction arose from a love of the tree, as we should like to think, we cannot say.

St. Peter's in Chepe is a rectory (says Stow), "the church whereof stood at the south-west corner of Wood Street, in the ward of Farringdon Within, but of what antiquity I know not, other than that Thomas de Winton was rector thereof in 1324."

The patronage of this church was anciently in the Abbot and Convent of St. Albans, with whom it continued till the suppression of their monastery, when Henry VIII., in the year 1546, granted the same to the Earl of Southampton. It afterwards belonged to the Duke of Montague. This church being destroyed in the fire and not rebuilt, the parish is united to the Church of St. Matthew, Friday Street. "In the year 1401," says Maitland, "licence was granted to the inhabitants of this parish to erect a shed or shop before their church in Cheapside. On the site of this building, anciently called the 'Long Shop,' are now erected four shops, with rooms over them."

Wordsworth has immortalised Wood Street by his plaintive little ballad—

THE REVERIE OF POOR SUSAN.

"At the corner of Wood Street, when daylight appears,
Hangs a thrush that sings loud, it has sung for three years;
Poor Susan has passed by the spot, and has heard
In the silence of morning the song of the bird.

"'Tis a note of enchantment ; what ails her ? she sees
A mountain ascending, a vision of trees ;
Bright volumes of vapour through Lothbury glide,
And a river flows on through the vale of Cheapside.

"Green pastures she views in the midst of the dale,
Down which she so often has tripped with her pail ;
And a single small cottage, a nest like a dove's,
The one only dwelling on earth that she loves.

"She looks, and her heart is in heaven ; but they fade,
The mist and the river, the hill and the shade ;
The stream will not flow, and the hill will not rise,
And the colours have all passed away from her eyes."

Perhaps some summer morning the poet, passing down Cheapside, saw the plane-tree at the corner wave its branches to him as a friend waves a hand, and at that sight there passed through his mind an imagination of some poor Cumberland servant-girl toiling in London, and regretting her far-off home among the pleasant hills.

St. Michael's, Wood Street, is a rectory situated on the west side of Wood Street, in the ward of Cripplegate Within. John de Eppewell was rector thereof before the year 1328. "The patronage was anciently in the Abbot and Convent of St. Albans, in whom it continued till the suppression of their monastery, when, coming to the Crown, it was, with the appurtenances, in the year 1544, sold by Henry VIII. to William Barwell, who, in the year 1588, conveyed the same to John Marsh and others, in trust for the parish, in which it still continues." Being destroyed in the Great Fire, it was rebuilt, in 1675, from the designs of Sir Christopher Wren. At the east end four Ionic pillars support an entablature and pediment, and the three circular-headed windows are well proportioned. The south side faces Huggin Lane, but the tower and spire are of no interest. The interior of the church is a large parallelogram, with an ornamented carved ceiling. In 1831 the church was repaired and the tower thrown open. We give a view of the interior on page 372. The vestry-books date from the beginning of the sixteenth century, and contain, among others, memoranda of parochial rejoicings, such as—"1620. Nov. 9. Paid for ringing and a bonfire, 4s."

The Church of St. Mary Staining being destroyed in the Great Fire, the parish was annexed to that of St. Michael's. The following is the most curious of the monumental inscriptions :—

" John Casey, of this parish, whose dwelling was
   In the north-corner house as to Lad Lane you pass ;
   For better knowledge, the name it hath now
   Is called and known by the name of the Plow ;
   Out of that house yearly did geeve
   Twenty shillings to the poore, their neede to releeve;
   Which money the tenant must yearlie pay
   To the parish and churchwardens on St. Thomas' Day.
   The heire of that house, Thomas Bowrman by name,
   Hath since, by his deed, confirmed the same ;
   Whose love to the poore doth hereby appear,
   And after his death shall live many a yeare.
   Therefore in your life do good while yee may,
   That when meagre death shall take yee away ;
   You may live like form'd as Casey and Bowrman—
   For he that doth well shall never be a poore man."

Here was also a monument to Queen Elizabeth, with this inscription, found in many other London churches :—

" Here lyes her type, who was of late
   The prop of Belgia, stay of France,
   Spaine's foile, Faith's shield, and queen of State,
   Of arms, of learning, fate and chance.
   In brief, of women ne'er was seen
   So great a prince, so good a queen.

" Sith Vertue her immortal made,
   Death, envying all that cannot dye,
   Her earthly parts did so invade
   As in it wrackt self-majesty.
   But so her spirits inspired her parts,
   That she still lives in loyal hearts."

There was buried here (but without any outward monument) the head of James, the fourth King of Scots, slain at Flodden Field. After the battle, the body of the said king being found, was closed in lead, and conveyed from thence to London, and so to the monastery of Shene, in Surrey, where it remained for a time. " But since the dissolution of that house," says Stow, " in the reign of Edward VI., Henry Gray, Duke of Suffolk, lodged and kept house there. I have been shown the said body, so lapped in lead. The head and body were thrown into a waste room, amongst the old timber, lead, and other rubble ; since which time workmen there, for their foolish pleasure, hewed off his head; and Launcelot Young, master glazier to Queen Elizabeth, feeling a sweet savour to come from thence, and seeing the same dried from moisture, and yet the form remaining with the hair of the head and beard red, brought it to London, to his house in Wood Street, where for a time he kept it for the sweetness, but in the end caused the sexton of that church to bury it amongst other bones taken out of their charnel."

"The parish church of St. Michael, in Wood Street, is a proper thing," says Strype, "and lately well repaired ; John Iue, parson of this church, John Forster, goldsmith, and Peter Fikelden, taylor, gave two messuages and shops, in the same parish and street, and in Ladle Lane, to the reparation of the church, the 16th of Richard II. In the year 1627 the parishioners made a new door to this church into Wood Street, where till then it had only one door, standing in Huggin Lane."

St. Mary Staining, in Wood Street, destroyed by the Great Fire, stood on the north side of Oat Lane, in the Ward of Aldersgate Within. "The additional epithet of *staining*," says Maitland, "is as uncertain as the time of the foundation ; some imagining it to be derived from the painters' stainers, who probably lived near it; and others from its being built with stone, to distinguish it from those in the City that were built with wood. The advowson of the rectory anciently belonged to the Prioress and Convent of Clerkenwell, in whom it continued till their suppression by Henry VIII., when it came to the Crown. The parish, as previously observed, is now united to St. Michael's, Wood Street. That this church is not of a modern foundation, is manifest from John de Lukenore's being rector thereof before the year 1328.

St. Alban's, Wood Street, in the time of Paul, the fourteenth Abbot of St. Alban's, belonged to the Verulam monastery, but in 1077 the abbot exchanged the right of presentation to this church for the patronage of one belonging to the Abbot of

Westminster. Matthew Paris says that this Wood Street Church was the chapel of King Offa, the founder of St. Alban's Abbey, who had a palace near it. Stow says it was of great antiquity, and that Roman bricks were visible here and there among the stones. Maitland thinks it probable that it was one of the first churches built by Alfred in London after he had driven out the Danes. The right of presentation to the church was

says Seymour, "is the name, by which it was first dedicated to St. Alban, the first martyr of England. Another character of the antiquity of it is to be seen in the manner of the turning of the arches to the windows, and the heads of the pillars. A third note appears in the Roman bricks, here and there inlaid amongst the stones of the building. Very probable it is that this church is, at least, of as ancient a standing as King Adelstane, the Saxon,

WOOD STREET COMPTER. *From a View published in* 1793. (*See page* 368.)

originally possessed by the master, brethren, and sisters of the Leper Hospital, which made way for St. James's Palace, and after the death of Henry VI. it was vested in the Provost and Fellows of Eton College. In the reign of Charles II. the parish was united to that of St. Olave, Silver Street, and the right of presentation is now exercised alternately by Eton College and the Dean and Chapter of St. Paul's. The style of the interior of the church is late pointed. The windows appear older than the rest of the building. The ceiling in the nave exhibits bold groining, and the general effect is not unpleasing.

"One note of the great antiquity of this church,"

who, as tradition says, had his house at the east end of this church. This king's house, having a door also into Adel Street, in this parish, gave name, as 'tis thought, to the said Adel Street, which, in all evidences, to this day is written King Adel Street. One great square tower of this king's house seemed, in Stow's time, to be then remaining, and 'to be seen at the north corner of Love Lane, as you come from Aldermanbury, which tower was of the very same stone and manner of building with St. Alban's Church.'"

About the commencement of the seventeenth century St. Alban's, being in a state of great decay, was surveyed by Sir Henry Spiller and Inigo

Jones, and in accordance with their advice, apparently, in 1632 it was pulled down, and rebuilt *anno* 1634; but, perishing in the flames of 1666, it was re-erected as it now appears, and finished in the year 1688, from Wren's design.

To be his comfort everywhere
    Now joyfull Alice is gone.
And for these three departed soules,
    Gone up to joyfull blisse,
Th' almighty praise be given to God,
    To whom the glory is."

THE TREE AT THE CORNER OF WOOD STREET, 1870 (*see page* **364**).

In the old church were the following epitaphs :—

    " Of William Wilson, Joane his wife,
      And Alice, their daughter deare,
    These lines were left to give report
      These three lye buried here ;
    And Alice was Henry Decon's wife,
      Which Henry lives on earth,
    And is the Serjeant Plummer
      To Queen ELIZABETH.
    With whom this Alice left issue here,
      His virtuous daughter Joan,

Over the grave of Anne, the wife of Laurence Gibson, gentleman, were the following verses, which are worth mentioning here :—

    " MENTIS VIS MAGNA.

    " What ! is she dead ?
      Doth he survive ?
    No ; both are dead,
      And both alive.
    She lives, hee's dead,
      By love, though grieving,

"In him, for her,
    Yet dead, yet living ;
Both dead and living,
    Then what is gone ?
One half of both,
    Not any one.
One mind, one faith,
    One hope, one grave,
In life, in death,
    They had and still they have."

The pulpit (says Seymour) is finely carved with an enrichment, in imitation of fruit and leaves ; and the sound-board is a hexagon, having round it a fine cornice, adorned with cherubims and other embellishments, and the inside is neatly finniered. The altar-piece is very ornamental, consisting of four columns, fluted with their bases, pedestals, entablature, and open pediment of the Corinthian order ; and over each column, upon acroters, is a lamp with a gilded taper. Between the inner columns are the Ten Commandments, done in gold letters upon black. Between the two, northward, is the Lord's Prayer, and the two southward the Creed, done in gold upon blue. Over the commandments is a Glory between two cherubims, and above the cornice the king's arms, with the supporters, helmet, and crest, richly carved, under a triangular pediment ; and on the north and south side of the above described ornaments are two large cartouches, all of which parts are carved in fine wainscot. The church is well paved with oak, and here are two large brass branches and a marble font, having enrichments of cherubims, &c.

In a curious brass frame, attached to a tall stem, opposite the pulpit is an hour-glass, by which the preacher could measure his sermon and test his listeners' patience. The hour-glass at St. Dunstan's, Fleet Street, was taken down in 1723, and two heads for the parish staves made out of the silver.

Wood Street Compter (says Cunningham) was first established in 1555, and on the Feast of St. Michael the Archangel in that year, the prisoners were removed from the Old Compter in Bread Street to the New Compter in Wood Street, Cheapside. This compter was burnt down in the Great Fire, but was rebuilt in 1670. It stood on the east side of the street, and was removed to Giltspur Street in 1791. There were two compters in London—the compter in Wood Street, under the control of one of the sheriffs, and the compter in the Poultry, under the superintendence of the other. Under each sheriff was a secondary, a clerk of the papers, four clerk sitters, eighteen serjeants-at-mace (each serjeant having his yeomen), a master keeper, and two turnkeys. The serjeants

wore blue and coloured cloth gowns, and the words of arrest were, "Sir, we arrest you in the King's Majesty's name, and we charge you to obey us." There were three sides — the master's side, the dearest of all ; 'the knights' ward, a little cheaper ; and the Hole, the cheapest of all. The register of entries was called the Black Book. "Garnish" was demanded at every step, and the Wood Street Compter was hung with the story of the prodigal son.

When the Compter gate was opened, the prisoner's name was enrolled in the black book, and he was asked if he was for the master's side, the Knight's ward, or the Hole. At every fresh door a fee was demanded, the stranger's hat or cloak being detained if he refused to pay the extortion, which, in prison language, was called "garnish." The first question to a new prisoner was, whether he was in by arrest or command ; and there was generally some knavish attorney in a threadbare black suit, who, for forty shillings, would offer to move for a habeas corpus, and have him out presently, much to the amusement of the villanous-looking men who filled the room, some smoking and some drinking. At dinner a vintner's boy, who was in waiting, filled a bowl full of claret, and compelled the new prisoner to drink to all the society ; and the turnkeys, who were dining in another room, then demanded another tester for a quart of wine to quaff to the new comer's health.

At the end of a week, when the prisoner's purse grew thin, he was generally compelled to pass over to the knight's side, and live in a humbler and more restricted manner. Here a fresh "garnish" of eighteenpence was demanded, and if this was refused, he was compelled to sleep over the drain ; or, if he chose, to sit up, to drink and smoke in the cellar with vile companions till the keepers ordered every man to his bed.

Fennor, an actor in 1617 (James I.), wrote a curious pamphlet on the abuses of this compter. "For what extreme extortion," says the angry writer, "is it when a gentleman is brought in by the watch for some misdemeanour committed, that he must pay at least an angell before he be discharged ; hee must pay twelvepence for turning the key at the master-side dore two shillings to the chamberleine, twelvepence for his garnish for wine, tenpence for his dinner, whether he stay or no, and when he comes to be discharged at the booke, it will cost at least three shillings and sixpence more, besides sixpence for the booke-keeper's paines, and sixpence for the porter. . . . And if a gentleman stay there but one night, he must pay for his garnish sixteene pence, besides a groate for his lodging, and so much for his sheetes. . . When a gentleman is upon his discharge, and hath given satisfaction for his executions, they must have fees for irons, three halfepence in the pound, besides the other fees, so that if a man were in for a thousand or fifteene hundred pound execution, they will if a man is so madde have so many three halfepence.

"This little Hole is as a little citty in a commonwealth, for as in a citty there are all kinds of officers, trades, and vocations, so there is in this place, as we may make a pretty resemblance between them. In steede of a Lord Maior, we have a master steward to over-see and correct all misdemeanours as shall arise. . . . And lastly, as in a citty there is all kinds of trades, so is there heere, for heere you shall see a cobler sitting mending olde showes, and singing as merrily as if hee were under a stall abroad ; not farre from him you shall see a taylor sit crosse-legged (like a witch) on his cushion, theatning the ruine of our fellow prisoner, the Ægyptian vermine ; in another place you may behold a saddler empannelling all his wits together how to patch this Scotchpadde handsomely, or mend the old gentlewoman's crooper that was almost burst in pieces. You may have a phisition here, that for a bottle of sack will undertake to give you as good a medicine for melancholly as any doctor will for five pounds. Besides, if you desire to bee removed before a judge, you shall have a tinker-like attorney not farre distant from you, that in stopping up one hole in a broken cause, will make twenty before hee hath made an end, and at last will leave you in prison as bare of money as he himself is of honesty. Heere is your cholericke cooke that will dresse our meate, when wee can get any, as well as any greasie scullion in Fleet Lane or Pye Corner."

At 25, Silver Street, Wood Street, is the hall of one of the smaller City companies—the Parish Clerks of London, Westminster, Borough of Southwark, and fifteen out parishes, with their master wardens and fellows. This company was incorporated as early as Henry III. (1233), by the name of the Fraternity of St. Nicholas, an ominous name, for "St. Nicholas's clerk" was a jocose *nom de guerre* for highwaymen. The first hall of the fraternity stood in Bishopsgate Street, the second in Broad Lane, in Vintry Ward. The fraternity was re-incorporated by James I. in 1611, and confirmed by Charles I. in 1636. The hall contains a few portraits, and in a painted glass window, David playing on the harp, St. Cecilia at the organ, &c. The parish clerks were the actors in the old miracle plays, the parish clerks of our churches dating only from the commencement of the Reformation. The "Bills of Mortality" were commenced by the Parish Clerks' Company in 1592, who about 1625 were licensed by the Star Chamber to keep a printing-press in their hall for printing the Bills, valuable for their warning of the existence or progress of the plague. The "Weekly Bill" of the Parish Clerks has, however, been superseded by the "Tables of Mortality in the Metropolis," issued weekly from the Registrar-General's Office, at Somerset House, since July 1st, 1837. The Parish Clerks' Company neither confers the freedom of the City nor the hereditary freedom.

There is in Wood Street a large gold refinery, through whose doors three tons of gold a day have been known to pass. Australian gold is here cast into ingots, value £800 each. This gold is one carat and three quarters above the standard, and when the first two bars of Australian gold were sent to the Bank of England they were sent back, as their wonderful purity excited suspicion. For refining, the gold is boiled fifteen minutes, poured off into hand moulds 18 pounds troy weight, strewn with ivory black, and then left to cool. You see here the stalwart men wedging apart great bars of silver for the melting pots. The silver is purified in a blast-furnace, and mixed with nitric acid in platinum crucibles, that cost from £700 to £1,000 apiece. The bars of gold are stamped with a trade-mark, and pieces are cut off each ingot to be sent to the assayer for his report.

"I read in divers records," says Stow, "of a house in Wood Street then called 'Black Hall ;' but no man at this day can tell thereof. In the time of King Richard II., Sir Henry Percy, the son and heir of Henry Percy, Earl of Northumberland, had a house in 'Wodstreate,' in London (whether this Black Hall or no, it is hard to trace), wherein he treated King Richard, the Duke of Lancaster, the Duke of York, the Earl Marshal, and his father, the Earl of Northumberland, with others, at supper."

The "Rose," in Wood Street, was a sponging-house, well known to the rakehells and spendthrifts of Charles II.'s time. "I have been too lately under their (the bailiffs') clutches," says Tom Brown, "to desire any more dealings with them, and I cannot come within a furlong of the 'Rose sponging-house without five or six yellow-boys in my pocket to cast out those devils there, who would otherwise infallibly take possession of me."

The "Mitre," an old tavern in Wood Street, was kept in Charles II.'s time by William Proctor, who died insolvent in 1665. "18th Sept., 1660," Pepys says, "to the 'Miter Taverne,' in Wood Street (a house of the greatest note in London). Here some of us fell to handycap, a sport that I never knew before." And again, "31st July, 1665. Proctor, the vintner, of the 'Miter,' in Wood Street, and his son, are dead this morning of the plague; he having laid out abundance of money there, and was the greatest vintner for some time in London for great entertainments."

In early life Thomas Ripley, afterwards a celebrated architect, kept a carpenter's shop and coffee house in Wood Street. Marrying a servant of Sir Robert Walpole, the Prime Minister of George I., this lucky pushing man soon obtained work from the Crown and a seat at the Board of Works, and supplanted that great genius who built St. Paul's, to the infinite disgrace of the age. Ripley built the Admiralty, and Houghton Hall, Norfolk, for his early patron, Walpole, and died rich in 1758.

Wood Street is associated with that last extraordinary outburst of the Civil War fanaticism — the Anabaptist rising in January, 1661.

On Sunday, January 6, 1661, we read in "Somers' Tracts," "these monsters assembled at their meeting-house, in Coleman Street, where they armed themselves, and sallying thence, came to St. Paul's in the dusk of the evening, and there, after ordering their small party, placed sentinels, one of whom killed a person accidentally passing by, because he said he was for God and King Charles when challenged by him. This giving the alarm, and some parties of trained bands charging them, and being repulsed, they marched to Bishopsgate, thence to Cripplegate and Aldersgate, where, going out, in spite of the constables and watch, they declared for King Jesus. Proceeding to Beech Lane, they killed a headborough, who would have opposed them. It was observed that all they shot, though never so slightly wounded, died. Then they hasted away to Caen Wood, where they lurked, resolved to make another effort upon the City, but were drove thence, and routed by a party of horse and foot sent for that purpose, about thirty being taken and brought before General Monk, who committed them to the Gate House.

PULPIT HOUR-GLASS (*see page* 368).

"Nevertheless, the others who had escaped out of the wood returned to London, not doubting of success in their enterprise; Venner, a wine-cooper by trade, and their head, affirming, he was assured that no weapons employed against them would prosper, nor a hair of their head be touched; which their coming off at first so well made them willing to believe. These fellows had taken the opportunity of the king's being gone to Portsmouth, having before made a disposition for drawing to them of other desperate rebels, by publishing a declaration called, 'A Door of Hope Opened,' full of abominable slanders against the whole royal family.

"On Wednesday morning, January 9, after the watches and guards were dismissed, they resumed their first enterprise. The first appearance was in Threadneedle Street, where they alarmed the trained bands upon duty that day, and drove back a party sent after them, to their main guard, which then marched in a body towards them. The Fifth Monarchists retired into Bishopsgate Street, where some of them took into an ale-house, known by the sign of 'The Helmet,' where, after a sharp dispute, two were killed, and as many taken, the same number of the trained bands being killed and wounded. The next sight of them (for they vanished and appeared again on a sudden), was at College Hill, which way they went into Cheapside, and so into Wood Street, Venner leading them, with a morrion on his head and a halbert in his hand. Here was the main and hottest action, for they fought stoutly with the Trained Bands, and received a charge from the Life Guards, whom they obliged to give way, until, being overpowered, and Venner knocked down and wounded and shot, Tufney and Crag, two others of their chief teachers, being killed by him, they began to give ground, and soon after dispersed, flying outright and taking several ways. The greatest part of them went down Wood Street to Cripplegate, firing in the rear at the Yellow Trained Bands, then in close pursuit of them. Ten of them took into the 'Blue Anchor' ale-house, near the postern, which house they maintained until Lieutenant-Colonel Cox, with his company, secured all the avenues to it. In the meantime, some of the aforesaid Yellow Trained Bands got upon the tiles of the next house, which they threw off, and fired in upon the rebels who were in the upper room, and even then refused quarter. At the same time, another file of musketeers got up the stairs, and having shot down the door, entered upon them. Six of them were killed before, another wounded, and one, refusing quarter, was knocked down, and afterwards shot. The others being asked why they had not begged quarter before, answered they durst not, for fear their own fellows should shoot them."

The upshot of this insane revolt of a handful of men was that twenty-two king's men were killed, and twenty-two of the fanatics, proving the fighting to have been hard. Twenty were taken, and nine or ten hung, drawn, and quartered. Venner, the leader, who was wounded severely, and some others, were drawn on sledges, their quarters were set on the four gates, and their heads stuck on poles on London Bridge. Two more were hung at the west end of St. Paul's, two at the Royal Exchange, two at the Bull and Mouth, two in Beech Lane, one at Bishopsgate, and another, captured later, was hung at Tyburn, and his head set on a pole in Whitechapel.

The texts these Fifth Monarchy men chiefly relied on were these :—" He shall use his people, in his hand as his battle-axe and weapon of war, for the bringing in the kingdoms of this world into subjection to Him." Another passage of Scripture which they distorted to their own ends was Isa. xli. 14th, 15th, and 16th verses. The prophet, speaking of Jacob, saith : " Behold, I will make thee a new sharp threshing instrument, having teeth ; thou shalt thresh the mountains, and beat them small, and shalt make the hills as chaff ; thou shalt fan them, and the wind shall carry them away," &c.

" Maiden Lane," says Stow, " formerly Engine Lane, is a good, handsome, well-built, and inhabited street. The east end falleth into Wood Street. At the north-east corner, over against Goldsmiths' Hall, stood the parish church of St. John Zachary, which since the dreadful fire is not rebuilt, but the parish united unto St. Ann's, Aldersgate, the ground on which it stood, enclosed within a wall, serving as a burial-place for the parish."

The old Goldsmiths' Church of St. John Zachary, Maiden Lane, destroyed in the Great Fire, and not rebuilt, stood at the north-west corner of Maiden Lane, in the Ward of Aldersgate ; the parish is annexed to that of St. Anne. Among other epitaphs in this church, Stow gives the following :—

" Here lieth the body of John Sutton, citizen, goldsmith, and alderman of London ; who died 6th July, 1450. This brave and worthy alderman was killed in the defence of the City, in the bloody nocturnal battle on London Bridge, against the infamous Jack Cade, and his army of Kentish rebels."

" Here lieth William Brekespere, of London, some time
    merchant,
Goldsmith and alderman, the Commonwele attendant,
With Margaryt his Dawter, late wyff of Suttoon,
And Thomas, hur Sonn, yet livyn undyr Goddy's tuitioon.
The tenth of July he made his transmigration.
She disissyd in the yer of Grase of Chryst's Incarnation,
A Thowsand Four hundryd Threescor and oon.
God assoyl their Sowls whose Bodys lye undyr this Stoon."

This church was rated to pay a certain annual sum to the canons of St. Paul's, about the year 1181, at which time it was denominated St. John Baptist's, as appears from a grant thereof from the Dean and Chapter of St. Paul's to one Zachary, whose name it probably received to distinguish it from one of the same name in Walbrook.

St. Anne in the Willows was a church destroyed by the Great Fire, rebuilt by Wren, and united to the parish of St. John Zachary. " It is so called," says Stow, " some say of willows growing thereabouts ; but now there is no such void place for willows to grow, more than the church-yard, wherein grow some high ash-trees."

" This church, standing," says Strype, " in the church-yard, is planted before with lime-trees that flourish there. So that as it was formerly called St. Anne-in-the-Willows, it may now be called St. Anne-in-the-Limes."

St. Anne's can be traced back as far as 1332. The patronage was anciently in the Dean and Canons of St. Martin's-le-Grand, in whose gift it continued till Henry VII. annexed that Collegiate Church, with its appendages, to the Abbey of Westminster. In 1553 Queen Mary gave it to the Bishop of London and his successors. One of the monuments here bears the following inscription :—

" Peter Heiwood, younger son of Peter Heiwood, one of the counsellors of Jamaica, by Grace, daughter of Sir John Muddeford, Kt. and Bart., great-grandson to Peter Heiwood, of Heywood, in County Palatine of Lancaster, who apprehended Guy Faux with his dark lanthorn, and for his zealous prosecution of Papists, as Justice of the Peace, was stabbed in Westminster Hall by John James, a Dominican Friar, An. Dom. 1640. Obiit, Novr. 2, 1701.
" Reader, if not a Papist bred,
    Upon such ashes gently tred."

The site of Haberdashers' Hall, in Maiden Lane, opposite Goldsmiths' Hall, was bequeathed to the Company by William Baker, a London haberdasher, in 1478 (Edward IV.). In the old hall, destroyed by the Great Fire, the Parliament

Commissioners held their meetings during the Commonwealth, and many a stern decree of confiscation was there grimly signed. In this hall there are some good portraits. The Haberdashers' Company have many livings and exhibitions in their gift; and almshouses at Hoxton, Monmouth, Newland (Gloucestershire), and Newport (Shrop-

one being hurrers, cappers, or haberdashers of hats; the other, haberdashers of ribands, laces, and small wares only. The latter were also called milliners, from their selling such merchandise as brooches, agglets, spurs, capes, glasses, and pins. "In the early part of Elizabeth's reign," says Herbert, "upwards of £60,000 annually was paid to foreign

INTERIOR OF ST. MICHAEL'S, WOOD STREET (*see page* 365).

shire); schools in Bunhill Row, Monmouth, and Newport; and they lend sums of £50 or £100 to struggling young men of their own trade.

The haberdashers were originally a branch of the mercers, dealing like them in merceries or small wares. Lydgate, in his ballad, describes the mercers' and haberdashers' stalls as side by side in the mercery in Chepe. In the reign of Henry VI., when first incorporated, they divided into two fraternities, St. Catherine and St. Nicholas. The

merchants for pins alone, but before her death pins were made in England, and in the reign of James I. the pinmakers obtained a charter."

In the reign of Henry VII. the two societies united. Queen Elizabeth granted them their arms: Barry nebule of six, argent and azure on a bend gules, a lion passant gardant; crest or, a helmet and torse, two arms supporting a laurel proper and issuing out of a cloud argent. Supporters, two Indian goats argent, attired and hoofed or; motto,

"Serve and Obey." Maitland describes their annual expenditure in charity as £3,500. The number of the Company consists of one master, four wardens, forty-five assistants, 360 livery, and a large company of freemen. This Company is the eighth in order of the chief twelve City Companies.

horns, tooth-picks, fans, pomanders, silk, and silver buttons.

The Haberdashers were incorporated by a Charter of Queen Elizabeth in 1578. The Court books extend to the time of Charles I. only. Their charters exist in good preservation. In their

INTERIOR OF HABERDASHERS' HALL (*see page* 374).

In the reign of Edward VI. there were not more than a dozen milliner's shops in all London, but in 1580 the dealers in foreign luxuries had so increased as to alarm the frugal and the philosophic. These dealers sold French and Spanish gloves, French cloth and frieze, Flemish kersies, daggers, swords, knives, Spanish girdles, painted cruises, dials, tablets, cards, balls, glasses, fine earthen pots, salt-cellars, spoons, tin dishes, puppets, pennons, ink-

chronicles we have only a few points to notice. In 1466 they sent two of their members to attend the coronation of Elizabeth, queen of Edward IV., and they also were represented at the coronation of the detestable Richard III. Like the other Companies, the Haberdashers were much oppressed during the time of Charles I. and the Commonwealth, during which they lost nearly £50,000. The Company's original bye-laws having been burnt in the Great Fire, a new code was drawn up, which in 1675 was sanctioned by Lord Chancellor Finch, Sir Matthew Hale, and Sir Francis North.

The dining-hall is a lofty and spacious room. About the year 1860 it was much injured by fire, but has been since restored and handsomely decorated. Over the screen at the lower end is a music gallery, and the hall is lighted from above by six sun-burners. Among the portraits in the edifice are whole lengths of William Adams, Esq., founder of the grammar school and almshouses at Newport, in Shropshire; Jerome Knapp, Esq., a former Master of the Company; and Micajah Perry, Esq., Lord Mayor in 1739; a half-length of George Whitmore, Esq., Lord Mayor in 1631; Sir Hugh Hammersley, Knight, Lord Mayor in 1627; Mr. Thomas Aldersey, merchant, of Bunbury, in Cheshire, who, in 1594, vested a considerable estate in this Company for charitable uses; Mr. William Jones, merchant adventurer, who bequeathed £18,000 for benevolent purposes; and Robert Aske, the worthy founder of the Haberdashers' Hospital at Hoxton.

Gresham Street, that intersects Wood Street, was formerly called Lad or Ladle Lane, and part of it Maiden Lane, from a shop sign of the Virgin. It is written Lad Lane in a chronicle of Edward IV.'s time, published by Sir Harris Nicolas, page 98. The "Swan with Two Necks," in Lad Lane, was for a century and more, till railways ruined stage and mail coach travelling, the booking office and head-quarters of coaches to the North.

Love Lane was so named from the wantons who once infested it. The Cross Keys Inn derived its name from the bygone Church of St. Peter before mentioned. As there are traditions of Saxon kings once dwelling in Foster Lane, so in Gutter Lane we find traditions of some Danish celebrities. "Gutter Lane," says Stow, that patriarch of London topography, "was so called by Guthurun, some time owner thereof." In a manuscript chronicle of London, written in the reign of Edward IV., and edited by Sir Harris Nicolas, it is called "Goster Lane."

Brewers' Hall, No. 19, Addle Street, Wood Street, Cheapside, is a modern edifice, and contains, among other pictures, a portrait of Dame Alice Owen, who narrowly escaped death from an archer's stray arrow while walking in Islington fields, in gratitude for which she founded an hospital. In the hall window is some old painted glass. The Brewers were incorporated in 1438. The quarterage in this Company is paid on the quantity of malt consumed by its members. In 1851 a handsome schoolhouse was built for the Company, in Trinity Square, Tower Hill.

In 1422 Whittington laid an information before his successor in the mayoralty, Robert Childe, against the Brewers' Company, for selling *dear ale*, when they were convicted in the penalty of £20; and the masters were ordered to be kept in prison in the chamberlain's custody until they paid it.

CHAPTER XXXII.

CHEAPSIDE TRIBUTARIES, NORTH (*continued*).

Milk Street—Sir Thomas More—The City of London School—St. Mary Magdalen—Honey Lane—All Hallows' Church—Lawrence Lane and St. Lawrence Church—Ironmonger Lane and Mercers' Hall—The Mercers' Company—Early Life Assurance Companies—The Mercers' Company in Trouble—Mercers' Chapel—St. Thomas Acon—The Mercers' School—Restoration of the Carvings in Mercers' Hall—The Glories of the Mercers' Company—Ironmonger Lane.

IN Milk Street was the milk-market of Mediæval London. That good and wise man, Sir Thomas More, was born in this street. "The brightest man," says Fuller, with his usual quaint playfulness, "that ever shone in that *via lactea*." More, born in 1480, was the son of a judge of the King's Bench, and was educated at St. Anthony's School, in Threadneedle Street. He was afterwards placed in the family of Archbishop Morton, till he went to Oxford. After two years he became a barrister at Lincoln's Inn, entered Parliament, and opposed Henry VII. to his own danger. After serving as law reader at New Inn, he soon became an eminent lawyer. He then wrote his "Utopia," acquired the friendship of Erasmus, and soon after became a favourite of Henry VIII., helping the despot in his treatise against Luther. On Wolsey's disgrace, More became chancellor, and one of the wisest and most impartial England has ever known. Determined not to sanction the king's divorce, More resigned his chancellorship, and, refusing to attend Anne Boleyn's coronation, he was attainted for treason. The tyrant, now furious, soon hurried him to the scaffold, and he was executed on Tower Hill in 1535.

This pious, wise, and consistent man is described

as having dark chestnut hair, thin beard, and grey eyes. He walked with his right shoulder raised, and was negligent in his dress. When in the Tower, More is said to have foreseen the fate of Anne Boleyn, whom his daughter Margaret had found filling the court with dancing and sporting.

"Alas, Meg," said the ex-chancellor, "it pitieth me to remember to what misery poor soul she will shortly come. These dances of hers will prove such dances that she will sport our heads off like foot-balls; but it will not be long ere her head will dance the like dance."

It is to be lamented that with all his wisdom, More was a bigot. He burnt one Frith for denying the corporeal presence; had James Bainton, a gentleman of the Temple, whipped in his presence for heretical opinons; went to the Tower to see him on the rack, and then hurried him to Smithfield. "Verily," said Luther, "he was a very notable tyrant, and plagued and tormented innocent Christians like an executioner."

The City of London School, Milk Street, was established in 1837, for the sons of respectable persons engaged in professional, commercial, or trading pursuits; and partly founded on an income of £900 a year, derived from certain tenements bequeathed by John Carpenter, town-clerk of London, in the reign of Henry V., "for the finding and bringing up of four poor men's children, with meat, drink, apparel, learning at the schools, in the universities, &c., until they be preferred, and then others in their places for ever." This was the same John Carpenter who "caused, with great expense, to be curiously painted upon a board, about the north cloister of Paul's, a monument of Death, leading all estates, with the speeches of Death, and answers of every state." The school year is divided into three terms—Easter to July; August to Christmas; January to Easter; and the charge for each pupil is £2 5s. a term. The printed form of application for admission may be had of the secretary, and must be filled up by the parent or guardian, and signed by a member of the Corporation of London. The general course of instruction includes the English, French, German, Latin, and Greek languages, writing, arithmetic, mathematics, book-keeping, geography, and history. Besides eight free scholarships on the foundation, equivalent to £35 per annum each, and available as exhibitions to the Universities, there are the following exhibitions belonging to the school:—The "Times" Scholarship, value £30 per annum; three Beaufoy Scholarships, the Solomons Scholarship, and the Travers Scholarship, £50 per annum each; the Tegg Scholarship, nearly £20 per annum; and

several other valuable prizes. The first stone of the school was laid by Lord Brougham, October 21st, 1835. The architect of the building was Mr. J. B. Bunning, of Guildford Street, Russell Square, and the entire cost, including fittings and furniture, was nearly £20,000. It is about 75 feet wide in front, next Milk Street, and is about 160 feet long; it contains a spacious theatre for lectures, &c. In 1879 it was resolved to remove the school to a new site at the east end of the Thames Embankment, between White and Black Friars. The lectures, founded by Sir Thomas Gresham, on divinity, astronomy, music, geometry, law, physics, and rhetoric, which upon the demolition of Gresham College, had been delivered at the Royal Exchange from the year 1773, were after the destruction of that building by fire, in January, 1838, read in the theatre of the City of London School until 1843; they were delivered each day during the four Law Terms, and the public in general were entitled to free admission.

In Milk Street stood the small parish church of St. Mary Magdalen, destroyed in the Great Fire. It was repaired and beautified at the charge of the parish in 1619. All the chancel window was built at the proper cost of Mr. Benjamin Henshaw, Merchant Taylor, and one of the City captains.

This church was burnt down in the Great Fire, and was not rebuilt. One amusing epitaph has been preserved:—

"HERE LIETH THE BODY OF SIR WILLIAM STONE, KNT.

"As the Earth the
Earth doth cover,
So under this stone
Lyes another;
Sir William *Stone*,
Who long deceased,
Ere the world's love
Him released;
So much it loved him,
For they say,
He answered Death
Before his day;
But, 'tis not so;
For he was sought
Of One that both him
Made and bought.
He remain'd
The Great Lord's Treasurer,
Who called for him
At his pleasure,
And received him.
Yet be it said,
Earth grieved that Heaven
So soon was paid.

"Here likewise lyes
Inhumed in one bed,
Dear Barbara,
The well-beloved wife

Of this remembered Knight ;
  Whose souls are fled
From this dimure vale
  To everlasting life,
Where no more change,
  Nor no more separation,
Shall make them flye
  From their blest habitation.
  Grasse of levitie,
  Span in brevity,
  Flower's felicity,
  Fire of misery,
  Wind's stability,
  Is mortality."

"Honey Lane," says good old Stow, "is so called not of sweetness thereof, being very narrow and small and dark, but rather of often washing and sweeping to keep it clean." With all due respect to Stow, we suspect that the lane did not derive its name from any superlative cleanliness, but more probably from honey being sold here in the times before sugar became common, when honey alone was used by cooks for sweetening.

On the site of All Hallows' Church, destroyed in the Great Fire, a market was afterwards established.

"There be no monuments," says Stow, "in this church worth the noting; I find that John Norman, Maior, 1453, was buried there. He gave to the drapers his tenements on the north side of the said church; they to allow for the beam light and lamp 13s. 4d. yearly, from this lane to the Standard.

"This church hath the misfortune to have no bequests to church or poor, nor to any publick use.

"There was a parsonage house before the Great Fire, but now the ground on which it stood is swallowed up by the market. The parish of St. Mary-le-Bow (to which it is united) hath received all the money paid for the site of the ground of the said parsonage."

All Hallows' Church was repaired and beautified at the cost of the parishioners in 1625.

Lawrence Lane derives its name from the church of St. Lawrence, at its north end. "Antiquities," says Stow, "in this lane I find none other than among many fair houses. There is one large inn for receipt of travellers, called 'Blossoms Inn,' but corruptly 'Bosoms Inn,' and hath for a sign 'St. Lawrence, the Deacon,' in a border of blossoms or flowers." This was one of the great City inns set apart for Charles V.'s suite, when he came over to visit Henry VIII. in 1522. At the sign of "St. Lawrence Bosoms" twenty beds and stabling for sixty horses were ordered.

The curious old tract about Bankes and his trained horse was written under the assumed names of "John Dando, the wier-drawer of Hadley, and Harrie Runt, head ostler of Besomes Inne," which is probably the same place.

St. Lawrence Church is situate on the north side of Cateaton Street, "and is denominated," says Maitland, "from its dedication to Lawrence, a Spanish saint, born at Huesca, in the kingdom of Arragon; who, after having undergone the most grievous tortures, in the persecution under Valerian, the emperor, was cruelly broiled alive upon a gridiron, with a slow fire, till he died, for his strict adherence to Christianity; and the additional epithet of Jewry, from its situation among the Jews, was conferred upon it, to distinguish it from the church of St. Lawrence Pulteney, now demolished.

"This church, which was anciently a rectory, being given by Hugo de Wickenbroke to Baliol College in Oxford, anno 1294, the rectory ceased; wherefore Richard, Bishop of London, converted the same into a vicarage; the advowson whereof still continues in the same college. This church sharing the common fate in 1666, it has since been beautifully rebuilt, and the parish of St. Mary Magdalen, Milk Street, thereunto annexed." The walls of the vestry-room are encased with carved oak, and the ceiling is enriched with plaster foliage, and also by a painting of the martyrdom of St. Lawrence, by Thornhill. Dr. Tillotson was married in this church in 1663–4, and buried in 1694, three years after his promotion to the see of Canterbury.

The famous Sir Richard Gresham lies buried here, as the inscription on his tomb shows.

There is also this epitaph :—

"Lo here the Lady Margaret North,
  In tombe and earth do lye ;
Of husbands four the faithfull spouse,
  Whose fame shall never dye.
One Andrew Franncis was the first,
  The second Robert hight,
Surnamed Chartsey, Alderman ;
  Sir David Brooke, a knight,
Was third. But he that passed all,
  And was in number fourth,
And for his virtue made a Lord,
  Was called Sir Edward North.
These altogether do I wish
  A joyful rising day ;
That of the Lord and of his Christ,
  All honour they may say.
    Obiit 2 die Junii, An. Dom. 1575."

In Ironmonger Lane, inhabited by ironmongers *temp.* Edward I., is Mercers' Hall, an interesting building.

The Mercers, though not formally incorporated till the 17th of Richard II. (1393), are traced back by Herbert as early as 1172. Soon afterwards they are mentioned as patrons of one of the great London charities. In 1214, Robert Spencer, a mercer, was mayor. In 1296 the mercers joined the company of merchant adventurers in establishing in Edward I.'s reign, a woollen manufacture in England, with a branch at Antwerp. In Edward II.'s reign they are mentioned as "the Fraternity of Mercers," and in 1406 (Henry I.) they are styled in a charter, "Brothers of St. Thomas à Becket."

Mercers were at first general dealers in all small wares, including wigs, haberdashery, and even spices and drugs. They attended fairs and markets, and even sat on the ground to sell their wares—in fact, were little more than high-class pedlers. The poet Gower talks of "the depression of such mercerie." In late times the silk trade formed the main feature of their business ; the greater use of silk beginning about 1573.

The mercers' first station, in Henry II.'s reign, was in that part of Cheap on the north side where Mercers' Hall now stands, but they removed soon afterwards higher up on the south side. The part of Cheapside between Bow Church and Friday Street became known as the Mercery. Here, in front of a large meadow called the "Crownsild," they held their little stalls or standings from Soper's Lane and the Standard. There were no houses as yet in this part of Cheapside. In 1329 William Elsing, a mercer, founded an hospital within Cripplegate, for 100 poor blind men, and became prior of his own institution.

In 1351 (Edward III.), the Mercers grew jealous of the Lombard merchants, and on Midsummer Day three mercers were sent to the Tower for attacking two Lombards in the Old Jewry. The mercers in this reign sold woollen clothes, but not silks. In 1371, John Barnes, mercer, mayor, gave a chest with three locks, with 1,000 marks therein, to be lent to younger mercers, upon sufficient pawn and for the use thereof. The grateful recipients were merely to say "De Profundis," a Pater Noster, and no more. This bequest seems to have started among the Mercers the kindly practice of assisting the young and struggling members of this Company.

In the reign of Henry VI. the mercers had become great dealers in silks and velvets, and had resigned to the haberdashers the sale of small articles of dress. It is not known whether the mercers bought their silks from the Lombards, or the London silk-women, or whether they imported them themselves, since many of the members of the Company were merchants.

Twenty years after the murder of Becket, the murdered man's sister, who had married Thomas

Fitz Theobald de Helles, built a chapel and hospital of Augustine Friars close to Ironmonger Lane, Cheapside. The hospital was built on the site of the house where Becket was born. He was the son of Gilbert Becket, citizen, mercer and portreve of London, who was said to have been a Crusader, and to have married a fair Saracen, who had released him from prison, and who followed him to London, knowing only the one English word "Gilbert." The hospital, which was called "St. Thomas of Acon," from Becket's mother having been born at Acre, the ancient Ptolemais, was given to the Mercers' Fraternity by De Hilles and his wife, and Henry III. gave the master and twelve brothers all the land between St. Olave's and Ironmonger Lane, which had belonged to two rich Jews, to enlarge their ground. In Henry V.'s reign that illustrious mercer Whittington, by his wealth and charity, reflected great lustre on the Mercers' Company, who at his death were left trustees of the college and almshouses founded by the immortal Richard on College Hill. The Company still preserve the original ordinance of this charity, with a picture of Whittington's death, and portraits of the first three wardens, Coventry, Grove, and Carpenter.

In 1414, Thomas Falconer, mercer and mayor, lent Henry V., towards his French wars, ten marks upon jewels.

In 1513, Joan Bradbury, widow of Thomas Bradbury, late Lord Mayor of London, left the Conduit Mead (now New Bond Street), to the Mercers' Company for charitable uses. In pursuance of the King's grant on this occasion, the Bishop of Norwich and others granted the Mercers' Company 29 acres of land in Marylebone, 120 acres in Westminster, and St. Giles, and St. Martin's-in-the-Fields, of the annual value of £13 6s. 8d., and in part satisfaction of the said £20 a year. The Company still possess eight acres and a half of this old gift, forming the north side of Long Acre and the adjacent streets, one of which bears the name of the Company. Mercer Street was described in a parliamentary survey in 1650 to have long gardens reaching down to Cock and Pye Ditch, and the site of Seven Dials. In 1544 the three Greshams (at the time the twelve Companies were appealed to) lent Henry VIII. upon mortgaged lands £1,673 6s. 8d. In 1561, the wardens of the Mercers' Company were summoned before the Queen's Council for selling their velvets, satins, and damasks so dear, as English coin was no longer base, and the old excuse for the former high charges was gone. The Mercers prudently bowed before the storm, promised reform, and begged her Majesty's Council to look after the Grocers. At this time the chief vendors of

Italian silks lived in Cheapside, St. Lawrence Jewry, and Old Jewry.

During the civil wars both King and Parliament bore heavily on the Mercers. In 1640 Charles I. half forced from them a loan of £3,030, and in 1642 the Parliament borrowed £6,500, and arms from the Company's armoury, valued at £88. They afterwards gave further arms, valued at £71 13s. 4d., and advanced as a second loan £3,200. The result now became visible. In 1698, hoping to clear off

whom the insurance was effected, should be at the rate of £30 for every £100 of subscription. It was stipulated that subscribers must be in good and perfect health at the time of subscription. It was decided that all married men of the age of thirty years or under, might subscribe any sum from £50 to £1,000; that all married men, not exceeding sixty years of age, might subscribe any sum not less than £50, and not exceeding £300. The Company's prospectus further stipulates 'that no person

THE "SWAN WITH TWO NECKS," LAD LANE (*see page* 374).

their debts, the Mercers' Company engaged in a ruinous insurance scheme, suggested by Dr. Assheton, a Kentish rector. It was proposed to grant annuities of £30 per cent. to clergymen's widows according to certain sums paid by their husbands.

"Pledging the rents of their large landed estates as security for the fulfilment of their contracts with usurers, the Mercers entered on business as life assurance agents. Limiting the entire amount of subscription to £100,000, they decided that no person over sixty years of age should become a subscriber; that no subscriber should subscribe less than £50—*i.e.*, should purchase a smaller contingent annuity than one of £15; that the annuity to every subscriber's widow, or other person for

that goes to sea, nor soldier that goes to the wars, shall be admitted to subscribe to have the benefit of this proposal, in regard of the casualties and accidents that they are more particularly liable to.' Moreover, it was provided that 'in case it should happen that any man who had subscribed should voluntarily make away with himself, or by any act of his occasion his own death, either by duelling, or committing any crime whereby he should be sentenced to be put to death by justice; in any or either of these cases his widow should receive no annuity, but upon delivering up the Company's bond, should have the subscription money paid to her.'

"The Mercers' operations soon gave rise to more

business-like companies, specially created to secure the public against some of the calamitous consequences of death. In 1706, the Amicable Life Assurance Office—usually, though, as the reader has seen, incorrectly, termed the First Life Insurance Office—was established in imitation of the

were fixed too high, and the Company had to sink to 18 per cent., and even this proved an insufficient reduction. In 1745 they were compelled to stop, and, after several ineffectual struggles, to petition Parliament for relief.

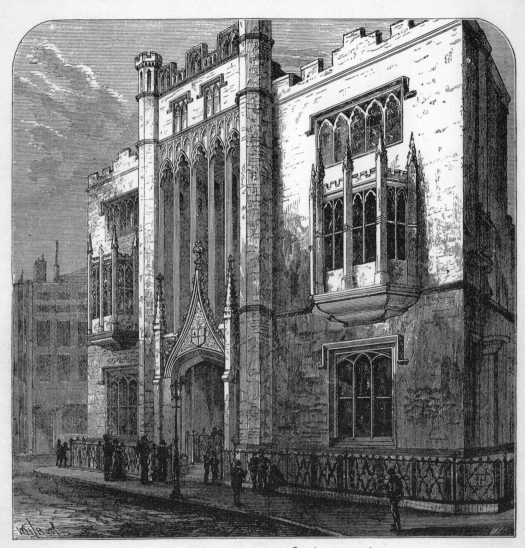

CITY OF LONDON SCHOOL, 1879 (*see page* 375).

ance Office—was established in imitation of the Mercers' Office. Two years later, the Second Society of Assurance, for the support of widows and orphans, was opened in Dublin, which, like the Amicable, introduced numerous improvements upon Dr. Assheton's scheme, and was a Joint-Stock Life Assurance Society, identical in its principles with, and similar in most of its details to, the modern insurance companies, of which there were as many as one hundred and sixty in the year 1859."

Large sums were subscribed, but the annuities

The petition showed that the Mercers were indebted more than £100,000. The annuities then out amounted to £7,620 per annum, and the subscriptions for future amounts reached £10,000 a year; while to answer these claims their present income only amounted to £4,100 per annum. The Company was therefore empowered by Act of Parliament, 4 George III., to issue new bonds and pay them off by a lottery, drawn in their own hall. This plan had the effect of completely retrieving their affairs, and restoring them to prosperity.

Strype speaks of the mercers' shops situated on the south side of Cheapside as having been turned from mere sheds into handsome buildings four or five storeys high.

Mercers' Hall and Chapel have a history of their own. On the rough suppression of monastic institutions, Henry VIII., gorged with plunder, granted to the Mercers' Company for £969 17s. 6d. the church of the college of St. Thomas Acon, the parsonage of St. Mary Colechurch, and sundry premises in the parishes of St. Paul, Old Jewry, St. Stephen, Walbrook, St. Martin, Ironmonger Lane, and St. Stephen, Coleman Street. Immediately behind the great doors of the hospital and Mercers' Hall stood the hospital church of St. Thomas, and at the back were court-yards, cloisters, and gardens in a great wide enclosure east and west of Ironmonger Lane and the Old Jewry.

St. Thomas's Church was a large structure, probably rich in monuments, though many of the illustrious mercers were buried in Bow Church, St. Pancras, Soper Lane, St. Antholin's, Watling Street, and St. Benet Sherehog. The church was bought chiefly by Sir Richard Gresham's influence, and Stow tells us "it is now called Mercers' Chappell, and therein is kept a free grammar school as of old time had been accustomed." The original Mercers' Chapel was a chapel toward the street in front of the "great old chapel of St. Thomas," and over it was Mercers' Hall. Aggas's plan of London (circa 1560) shows it was a little above the Great Conduit of Cheapside. The small chapel was built by Sir John Allen, mercer and mayor (1521), and he was buried there; but the Mercers removed this tomb into the hospital church, and divided the chapel into shops. Guy, the founder of the hospital, was apprenticed to a bookseller who occupied one of these shops, and after the Fire of London he himself carried on the same trade in a shop which was built on the same site. Before the suppression, the Mercers occupied only a part of the present front, the modern Mercers' Chapel standing, says Herbert, exactly on the site of part of the hospital church.

The old hospital gate, which forms the present hospital entrance, had an image of St. Thomas à Becket; but this was pulled down by Elizabethan fanatics. The interior of the chapel remains unaltered. There is a large ambulatory before it supported by columns, and a stone staircase leads to the hall and court-rooms. The ambulatory contains the recumbent figure of Richard Fishborne, Mercer, dressed in a fur gown and ruff. He was a great benefactor to the Company, and died in 1623 (James I.).

Many eminent citizens were buried in St. Thomas's, though most of the monuments had been defaced even in Stow's time. Among them were ten Mercer mayors and sheriffs, ten grocers (probably from Bucklersbury, their special locality), Sir Edward Shaw, goldsmith to Richard III., two Earls of Ormond, and Stephen Cavendish, draper and mayor (1362), whose descendants were ancestors of the great family of Cavendish, Duke of Devonshire.

William Downer, of London, gent., by his last will, dated 26th June, 1484, gave orders for his body to be buried within the church of St. Thomas Acon's, of London, in these terms:—"So that every year, yearly for evermore, in their foresaid churche, at such time of the year as it shal happen me to dy, observe and keep an *obyte*, or an anniversary for my sowl, the sowles of my seyd wyfe, the sowles of my fader and moder, and al Christian sowles, with *placebo* and dirige on the even, and mass of requiem on the morrow following solemnly by note for evermore."

Previous to the suppression, Henry VIII. had permitted the Hospital of St. Thomas of Acon, which wanted room, to throw a gallery across Old Jewry into a garden which the master had purchased, adjoining the Grocers' Hall, and in which Sir Robert Clayton afterwards built a house, of which we shall have to speak in its place. The gallery was to have two windows, and in the winter a light was ordered to be burned there for the comfort of passers-by. In 1536, Henry VIII. and his queen, Jane Seymour, stood in the Mercers' Hall, then newly built, and saw the "marching watch of the City" most bravely set out by its founder, Sir John Allen, mercer and mayor, and one of the Privy Council.

In the reign of James I., Mercers' Chapel became a fashionable place of resort; gallants and ladies crowded there to hear the sermons of the learned Italian Archbishop of Spalatro, in Dalmatia, one of the few prize converts to Protestantism. In 1617 we look in and find among his auditors the Archbishop of Canterbury, the Lord Chancellor, the Earls of Arundel and Pembroke, and Lords Zouch and Compton. The chapel continued for many years to be used for Italian sermons preached to English merchants who had resided abroad, and who partly defrayed the expense. The Mercers' School was first held in the hospital and then removed to the mercery.

The present chapel front in Cheapside is the central part alone of the front built after the Great Fire. Correspondent houses, five storeys high, formerly gave breadth and effect to the whole mass.

Old views represent shops on each side with un-sashed windows. The first floors have stone balconies, and over the central window of each room is the bust of a crowned virgin. It has a large doorcase, enriched with two genii above, in the act of mantling the Virgin's head, the Company's cognomen displayed upon the keystone of the arch. Above is a cornice, with brackets, sustaining a small gallery, from which, on each side, arise Doric pilasters, supporting an entablature of the same order; between the intercolumns and the central window are the figures of Faith and Hope, in niches, between whom, in a third niche of the entablature, is Charity, sitting with her three children. The upper storey has circular windows and other enrichments.

The entrance most used is in Ironmonger Lane, where is a small court, with offices, apparently the site of the ancient cloister, and which leads to the principal building. The hall itself is elevated as anciently, and supported by Doric columns, the space below being open one side and forming an extensive piazza, at the extremity whereof is the chapel, which is neatly planned, wainscoted, and paved with black and white marble. A high flight of stairs leads from the piazza to the hall, which is a very lofty apartment, handsomely wainscoted and ornamented with Doric pilasters, and various carvings in compartments.

In the hall, besides the transaction of the Company's business, the Gresham committees are held, which consist of four aldermen, including the Lord Mayor *pro tempore*, and eight of the City corporation, with whom are associated a select number of the assistants of the Mercers. In this hall also the British Fishery Society, and other corporate bodies, were formerly accustomed to hold their meetings.

The chief portraits in the hall are those of Sir Thomas Gresham (original), a fanciful portrait of Sir Richard Whittington, a likeness of Count Tekeli (the hero of the old opera), Count Panington; Dean Colet (the illustrious friend of Erasmus, and the founder of St. Paul's school); Thomas Papillon, Master of the Company in 1698, who left £1,000 to the Company, to relieve any of his family that ever came to want; and Rowland Wynne, Master of the Company in 1675. Wynne gave £400 towards the repairing of the hall after the Great Fire.

In Strype's time (1720), the Mercers' Company gave away £3,000 a year in charity. In 1745 the Company's money legacies amounted to £21,699 5s. 9d., out of which the Company paid annually £573 17s. 4d. In 1832, the lapsed legacies of the Company became the subject of a Chancery suit; the result was that money is now lent to liverymen or freemen of the Company requiring assistance in sums of £100, and not exceeding £500, for a term, without interest, but only upon approved security

The present Mercers' School is a very elegant stone structure, adjoining St. Michael's Church, College Hill, on the site of Whittington's Almshouses, which were removed to Highgate, to make room for it.

Some scholarships are in the gift of the Mercers' Company; and it must not be forgotten that Caxton, the first great English printer, was a member of this livery.

Subsequently to the Great Fire, says Herbert, there was some discussion with Parliament on rebuilding the Mercers' School on the former site of St. Mary Colechurch. That site, however, was ultimately rejected, and by the Rebuilding Act, 22 Charles II. (1670), it was expressly provided that there should be a plot of ground, on the western side of the Old Jewry, "set apart for the Mercers' School." Persons who remember the building, says Herbert, describe it whilst here as an old-fashioned house for the masters' residence, with projecting upper storeys, a low, spacious building by the side of it for the schoolroom, and an area behind it for a playground, the whole being situate on the west side of the Old Jewry, about forty yards from Cheapside.

The great value of ground on the above spot, and a desire to widen, as at present, the entrance to the Old Jewry, occasioned the temporary removal of the Mercers' School, in 1787, to No. 13, Budge Row, about thirty yards from Dowgate Hill (a house of the Company's, which was afterwards burnt down). In 1804 it was again temporarily removed to No. 20, Red Lion Court, Watling Street; and from thence, in 1808, to its present situation on College Hill. The latter premises were hired by the Company, at the rent of £120, and the average expense of the school was £677 1s. 1d.

The salary of the master of the Mercers' School was formerly £200, and £50 gratuity, with a house to live in, rent and taxes free; but of late years the salary has been increased, and the residence for the master is no longer provided by the Mercers' Company. There are two exhibitions belonging to the school.

With the Mercers' Hospital, in the Middle Ages, many curious old City customs were connected. The customary devotions of the new Lord Mayor, at St. Thomas of Acon Church, in the Catholic times, identify themselves in point of locality with the Mercers' Company, and are to be ranked amongst that Company's observances. Strype has described these, from an ancient MS. he met with on the subject. The new Lord Mayor, it states, "*after dinner*" on his inauguration day (the ceremony would have suited much better *before* dinner in modern days), "was wont to go from his house to the Church of St. Thomas of Acon, those of his livery going before him ; and the aldermen in like manner being there met together, they came to the Church of St. Paul, whither, when they were come, namely, in the middle place between the body of the church, between two little doors, they were wont to pray for the soul of the Bishop of London, William Norman, who was a great benefactor to the City, in obtaining the confirmation of their liberties from William the Conqueror, a priest saying the office *De Profundis* (called a dirge) ; and from thence they passed to the churchyard, where Thomas à Becket's parents were buried, and there, near their tomb, they said also, for all the faithful deceased, *De Profundis* again. The City procession thence returned through Cheapside Market, sometimes with wax candles burning (if it was late), to the said Church Sanctæ Thomæ, and there the mayor and aldermen offered single pence, which being done, every one went to his home."

On all saints' days, and various other festivals, the mayor with his family attended at this same Church of St. Thomas, and the aldermen also, and those that were " of the livery of the mayor, with the honest men of the mysteries," in their several habits, or suits, from which they went to St. Paul's to hear vespers. On the Feast of Innocents they heard vespers at St. Thomas's, and on the morrow mass and vespers.

The Mercers' election cup, says Timbs, of early sixteenth century work, was silver-gilt, decorated with fret-work and female busts ; the feet, flasks ; and on the cover is the popular legend of an unicorn yielding its horn to a maiden. The whole is enamelled with coats of arms, and these lines—

"To elect the Master of the Mercerie hither am I sent,
And by Sir Thomas Leigh for the same intent."

The Company also possess a silver-gilt wagon and tun, covered with arabesques and enamels, supposed to be German, of sixteenth century work. The hall is decorated with carvings ; the main stem of deal, the fruit, flowers, &c., of lime, pear, and beech. These becoming worm-eaten, were long since removed from the panelling and put aside ; but they have been restored by Mr. Henry Crace, who thus describes the process :—

" The carving is of the same colour as when taken down. I merely washed it, and with a gimlet bored a number of holes in the back, and into every projecting piece of fruit and leaves on the face, and placing the whole in a long trough, fifteen inches deep, I covered it with a solution prepared in the following manner :—I took sixteen gallons of linseed oil, with 2 lbs. of litharge, finely ground, 1 lb. of camphor, and 2 lbs. of red lead, which I boiled for six hours, keeping it stirred, that every ingredient might be perfectly incorporated. I then dissolved 6 lbs. of bees'-wax in a gallon of spirits of turpentine, and mixed the whole, while warm, thoroughly together.

" In this solution the carving remained for twenty-four hours. When taken out, I kept the face downwards, that the oil might soak down to the face of the carving ; and on cutting some of the wood nearly nine inches deep, I found it had soaked through, for not any of the dust was blown out, as I considered it a valuable medium to form a substance for the future support of the wood. This has been accomplished, and, as the dust became saturated with the oil, it increased in bulk, and rendered the carving perfectly solid."

The Company is now governed by a master, three wardens, and a court of thirty-one or more assistants. The livery fine is 53s. 4d. The Mercers' Company, though not by any means the most ancient of the leading City companies, takes precedence of all. Such anomalous institutions are the City companies, that, curious to relate, the present body hardly includes one mercer among them. In Henry VIII.'s reign the Company (freemen, householders, and livery) amounted to fifty-three persons ; in 1701 it had almost quadrupled. Strype (1754) only enumerates fifty-two mayors who had been mercers, from 1214 to 1701 ; this is below the mark. Halkins over-estimates the mercer mayors as ninety-eight up to 1708. Few monarchs have been mercers, yet Richard II. was a free brother, and Queen Elizabeth a free sister of the Company.

Half our modern nobility have sprung from the trades they now despise. Many of the great mercers became the founders of noble houses ; for instance—Sir John Coventry (1425), ancestor of the present Earl of Coventry ; Sir Geoffrey Bullen, grandfather of Queen Elizabeth ; Sir William Hollis, ancestor of the Earls of Clare. From Sir Richard Dormer (1542) sprang the Lords Dormer ; from Sir Thomas Baldry (1523) the Lords Kensington (Rich) ; from Sir Thomas Seymour (1527) the Dukes of Somerset ; from Sir Baptist Hicks, the great mercer of James I., who built Hicks' Hall, on Clerkenwell Green, sprang the Viscounts Campden ;

from Sir Rowland Hill, the Lords Hill; from James Butler (Henry II.) the Earls of Ormond; from Sir Geoffrey Fielding, Privy Councillor to Henry II. and Richard I., the Earls of Denbigh.

The costume of the Mercers became fixed about the reign of Charles I. The master and wardens led the civic processions, "faced in furs," with the lords; the livery followed in gowns faced with satins, the livery of all other Companies wearing facings of fringe.

"In Ironmonger Lane," says Stow, giving us a glimpse of old London, "is the small parish church of St. Martin, called Pomary, upon what occasion certainly I know not; but it is supposed to be of apples growing where now houses are lately builded, for myself have seen the large void places there." The church was repaired in the year 1629. Mr. Stodder left 40s. for a sermon to be preached on St. James's Day by an unbeneficed minister, in commemoration of the deliverance in the year 1588 (Armada); and 50s. more to the use of the poor of the same parish, to be paid by the Ironmongers.